# ADAPTIVE EDUCATIONAL TECHNOLOGIES FOR LITERACY INSTRUCTION

While current educational technologies have the potential to fundamentally enhance literacy education, many of these tools remain unknown to or unused by today's practitioners due to a lack of access and support. *Adaptive Educational Technologies for Literacy Instruction* presents actionable information for educators, administrators, and researchers about available educational technologies that provide adaptive, personalized literacy instruction to students of all ages. These accessible, comprehensive chapters, written by leading researchers who have developed systems and strategies for classrooms, introduce effective technologies for reading comprehension and writing skills.

**Scott A. Crossley** is Associate Professor of Applied Linguistics at Georgia State University, USA.

**Danielle S. McNamara** is Professor in Cognitive and Learning Sciences and ISTL Senior Investigator at Arizona State University, USA.

# ADAPTIVE EDUCATIONAL TECHNOLOGIES FOR LITERACY INSTRUCTION

*Edited by Scott A. Crossley and Danielle S. McNamara*

NEW YORK AND LONDON

First published 2017
by Routledge

711 Third Avenue, New York, NY 10017
and by Routledge
2 Park Square, Milton Park, Abingdon, Oxon OX14 4RN

*Routledge is an imprint of the Taylor & Francis Group, an informa business*

© 2017 Taylor & Francis

The right of Scott A. Crossley and Danielle S. McNamara to be identified as the authors of the editorial material of this work, and of the authors for their individual chapters, has been asserted by them in accordance with sections 77 and 78 of the Copyright, Designs and Patents Act 1988.

All rights reserved. No part of this book may be reprinted or reproduced or utilized in any form or by any electronic, mechanical, or other means, now known or hereafter invented, including photocopying and recording, or in any information storage or retrieval system, without permission in writing from the publishers.

*Trademark notice*: Product or corporate names may be trademarks or registered trademarks, and are used only for identification and explanation without intent to infringe.

*Library of Congress Cataloging in Publication Data*
Names: Crossley, Scott A., editor. | McNamara, Danielle S., editor.
Title: Adaptive educational technologies for literacy instruction / edited by Scott A. Crossley and Danielle S. McNamara.
Description: New York, NY : Routledge, 2016. | Includes bibliographical references and index.
Identifiers: LCCN 2015047773| ISBN 9781138125438 (hardback) | ISBN 9781138125445 (pbk.) | ISBN 9781315647500 (ebook)
Subjects: LCSH: Language arts—Computer-assisted instruction. | Computers and literacy. | Educational technology.
Classification: LCC LB1576.7 .A35 2016 | DDC 428.40785—dc23
LC record available at http://lccn.loc.gov/2015047773

ISBN: 978-1-138-12543-8 (hbk)
ISBN: 978-1-138-12544-5 (pbk)
ISBN: 978-1-315-64750-0 (ebk)

Typeset in Bembo
by Swales & Willis Ltd, Exeter, Devon, UK

Printed and bound in the United States of America by Publishers Graphics, LLC on sustainably sourced paper.

# CONTENTS

List of Figures *viii*
List of Tables *xii*
List of Contributors *xiii*

1 Educational Technologies and Literacy Development 1
  *Scott A. Crossley and Danielle S. McNamara*

2 Challenges and Solutions when Using Technologies
  in the Classroom 13
  *Amy M. Johnson, Matthew E. Jacovina, Devin G. Russell, and Christian M. Soto*

**PART I**
**Reading and Comprehension Technologies
for the Classroom** **31**

3 Assessment-to-Instruction (A2i): An Online Platform for
  Supporting Individualized Early Literacy Instruction 33
  *Sarah W. Ingebrand and Carol McDonald Connor*

4 Common Core TERA: Text Ease and Readability Assessor 49
  *G. Tanner Jackson, Laura K. Allen, and Danielle S. McNamara*

5 Dynamic Support of Contextual Vocabulary Acquisition for Reading (DSCoVAR): An Intelligent Tutor for Contextual Word Learning     69
*Gwen A. Frishkoff, Kevyn Collins-Thompson, SungJin Nam, Leslie Hodges, and Scott A. Crossley*

6 Intelligent Tutoring of the Structure Strategy: A Reading Strategy Tutor     82
*Bonnie J. F. Meyer and Kausalai K. Wijekumar*

7 iSTART-2: A Reading Comprehension and Strategy Instruction Tutor     104
*Erica L. Snow, Matthew E. Jacovina, G. Tanner Jackson, and Danielle S. McNamara*

8 TuinLEC: An Intelligent Tutoring System to Teach Task-Oriented Reading Skills to Young Adolescents     122
*Eduardo Vidal-Abarca, Maria-Ángeles Serrano, Luis Ramos, Laura Gil, and Antonio Ferrer*

## PART II
## Writing Technologies for the Classroom     143

9 Commercialized Writing Systems     145
*Laura K. Allen and Cecile A. Perret*

10 The *Criterion®* Online Writing Evaluation Service     163
*Chaitanya Ramineni and Paul Deane*

11 We-Write: A Web-Based Intelligent Tutor for Supporting Elementary Classroom Teachers in Persuasive Writing Instruction     184
*Kausalai K. Wijekumar, Karen R. Harris, Steve Graham, and Bonnie J. F. Meyer*

12 The Writing Pal: A Writing Strategy Tutor     204
*Scott A. Crossley, Laura K. Allen, and Danielle S. McNamara*

13 Computer-Assisted Research Writing in the Disciplines     225
*Elena Cotos*

14  Writing to Learn and Learning to Write through SWoRD  243
    *Christian Schunn*

## PART III
## Future Technologies for the Classroom                                    **261**

15  Project LISTEN's Reading Tutor                                           263
    *Jack Mostow*

16  EMBRACEing Dual Language Learners                                        268
    *Arthur M. Glenberg, Erin A. Walker, and
    M. Adelaida Restrepo*

17  The *Language Muse Activity Palette*: Technology for
    Promoting Improved Content Comprehension for
    English Language Learners                                                275
    *Jill Burstein and John Sabatini*

18  The Reading Strategy Assessment Tool:
    A Computer-Based Approach for Evaluating
    Comprehension Processes during Reading                                   282
    *Joseph P. Magliano, Melissa Ray, and Keith K. Millis*

19  Reading Comprehension Lessons in AutoTutor for the
    Center for the Study of Adult Literacy                                   288
    *Arthur C. Graesser, Zhiqiang Cai, Whitney O. Baer,
    Andrew M. Olney, Xiangen Hu, Megan Reed,
    and Daphne Greenberg*

20  Udio: Rich and Authentic Literacy Experiences for
    Struggling Middle School Readers                                         294
    *Alyssa R. Boucher, Miriam Evans, and Steve Graham*

*Index*                                                                     *302*

# FIGURES

| | | |
|---|---|---|
| 2.1 | TPACK Framework's Knowledge Components | 22 |
| 3.1 | Students' Reading Grade Equivalent Versus Recommended Minutes Per Day of Instruction | 37 |
| 3.2 | Welcome Screen for A2i | 38 |
| 3.3 | Classroom View Display | 39 |
| 3.4 | Student Information Page | 40 |
| 3.5 | Student Information Page | 41 |
| 3.6 | Lesson Plan Page (Top and Bottom) | 42 |
| 3.7 | Assessments Page | 43 |
| 3.8 | Graphs Tab Showing Results of Word Match Game | 44 |
| 3.9 | Classroom Settings Page | 45 |
| 3.10 | Classroom Settings Page | 46 |
| 4.1 | Different Aspects of the TERA Component Scores | 53 |
| 4.2 | Login and Creation Page for TERA Website | 57 |
| 4.3 | Screenshot of Library Tool | 58 |
| 4.4 | My Texts Page | 59 |
| 4.5 | Input New Text Feature | 60 |
| 4.6 | Partial Screenshot of Texts to Compare Page | 61 |
| 5.1 | Strategy Training Module | 73 |
| 5.2 | Contextual Word Learning Module | 74 |
| 5.3 | Teacher Dashboard | 75 |
| 6.1 | Screenshot of I.T. Guidance Page | 87 |
| 6.2 | Screenshot of I.T. Modeling Use of the Comparison Structure | 88 |
| 6.3 | Identifying the Text Structure in ITSS | 88 |
| 6.4 | Clicking on Signaling Words in ITSS | 89 |
| 6.5 | Writing a Main Idea with the Passage in View in ITSS | 89 |

| | | |
|---|---|---|
| 6.6 | Expanded Text Structure Key | 90 |
| 6.7 | Screenshot on Correcting Your Work | 91 |
| 6.8a | Matrix of Topics Crossed with Issues | 92 |
| 6.8b | Format of Thorough Main Idea | 92 |
| 6.9a | Students' Constructed Main Ideas to Use as Guides When Writing Recalls | 93 |
| 6.9b | Students' Constructed Main Ideas to Use as Guides When Writing Recalls | 93 |
| 6.10a | Examples of Other Types of Questions Less Frequently Practiced in ITSS | 94 |
| 6.10b | Examples of Other Types of Questions Less Frequently Practiced in ITSS | 94 |
| 6.11 | Games Related to Text Structure Skills | 95 |
| 6.12 | Games Related to Text Structure Skills | 95 |
| 6.13 | Example of Further development of ITSS | 98 |
| 6.14 | Menu for the ITSS Management and Administration Tool | 99 |
| 7.1 | Screen Shot of One of the iSTART-2 Strategy Training Videos | 108 |
| 7.2 | Practice Phase within the Interactive Game-Based Interface | 108 |
| 7.3 | Map Conquest | 109 |
| 7.4 | Bridge Builder | 110 |
| 7.5 | Account Creation Process | 115 |
| 7.6 | Teacher Interface | 115 |
| 7.7 | Example of iSTART-2 Breaking Text into Individual Sentences | 116 |
| 7.8 | Lesson Progress Page | 117 |
| 8.1a | Screenshot of Instructional Modules Screen | 127 |
| 8.1b | Screenshot of Instructional Modules Screen | 129 |
| 8.2a | Identification of Different Types of Questions | 130 |
| 8.2b | Identification of Different Types of Questions | 131 |
| 8.3 | Screenshot of a Practice Module Screen | 132 |
| 8.4 | Screenshot of the Binoculars Help Used in a Question | 132 |
| 8.5 | Different Types of Feedback Presented in Distinct Modes | 133 |
| 8.6 | A Module Chart in the Student Interface | 134 |
| 8.7 | Welcome Screen | 136 |
| 8.8 | Registration Form Showing Dropdown Field "Type of Account" | 137 |
| 8.9 | Monitoring Students' Progress | 138 |
| 8.10 | Monitoring Table | 139 |
| 8.11 | Graphic Display of Main Indicators | 139 |
| 10.1 | The General Theory of Action Underlying *Criterion* | 166 |
| 10.2 | Example of the Planning Template for Cause/Effect | 167 |
| 10.3 | Descriptors for Performance | 169 |

## x Figures

| | | |
|---|---|---|
| 10.4 | Graphic Descriptors | 171 |
| 10.5 | Assistance with Errors | 171 |
| 10.6 | Assistance with Errors | 172 |
| 10.7 | Instructor's Home Page | 175 |
| 10.8a | Creating Assignments | 176 |
| 10.8b | Creating Assignments | 176 |
| 10.9 | *Criterion* Score by Student—Revision Attempts | 177 |
| 10.10 | Student Scores | 177 |
| 10.11 | Error Reports | 178 |
| 11.1 | Teacher Dashboard | 195 |
| 11.2 | We-Write Teacher and Computer Lesson Sequence Guide | 197 |
| 11.3 | Creating Custom Lessons | 198 |
| 11.4 | Tracking Student Progress | 198 |
| 11.5 | Student Picks out TREE from Model Essay in Early SRSD Stage | 199 |
| 12.1 | Screenshot of One of the W-Pal Lesson Videos | 210 |
| 12.2 | "Lessons Tab" in the W-Pal Interface | 210 |
| 12.3 | Screenshot of a W-Pal Game | 211 |
| 12.4 | Formative Feedback | 213 |
| 12.5 | Welcome Screen for the W-Pal System | 216 |
| 12.6 | W-Pal Teacher Interface | 217 |
| 12.7 | Screenshot of the Scoreboard Tab | 218 |
| 12.8 | Screenshot of the Assignment Creation Window | 218 |
| 12.9 | Screenshot of the Lessons Tab | 219 |
| 13.1 | Screenshot Illustrating Use of Gloss | 230 |
| 13.2 | Screenshot Showing Examples of Step Identifying a Gap | 230 |
| 13.3 | Visualization of Macro-Level Feedback | 231 |
| 13.4 | Functional steps Operationalized through Macro-Level and Micro-Level Feedback | 232 |
| 13.5 | Student Interaction with Micro-Level Feedback | 233 |
| 13.6 | Creating a Profile | 233 |
| 14.1 | The Student Assignment Time Line View | 247 |
| 14.2 | Reviewing Form | 248 |
| 14.3 | Authors Rating Helpfulness of Received Comments | 249 |
| 14.4 | Comparison of Student's Ratings to Mean Ratings | 250 |
| 14.5 | Teacher Display of Available Student Activity Information | 251 |
| 14.6 | Teacher Display of Inter-Rater Agreement | 251 |
| 14.7 | Reviewer Comments | 252 |
| 15.1 | Screenshot of Child Reading Story | 264 |
| 16.1 | Images of Toys to Assist with Reading Stories | 270 |
| 16.2 | Extension of *EMBRACE* for Use with Other Texts | 272 |
| 17.1 | Generating Language-Based Activities for Classroom Texts | 277 |

| | | |
|---|---|---|
| 17.2 | Generating Language-Based Activities for Classroom Texts | 278 |
| 18.1 | Sample Screen Shots Demonstrating Direct or Indirect Questions | 283 |
| 19.1 | Example of Trialogue Design Found in CSAL AutoTutor | 289 |
| 20.1 | How Udio Works to Improve Reading and Comprehension Skills | 295 |
| 20.2 | Variety of Texts Available from Udio | 296 |
| 20.3 | Designing a Project | 298 |
| 20.4 | Student Dashboard | 299 |

# TABLES

| | | |
|---|---|---|
| 3.1 | Examples of Activities and Dimensions in A2i | 36 |
| 4.1 | Text Excerpts for Similar Grade Levels | 52 |
| 4.2 | TERA Features and How They May Be Used To Facilitate Educational Goals and Classroom Pedagogy | 63 |
| 5.1 | Examples of Student Responses to the Tier 2 Word *Garish* | 76 |
| 7.1 | The Five Comprehension Strategies in the iSTART-2 Program | 106 |
| 7.2 | iSTART-2 and the Common Core Alignment Examples | 112 |
| 8.1 | Strategy Content of Modules Used in TuinLEC | 125 |
| 8.2 | Overview of Modules Used in TuinLEC | 128 |
| 10.1 | Features Included in the *e-rater* Scoring Model Grouped by Construct Dimension | 168 |
| 10.2 | Examples of Detailed Feedback Analysis Based on NLP Techniques | 170 |
| 11.1 | The Six Stages of the SRSD Approach | 185 |
| 11.2 | Samples of Operationalization of SRSD in We-Write | 191 |
| 12.1 | Summary of Writing Strategy Module Content and Practice Games | 209 |
| 12.2 | Brief Descriptions of Writing Pal Practice Games | 212 |
| 12.3 | The Writing Pal and Common Core State Standards Alignment | 220 |

# CONTRIBUTORS

**Laura K. Allen** is a graduate student in the Department of Psychology and the Institute for the Science of Teaching & Learning at Arizona State University. Her research investigates the cognitive individual differences that contribute to proficiency in reading comprehension and writing, as well as the application of cognitive principles to educational practice. The majority of her current research projects focus on the application of natural language processing techniques to better understand cognition, particularly with respect to text-based communication.

**Whitney O. Baer** is the Project Manager for several grants with the Institute for Intelligent Systems (IIS) at the University of Memphis. She has a Bachelor of Arts in English and History from Colgate University. Prior to joining the team at the University of Memphis, she worked for many years in educational publishing and gained experience with course redesign, learning management systems, and educational research and development. In the IIS, she is responsible for helping to develop curriculum and managing the process of interpreting scripted conversation into the AutoTutor framework.

**Alyssa R. Boucher** is an Associate Research Scientist with expertise in speech and language development and disabilities at CAST. Her primary research focuses on emergent literacy skills in children, particularly those with communication delays and disorders. She is also interested in minimizing barriers within the curriculum that affect expression, language processing, and comprehension. She is an ASHA-certified speech-language pathologist who uses her clinical experience, along with her understanding of Universal Design for Learning, to contribute to CAST's research and development activities.

**Jill Burstein** is a Research Director of the Natural Language Processing group in ETS's Research Division. She is a computational linguist and an expert in the design and application of automated capabilities for educational technology, specializing in automated writing evaluation. Her research is highly cross-disciplinary, as reflected in her publications with research colleagues from the writing and reading studies, English language learning, and psychometric communities. She led the team that invented e-rater®, ETS's commercially deployed automated writing evaluation system. She holds 14 patents for NLP-based, educational technology inventions.

**Zhiqiang Cai** is a Research Assistant Professor with the Institute for Intelligent Systems at the University of Memphis. He received a Master of Science degree in computational mathematics in 1985 from Huazhong University of Science and Technology, P. R. China. His current research interests are in algorithm design and software development for tutoring systems and natural language processing. He is the chief software designer and developer of QUAID, Coh-Metrix, and AutoTutor systems.

**Kevyn Collins-Thompson** is an Associate Professor of Information and Computer Science at the University of Michigan. His expertise lies in human language technology, data mining, and machine learning. He is co-PI with Dr. Frishkoff on the DSCoVAR project and was a key contributor to the development of the REAP system (http://reap.cs.cmu.edu). In related work, he pioneered the use of automated methods for assessing reading difficulty and developed the algorithmic approach called MESA (Markov Estimation of Semantic Association), which is used for fine-grained and incremental assessment of partial word knowledge.

**Carol McDonald Connor** is a Professor in Developmental Psychology at Arizona State University. Her research has focused on examining the links between young children's language and literacy development with the goal of illuminating reasons for the perplexing difficulties that children who are atypical and diverse learners have when developing basic and advanced literacy skills. Most recently, her research interests have focused on children's learning in the classroom—from preschool through fifth grade. She has been awarded the Presidents' Early Career Award for Scientists and Engineers (PECASE, 2008), the Society for Research in Child Development (SRCD, 2009) Early Career Award, and the Richard Snow Award (APA, 2008).

**Elena Cotos** is an Assistant Professor in the Department of English at Iowa State University. She holds a doctoral degree in Applied Linguistics and Technology and a Masters in Philology. Her research interests include automated writing evaluation, academic writing, corpus-based genre analysis, and computer-assisted language learning and assessment. She also contributed to a number of edited volumes and has recently published her monograph *Genre-Based Automated Writing Evaluation for L2 Research Writing*.

**Scott A. Crossley** is Associate Professor of Applied Linguistics at Georgia State University. His interests include the application and development of natural language processing tools in educational technology. He has published articles on the use of natural language processing tools to examine lexical acquisition, writing proficiency, reading comprehension, discourse processing, language assessment, and automatic feedback in intelligent tutoring systems. He is a consultant on the DSCoVAR project and collaborated with Dr. Frishkoff and Dr. Collins-Thompson on a seed grant from the Language & Literacy Initiative (GSU), which provided initial funding for this project.

**Paul Deane** is a Principal Research Scientist in the Natural Language Processing and Speech Group at Educational Testing Service. He received his PhD in Linguistics from the University of Chicago in 1987. His primarily research interests focus on reading, writing, and vocabulary assessment, automated essay scoring, and support for learning based on the cognitive and learning sciences. He is currently working on innovative designs for assessment in the English Language Arts and the use of automated methods, including keystroke log analysis, to support writing assessment.

**Miriam Evans** is an Associate Research Scientist at CAST. Her research interests focus on the social-emotional aspects of learning for students with disabilities, including the roles of motivation, self-determination, and peer relationships. She was the lead content developer for Udio and was responsible for implementing exploratory research on the use of Udio with adolescents with low-incidence disabilities. In addition to her role at CAST, she is an adjunct lecturer at the Lynch School of Education at Boston College.

**Antonio Ferrer** is an Associate Professor of Educational Psychology at the University of Valencia. His research interests are reading literacy processes, learning from text, reading in populations with developmental disabilities, and technology for learning and reading literacy. He is currently working on the improvement of the tutoring system, TuinLEC, on the study of feedback effects while reading science texts for learning in middle school and on checking guidelines for easy-to-read texts in the deafness and intellectual disabilities population.

**Gwen A. Frishkoff** is an Assistant Professor of Psychology at Georgia State University. She combines her expertise in cognitive psychology, linguistics, and neuroscience with an interest in vocabulary acquisition. She is co-Principal Investigator with Dr. Kevyn Collins-Thompson on the DSCoVAR project, which was funded by the Institute of Educational Sciences (IES, Department of Education). She also contributed to project REAP (http://reap.cs.cmu.edu), an IES-funded project on computer-assisted word learning and comprehension.

**Laura Gil** is an Associate Professor at the University of Valencia. Her interests include the assessment of reading literacy skills and the development of educational tools for improving students' reading literacy. During the last years, she has collaborated in the development of an automated tutoring system for teaching students reading literacy skills called TuinLec. She is currently working on the analyses of students' reading processes when they are learning with multiple documents.

**Arthur M. Glenberg** is a Professor in the Department of Psychology at Arizona State University and an emeritus professor at the University of Wisconsin-Madison. He conducts basic research in cognitive psychology and cognitive neuroscience. He has also developed a reading comprehension intervention for children in the early elementary grades based on principles of embodied cognition, and he has extended the intervention for English Language Learning children. He has published a textbook (in its third edition), an edited volume, and over 100 peer-reviewed articles.

**Arthur C. Graesser** is a Distinguished University Professor of Interdisciplinary Research in the Department of Psychology and the Institute of Intelligent Systems at the University of Memphis and is an Honorary Research Fellow in the Oxford University Centre for Educational Assessment at the University of Oxford. His primary research interests are in cognitive science, discourse processing, computational linguistics, and the learning sciences. He has developed automated tutoring systems with conversational agents (such as AutoTutor) and automated text analysis systems (Coh-Metrix, QUAID).

**Steve Graham** is the Warner Professor at Mary Lou Fulton Teachers College at Arizona State University and a Research Professor in the Learning Science Institute at the Australian Catholic University, Brisbane. He is the co-author of the Handbook of Writing Research, Handbook of Learning Disabilities, and APA Handbook of Educational Psychology. He is also the author of three influential Carnegie Corporation reports: *Writing Next*, *Writing to Read*, and *Informing Writing*. Steve was the chair of the What Works Clearinghouse guide, Teaching Elementary School Students to be Effective Writers.

**Daphne Greenberg** is the distinguished Professor of Educational Psychology in the College of Education and Human Development at Georgia State University. Her primary research focus is adult literacy, and she is currently the Principal Investigator of the Center of the Study of Adult Literacy (csal.gsu.edu), a national research center on adult literacy funded by the Institute of Education Sciences, U.S. Department of Education. She is a founding member of the Georgia Adult Literacy Advocacy group and the Literacy Alliance of Metro Atlanta. She has tutored native and nonnative English speaking adults and has helped communities organize and develop adult literacy programs.

**Karen R. Harris** is the Warner Professor at Fulton Teachers College, Arizona State University. Her research focuses on children's writing, as well as theoretically based interventions for the development of self-regulation of the writing process and learning to compose. She developed the Self-Regulated Strategy Development (SRSD) model of strategies instruction. For the past decade, she has been working on the development and validation of a practice-based professional development model for SRSD, resulting in randomized controlled trials now published or under review. She has authored over 200 publications and spent over 30 years working in schools.

**Leslie Hodges** is a doctoral student in Developmental Psychology at Georgia State University. She received her BA in psychology, with a minor in linguistics, from the University of Colorado, and then went on to teach high school and junior high social studies for several years. She contributed to the development of a high-quality corpus of annotated contexts—used in contextual word learning research (including her master's thesis) and, in the present project, for implementation of DSCoVAR.

**Xiangen Hu** is a Professor in the Department of Psychology and Department of Electrical and Computer Engineering at the University of Memphis (UofM) and Senior Researcher at the Institute for Intelligent Systems (IIS) at the UofM, and Visiting Professor at Central China Normal University. His primary research areas include mathematical psychology, research design and statistics, and cognitive psychology. He is the Director of the Advanced Distributed Learning (ADL) Center for Intelligent Tutoring Systems (ITS) Research & Development and Senior Researcher in the Chinese Ministry of Education's Key Laboratory of Adolescent Cyberpsychology and Behavior.

**Sarah W. Ingebrand** is a doctoral student in the Department of Psychology at Arizona State University. She is pursuing doctoral research in the area of Developmental Psychology. She received her Master's degree from Florida State University where she was a Predoctoral Interdisciplinary Research Training (PIRT) Fellow through the Florida Center for Reading Research. Her research focuses on the development of reading, writing, and spelling skills in elementary and middle school students.

**G. Tanner Jackson** is a Managing Research Scientist at Educational Testing Service. His work focuses on innovative educational systems and student process data. His main efforts involve the development and evaluation of conversation-based formative assessments and educational games. He is interested in how users interact with complex systems and leverages these environments to examine and interpret continuous and live data streams, including user interactions across time within educational systems.

**Matthew E. Jacovina** is an Assistant Research Professor in the Institute for the Science of Teaching & Learning at Arizona State University. He received his PhD in cognitive psychology from Stony Brook University. He studies the cognitive processes that guide comprehension and communication, focusing on situations in which success is complicated by mismatches between discourse content and prior knowledge, preferential biases, or time pressure. He is interested in how individual differences influence success in these situations and how educational technology can leverage these understandings to personalize and improve learning. He is currently working on the optimization of iSTART-2 and Writing Pal, game-based tutoring systems teaching reading and writing strategies.

**Amy M. Johnson** is an Assistant Research Professor in the Science of Learning and Educational Technology (SoLET) Lab at Arizona State University. She received her PhD in Cognitive Psychology from the University of Memphis in 2011. She is interested in learners' knowledge construction through integration of textual and pictorial information within multimedia and hypermedia environments and the use of multiple external representations when regulating learning. She is currently working on adapting iSTART-2 to the unique requirements of struggling adult readers.

**Joseph P. Magliano** is a Presidential Research Professor of Psychology and the co-director of the Center for the Interdisciplinary Study of Language and Literacy at Northern Illinois University. He studies how we understand and use texts and visual media in academic and non-academic settings. He also studies how to use computer-based technologies to both assess and help students to be successful in their academic reading. He has published over 80 scholarly articles and book chapters and has received funding for his research from the Institute of Education Sciences and the National Science Foundation.

**Danielle S. McNamara** is Professor in Cognitive and Learning Sciences and ISTL Senior Investigator at Arizona State University. Her research interests involve better understanding processes such as comprehension and writing. She develops educational technologies (e.g., iSTART and Writing Pal) to help students learn how to understand challenging text and learn strategies that support more effective writing. She also works on the development of text analysis tools that provide a wide range of information about text, including the difficulty of text and the quality of writing. More information about her work is available at soletlab.com.

**Bonnie J. F. Meyer** is a Professor of Educational Psychology at The Pennsylvania State University. Her current research focuses on upper elementary through middle school students' understanding of text structures and signaling words. She studies how structure strategy applications can improve reading, writing, and decision-making. She has over 50 publications on the structure strategy including the book, *Memory Improved*, which presented a well-designed, empirical study documenting positive effects of intervention with the strategy. Structure strategy instruction via ITSS is built on her theoretical work and instruction to improve reading comprehension by strategically using text structure.

**Keith K. Millis** is a Professor in the Department of Psychology at Northern Illinois University. He has a Master's degree in Cognitive Science and a Ph.D. in Cognitive Psychology from the University of Memphis. His research areas include discourse comprehension, reading assessment, and intelligent tutors/serious games. He was the PI on Operation ARA, a serious game that teaches scientific enquiry, and co-PI on the creation of the Reading Strategy Assessment Tool (RSAT) (with Dr. Magliano), both of which were funded from the U.S. Department of Education.

**Jack Mostow** is an Emeritus Research Professor of Robotics, Machine Learning, Language Technologies, and Human-Computer Interaction at Carnegie Mellon University. In 1992, he founded Project LISTEN (www.cs.cmu.edu/~listen), which developed an automated Reading Tutor that listens to children reading aloud, winning a United States patent and the Allen Newell Medal of Research Excellence. Dr. Mostow was elected International Artificial Intelligence in Education Society President in 2010 and now leads Carnegie Mellon's $15m Global Learning XPRIZE effort to develop an Android tablet app that enables children in developing countries to learn basic reading, writing, and numeracy despite little or no access to schools.

**SungJin Nam** is a doctoral student in School of Information at the University of Michigan. With backgrounds in psychology and data science, he is interested in interpreting human behavior by data-driven methods. He is a research assistant on the DSCoVAR project, contributing as a programmer and data analyst.

**Andrew M. Olney** is an Associate Professor in both the Institute for Intelligent Systems and Department of Psychology and is Director of the Institute for Intelligent Systems at the University of Memphis. He received a BA in Linguistics with Cognitive Science from University College London in 1998, an MS in Evolutionary and Adaptive Systems from the University of Sussex in 2001, and a PhD in Computer Science from the University of Memphis in 2006. His primary research interests are in natural language interfaces. Specific interests include vector space models, dialogue systems, unsupervised grammar induction, robotics, and intelligent tutoring systems.

**Cecile A. Perret** is a Research Technician in the Science of Learning and Educational Technology (SoLET) Lab at Arizona State University's (ASU) Institute for the Science of Teaching and Learning. She graduated from ASU with a BS in Psychology in 2014 and has assisted the SoLET Lab in their research since 2012. She is interested in how intelligent tutoring systems can help students develop and apply their critical thinking skills to various tasks, particularly tasks that require integrating information from complex sources.

**Chaitanya Ramineni** is a Research Scientist in the Assessment Innovations Research Center at Educational Testing Service (ETS), Princeton, NJ. She received her PhD in Research Methodology and Evaluation from the University of Delaware in 2009. She is interested in the use of automated technologies for assessment and instruction, constructed response scoring, and linking assessment and learning outcomes. She is currently working on enhancing the reliability of automated features for scoring and feedback and using automated features to link standardized assessments to external criterion of interest, a project for which she is a co-recipient of the 2015 NCME Bradley Hanson award for significant contributions to educational measurement.

**Luis Ramos** is a school psychologist. He recently earned his PhD at the University of Valencia with a doctoral dissertation about TuinLEC. He has considerable experience in reading comprehension instruction and reading assessment. He is involved in the instructional applications of TuinLEC in the context of the school classrooms. Nowadays, he combines his work as a school psychologist with teaching psychology as Adjunct Professor at the School for Teachers of the University of Valencia.

**Melissa Ray** is a Research Scientist at Northern Illinois University and is affiliated with the Center for the Interdisciplinary Study of Language and Literacy (CISLL). Her research interests include college readiness, individual differences in reading comprehension, and the relationship between text structure and comprehension.

**Megan Reed** is a Graduate Research Assistant with the Institute for Intelligent Systems at the University of Memphis. She is currently completing a Graduate Certificate in Cognitive Science under the supervision of Dr. Arthur C. Graesser. She is a script author for the Center for the Study of Adult Literacy (CSAL) and develops content for lessons in CSAL AutoTutor. Before entering the field of learning sciences and intelligent systems, she studied public relations and worked as a media relations assistant. She has a BA in Journalism and Psychology from the University of Memphis. Her current research interests are in language learning and development, applied linguistics, cognitive science, and intelligent tutoring systems.

**M. Adelaida Restrepo** is a Professor in the Department of Speech and Hearing Science at Arizona State University. She is the director of the Bilingual Language and Literacy Laboratory. The main mission at the lab is to research best language assessment and intervention practices for bilingual children. She specializes in oral language and emergent literacy development and in prevention of academic difficulties in bilingual children.

**Devin G. Russell** is a doctoral student in Cognitive Psychology at Arizona State University and is working as a graduate research assistant in the Science of Learning and Educational Technology (SoLET) Lab. His research interests include memory, motivation, attention, strategy use and acquisition, intelligent tutoring systems, and games. He currently works on the iSTART-2 and Writing Pal projects, investigating reading and writing educational technologies.

**John Sabatini** is a Principal Research Scientist in the Center for Global Assessment in ETS's Research Division. His research interests include reading literacy development, disabilities, assessment, cognitive psychology, and educational technology, with a primary focus on adults and adolescents. He has been the principal investigator of an IES-funded grant to develop pre-K-12 comprehension assessments as part of the Reading for Understanding initiative. He is co-investigator on projects exploring the reading processes of adolescents and English language learners. He provides technical consulting to national and international surveys including the PIAAC and PISA.

**Christian Schunn** is a Senior Scientist at the Learning Research and Development Center and a Professor of Psychology, Learning Sciences and Policy, and Intelligent Systems at the University of Pittsburgh. He directs a number of research and design projects in science, mathematics, and engineering education. This work includes supporting and studying web-based peer assessment in diverse contexts, building innovative technology-supported STEM curricula, and studying factors that influence student and teacher learning and engagement. He is a Fellow of AAAS, APA, and APS.

**Maria-Ángeles Serrano** is a PhD candidate in Educational Psychology at the University of Valencia. Her research interests include individual differences in reading literacy skills, particularly in self-regulation strategies, and how educational technology can enhance strategy use and learning. She is currently working on the tutoring system, TuinLEC, and collaborating with Dr. Danielle S. McNamara in the development of preliminary studies to test the Spanish version of iSTART (iSTART-E).

**Erica L. Snow** is the learning analytics lead scientist at SRI international. She recently completed her PhD in Cognitive Science at Arizona State University. Her current research explores how information from adaptive learning environments can be leveraged to understand better students' cognitive and learning processes.

**Christian M. Soto** is an Educational Psychologist with a PhD in the field of psycholinguistics at the University of Conception in Chile. He has considerable experience as an educational consultant intervening in schools and generating studies about educational topics. He is especially interested in the theory and application of metacognition to reading comprehension and learning, considering specifically the regulation and monitoring process. He is currently collaborating with the Science of Learning and Educational Technology (SoLET) Lab on the elaboration of the Spanish version of iSTART (iSTART-E) and on the development of preliminary studies on the system.

**Eduardo Vidal-Abarca** is a Professor of Developmental and Educational Psychology at the University of Valencia and Director of the Interdisciplinary Research Structure on Reading at the University of Valencia. He is interested in discourse processing and technology for the assessment and teaching of reading skills. He has developed automated reading literacy assessment tools (such as e-CompLEC).

**Erin A. Walker** is an Assistant Professor in the School of Computing, Informatics, and Decision Systems Engineering at Arizona State University. She received her PhD at Carnegie Mellon University in Human-Computer Interaction in 2010 and was then awarded a NSF/CRA Computing Innovation Fellowship to conduct postdoctoral work. Her research interests involve the development of personalized learning environments for higher-order skills that span multiple contexts. She is currently working on various projects that attempt to incorporate social and contextual adaptation into learning technologies, including designing a teachable robot for mathematics learning and reimagining the digital textbook.

**Kausalai K. Wijekumar** is Professor of Education at Texas A&M University. Her interests include the effects of technologies on human cognition, learning, and problem solving. Her interests also extend to the application of intelligent tutoring systems to improve reading comprehension in monolingual and bilingual learners and writing. She is the recipient of numerous grants to support the development and large scale testing of intelligent tutoring systems for content area reading comprehension, Spanish-speaking English language learners, and persuasive writing.

# 1
# EDUCATIONAL TECHNOLOGIES AND LITERACY DEVELOPMENT

*Scott A. Crossley and Danielle S. McNamara*

## Introduction

The purpose of this handbook is to provide actionable information to educators, administrators, and researchers about current, available research-based educational technologies that provide adaptive (personalized) instruction to students on literacy, including reading comprehension and writing. This handbook is comprised of chapters by leading researchers who have developed educational technologies for use in the classroom. Each major chapter in this handbook introduces a currently available educational technology that focuses on the instruction of reading comprehension or writing literacies. The final chapters in this handbook are shorter and introduce technologies that are currently under development.

Educational technologies, such as intelligent tutoring systems (ITS), automated writing evaluation (AWE) systems, and text readability tools, have the potential to fundamentally augment and enhance literacy education. However, many of these technologies remain unused in the contemporary classroom even though numerous studies have indicated their strengths in enhancing learning across a variety of student populations. There are a number of potential reasons such technologies are not found in the classroom, ranging from hesitancy on the part of teachers and administrators to adopt technologies, lack of technology support, and a potential digital divide between teachers, administrators, and students. However, another possible cause stems from a lack of adequate information provided to educators about available technologies for the classroom. Educators do not have easily accessible information about technologies that are potentially usable in their classrooms. A primary reason for this is that researchers generally disseminate such information in academic journals and conference proceedings, which are not readily available to teachers and administrators. Information about technologies is dispersed, rendering it difficult and time consuming to discover whether the right technology exists and to consider a technology's potential usability in schools. Perhaps most importantly, research articles are often not targeted to the education practitioner and are thus often inaccessible. The purpose of this handbook is to help bridge this divide between teachers, administrators, and educational technology researchers focusing on the development of literacy skills in students of all ages.

Thus, the goal of this book is to provide teachers and administrators with a resource that reviews available educational technologies that have empirical data to demonstrate their success and benefits and provides teachers and administrators with a means to access these technologies. That these available educational technologies focus specifically on reading comprehension and writing, is not unintentional. The recent focus on the common core in the United States renders literacy increasingly important to a wide range of teachers, including those who traditionally focus on literacy such as English Language Arts teachers, but also those who teach content areas such as history and science.

The technologies described in this volume provide evidence that teachers and administrators can facilitate and enhance literacy instruction using adaptive, personalized techniques on a large scale that is only possible with the use of advanced technology. While there are a burgeoning number of educational technologies, there are still too few. We believe that this volume is particularly timely, because there is an increasing number of adaptive reading and writing educational technologies. Our hope is that providing information about available technologies to educators will bolster wider use of these technologies and stimulate the development and dissemination of newer and better literacy technologies for the future.

The following two sections discuss the importance of literacy and describe the need for educational technologies to support literacy. We then briefly describe the chapters and the educational technologies in this volume.

## Literacy Skills

Literacy is an important component not only of educational success but also success in business and in life (Geiser & Studley, 2001; Powell, 2009). However, literacy is not acquired quickly. Becoming literate is a long, complex, and difficult undertaking that requires the coordination of a number of cognitive and knowledge skills (National Assessment of Educational Progress, 2011). Importantly, as text becomes more common in e-mails, text messages, and social media posts, the need for strong literacy skills will continue to increase (Barton & Lee, 2013; National Assessment Governing Board, 2011; National Writing Project, 2010).

However, national and international assessments indicate that students struggle to develop strong literacy skills in core areas, such as reading and writing (Carnegie Council on Advancing Adolescent Literacy, 2010). For instance, 25 percent or more of students in the 8th and 12th grades in the United States perform below a basic level of reading comprehension (U.S. Department of Education, 2011). Importantly, those students who fail to achieve proficiency in basic literacy skills have an increased risk of being referred to special education classes, missing grade level advancements, and dropping out of school (Reynolds & Ou, 2004; Shonkoff & Phillips, 2000).

Problems in literacy within the United States are compounded by the number of English language learners (ELLs) enrolled in public schools (National Clearinghouse for Language Acquisition, 2011). By definition, these students are developing English skills and typically read and write at lower levels than native speakers. The lower-level writing skills of ELL's are evidenced in national test scores in the United States. For instance, as of 2009, Hispanic non-ELL 4th grade students scored, on average, 29 points higher on standardized reading tests than Hispanic ELL students. Hispanic non-ELL 8th grade students scored, on average, 39 points higher on standardized reading tests than Hispanic ELL students. Regrettably, the 2009 statistics for 4th and 8th grade students are not statistically different from the statistics collected in 1998 or 2007, indicating that reading proficiency levels of ELL students are neither increasing nor declining.

Literacy problems in public schools in the United States continue long after students graduate or drop out of school. For instance, studies investigating adult literacy at the international level demonstrate that adults in the United States score below international levels of print and math literacy as well as analytic skills in technological environments (Goodman, Finnegan, Mohadjer, Krenzke, & Hogan, 2013). These literacy problems lead to expenditures for adult literacy programs that serve almost two million students in the United States (Graesser et al., this volume).

## The Need for Supplemental Literacy Instruction

The national and international statistics on literacy are not promising. Currently, most students struggle to attain proficient levels of literacy, and teachers do not have enough classroom time or resources to dedicate adequate time to each individual student. Hence, many students still struggle to read at basic levels. Such difficulties may stem from a lack of necessary skills or the knowledge needed to gain a deep understanding of the content embedded within texts (O'Reilly & McNamara, 2007).

From a reading perspective, there is a lack of reading comprehension instruction in elementary classrooms (e.g. Ness, 2011; Pressley, Wharton-McDonald, Mistretta-Hampston, & Echevarria, 1998; Taylor, Pearson, Clark, & Walpole, 2000). A possible explanation for this absence may be that many teachers do not understand the active reading components that are the critical foundation of reading comprehension and many do not appear to be adequately prepared to undertake this challenging task (Pressley, 2006). Furthermore, the teaching of reading literacy strategies is complicated by the explicitness of instruction and the challenge of finding appropriated texts and comprehension questions that fit the huge variety of task-oriented reading activities that people accomplish in ordinary life (White, Chen, & Forsyth, 2010).

From a writing perspective, research also indicates that many teachers are not adequately trained in writing instruction through either pre- or in-service preparation and, as a result, often do not implement evidence-based writing interventions. This may be because, like reading skills, writing is a complex skill that relies on self-regulation, social awareness of writing purposes, idea generation, knowledge telling, linguistic abilities, and knowledge of the writing process, writing genres, and writing strategies (Flower & Hayes, 1981; Harris & Graham, 2009; Kellogg & Whiteford, 2009).

Of course, reading and writing are intricately linked and both are essential for success in school. For instance, writing about material read or presented in class enhances students' learning of both the subject matter and literacy skills in general (Bangert-Drowns, Hurley, & Wilkinson, 2004; Graham & Hebert, 2010). There is also overlap between the types of effective, evidence-based instruction used in both reading and writing pedagogy. This instruction includes deliberate practice, individualized feedback, and strategy instruction. In terms of deliberate practice, research strongly supports the notion that proficiency in reading and writing is promoted though practice that is purposeful and persistent, allowing students opportunities to read and write text across multiple domains and genres (Duke & Pearson, 2002; Graham & Harris, 2013; Kellogg & Raulerson, 2007; Snow, Burns, & Griffin, 1998). Research indicates that practice is not just helpful; it is necessary for literacy acquisition (Ericsson, Krampe, & Tesch-Römer, 1993; Johnstone, Ashbaugh, & Warfield, 2002; Kellogg & Raulerson, 2007).

However, deliberate practice alone will not lead to proficient literacy. Previous research suggests that the best method for developing overall literacy skills is for students to practice reading and writing in a purposeful manner and in a manner in which they simultaneously receive formative feedback. While formative feedback is important, it is also crucial that the feedback students receive is individualized (Graham & Harris, 2013; Kellogg & Raulerson, 2007). Such feedback can help support writing quality through multiple rounds of revision (Graham & Harris, 2013) as well as motivate students through the revision process (Beach & Friedrich, 2006; Ferris, 2003).

In addition to deliberate practice and formative feedback, best practices in literacy instruction also include strategy instruction. Strategies are effortful and purposeful procedures that are enacted in order to achieve a goal or accomplish a task (Alexander, Graham, & Harris, 1998; Healy, Schneider, & Bourne, 2012). Strategy instruction helps students learn by providing them with concrete information and heuristics (Alexander et al., 1998) that allow them to break up complex tasks into more manageable pieces (Healy et al., 2012). The use of strategies can help students coordinate the different aspects of reading and/or writing a text (Elliot & Klobucar, 2013). Thus, better readers employ a greater number of reading strategies, such as self explaining texts (McNamara, 2004;

O'Reilly, Taylor, & McNamara, 2006), and better writers are better at successfully using strategies during complex writing tasks (McCutchen, 2006). Thus, to improve students' literacy skills, it is critical that students are taught the components of the reading and writing processes as well as strategies that can help them to engage in these processes. Strategies can also help lower-level learners overcome skill deficits in vocabulary or domain knowledge, both of which are important components of literacy (Graham, Harris, & Mason, 2005).

Of course, none of these educational practices operate in isolation; rather, they are dependent on one another to maximize learning. Thus, in order to cement newly learned strategies, students need to be provided with opportunities for sustained and deliberate writing practice (Kellogg, 2008), which can help them understand how and when to use strategies appropriately (Plant, Ericsson, Hill, & Asberg, 2005). At the same time, students should receive individualized feedback to help them to select when to use learned strategies more effectively and appropriately (Shute, 2008). Thus, sustained and deliberate practice combined with individualized feedback help students to develop effective strategies, because practice and feedback allow strategies to be used in practical settings, which staves off strategy forgetting or misapplication (Rohrer & Pashler, 2010).

## Overview of Chapters

The purpose of this volume is to provide educators with information about and access to educational technologies for literacy. However effective these technologies might be, we also fully recognize that implementing technology in the classroom is not an easy task. So, we begin with a chapter (Johnson, Jacovina, Russell, & Soto) that discusses these challenges and offers some potential solutions. While there has been some increase in levels of support for technology, teachers often report that the smooth and effective integration of new educational technologies remains challenging. These challenges range from the acquisition of equipment, the adaptation of curricula and teaching techniques to incorporate new educational tools, software training, technical, administrative, and peer support, as well as teacher attitudes, beliefs, and skills. Johnson and colleagues provide a number of suggestions to help integrate technology, all of which revolve around the need for collaborative efforts among teachers, educational technology professionals, school administrators, researchers, and educational software personnel.

The remaining chapters in this volume describe educational technologies that provide adaptive instruction for understanding text or writing. Each chapter provides a description of the technology, why it is needed, who will benefit from using the technology, and evidence for its effectiveness. Importantly, the authors also provide information on how to access each system. These chapters comprise three major parts. The first part describes educational technologies that focus on providing adaptive instruction in reading text and comprehending text at deeper levels. The second part comprises chapters describing technologies for writing.

These technologies provide students with deliberate practice, individualized feedback, and strategy instruction to improve writing quality. The third part describes educational technologies that are representative of our future. In the future, we expect to see a proliferation of writing and reading technologies that actively engage the learner. These short overviews provide a glimpse of upcoming technologies that will be available for classroom use in future years.

## Part I: Reading

The first part of this volume focuses on adaptive technologies for reading. The majority of current literacy technologies focus on providing adaptive instruction to the student. By contrast, the first two chapters in this part focus on providing direct support to teachers. Chapter 3 (Ingebrand & Connor) describes A2i, a digital platform that provides K-3 teachers with information about the types and amount of reading instruction needed by developing readers, allowing teachers to more effectively individualize reading instruction for students. The system does so by monitoring student progress across the school year, and suggesting groups of students who need similar types of instruction, such as code focused (e.g., word decoding) or meaning focused (e.g., comprehension) instruction.

Chapter 4 (Jackson, Allen, & McNamara) describes a tool that provides teachers with information about the difficulty of texts read by students. Text difficulty is often described solely in terms of the challenges posed by the words and the sentences. By contrast, the tool for Text Ease and Readability Assessor (TERA) provides a profile of text difficulty encompassing multiple dimensions, including: *narrativity (genre), syntax, word concreteness, referential cohesion,* and *deep cohesion*. Jackson and colleagues describe these dimensions and provide recommendations to teachers on student needs and instructional approaches that align with these dimensions.

Chapters 5 through 8 describe technologies that provide adaptive reading instruction to students. The first level of instruction is toward learning vocabulary. Indeed, there are several available educational technologies that provide students with practice and feedback on learning new vocabulary. We include Chapter 5 as a representative technology and one of the newest technologies that focus on word learning. DSCoVAR (Dynamic Support of Contextual Vocabulary Acquisition for Reading: Frishkoff, Collins-Thompson, Nam, Hodges, & Crossley) is appropriate for intermediate readers (adolescents to adults), presenting challenging words in various contexts and providing individualized feedback to promote robust word learning.

Chapter 6 describes Intelligent Tutoring of the Structure Strategy (ITSS: Meyer & Wijekumar). ITSS provides students in grades 4–8 with instruction to understand text structure (e.g., comparison, description, cause, and effect) and then to use that structure to comprehend and describe information depicted in expository and persuasive texts.

While ITSS is appropriate for young readers who are learning how to recognize important cues in non-fiction text, generating connections among ideas in the text and with background knowledge becomes increasingly important for developing readers. Chapter 7 describes Interactive Strategy Training for Active Reading and Thinking (iSTART), a technology that focuses on providing students in grades 7–14 with comprehension strategies that promote effective inferencing. iSTART-2 (Snow, Jacovina, Jackson, & McNamara) is a game-based educational technology designed to improve students' comprehension skills by providing them with instruction on how to self-explain text using comprehension strategies, such as paraphrasing and making bridging inferences. The system is designed for students in middle school, high school, and college and has been shown to improve students' reading comprehension skills, particularly for complex texts.

Recognizing the importance of developing technologies for ELLs, the developers of ITSS and iSTART have also created versions of their tutoring technologies for Spanish speaking learners. Chapter 8 (Vidal-Abarca, Serrano, Ramos, Gil, & Ferrer) describes TuinLEC, an educational technology designed specifically for Spanish speaking students at the upper elementary level. TuinLEC focuses on teaching students strategies to answer multiple-choice questions that are typical of standardized assessments. Students learn to develop a better understanding of the text before answering questions, and when to refer back to the text when it is available.

## *Part II: Writing*

The second part of the book contains chapters that focus on providing students with deliberate practice, individualized feedback, and strategy instruction for writing. Systems that provide students with deliberate practice and language specific feedback for writing are commonly found in the commercial sector. The sheer number of these systems precludes an individual chapter for each system. Hence, Chapter 9 (Allen & Perret) provides an overview of many of the available systems. All of the systems vary in their specific properties, but commonalities include automated essay scoring (AES) engines to assign scores to essays and AWE systems to provide students with some form of feedback on their writing. This feedback can range from the detection of lower-level spelling and grammar errors to higher-level components related to rhetorical language use. Chapter 10 provides a detailed account of the earliest and best known of commercialized systems, *Criterion®* (Ramineni & Deane). *Criterion®* Online Writing Evaluation Service is a writing tool that affords the collection of writing samples, scoring of those writing samples, and immediate feedback to the writer through the *e-rater®* AES engine (Burstein, Tetreault, & Madnani, 2013).

The following two chapters in the writing section move beyond only essay quality and feedback and provide students with writing strategy training. Chapter 11 provides an overview of We-Write (Wijekumar, Harris, Graham, & Myer). We-Write modules include teacher-led and computer supported modeling, practice tasks, assessment, feedback, and scaffolding. The focus of We-Write is on self-regulated strategies development, which helps students in grades 4–5 plan, draft, revise, and reflect on persuasive writing tasks.

Chapter 12 describes the Writing-Pal (W-Pal; Crossley, Allen, & McNamara). W-Pal targets adolescent writers, but can be used effectively from middle school to first-year college classes. W-Pal is an automated tutoring system that provides instruction on writing strategies through lessons, game-based practice on these strategies, essay writing practice, automated essay scoring, and practical feedback for essay revision.

Chapter 13 (Cotos) focuses on a technology that helps advanced students develop and write research articles. The *Research Writing Tutor* (RWT) employs the conventions of scientific argumentation to facilitate the learning of scientific writing conventions. RWT also provides rhetorical feedback to writers to help them engage in interactive writing to promote meaningful text revision.

Chapter 14 describes SWoRD (recently renamed Peerceptiv; Schunn), a system designed to support peer review of essays for high school and college students. Like *Criterion®* and RWT, SWoRD provides students with feedback on their writing, but, uniquely, this system provides an automated approach for effective peer review. The objective of the system is to harness the power of peer reviewing to produce accurate ratings of essay quality and useful feedback for writing improvement.

## *Part III: Future Technologies*

The last part of the volume focuses on educational technologies for literacy that are under development. These chapters are short overviews that provide a glimpse of upcoming technologies that will soon be available for classroom use. Chapter 15 describes Project Listen (Mostow), an educational tool that improves reading fluency by reading along and providing feedback to young children in grades 1–3. Chapter 16 introduces EMBRACE (Glenberg, Walker, & Restrepo), which is designed to improve both general and STEM reading comprehension for young ELLs (grades 2–5). Chapter 17 provides an overview of PALETTE (Burstein & Sabatini), a tool that can automatically generate activities for middle school ELLs to support students' language development and content comprehension. Chapter 18 introduces RSAT (Magliano, Ray, & Millis), which provides teachers with direct evaluations of what students do as they read. Chapter 19 discusses an iteration of the AutoTutor ITS that provides reading strategy instruction for adult literacy learners (Graesser et al., this volume). Fittingly, our final chapter focuses on a system that merges both reading and writing instruction, Udio (Boucher, Evans, & Graham). Udio provides students with a wide variety of high-interest and age-relevant readings along with opportunities to write projects in support of these readings.

## Conclusions

As discussed in multiple chapters throughout this book, providing students with deliberate practice, individualized feedback, and strategy training is difficult to accomplish in the classroom, because of time constraints and class sizes. Literacy skills are only one of many skills taught in the classroom and finding time to allot to deliberate and guided practice is difficult. In addition, with larger class sizes, teachers do not have the time to read and process large quantities of student text (National Commission on Writing, 2004). This is especially true for writing assignments for which it is more time consuming to review each student's writing and give individualized, formative feedback (Grimes & Warschauer, 2010; Roscoe, Varner, Snow, & McNamara, 2014).

Fortunately, educational technologies, such as those described in this volume, can provide supplemental instruction to help teachers address restrictions that result from large class sizes and limited classroom time. In fact, the expressed purpose of these educational technologies is to afford students opportunities for deliberative practice in reading and/or writing. In many cases, the technologies can also provide individualized feedback to the learner, and many of the educational technologies contained in this book can help students develop better literacy strategies to help them independently increase their reading and writing proficiency.

The educational technologies described within this volume offer exciting opportunities for supplemental classroom activities to support increased literacy skills. Importantly, the technologies provide students with opportunities for deliberate practice, individualized feedback, and strategy instruction, all hallmarks of efficient literacy instruction. In addition, and perhaps most importantly, these technologies lead to learning gains for students in terms of reading comprehension and writing proficiency. In sum, the technologies work.

## Acknowledgments

The research reported here was supported by the Institute of Education Sciences, IES R305G020018–02, R305G040046, R305A080589, R305A130124), the National Science Foundation (NSF REC0241144, IIS-0735682), and the Office of Naval Research (ONR N000141410343). The opinions expressed are those of the authors and do not represent the views of these granting agencies.

## References

Alexander, P. A., Graham, S., & Harris, K. R. (1998). A perspective on strategy research: Progress and prospects. *Educational Psychology Review, 10*(2), 129–154.

Bangert-Drowns, R. L., Hurley, M. M., & Wilkinson, B. (2004). The effects of school-based writing-to-learn interventions on academic achievement: A meta-analysis. *Review of Educational Research, 74*(1), 29–58.

Barton, D., & Lee, C. (2013). *Language Online: Investigating Digital Texts and Practices.* New York: Routledge.

Beach, R., & Friedrich, T. (2006). Response to writing. In C. A. MacArthur, S. Graham & J. Fitzgerald (Eds.), *Handbook of Writing Research* (pp. 222–234). New York: Guilford Press.

Burstein, J., Tetreault, J., & Madnani, N. (2013). The e-rater automated essay scoring system. In M. D. Shermis & J. Burstein (Eds.), *Handbook of Automated Essay Evaluation: Current Applications and New Directions* (pp. 55–67). New York: Routledge.

Carnegie Council on Advancing Adolescent Literacy. (2010). *Time to Act: An Agenda for Advancing Adolescent Literacy for College and Career Success.* New York: Carnegie Corporation of New York.

Duke, N. K., & Pearson, P. D. (2002). Effective practices for developing reading comprehension. In A. E. Farstrup & Samuels, S. J. (Eds.), *What Research Has to Say about Reading Instruction* (3rd ed., pp. 205–242). Newark, DE: International Reading Association.

Elliot, N., & Klobucar, A. (2013). Automated essay evaluation and the teaching of writing. In M. D. Shermis, J. Burstein & S. Apel (Eds.), *Handbook of Automated Essay Evaluation: Current Applications and New Directions* (pp. 16–35). London: Routledge.

Ericsson, K. A., Krampe, R. T., & Tesch-Römer, C. (1993). The role of deliberate practice in the acquisition of expert performance. *Psychological Review, 100*(3), 363.

Ferris, D. R. (2003). *Response to Student Writing: Implications for Second Language Students.* Mahwah, NJ: Lawrence Erlbaum Associates.

Flower, L., & Hayes, J. R. (1981). A cognitive process theory of writing. *College Composition and Communication, 32*(4), 365–387.

Geiser, S., & Studley, R. (2001). UC and the SAT: Predictive validity and differential impact of the SAT I and SAT II at the University of California. University of California, Office of the President.

Goodman, M., Finnegan, R., Mohadjer, L., Krenzke, T., & Hogan, J. (2013). *Literacy, Numeracy, and Problem Solving in Technology-Rich Environments Among U.S. Adults: Results from the Program for the International Assessment of Adult Competencies 2012: First Look* (NCES 2014–008). U.S. Department of Education. Washington, DC: National Center for Education Statistics. Retrieved from http://nces.ed.gov/pubsearch.

Graham, S., & Harris, K. R. (2013). Designing an effective writing program. In S. Graham, C. A. MacArthur & J. Fitzgerald (Eds.), *Best Practices in Writing Instruction* (pp. 3–25). New York: The Guilford Press.

Graham, S., & Hebert, M. (2010). *Writing to Read: Evidence for How Writing Can Improve Reading.* Alliance for Excellence in Education. Washington, D.C.

Grimes, D., & Warschauer, M. (2010). Utility in a fallible tool: A multi-site case study of automated writing evaluation. *Journal of Technology, Learning, and Assessment, 8*(6).

Graham, S., Harris, K. R., & Mason, L. (2005). Improving the writing performance, knowledge, and motivation of struggling young writers: The effects of self-regulated strategy development. *Contemporary Educational Psychology, 30*, 207–241.

Harris, K. R., & Graham, S. (2009). Self-regulated strategy development in writing: Premises, evolution, and the future. *British Journal of Educational Psychology* (monograph series), *6*, 113–135.

Healy, A., Schneider, V., & Bourne, L. (2012). Empirically valid principles of training. In A. Healy & L. Bourne (Eds.), *Training Cognition: Optimizing Efficiency, Durability, and Generalizability* (pp. 13–39). New York: Psychology Press.

Johnstone, K. M., Ashbaugh, H., & Warfield, T. D. (2002). Effects of repeated practice and contextual-writing experiences on college students' writing skills. *Journal of Educational Psychology, 94*(2), 305–315.

Kellogg, R. T. (2008). Training writing skills: A cognitive developmental perspective. *Journal of Writing Research*, *1*(1), 1–26.

Kellogg, R. T., & Raulerson, B. A. (2007). Improving the writing skills of college students. *Psychonomic Bulletin & Review*, *14*(2), 237–242.

Kellogg, R. T., & Whiteford, A. P. (2009). Training advanced writing skills: The case for deliberate practice. *Educational Psychologist*, *44*(4), 250–266.

McCutchen, D. (2006). Cognitive factors in the development of children's writing. In C. A. MacArthur, S. Graham & J. Fitzgerald (Eds.), *Handbook of Writing Research*, (pp. 115–130). New York: The Guilford Press.

McNamara, D. S. (2004). SERT: Self-explanation reading training. *Discourse Processes*, *38*(1), 1–30.

National Assessment of Educational Progress. (2011). *The Nation's Report Card: Writing 2011*. Retrieved from http://nationsreportcard.gov/writing_2011/writing_2011_report/

National Assessment Governing Board. (2011). *Writing Framework for the 2011 National Assessment of Education Progress* (ERIC No. 512552). Retrieved from http://files.eric.ed.gov/fulltext/ED512552.pdf

National Clearinghouse for English Language Acquisition. (2011). *The Growing Numbers of English Learner Students*. Washington, DC: Author. Retrieved from https://ncela.ed.gov/files/uploads/9/growing_EL_0910.pdf

The National Commission on Writing. (2004). *Writing: A Ticket to Work. Or a Ticket Out*. College Board.

National Writing Project, DeVoss, D. N., Eidman-Aadahl, E., & Hicks, T. (2010). *Because Digital Writing Matters: Improving Student Writing in Online and Multimedia Environments*. San Francisco, CA: Wiley.

Ness, M. (2011). Explicit reading comprehension instruction in elementary classrooms: Teacher use of reading comprehension strategies. *Journal of Research in Childhood Education*, *25*(1), 98–117.

O'Reilly, T., & McNamara, D. S. (2007). The impact of science knowledge, reading skill, and reading strategy knowledge on more traditional "High-Stakes" measures of high school students' science achievement. *American Educational Research Journal*, *44*, 161–196.

O'Reilly, T., Taylor, R. S., & McNamara, D. S. (2006). Classroom based reading strategy training: Self-explanation vs. reading control. In R. Sun & N. Miyake (Eds.), *Proceedings of the 28th Annual Conference of the Cognitive Science Society* (p. 1887). Mahwah, NJ: Erlbaum.

Plant, E. A., Ericsson, K. A., Hill, L., & Asberg, K. (2005). Why study time does not predict grade point average across college students: Implications of deliberate practice for academic performance. *Contemporary Educational Psychology*, *30*(1), 96–116.

Powell, P. R. (2009). Retention and writing instruction: Implications for access and pedagogy. *College Composition and Communication*, *60*(4), 664–682.

Pressley, M. (2006). *Reading Instruction That Really Works*. New York: The Guilford Press.

Pressley, M., Wharton-McDonald, R., Mistretta-Hampston, J., & Echevarria, M. (1998). Literacy instruction in 10 fourth-grade classrooms in upstate New York. *Scientific Studies of Reading*, *2*(2), 159–194.

Reynolds, A. J., & Ou, S. R. (2004). Alterable predictors of child well-being in the Chicago longitudinal study. *Children and Youth Services Review*, *26*(1), 1–14.

Rohrer, D., & Pashler, H. (2010). Recent research on human learning challenges conventional instructional strategies. *Educational Researcher*, *39*(5), 406–412.

Roscoe, R. D., Varner (Allen), L. K., Snow, E. L., & McNamara, D. S. (2014). Designing usable automated formative feedback for intelligent tutoring of writing. In J. L. Polman,

E. A. Kyza, D. K. O'Neill, I. Tabak, W. R. Penuel, A. S. Jurow, K. O'Connor, T. Lee & L. D'Amico (Eds.), *Proceedings of the 11th International Conference of the Learning Sciences (ICLS), Volume 3*, (pp. 1423–1425). Boulder, CO.

Shonkoff, J. P., & Phillips, D. A. (2000). Committee on Integrating the Science of Early Childhood Development, Board on Children, Youth, and Families. *From Neurons to Neighborhoods: The Science of Early Childhood Programs*. National Academies Press.

Shute, V. J. (2008). Focus on formative feedback. *Review of Educational Research*, 78(1), 153–189.

Snow, C. E., Burns, M. S., & Griffin, P. (Eds.). (1998). *Preventing Reading Difficulties in Young Children*. Washington, DC: National Academy Press.

Taylor, B. M., Pearson, P. D., Clark, K., & Walpole, S. (2000). Effective schools and accomplished teachers: Lessons about primary-grade reading instruction in low-income schools. *The Elementary School Journal*, 121–165.

U.S. Department of Education. (2011). *Reading 2011: National Assessment of Educational Progress at Grades 4 and 8*. (NCES 2012–455). Washington DC: National Center for Education Statistics.

White, S., Chen, J., & Forsyth, B. (2010). Reading-related literacy activities of American adults: Time spent, task types, and cognitive skills used. *Journal of Literacy Research*, 42(3), 276–307.

# 2
# CHALLENGES AND SOLUTIONS WHEN USING TECHNOLOGIES IN THE CLASSROOM

*Amy M. Johnson, Matthew E. Jacovina, Devin G. Russell, and Christian M. Soto*

## Introduction

Technology is perhaps the strongest factor shaping the educational landscape today. Many school districts are showing support for increased levels of technology in the classroom by providing hardware such as tablets and computers, enhancing internet connectivity, and implementing programs designed to improve computer literacy for both teachers and students. Although teachers generally appreciate the benefits of educational technologies, they often find smooth and effective integration of new educational technologies challenging. From acquisition of new technology equipment to adaptation of curricula and teaching techniques to incorporate new educational tools, technology integration presents significant challenges to educators at each level of school systems.

The purpose of this chapter is to present common challenges faced by educators when attempting to integrate technology in the classroom, and offer potential solutions to those problems. Examination of these issues should be valuable to current and future educators, school administrators, as well as educational technology researchers. The chapter begins by introducing the challenges to technology integration that are external (extrinsic) to the teacher, including access to resources, training, and support. We then present barriers that are internal to teachers, including their attitudes and beliefs, resistance toward technology in the classroom, and their knowledge and skills. The next section presents international perspectives on the technology integration problem, focusing on a case in Chile. The chapter concludes with a short summary of the chapter and condensed recommendations for effective technology implementation.

## External Challenges to Classroom Technology

First-order barriers to the successful integration of technology into the classroom are factors external to teachers implementing technology. External barriers must be addressed at the institutional level and changes are typically incremental (e.g., rolling out access to technology one level at a time). Although there is growing evidence that, in the United States, first-order barriers are being tackled (Ertmer, Ottenbreit-Leftwich, Sadik, Sendurur, & Sendurur, 2012), more effort is needed to entirely overcome these challenges. In this section, we introduce some of the external barriers to classroom technology integration and present strategies to address them.

First, we address issues surrounding insufficient equipment or connectivity, termed the *access* constraint. If a teacher's school does not possess adequate computers and fast internet connection, the implementation of educational technology is not feasible. Next, we introduce the challenge of inadequate *training* related to technology. If teachers are not provided with effective professional development on new technologies, they will not be capable of using it to its full potential. Finally, we discuss factors related to the *support* constraint. Support barriers to technology integration include inadequate technical support and administrative/peer support.

### *Access*

Early accounts of technology integration focused much of their interest on increasing the availability of computers in schools (Fisher, Dwyer, & Yocam, 1996). Certainly, the most basic step toward effective technology integration is widespread access to equipment necessary to run educational computer programs. If computer lab time is limited to one hour per week, persistent use of educational technology is not viable. While many schools across the country are making the transition to one-to-one (1:1) computing (Warschauer, Zheng, Niiya, Cotten, & Farkas, 2014), many students do not have regular and reliable access to a computer. Inconsistent computer access makes it extremely difficult for instructors to integrate technology into existing lesson plans. Routine access to hardware (i.e., laptops or tablets), software (e.g., reading and writing software, internet browsers), and internet connection is a fundamental requirement.

Research demonstrates that much progress has been made to improve equipment and internet access in schools over the last 20 years. Results from the National Center for Education Statistics' (NCES) 2009 survey of public school teachers revealed that 97 percent of all teachers have at least one computer in their classroom every day (Gray, Thomas, & Lewis, 2010). Compare this result to the 1999 survey, which found that only 84 percent of public school teachers had computers available in the classroom (Smerdon et al., 2000). The 2009 results indicated that, on average, classrooms had 5.3 students to every computer in the classroom (Gray et al., 2010). Results also showed that 93 percent of classroom computers had internet access by 2009 (compared to 64 percent in the 1999 survey; Smerdon et al., 2000). These results demonstrate that, by the year 2009, the ideal 1:1 computing model had not been broadly realized, but computers are widely accessible in the modern classroom. Further advances have presumably been made since the 2009 study, but up-to-date statistics are not available.

Although impressive recent advances have been made, effective use of educational technologies for literacy may require more frequent instructional time on computers than currently afforded by the ratio of students to computers. Intelligent tutoring systems, such as those detailed in this book, can individualize instruction to student progress within the system, but consistent 1:1 computer access is highly desirable given this pedagogical approach. With limited federal, state, and local funding, schools may often need to pursue unconventional funding options for obtaining classroom technologies. Budgets may be supplemented using crowdfunding sites, some of which specifically target education funding (e.g., AdoptAClassroom, DonorsChoose, IncitED). One challenge with crowdfunding is retaining donors; a recent study by Althoff and Leskovec (2015) reported that 74 percent of donors only contribute to one project. The authors found that donors were more likely to make additional donations when teachers are prompt in sending recognition messages to donors and in communicating the eventual impact. Thus, teachers who use crowdfunding sites must consider more than how useful a project is; they must also consider how best to communicate with donors to increase the likelihood of repeat donations. Educators can also apply for grants to support technology infrastructure, and websites make identifying funding opportunities easier (e.g., Edutopia, Fund for Teachers). Additionally, schools or teachers may seek support through partnerships with local businesses or universities. Some schools have also moved toward a Bring Your Own Device (BYOD) strategy in which students bring their own computing device to school to use for educational purposes. BYOD has obvious cost-cutting benefits, but schools must also be prepared with a network infrastructure that can accommodate the additional number of devices and that is appropriately secure (Afreen, 2014).

## *Training*

According to Ertmer et al. (2012), the most commonly cited reason for lack of technology implementation in the classroom is inadequate professional development and training. The National Education Association (NEA) includes expanding professional development in technology as one of their policy recommendations (NEA, 2008). According to NEA results (2008), teachers today report increasing confidence using classroom technology, operating software, and searching the internet, but given that technology is constantly changing, it is more important than ever that teachers stay up-to-date with their technological expertise. Even if a school district were to hire only teachers who were literate in current classroom technology, countless new technologies will be developed during their teaching careers, and they will need to undergo additional training to keep their skills current. Without the necessary resources to provide continuous technological training, schools and districts will continue to cite inadequate professional development as a major barrier to technology implementation.

Survey results from public school teachers suggest that educational technology professional development is reasonably widespread. In a 2009 survey, only 18 percent of teachers reported having completed no educational technology training over the previous year; the majority (53 percent) reported completing 1 to 8 hours training (Gray et al., 2010). Further, they generally had positive perceptions of their training. Eighty-one percent agreed with the statement "It met my goals and needs" and 88 percent agreed with the statement "It supported the goals and standards of my state, district, and school." Unfortunately, some research suggests that professional development has a greater impact on teachers' noninstructional (e.g., research, administrative) tasks than on student instruction. A 2006 survey revealed that around two-thirds of teachers felt their training was adequate for using the internet for research, using technology equipment, and using administrative software (NEA – AFT, 2008). Fewer teachers regarded the training adequate for the following instructional goals: evaluating student progress (57.6 percent); integrating technology into instruction (55.7 percent); and designing individual lessons (45.6 percent). Given limited budgets for professional development at the institution level, schools should verify their chosen training focuses on technology for student instruction. As with issues regarding technology access, more recent progress has likely been made in addressing these issues, but more recent survey results from NCES or NEA were not available at the time of writing this chapter.

The specific type of training that is available to teachers is also an important consideration. For example, many schools are purchasing iPads; however, the usefulness of iPads for education is not always immediately clear. One weakness of the iPad is the difficulty in typing using the touch keyboard, making it less ideal for activities requiring students to generate text, such as writing practice. One recent study with a sample of 21 teachers who had access to at least 1 iPad reported that the perceived usefulness of iPads was mixed, with an average rating of 2.75 on a 5 point scale. Several teachers reported not using the iPads frequently, with one explanation being lack of familiarity with apps that would be useful for particular lessons. In another study, nine teachers were provided with professional development that focused on using iPads in science and math classrooms (Hu & Garimella, 2014). A pre-post comparison showed that teachers perceived the iPad as being more useful and felt more proficient in using particular apps (including organizational and communication apps, such as Dropbox and Evernote) after completing the professional development. Additionally, teachers felt more confident overall about using the iPad and planned to integrate it into their classes.

This study thus demonstrates the effectiveness of professional development that is targeted to a specific technology. The iPad and mobile devices in general, are particularly appropriate technologies to target given their pervasiveness and the abundance of educational software available that is often difficult to sort through.

To realize effective technology integration, school administrators should seek assistance to identify and provide ongoing training. The International Society for Technology in Education approves materials aligned to their standards for integration of technology into the classroom (http://www.iste.org/standards/iste-standards), including student curricula that integrate technology (addressing student standards), professional development resources (training teacher standards), as well as assessments (evaluating student standards). Professional development programs approved by the ISTE include face-to-face instruction, online courses, online communities of learning, online learning modules, in-class mentoring, and target development of different levels of teacher technology skills. Using guidance provided by ISTE, schools can identify professional development programs that best fit their needs. Additionally, some school districts use master teachers successful in implementing educational technologies to lead professional learning communities, meeting regularly to train and support technology integration. Finally, schools and teachers should pursue training from educational software companies and educational technology researchers. Many software companies offer free professional development courses, online training, and continuing support to educators. For example, Apple sales representatives offer formal training for iPads (Vu, McIntyre, & Cepero, 2014).

## *Support*

Though we cannot say for certain how the future will impact professional development, it is clear that the teachers of today do not have optimal access to technological support. According to statistics reported by the U. S. Department of Education (2010), 68 percent of school districts reported having adequate support for educational technology. While it is encouraging to see that the majority of responding districts feel that they have access to adequate support, there is clearly room for improvement. With additional technology support, teachers can worry less about technological barriers and instead focus on teaching their students.

Adopting a new educational technology can be a time-consuming process. If a technology is adopted school-wide, teachers should have access to extended support from trained professionals, as opposed to a single hour-long meeting before the school day begins. Of course, this will most likely require additional funding for schools, but creators of educational technologies should also place increased emphasis on user support. With high quality support from both creators of educational technologies and school employees, teachers will have access to the resources they deserve. The knowledge that support is readily available may in turn increase acceptance of classroom technologies.

Ertmer (1999) notes that the most essential form of support to teachers can change as the technology integration project matures. During the earlier phases of a project, teachers require more technical support just to use the new technology, which could be accomplished by hiring educational technology and information technology professionals. As teachers become more proficient in the technical skills required for the new technology, their needs may shift to administrative and peer support to help develop and apply new uses for the technology in their classrooms. This type of support may be provided in professional learning communities through regular discussions regarding novel, domain-relevant uses of the technology.

## Internal Challenges to Classroom Technology

In the previous section, we discussed external barriers to the classroom integration of educational technologies. Of course, as Ertmer (1999) points out, even with first-order barriers removed, digital technology would not appear immediately and seamlessly within all classrooms using appropriate pedagogy. Individual educators are ultimately responsible for using technology, and thus even when given resources, they have choices about how to use technology. In this section, we describe barriers that relate specifically to teachers, their beliefs, and their knowledge. These issues are, by their nature, personal and thus vary greatly from teacher to teacher even within the same environment. Consequently, it is difficult to address these issues broadly. However, we attempt to provide an overview of common frameworks, provide examples of the research being done using these frameworks as guides, and discuss implications with regard to literacy technology.

First, we will discuss educators' attitudes and beliefs, referred to as second-order barriers (Ertmer, 1999). If teachers do not expect new technology to be useful or do not think they have the required experience to use such technologies, they are more likely to persist using more traditional methods. Closely related to the attitudes and beliefs, teacher resistance may present a barrier to technology integration. Finally, we discuss the influence of teachers' skills and knowledge as they pertain to technology.

### *Teacher Attitudes and Beliefs*

Teachers' attitudes and beliefs are crucial factors in determining the role and effectiveness of technology in classrooms. Attitudes and beliefs about both educational technology and pedagogy in general will ultimately influence how teachers implement technology. In the following sections, we discuss these issues and ways to promote positive attitudes that can optimize technology use. Now that technology is being widely used in schools, perhaps the most important question is *how* best to implement technology, rather than *whether* technology will be used (Ertmer, 1999; Ertmer et al., 2012; Keengwe, Onchwari, & Wachira, 2008; Lowther, Inan, Strahl, & Ross, 2008).

## Confidence in Skills and Knowledge

Given the abundance of available educational technology, it is essential that teachers feel comfortable and confident about their ability to use them effectively. Many current teachers grew up without access to technologies like the personal computer and the internet, but students today are raised in an environment saturated by computer technology. These "digital natives" can intimidate teachers, especially teachers with little technological experience. If teachers feel they do not have the necessary competencies when using technology, they may feel less in control of the class, use less technology, and be unlikely to explore new possibilities that utilize technology when designing their classes (Hughes, 2005; Rakes & Casey, 2002). By sticking to traditional teaching methods, teachers who are less fluent with technology maintain a feeling of control in the classroom and will not have to prepare to face the challenges of instructing digital natives in a digital environment.

In a survey of 764 teachers, Wozney, Venkatesh, and Abrami (2006) found that one of the two strongest predictors of teachers' technology use was confidence in achieving instructional goals using technology. Teachers who believe they lack training can decide either to work with technology at their current level of expertise, or postpone the use of technology until they consider that they have sufficient competence (Ertmer, 1999). To build teachers' knowledge to a sufficient level, boosting confidence in the process, training, and support from the educational administrators is necessary.

## About Technology and Learning

Teachers may use technology throughout the curriculum or to complement a specific lesson. Variations in technology usage reflect important differences in teachers' beliefs about the utility of technology in the educational process. Ertmer found that "teachers were able to enact technology integration practices that closely aligned with their beliefs" (Ertmer et al., 2012). These beliefs are greatly influenced by the teachers' philosophy regarding how students learn. If the teacher regards student learning as primarily dependent on explicit teacher teaching, classroom activities will be driven by the traditional chalk-and-talk approach. More traditional educational beliefs have been related to less integration of computer-based technology in classrooms (Hermans, Tondeur, van Braak, & Valcke, 2008). Thus, the use of technology will likely be limited to supplementary demonstrative activities within particular educational units.

For teachers to achieve effective use of computers, they must experience a paradigm shift from the teacher-centered classroom to the student-centered classroom (Adams & Burns, 1999; Bitner & Bitner, 2002; Hannafin & Savenye, 1993; Harris & Grandgenett, 1999; Mandinach & Cline, 2000). In this situation, educational technologies will likely have a more central role, because they permit active student learning activities in which the teacher serves as facilitator of the learning process. Ravitz, Becker, and Wong (2000) reported that teacher implementation of constructivist learning environments were often limited by difficulties meeting individual student needs, balancing multiple objectives, and responding to external forces and expectations. Teachers in these situations will thus more frequently use technology when they believe that it connects directly with their specific content areas and/or grade levels, allowing them more readily to meet their classroom goals (Hughes, 2005; Snoeyink & Ertmer, 2001).

The increasing acceptance of constructivist learning philosophies, along with intelligent learning technologies offer new possibilities to address individual differences of the student, one of the emphases of modern educational pedagogy. However, new technologies should incorporate student performance visualization tools that permit teachers to easily understand student progress on their educational objectives. Although technologies can be powerful means to improve learning, the teacher remains the critical factor to student success, and must be informed of student progress in order to intervene directly with their students.

## *Teacher Resistance to Technology in the Classroom*

Browsing online teacher forums makes it clear that implementing new technologies into lesson plans can be a difficult task. Perhaps the most common reason mentioned by teachers for not actively integrating new technologies is that many teachers are satisfied with their current lesson plans. A teacher's desire for their students to learn effectively drives classroom instruction, and if current lesson plans meet the needs of students, there is very little motivation for the teacher to alter them. Educators spend countless hours creating lesson plans that will hold attention and make learning exciting. Revising lesson plans means several hours of additional work for the teacher, which is problematic given an already demanding schedule.

Simply revising lesson plans can occupy a great deal of time, but revising lesson plans to incorporate technology is even more labor intensive. When adopting new classroom technologies, educators face the problem known online as the "double innovation" problem (Cleaver, 2014). Double innovation essentially adds an additional layer of preparation teachers must work through. The teacher must first learn the technology well enough to utilize it in a classroom setting before deciding how to integrate the technology with classroom objectives and curriculum. While educational technologies are becoming easier to learn, the double innovation problem still results in additional preparation time. Data collected from teacher interviews conducted by Ertmer et al. (2012) showed time as being the sixth most influential barrier to integrating new classroom technologies. A teacher's time is extremely valuable, and it should come as no surprise that time is one of the most commonly cited barriers to integrating new technologies in the classroom.

Clearly, there are numerous reasons a teacher might shy away from new technology in the classroom, but once teachers decide to further incorporate technology into lesson plans, they must first choose what technologies to use. There are thousands of internet technologies, tutoring systems, and learning environments for teachers to choose from, so deciding which ones will enhance the student learning experience and align with curricula is a daunting task. Even if teachers find a technology they believe will help their students, it is not always clear if these programs are actually effective. Many technologies claim to improve the academic and cognitive abilities of students, but claims can be false and are often only created as advertisement. Having to verify the truthfulness of these claims is an additional burden placed on the educator, who may not have time to search for classroom technologies in the first place. Perhaps, as a consequence, decisions about technology are often made by school or district administrators without input from teachers. In some ways, this can be helpful by saving teachers the time and effort required to evaluate technologies, but lack of choice can also negatively impact an instructor's perception of the technology. Teachers may view the new technology as an imposition, when in reality the technology may make their teaching experience easier and more enjoyable.

## *Solutions to Increase Acceptance of Classroom Technology*

Time will inevitably bring about the increased adoption of classroom technology on a large scale, so here we suggest some strategies that can be used by educators and researchers alike to encourage technology integration now. First, it is extremely important that teachers have a say in what technologies they will use in their instruction. Teaching is a deeply personal experience, and when educators feel as though they have lost the ability to teach in a manner that best suits them, it can be frustrating and discouraging. No single educational technology will be perfect for every teacher, and educators should have the ability to select a technology that they feel most comfortable with. By allowing teachers more freedom of choice they will retain the very important sense of classroom control.

While the importance of teacher autonomy in the selection of educational technology cannot be understated, it does introduce the burden of sifting through a vast number of available technologies. A second solution to encouraging acceptance of classroom technology is a call for better organization of available technologies. While a typical internet search will turn up thousands of results for educational technology tools, there are very few places that effectively organize and evaluate available technologies. Teachers should be able to easily find and access rigorously tested technologies within a specific learning domain. In fact, this book can serve as a valuable resource to teachers looking to find such technologies. Better organization of empirically validated educational technologies will serve to save valuable time and will place less of a burden on the teacher.

## Teacher Skills and Knowledge

Pedagogical content knowledge (PCK) has long been discussed as crucial for effective teaching (Shulman, 1986). Effective educators must not only be domain experts, but also understand how to use flexibly the affordances of different pedagogies for particular content topics. With the advent of numerous novel technologies over the past decades, educators have an abundance of technologies to leverage to make their teaching more effective. Although the potential benefits are clear, the sheer number of possible combinations of technologies and pedagogies for different tasks and students is overwhelming. The technological pedagogical content knowledge (TPACK) framework expands on the focus of PCK to also include technology as a knowledge domain (Mishra & Koehler, 2006). TPACK focuses on technology, pedagogy, and content knowledge individually, and also on their interactive combinations; this leads to a sum of seven types of knowledge that TPACK supporters argue are crucial for ideal integration: content knowledge, pedagogical knowledge, technological knowledge, PCK, technological content knowledge, technological pedagogical knowledge (TPK), and TPACK (see Figure 2.1).

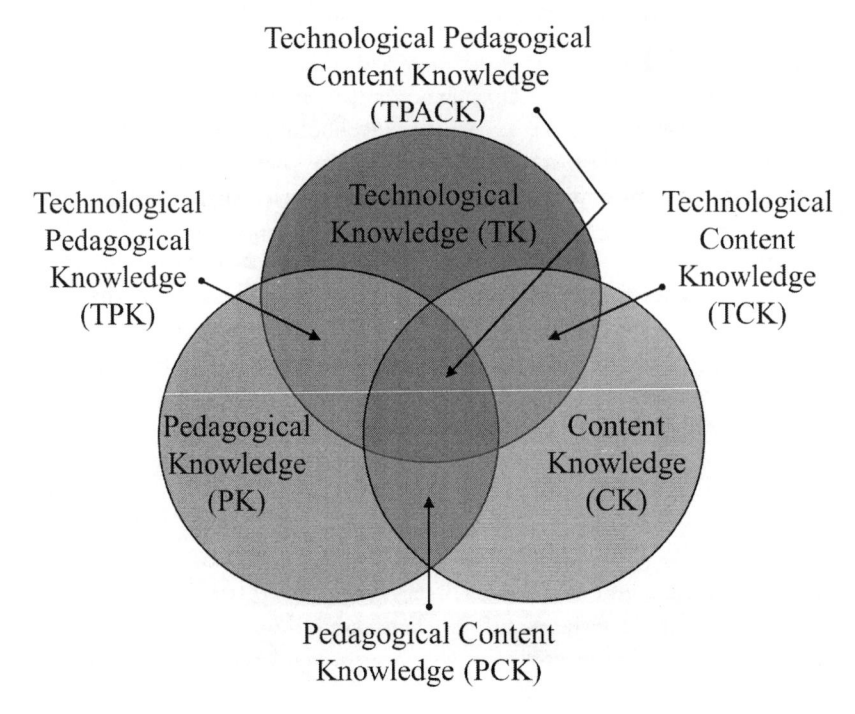

**FIGURE 2.1** TPACK Framework's Knowledge Components (adapted from Koehler & Mishra, 2009).

Clearly, educators with expertise in the three core knowledge types will have some proficiency in the combined types. However, there is specialized knowledge in the combined domains. TPK requires more than knowing useful pedagogical techniques and familiarity with technologies; it requires an understanding of how particular technologies can provide support for particular pedagogical strategies or techniques. As an example, the selection of a social networking tool for collaborative learning must be informed by the affordances specific to each platform (e.g., Twitter might encourage a great number of messages to be shared, but following threads of conversations between numerous students would be very difficult). TPACK additionally requires an understanding of how technologies can support pedagogies for specific domains.

How can the TPACK framework be useful? It has been conceptualized in different ways, but most relevant for our current discussion is that it is often viewed as the complete set of knowledge necessary to teach with technology (Mishra & Koehler, 2006). Thus, a goal is to promote these knowledge domains; clearly, most of these knowledge domains are *already* heavily emphasized during teacher training and professional development (e.g., mastering the content in which a teacher specializes). The intersections between technological knowledge and content/pedagogical knowledge, however, is more specialized and less frequently taught. For example, consider the case of writing instruction. Teaching writing techniques and strategies (requiring content knowledge) through deliberate writing practice and feedback (requiring pedagogical knowledge) is something successful writing teachers do and an example of PCK. Digital technology can further support instruction by allowing teachers to provide feedback through word documents. This is an example of TPACK; however, training on the capabilities of different technologies might allow teachers to further optimize the experience for students. Programs such as myAccess or the Writing Pal can provide automated immediate feedback, increasing the efficiency with which students receive feedback (Allen, Jacovina, & McNamara, 2015). Without training, teachers are unlikely to understand exactly how these feedback mechanisms work and therefore will not optimize their effectiveness (e.g., Grimes & Warschauer, 2010). Thus, training on TPACK might be helpful for writing instructors. TPACK can be taught effectively, making this goal tenable. Researchers investigating how TPACK knowledge in preservice teachers developed over an 11-month Master of Arts in Education program generally showed positive increases in knowledge (Hofer & Grandgenett, 2012).

Brantley-Dias and Ertmer (2013) urge caution in extending TPACK too far. Although it might seem advantageous to encourage teachers to develop their knowledge in each of the seven domains, there is little evidence that such a practice leads to more effective teaching. We respect this caution and view TPACK as something that teachers should be aware of and discuss, but that does not have a definitive end goal. Despite any weaknesses in the TPACK framework, there have been interesting, though not strongly empirically supported, activities and suggestions that have come from it. First, it does provide common language for educators to discuss methods and techniques for improving knowledge related to technology. Second, these discussions can be made into activities that promote flexible thinking about technology affordances. For example, a TPACK game has been used by various groups as part of professional development (Richardson, 2010; https://www.youtube.com/watch?v=7z3aP_Chj6c). Such activities are ways for teachers to increase their knowledge of technology.

## Considerations from an International Perspective

When educators or researchers grapple with technology integration issues in only their own country, they may lose perspective regarding variables that could influence results when using technology in the classroom. Thus, examination of comparative studies across various nations may help us to reconsider important factors in the planning of school interventions. Ample evidence indicates that, in the U.S., many first-order barriers have largely been conquered (Ertmer et al., 2012). Thus, current challenges relate to identifying and implementing methods to integrate technology most effectively in the educational context. Measuring integration success is potentially an even more difficult task. Will it be possible to assess the progress made in the U.S. and other countries, and compare outcomes across countries? The answer is potentially linked to diverse standards adopted by different countries regarding educational technology development. The U.S. follows educational technology standards defined by the ISTE, the United Kingdom the Qualified Teacher Status (QTS), and other European countries often follow the European Pedagogical Informational and Communication Technology (ICT), and so on. Because different criteria are used, researchers seeking evidence concerning international experiences in educational technology integration face substantial challenges.

When considering the educational technology progress in various countries, one discovers provocative cases of failures and successes. For example, in Chile, progress may be different to other countries of Latin America. The Education Ministry of Chile has been promoting systematic development in educational technology since 1992, with the aim of contributing to improving the quality and equity of public education (Cancino & Donoso, 2004). In terms of access to technology, the ENLACES program has made Chile a pioneer country in Latin America. From 2000 to 2010, the number of Chilean students per computer went from 80 to approximately 10 students per computer. Furthermore, in 1998, fewer than 1,000 schools in Chile had access to the internet; in 2008, around 7,000 schools had access, reaching broad national coverage.

Currently, one of the key challenges in Chile is the struggle to secure sufficient professional development and technology support for teachers through collaboration with and support of different institutions (universities, government, administrators, ENLACES, and schools). On this issue, the experiences in the U.S. could be invaluable, given its relative successes in educational technology implementation (Ertmer et al., 2012). Once technology integration policies are adopted, a further challenge concerns establishment of valid instruments and methods to assess the impact of programs and determine how use of technology is affecting academic learning outcomes. Policy-makers in Chile considered whether to adopt an existing international standard, eventually deciding instead to create their own separate standards related to educational technology (Toro, 2010).

Careful deliberation of comparative studies across multiple countries may also be useful in determining a sound assessment approach. For example, a 2012 international study evaluated the impact of educational technology on academic performance, examining different factors related to educational technology and their impact on the PISA test reading results (San Martín, Jara, Preiss, Claro, & Farina, 2012). Spanish speaking countries in South America (Uruguay and Chile) were compared with countries in Europe, which share characteristics (Spain and Portugal). Results revealed that the use of the educational technology led to varied improvements depending on an additional factor, class time devoted to reading. Students in Spain and Portugal spent more time reading than their counterparts in Chile and Uruguay, and the correlation between use of technology in class and PISA reading scores was higher in Chile and Uruguay. One of the more interesting conclusions of the San Martin study is that when traditional reading time is low, reading through technology contributes positively to reading outcomes (San Martín et al., 2012). Studies by Jackson and colleagues with U.S. students seem to lend support to this interpretation (Jackson et al., 2006; Jackson, Von Eye, Witt, Zhao, & Fitzgerald, 2011). The authors conclude that more internet use over time is associated with better reading results for students with low reading skills. One explanation for this is that because the internet is largely based on reading written text, its use encourages the students to read more than they typically do when not on the internet.

Reviewing international experiences may be a valuable way to obtain essential information about public policies on educational technology, helping to generate plans for implementation of key processes like teacher training and support. Moreover, international comparison studies could serve as valuable resources for assessment adoption or development, and can help us understand how technology impact learning and when other factors moderate those effects.

## Conclusion

Although the task of technology integration presents significant challenges to school districts, school administrators, and teachers alike, exciting new educational technologies are increasingly available that offer teachers novel ways of presenting material to students. Research on the reading and writing technologies reviewed throughout this book demonstrates they can have considerable positive impacts on student performance. Furthermore, efforts to adopt new educational technologies in the classroom will be rewarded, albeit with some potential barriers.

Recent research on technology use in the classroom indicates that significant advances have been made to overcome the first-order (external) barriers to technology integration, especially concerning access to computing resources. Recommendations to make further improvement include the following: (1) obtain funds for resources via non-traditional sources (e.g., crowdfunding, grants); (2) seek guidance from the ISTE to identify effective professional development programs; (3) exploit the expertise of master teachers in professional learning communities; (4) request training on newly adopted educational software directly from software companies; and (5) ensure that adequate technical, administrative, and peer support is available to teachers during the implementation. In comparison, overcoming second-order (internal) barriers to technology integration will likely be a more difficult hurdle. Our suggestions to confront the challenges internal to the teacher (i.e., attitudes, beliefs, skills, and knowledge) include the following: (1) provide teacher training that highlights constructivism and student-centered education; (2) focus professional development efforts toward those which emphasize the use of technology in instruction, rather than for administrative tasks; (3) include visualization tools in student tracking technologies, which allow teachers to easily interpret student progress; (4) involve teachers in the decision-making process when adopting new technologies; and (5) offer teachers training on the intersection of technological knowledge, pedagogical knowledge, and content knowledge (TPACK). Technology integration in the classroom will require the ongoing collaborative efforts of teachers, educational technology professionals, school administrators, researchers, and educational software personnel. Fortunately, the benefits to schools, teachers, and students will yield tremendous returns.

## Acknowledgments

The authors would like to recognize the support of the Institute of Education Sciences, U.S. Department of Education, through Grants R305A130124 and R305A120707, and the Office of Naval Research, through Grant N00014140343, to Arizona State University. The opinions expressed are those of the authors and do not represent the views of the Institute or the U.S. Department of Education.

## References

Adams, M., & Burns, M. (1999). *Connecting Student Learning and Technology*. Austin, TX: Southwest Educational Development Laboratory.

Afreen, R. (2014). Bring your own device (BYOD) in higher education: Opportunities and challenges. *International Journal of Emerging Trends & Technology in Computer Science, 3*, 233–236.

Allen, L. K., Jacovina, M. E., & McNamara, D. S. (2015). Computer-based writing instruction. In C. A. MacArthur, S. Graham & J. Fitzgerald (Eds.), *Handbook of Writing Research* (2nd ed. pp. 316–329). New York: Guilford Press.

Althoff, T., & Leskovec, J. (2015). Donor retention in online crowdfunding communities: A case study of DonorsChoose.org. *Proceedings of the 24th International Conference on World Wide Web*, 34–44.

Bitner, N. & Bitner, J. (2002). Integrating technology into the classroom: Eight keys to success. *Journal of Technology and Teacher Education, 10*(1), 95–100. Norfolk, VA: Society for Information Technology & Teacher Education.

Brantley-Dias, L., & Ertmer, P. A. (2013). Goldilocks and TPACK: Is the construct "Just Right?" *Journal of Research on Technology in Education, 46*, 103–128.

Cancino, V. & Donoso, S. (2004). El programa de informática educativa de la reforma educativa chilena: análisis crítico. *Revista Iberoamericana de Educación, 8*(36), 129–154.

Cleaver, S. (2014). *Technology in the Classroom: Helpful or Harmful?* Retrieved from http://www.education.com/magazine/article/effective-technology-teaching-child/

Ertmer, P. A. (1999). Addressing first-and second-order barriers to change: Strategies for technology integration. *Educational Technology Research and Development, 47*(4), 47–61.

Ertmer, P. A., Ottenbreit-Leftwich, A., Sadik, O., Sendurur, E., & Sendurur, P. (2012). Teacher beliefs and technology integration practices: A critical relationship. *Computers & Education, 59*, 423–435.

Fisher, C., Dwyer, D. C., & Yocam, K. (Eds.). (1996). *Education and Technology: Reflections on Computing in Classrooms.* San Francisco, CA: Jossey-Bass.

Gray, L., Thomas, N., & Lewis, L. (2010). *Teachers' Use of Educational Technology in U.S. Public Schools: 2009* (NCES 2010–040). Washington, DC: National Center for Education Statistics, Institute of Education Sciences, U.S. Department of Education.

Grimes, D., & Warschauer, M. (2010). Utility in a fallible tool: A multi-site case study of automated writing evaluation. *Journal of Technology, Learning, and Assessment, 8*(6), n6.

Hannafin, R. D., & Savenye, W. C. (1993). Technology in the classroom: The teacher's new role and resistance to it. *Educational Technology, 33*(6), 26–31.

Harris, J. B., & Grandgenett, N. (1999). Correlates with use of telecomputing tools: K-12 teachers' beliefs and demographics. *Journal of Research on Computing in Education, 31*(4), 327–340.

Hermans, R., Tondeur, J., Van Braak, J., & Valcke, M. (2008). The impact of primary school teachers' educational beliefs on the classroom use of computers. *Computers and Education, 51*(4), 1499–1509.

Hofer, M., & Grandgenett, N. (2012). TPACK development in teacher education: A longitudinal study of preservice teachers in a secondary M.A.Ed. program. *Journal of Research on Technology in Education, 45*, 83–106.

Hu, H. & Garimella, U. (2014). iPads for STEM teachers: A case study on perceived usefulness, perceived proficiency, intention to adopt, and integration in K-12 instruction. *Journal of Educational Technology Development and Exchange, 7*, 49–66.

Hughes, J. (2005). The role of teacher knowledge and learning experiences in forming technology-integrated pedagogy. *Journal of Technology and Teacher Education, 13*(2), 277–302.

Jackson, L., Von Eye, A., Witt, E., Zhao, Y., & Fitzgerald, H. (2011). A longitudinal study of the effects on internet use and videogame playing on academic performance and the roles of gender, race and income in these relationships. *Computers in Human Behavior, 27*, 228–239.

Jackson, L., Von Eye, A., Biocca, F., Barbatsis, G., Zhao, Y., & Fitzgerald, H. (2006). Does home internet use influence the academic performance of low-income children? *Developmental Psychology, 42,* 429–435.

Keengwe, J. G., Onchwari, G., & Wachira, P. (2008). Computer technology integration and student learning: Barriers and promise. *Journal of Science Education and Technology, 17*(6), 560–565.

Koehler, M. J., & Mishra, P. (2009). What is technological pedagogical content knowledge (TPACK)? *Contemporary Issues in Technology and Teacher Education, 9,* 60–70.

Lowther, D. L., Inan, F. A., Strahl, J. D., & Ross, S. M. (2008). Does technology integration "work" when key barriers are removed? *Educational Media International, 45*(3), 189–206.

Mandinach, E. B., & Cline, H. F. (2000). It won't happen soon: Practical, curricular, and methodological problems in implementing technology-based constructivist approaches in classrooms. In S. P. Lajoie (Ed.), *Computers as Cognitive Tools. No More Walls* (pp. 377–395). Mahwah, NJ: Lawrence Erlbaum Associates.

Mishra, P., & Koehler, M. J. (2006). Technological pedagogical content knowledge: A framework for integrating technology in teacher knowledge. *Teachers College Record, 108,* 1017–1054.

NEA. (2008). *Technology in Schools: The Ongoing Challenge of Access, Adequacy and Equity.* Washington, DC: NEA Policy and Practice Department. Retrieved from http://www.nea.org/assets/docs/PB19_Technology08.pdf.

NEA – American Federation of Teachers (AFT). (2008). *Access, Adequacy, and Equity in Education Technology: Results of a Survey of America's Teachers and Support Professionals on Technology in Public Schools and Classrooms.* Washington, DC: NEA. Retrieved from http://www.edutopia.org/pdfs/NEA-Access,Adequacy,andEquityinEdTech.pdf.

Rakes, G. C., & Casey, H. B. (2002). An analysis of teacher concerns toward instructional technology. *International Journal of Educational Technology, 3*(1).

Ravitz, J. L., Becker, H. J., & Wong, Y. T. (2000). *Constructivist-Compatible Beliefs and Practices among U.S. Teachers (Report no. 4).* Irvine, CA: Teaching, Learning and Computing.

Richardson, K. W. (2010). TPACK: Game on. *Learning & Leading with Technology, 37,* 34–35.

San Martín, E., Jara, I., Preiss, D., Claro, M., & Farina, P. (2012) *¿Cuán relevante es el aporte de diversos usos de TIC para explicar el rendimiento lector en PISA?. Modelando el aporte neto TIC en Chile, Uruguay, España, Portugal y Suecia.* Informe de investigación Proyecto FONIDE N°: FE11124. Chile.

Shulman, L. (1986). Those who understand: Knowledge growth in teachers. *Educational Researcher, 15,* 4–14.

Smerdon, B., Cronen, S., Lanahan, L., Anderson, J., Iannotti, N., & Angeles, J. (2000). *Teachers' Tools for the 21st Century: A Report on Teachers' Use of Technology. Statistical Analysis Report.* (NCES 2000–102). U.S. Department of Education, National Center for Education Statistics. Washington, DC: U.S. Government Printing Office.

Snoeyink, R., & Ertmer, P. A. (2001). Thrust into technology: How veteran teachers respond. *Journal of Educational Technology Systems, 30*(1), 85–11

Toro, P. (2010) Enlaces: contexto, historia y memoria. In A. Bilbao & A. Salinas (Eds.), *El Libro Abierto de la informática educativa, lecciones y desafíos de la red Enlaces* (pp. 38–50). Santiago de Chile: Enlaces, Centro de Educacion y Tecnologia del Ministerio de Education.

U.S. Department of Education, Office of Educational Technology. (2010). *Transforming American education: Learning powered by technology.* National Educational Technology Plan 2010. Retrieved from http://nces.ed.gov/pubs2007/2007020.pdf.

Vu, P., McIntyre, J., & Cepero, J. (2014). Teachers' use of the iPad in classrooms and their attitudes toward using it. *Journal of Global Literacies, Technologies, and Emerging Pedagogie, 2*, 58–76

Warschauer, M., Zheng, B., Niiya, M., Cotten, S., & Farkas, G. (2014). Balancing the one-to-one equation: Equity and access in three laptop programs. *Equity & Excellence in Education, 47*(1), 46–62.

Wozney, L., Venkatesh, V., & Abrami, P. (2006). Implementing computer technologies: Teachers' perceptions and practices. *Journal of Technology and Teacher Education, 14*, 173–207.

# PART I
# Reading and Comprehension Technologies for the Classroom

This section focuses on adaptive technologies for reading. The section begins with two chapters that focus on providing direct support to teachers, followed by chapters that describe systems directed toward providing adaptive instruction to the student. These systems each vary in method of instruction as well as topic of instruction, each depicting tutoring technologies that target different levels of reading comprehension. The first chapter introduces a system that offers training on providing practice and feedback for learning new vocabulary. The next chapter presents a system that instructs students on proper text structure and how to recognize important cues in non-fiction text. However, when reading more complex texts, students must also be able to use their background knowledge to generate connections among ideas—thus, the following chapter presents a system intended to accomplish this. The first few chapters focus on systems developed for native speakers of English (although many of these systems also offer versions of their tutoring technologies to improve the English literacy for Spanish speakers). By contrast, the final chapter in this section describes an educational technology designed specifically for Spanish speaking students.

# 3

# ASSESSMENT-TO-INSTRUCTION (A2i)

## An Online Platform for Supporting Individualized Early Literacy Instruction

*Sarah W. Ingebrand and Carol McDonald Connor*

Literacy is a vital skill that students must master if they are to succeed in educational and life endeavors (NICHD, 2000; Snow, 2001). Students who fail to achieve proficient levels of literacy are at increased risk of grade retention, referral to special education, and dropping out of high school (Reynolds & Ou, 2004; Shonkoff & Phillips, 2000). The kindergarten through third grade years are a particularly important time for students to gain a strong foundation in reading, because those who continue to struggle with reading in third grade are significantly less likely to achieve reading proficiency (Spira, Bracken, & Fischel, 2005). One of the reasons many students fail to attain proficient literacy skills is that they do not receive the amounts and types of instruction needed to meet their potential, because one size does not fit all, especially with regard to early literacy instruction (Connor et al., 2009; Taylor, Roehrig, Connor, & Schatschneider, 2010).

A majority of the available reading-focused educational technologies, including those presented in this book, are aimed at providing literacy instruction directly to students. Assessment-to-Instruction (A2i) is unique in that the intended user is the teacher. This platform aims to provide teachers with information about the types and amounts of instruction their students need as well as serves as a tool to monitor progress across the school year.

Teachers need information on what students know, what they need to know, and how much progress they are making. In order to determine how students are doing and whether they are making progress toward their learning goals, formative assessment and progress monitoring can be utilized. Formative assessment is an instructional strategy that is classroom management positioned and focused on an individualized instruction framework for progress monitoring (Heritage, 2011). Formative assessments are classroom activities that are used regularly to monitor a student's progress. Such assessments allow a teacher to verify a student instruction framework for progress monitoring (Heritage, 2011). The information provided by A2i is computed using student assessment scores. A2i has three such assessments embedded in the system as well as the capacity to use additional data when available.

There is increasing evidence that effective teachers individualize reading instruction and are able to use assessment information appropriately to guide the personalized (or individualized or differentiated) instruction they provide (Fuchs, Fuchs, & Phillips, 1994). However, teachers report that using assessment to guide instruction is difficult (Roehrig, Duggar, Moats, Glover, & Mincey, 2008). In part, A2i was created to assist teachers in delivering this effective but complicated type of instruction. A2i serves as a tool to encourage individualized teaching and helps to remove the inherent difficulty in using assessments to inform reading instruction by providing teachers with concrete instructional recommendations for each student.

As an effort to assist teachers, a classroom-based literacy intervention called the Individualizing Student Instruction or ISI classroom intervention was developed by Dr. Connor and colleagues, beginning in 2003. Today, the ISI classroom instructional intervention, which is supported by A2i online software, has been evaluated through a series of randomized controlled trials (RCTs) (Al Otaiba et al., 2011; Connor, 2011; Connor et al., 2009, 2011a, 2011b; Connor, Morrison, Fishman, Schatschneider, & Underwood, 2007). These studies reveal that when teachers precisely follow recommendations for individualizing instruction (provided as part of the ISI intervention), students in kindergarten, first, second, and third grade gain, on average, a two-month advantage in reading ability over peers who do not receive individualized instruction. Plus, this effect accumulates as children spend more time in ISI classrooms (Connor et al., 2013).

## An Introduction to A2i

The overall aim of the A2i online platform is to assist teachers in planning and providing ISI instruction to ensure that every student is reading at or above grade level and is making a minimum of one year's worth of progress across the school year, regardless of their incoming skills. While the A2i platform utilizes assessment information across multiple literacy areas, the overall target of this intervention is to improve student reading ability: both decoding and comprehension. A2i uses individual standardized student assessment scores for word knowledge (e.g., vocabulary), decoding, and comprehension to recommend the amount of four different types of literacy instruction (discussed below) for each student in the classroom using computer algorithms (Connor, 2013). These instruction recommendations are calculated for every student individually, based on their assessments scores. Then, the instructional recommendations are communicated to the teacher for every individual student through the classroom view. From there, A2i recommends which children should participate in lessons together, based on a previously selected number of small groups. The number of small groups desired by the teacher may depend on the number of aids available to them, their comfort level with running small groups, the age of their students, along with other factors. Regardless of the number of small groups desired, A2i recommends groups of children who have similar instructional needs, which allows the teacher or aid to deliver the precise amount and type of instruction needed by that group of students.

A2i conceptualizes literacy instruction across two dimensions—content and management. The instructional content recommendations fall into two major categories of reading instruction: code-focused instruction and meaning-focused instruction. Code-focused instruction includes any activity in which students explicitly focus on the task of decoding, such as learning the alphabet principle (e.g., relating phonemes to letters, learning to blend them to decode words), phonological awareness, phonics, and letter and word fluency. Meaning-focused activities require students to actively extract and construct meaning from text. Meaning-focused instructional activities may include reading aloud, reading independently, writing, language, vocabulary, and comprehension strategies. In addition to the code and meaning-focused recommendations, A2i identifies how much time (per day and per week) a student should spend with the teacher (teacher/student managed) versus alone or with peers (student/peer managed). Examples of these activities and dimensions can be seen in Table 3.1. Using these two dimensions, any evidence-based literacy activity falls into one of the four types—keeping in mind that most children, particularly in kindergarten and first grade, will make greater gains if they receive all four types of instruction. However, the amount of each will vary depending on word knowledge, decoding, and reading comprehension skills. Examples of these differences are illustrated in Figure 3.1. Notice that the recommended amount of each type of instruction varies depending on a student's constellation of skills in grade equivalents (GE)—and the relation is not a simple straight line.

Within A2i, teachers can edit the details of their students as well as view the content and management recommendations. In addition, A2i offers three integrated online assessments that can be taken by students, the option to upload additional standardized test scores, recommended but customizable student groupings, and a calendar where teachers can develop and prepare individualized lessons plans and graphical displays that chart student growth across the school year.

Teachers carry out the instructional recommendations in the classroom by utilizing small groups. Small groups allow for flexibility and a low child-teacher ratio, providing teachers with concrete techniques for ensuring that each student receives the recommended instructional minutes. Many teachers set up stations and provide color-coded folders and organizational charts to help their students work independently or with peers while they meet with small groups of students at the teacher station. Based on numerous research studies and trials, it has been found that the closer teachers match their actual instruction to the recommended amounts and types of instruction, the better their students' literacy outcomes are

**TABLE 3.1** Examples of Activities and Dimensions in A2i.

|  | Teacher/Child Managed (TM) | Child/Peer Managed (CM) |
|---|---|---|
| **Code-focused (CF)** | The teacher is working with a small group of children on how to decode compound words such as "cowboy" and "baseball". She says: "What word do you have when you take the 'boy' out of 'cowboy'?" | Children are working together to sound out and then write words that have the rime "-ake". They have written the words "bake" and "cake" on the white board. |
| **Meaning-focused (MF)** | The teacher is discussing the story "Stone Soup" with the class. She starts by asking the children: "What is the main idea of the story and what are the supporting details?" She then tells them to: "Think, pair, share" so the children turn to their partner to discuss the main idea and supporting details. After the children have discussed with their partner, the teacher asks the pairs to share their ideas. | Children are silently reading a book of their choice at their desks. Other children are writing in their journals. |

at the end of the year. In addition, the amount of time teachers spent logged in and *using* the A2i software predicted better student reading outcomes at the end of the year (Connor et al., 2009, 2011a, 2011b).

In addition to the instructional recommendations that are the backbone of A2i, the software provides a number of additional services. First, is the ability to effectively individualize instruction based on student needs. The recommended groupings provided by the program divide students into meaningful groups, which saves a teacher the time and effort it would take to consider multiple test scores and skill levels when forming teacher-led small groups for reading. The second added benefit of the A2i technology is the system's ability to track student progress across the school year. This system also provides teachers with a notification system that identifies students who are not progressing across the year as expected. Overall, A2i provides teachers with the information they need to individualize their literacy instruction along with feedback about how students are actually progressing. The methods and tools the A2i software utilizes to do this are described in the following section.

Assessment-to-Instruction (A2i) **37**

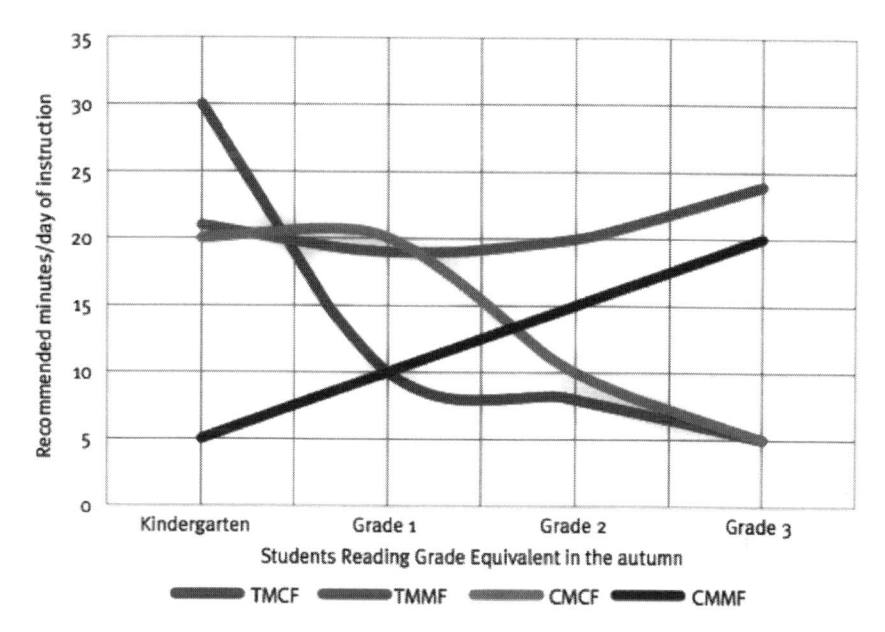

**FIGURE 3.1** Students' Reading Grade Equivalent Versus Recommended Minutes Per Day of Instruction.

## Details of the A2i Technology

The A2i online software provides teachers with an effective way to take assessment data information and apply that information directly to their instruction. This is helpful for two reasons. First, A2i uses a number of complex algorithms that utilize student assessment data on vocabulary, decoding, and comprehension, and produce instructional recommendations. These recommendation algorithms require scores from reliable and valid standardized tests. To date, A2i has used the Woodcock-Johnson III Picture vocabulary, letter-word identification, and passage comprehension tests (Woodcock, McGrew, & Mather, 2001) and the DIBELS (University of Oregon, 2007), as well as three integrated online assessments. Assessment scores on the three areas of vocabulary, decoding, and comprehension are used so the full constellation of students' skills related to literacy ability are considered when the recommendations are generated.

Second, the use of grouping algorithms provides recommended groupings for students based on their most current assessment scores, although the teacher can change group membership as needed. As discussed earlier, the teacher is provided with information on which groups of students need specific types and durations of instruction, effectively individualizing instruction at the small group level. As students progress and are re-assessed, the groups can be automatically updated when new scores are entered. This allows for dynamic individualizing with no additional work for the teacher. Once new assessment scores are entered onto

**38** S.W. Ingebrand and C.M. Connor

the A2i system, or students take the integrated online assessments, A2i is able to generate updated instructional recommendations and groupings in real time with no additional burden on the teacher.

The specific features of A2i are described below in the order that teachers often navigate these screens and in the order that the links appear on the Welcome to A2i! screen (see Figure 3.2).

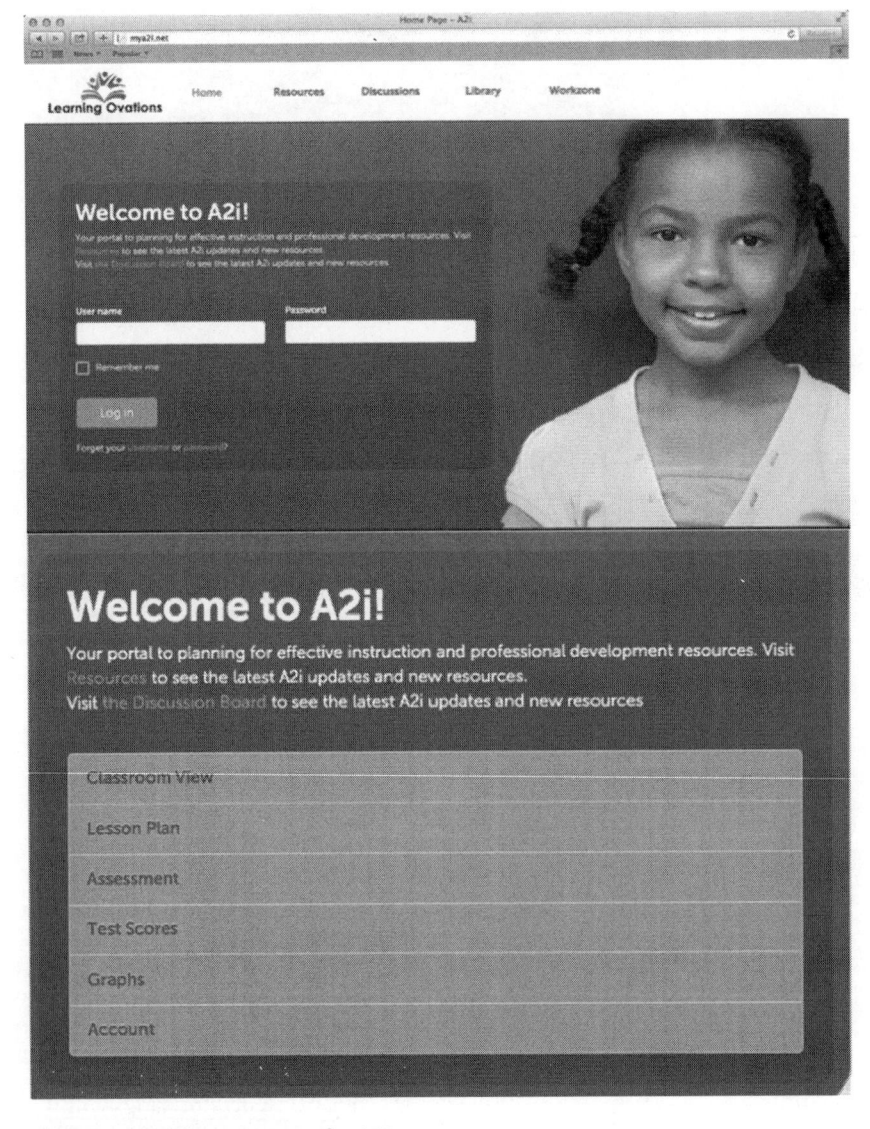

**FIGURE 3.2** Welcome Screen for A2i.

The **Classroom View** (Figure 3.3) display is the control center for teachers using A2i. On this screen, a teacher is able to use the Student Actions button to remove students from the classroom, shift students between groups, and view recommended instruction times on a daily or weekly scale. There is also a "reset to recommended groups" option at the bottom of the page that allows teachers to update groups automatically after new assessment data is added. This option also allows them to reset changes they have made to student groupings.

For example, in Figure 3.3, Jenn Law has been assigned to Group 1 and it is recommended that she spend 14 minutes in teacher-managed/meaning-focused instruction and 22 minutes in teacher-managed/code-focused instruction during the literacy period. Her daily recommendation shows 13 minutes of meaning-focused and

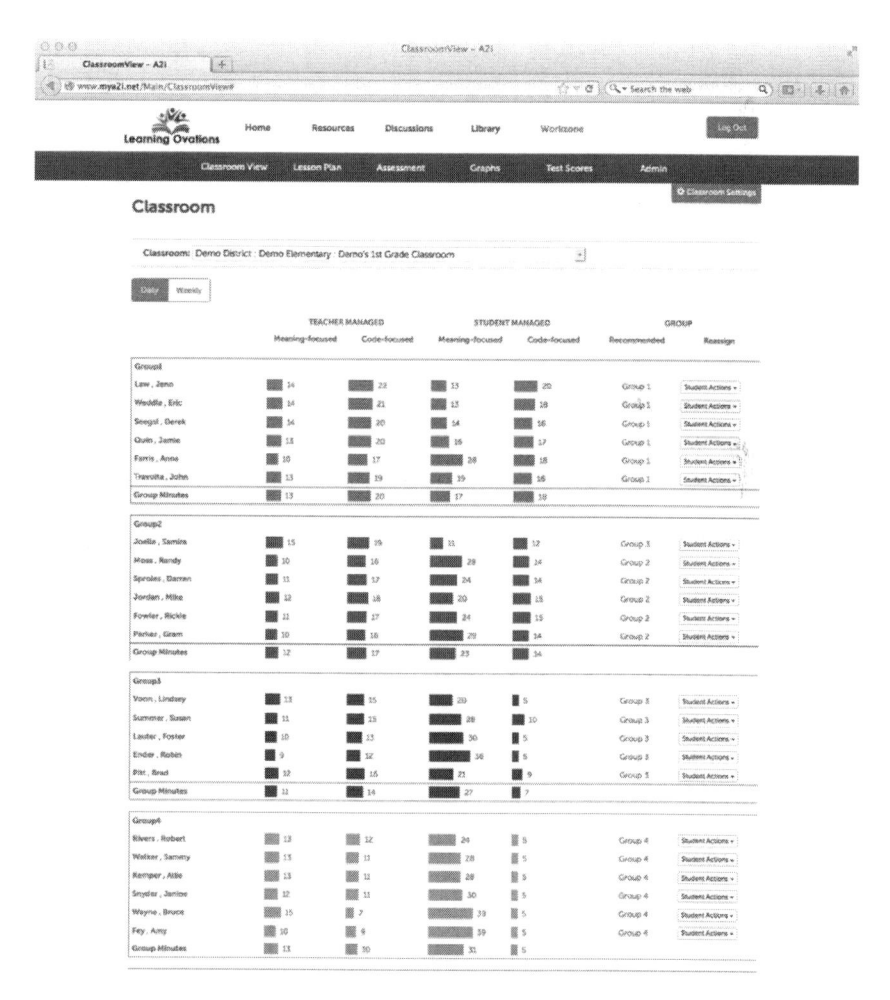

**FIGURE 3.3** Classroom View Display.

20 minutes of code-focused instruction in the student managed context. In contrast, students assigned to Group 4 require more meaning-focused and less code-focused instruction in both their teacher and student managed time. Recommendation times can be displayed as daily or weekly amounts and the teacher can select the total number of student groups created as well as the days they plan to meet with each group.

If a student is selected on the Classroom View page, the Student Information page appears (Figures 3.4 and 3.5). This page displays all of the student information (name, birth date, ID number, etc.) along with that child's assessment data in a table. The graph window displays a chart of the student's specific scores or a graph of the assessment scores for the entire class.

The Lesson Plan page displays the students in each group along with the average vocabulary, decoding, and comprehension score for that group (Figure 3.6). Below this display is a weekly lesson planner that can be populated with activities. These activities can be selected one at a time by the teacher, based on the library of indexed curriculum, or the recommend feature can be used to populate the entire week of lessons. The recommended activities are selected from a specific curriculum (selected by the teacher), are aligned with the average reading level of the student groups, and take approximately the same amount of time to complete as their instructional time recommendations. Each activity that is recommended includes information on where the lesson materials can be

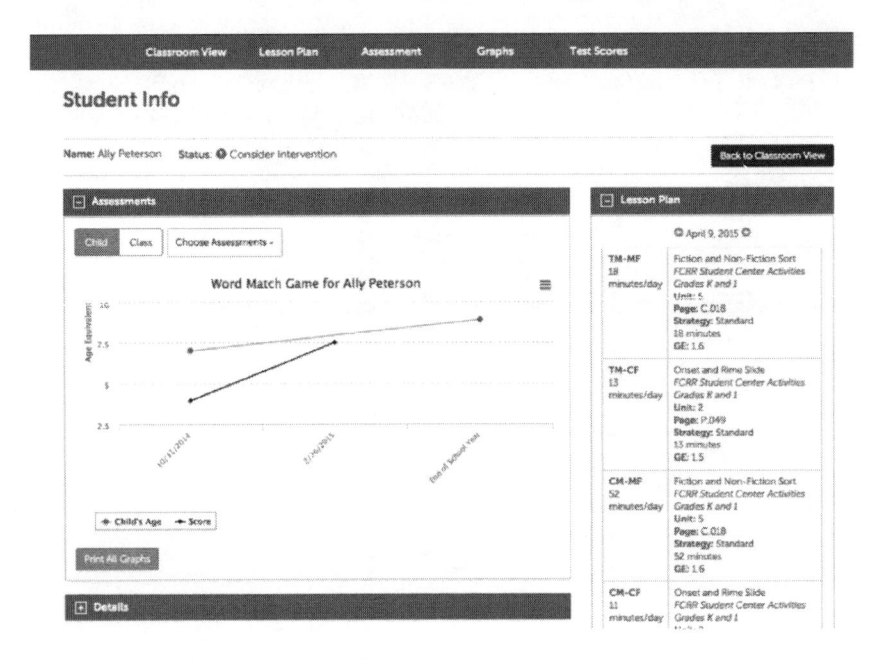

**FIGURE 3.4** Student Information Page.

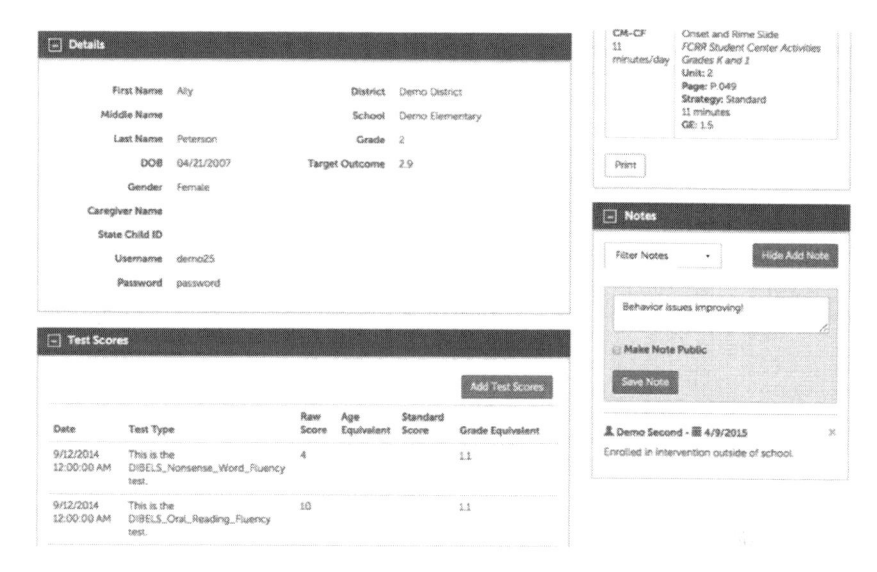

**FIGURE 3.5** Student Information Page.

found, whether it is in the teacher's edition curriculum manual already in use by a teacher/school, or whether it is available through an online source (with a link to download). Information is also provided on how long the lesson will take, which common core standard the lesson addresses, and the grade level equivalent of the lesson material.

A separate lesson planner can be generated for each group so the burden of individualizing instruction based on students' reading level for each group is no longer solely the responsibility of the teacher. That being said, this system also provides enough flexibility for teachers to overrule recommended activities with a different lesson. Once a lesson has been taught, the teacher can mark an activity as 'complete' by clicking a small checkbox (turning that calendar square green) to record the progress being made in each group and what topics are being covered.

The Assessments page links students to the assessments that have been developed by the A2i researchers and are integrated into the A2i system (Figure 3.7). Teachers can access each student's username and password on the Student Information page. Students log in to take the assessments. These assessments center on the three skill areas required by the recommendation algorithms. All three assessments are taken online and are adaptive, meaning the questions a student answers are determined by how well they have done on the previous questions. This allows the tests to be highly accurate but also brief. There is also a large bank of test items, meaning these assessments can be taken as often as once a month. Additionally, all three assessments have undergone item response theory (IRT) analyses and show good psychometric properties. IRT provides the difficulty levels for the adaptive aspect of the assessments.

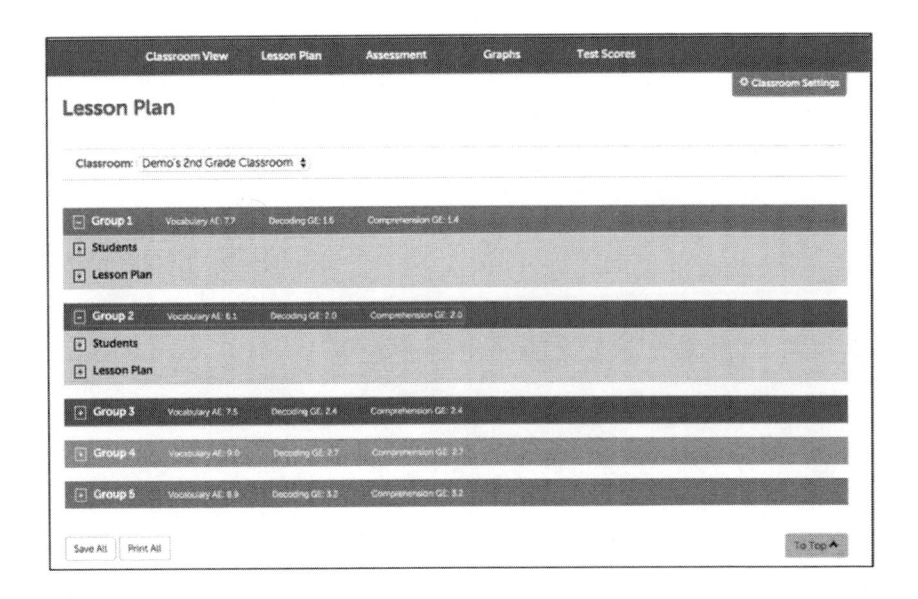

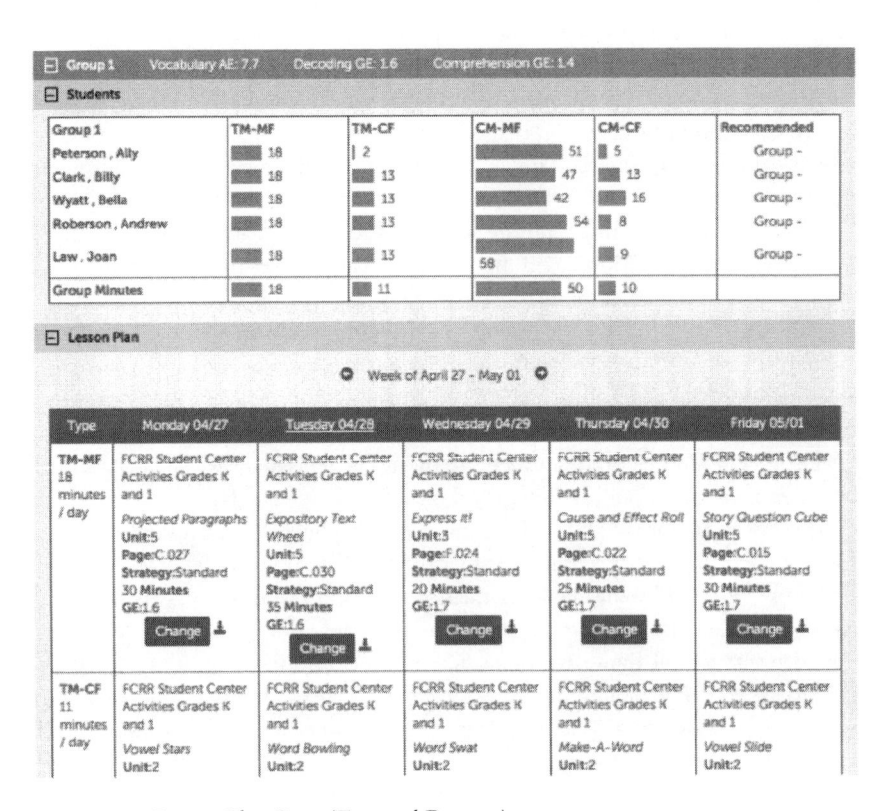

**FIGURE 3.6** Lesson Plan Page (Top and Bottom).

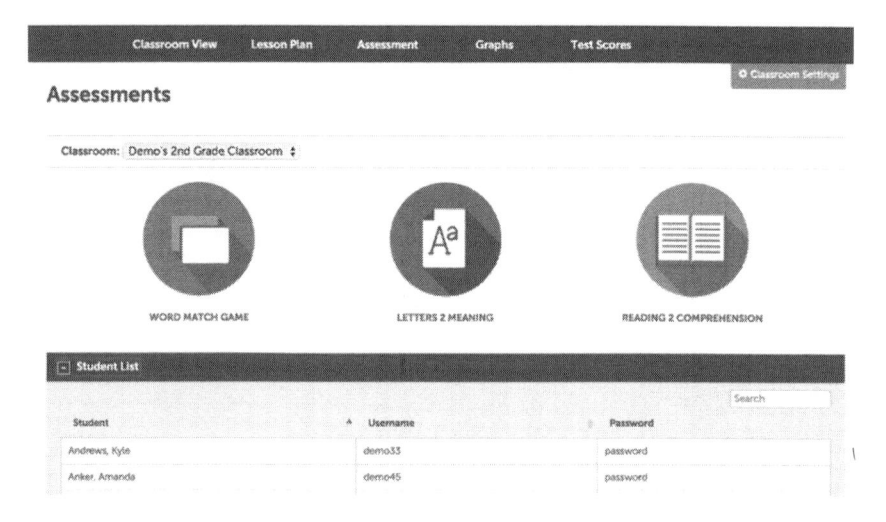

**FIGURE 3.7** Assessments Page.

The first assessment that was developed is the *Word Match Game*. This assessment measures a student's vocabulary ability by asking the students to select words that go together (e.g., cat and kitten). The directions and target words are read aloud to the student to limit the influence of reading ability on the vocabulary score. The second assessment is *Letters 2 Meaning*. This assessment was designed to capture student's decoding, word reading, spelling, and composition skills. Initially, students must select a letter based on the letter name or sound they hear as their prompt. As they progress through the test, the tasks get more difficult and they are asked to select the correct word from a list, spell words correctly, and put words together to form sentences. Finally, the *Reading 2 Comprehension* assessment provides a measure of reading comprehension. The students are asked to fill in missing words within a passage they are asked to read. All three of the assessments are adaptive and last only 5 to 15 minutes per child. They also include a large test bank of items so children can be assessed multiple times during the year without seeing the same questions. The results from each of the assessments are used to determine in which group a student should be placed and to allow their progress to be tracked. In addition, these assessments provide teachers with a short, quick, and accurate way to obtain the three reading ability skill levels required by the algorithms: decoding, vocabulary, and comprehension. As soon as a student finishes an assessment, the scores appear in A2i on the Student Information page as well as on the Graphs page and Test Scores spreadsheet.

The Graphs tab displays the assessment data and target outcomes for all students in a class (Figure 3.8). Each assessment is displayed on a separate chart that also depicts the time the assessment was taken and how close each student is to their target outcomes for that year. These graphs can also be downloaded or

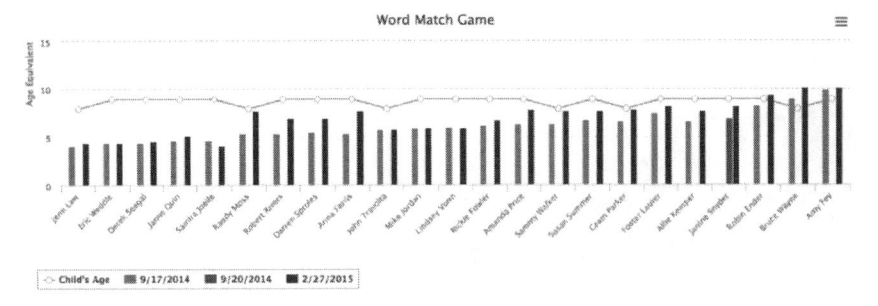

**FIGURE 3.8** Graphs Tab Showing Results of Word Match Game.

printed and the target line can be turned on or off depending on the type of information that a teacher requires.

The Test Scores grid is a display of all of the tests scores in the system. The scores can be searched using any criteria on the page. They can also be sorted by clicking at the top of any of the columns, similar to most digital spreadsheets. An *Add Scores* feature allows scores to be entered for one student or an entire class by typing them into the spreadsheet and selecting a specific test type. An *Import Test Scores* feature allows scores for any or all students to be seamlessly uploaded into A2i from a spreadsheet.

On each of these pages there is a tab that appears in the upper right corner labeled Classroom Settings. This link opens a pop-up window that allows teachers to customize further the specific features of their classroom, which allows them to utilize fully the recommendations provided by A2i. In this window, teachers can select specific days they will or will not be teaching specific small groups (which in turn adjusts the recommended minutes and lesson activity suggestions). In this window, the teacher can also add teacher-aids or parent volunteers who are able to provide instruction in small groups, again affecting the number of small groups that can receive teacher-managed instruction within the allotted literacy block. Finally, this display allows teachers to enter the amount of time they will dedicate to literacy instruction (i.e., the literacy block) and provides teachers with a link that allows them to enter test scores. See Figure 3.9 and Figure 3.10 for more details.

Along with these core features, A2i has a number of features that further increase usability, many of them created based on teacher recommendations, feedback, and discussions during software development. The first is an option to create different user profiles. This allows additional security across a school, because a teacher can only view the students in their classroom, but a principal or literacy coach may have access to any number of classrooms. These higher security users also have access to user reports that track and display how often each user has logged in to the A2i website and how much time they have spent on each of the screens described above. Another useful feature is student uploading. To aid in data management, A2i allows not only test scores, but also student names and detail

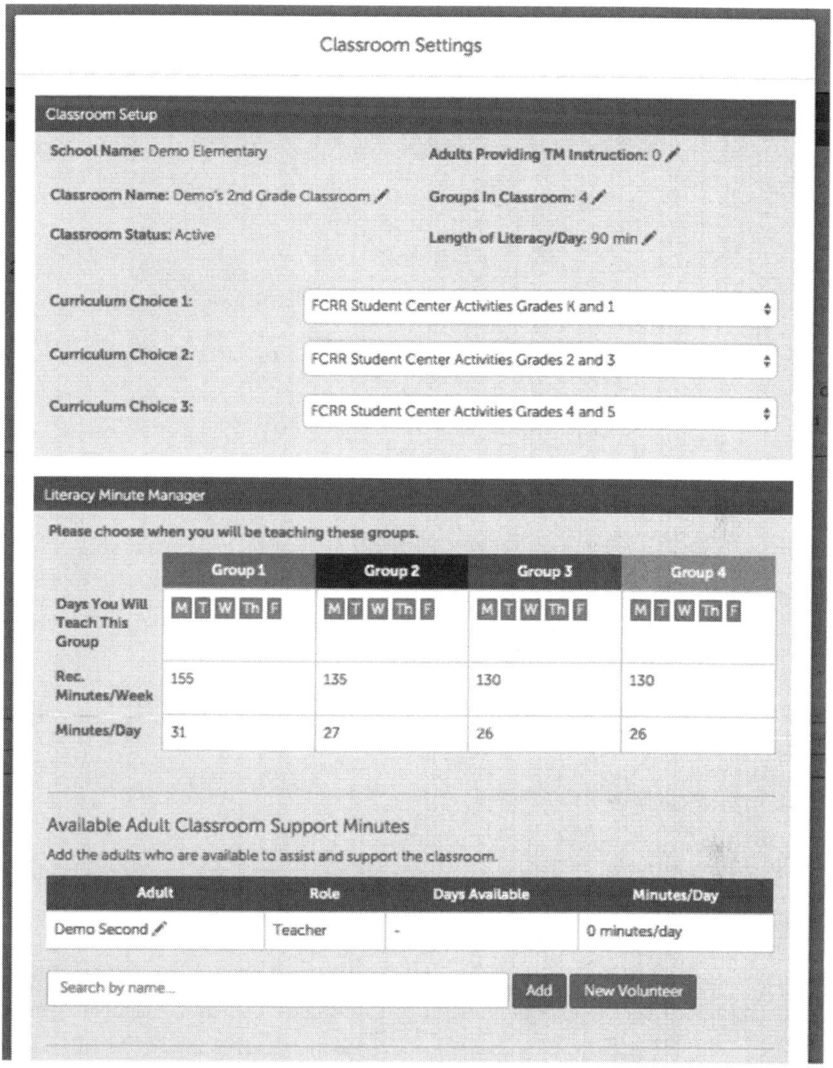

## Classroom Settings

**Classroom Setup**

School Name: Demo Elementary
Classroom Name: Demo's 2nd Grade Classroom
Classroom Status: Active

Adults Providing TM Instruction: 0
Groups In Classroom: 4
Length of Literacy/Day: 90 min

Curriculum Choice 1: FCRR Student Center Activities Grades K and 1
Curriculum Choice 2: FCRR Student Center Activities Grades 2 and 3
Curriculum Choice 3: FCRR Student Center Activities Grades 4 and 5

**Literacy Minute Manager**

Please choose when you will be teaching these groups.

|  | Group 1 | Group 2 | Group 3 | Group 4 |
|---|---|---|---|---|
| Days You Will Teach This Group | M T W Th F | M T W Th F | M T W Th F | M T W Th F |
| Rec. Minutes/Week | 155 | 135 | 130 | 130 |
| Minutes/Day | 31 | 27 | 26 | 26 |

**Available Adult Classroom Support Minutes**

Add the adults who are available to assist and support the classroom.

| Adult | Role | Days Available | Minutes/Day |
|---|---|---|---|
| Demo Second | Teacher | - | 0 minutes/day |

Search by name... [Add] [New Volunteer]

**FIGURE 3.9** Classroom Settings Page.

information to be uploaded. This allows teachers to set up their classrooms at the beginning of the year with minimal typing.

## Evidence on Effectiveness

The A2i software, used in tandem with the ISI intervention, has been tested across a number of RCTs. The research has shown this system to be effective for students in kindergarten through third grade. In addition, students who received

**FIGURE 3.10** Classroom Settings Page.

the intervention across multiple years achieved higher scores on standardized reading measures than children who only experienced one year of the intervention, revealing that the effectiveness of this intervention may accumulate across years (Connor et al., 2007).

In addition to the improvement in reading outcomes, A2i provides a tool for teachers to aid in individualizing instruction. Study results show that teachers using the A2i tool, along with training and support, were able to provide more effective literacy instruction. This effect was found regardless of a teacher's initial ability, revealing that A2i has the potential to assist struggling teachers in becoming more effective educators, as well as to make good teachers better (Connor et al., 2013).

The effectiveness of A2i can also be discussed in terms of development. The initial conception of A2i was developed as a research-based tool for teachers to use for a one-year study. Since that time, many teachers, literacy coaches, school administrators, and principals have provided advice, support, and feedback for A2i and its features. Recently, the A2i system has evolved from a basic research tool into a dynamic, professionally designed software platform that teachers can easily adopt as a central guide for literacy instruction. An efficacy study centered on the latest iteration of A2i is taking place as part of a randomized control trial being carried out over the 2015–2016 school year.

## Accessing the Technology

A2i is a completely online tool. The website can be accessed by using the URL http://mya2i.net. The site is best supported on the Google Chrome web browser. To log into a demonstration classroom, enter the **username: demofirst** and **password: password**. All features available to teachers using A2i are available in this demo, with the exception of the upper-level administrative features. Having an active log in also provides the user with access to the A2i Resources page. This page provides teachers with access to information and videos on how ISI and A2i have been implemented in classrooms along with frequently asked questions, a A2i professional development manual, and additional articles. More information about the research supporting A2i, specific information about professional development, the theory behind A2i, and information for parents can be found on the Learning Ovations website: http://learningovations.com. A2i is commercially available. Questions about A2i or teachers and educational leaders interested in utilizing A2i in their classrooms should contact Learning Ovations for more information about access and cost.

## Final Thoughts

To quote a teacher, "The greatest challenge is getting to know each learner as an individual and identifying their unique needs and preferred learning modalities." One of the goals of the A2i software is to ease this burden for teachers. The A2i online software provides teachers with a tool to aid in effectively individualizing literacy instruction in any classroom. This tool has the potential to assist teachers in becoming more effective educators, as well as make high-quality teachers even better (Connor et al., 2013). The use of A2i, along with the ISI intervention, has improved student outcomes across classrooms, schools, and districts. As teachers learn about A2i and start using the system, the goal of having all students reading at or above proficient levels by third grade gets closer.

## References

Al Otaiba, S., Connor, C. M., Folsom, J. S., Greulich, L., Meadows, J., & Li, Z. (2011). Assessment data-informed guidance to individualize kindergarten reading instruction: Findings from a cluster-randomized control field trial. *Elementary School Journal, 111*(4), 535–560.
Connor, C. M. (2011). Child by instruction interactions: Language and literacy connections. In S. B. Neuman & D. K. Dickinson (Eds.), *Handbook on Early Literacy* (3rd ed., pp. 256–275). New York: Guilford Press.

Connor, C. M. (2013). US Patent No. 8506304. United States Patent Office.
Connor, C. M., Morrison, F. J., Fishman, B. J., Schatschneider, C., & Underwood, P. (2007). THE EARLY YEARS: Algorithm-guided individualized reading instruction. *Science, 315*(5811), 464–465. doi: 10.1126/science.1134513
Connor, C. M., Morrison, F. J., Fishman, B., Crowe, E. C., Al Otaiba, S., & Schatschneider, C. (2013). A longitudinal cluster-randomized controlled study on the accumulating effects of individualized literacy instruction on students' reading from first through third grade. *Psychological Science, 24*(8), 1408–1419. doi: 10.1177/0956797612472204
Connor, C. M., Piasta, S. B., Fishman, B., Glasney, S., Schatschneider, C., Crowe, E.,... Morrison, F. J. (2009). Individualizing student instruction precisely: Effects of child by instruction interactions on first graders' literacy development. *Child Development, 80*(1), 77–100.
Connor, C. M., Morrison, F. J., Fishman, B., Giuliani, S., Luck, M., Underwood, P.,... Schatschneider, C. (2011a). Testing the impact of child characteristics × instruction interactions on third graders' reading literacy instruction. *Reading Research Quarterly, 46*(3), 189–221.
Connor, C. M., Morrison, F. J., Schatschneider, C., Toste, J., Lundblom, E. G., Crowe, E., & Fishman, B. (2011b). Effective classroom instruction: Implications of child characteristic by instruction interactions on first graders' word reading achievement. *Journal of Research on Educational Effectiveness, 4*(3), 173–207.
Fuchs, L. S., Fuchs, D., & Phillips, N. (1994). The relation between teachers' beliefs about the importance of good student work habits, teacher planning, and student achievement. *Elementary School Journal, 94*(3), 331–345.
Heritage, M. (2011). *Formative Assessment: An Enabler of Learning.* Johns Hopkins University New Horizons for Learning. Retrieved from http://education.jhu.edu/PD/newhorizons/Better/articles/ Spring2011.html
NICHD. (2000). *National Institute of Child Health and Human Development, National Reading Panel Report: Teaching Children to Read: An Evidence-Based Assessment of the Scientific Research Literature on Reading and its Implications for Reading Instruction.* Washington DC: U.S. Department of Health and Human Services, Public Health Service, National Institutes of Health, National Institute of Child Health and Human Development.
Reynolds, A. J., & Ou, S. R. (2004). Alterable predictors of child well-being in the Chicago longitudinal study. *Children and Youth Services Review, 26,* 1–14.
Roehrig, A. D., Duggar, S. W., Moats, L. C., Glover, M., & Mincey, B. (2008). When teachers work to use progress monitoring data to inform literacy instruction: Identifying potential supports and challenges. *Remedial and Special Education, 29,* 364–382.
Shonkoff, J. P., & Phillips, D. A. (Eds.). (2000). *From Neurons to Neighborhoods: The Science of Early Childhood Development.* Washington DC: National Academy Press.
Snow, C. E. (2001). *Reading for Understanding.* Santa Monica, CA: RAND Education and the Science and Technology Policy Institute.
Spira, E. G., Bracken, S. S., & Fischel, J. E. (2005). Predicting improvement after first-grade reading difficulties: The effects of oral language, emergent literacy, and behavior skills. *Developmental Psychology, 41*(1), 225–234.
Taylor, J. E., Roehrig, A. D., Connor, C. M., & Schatschneider, C. (2010). Teacher quality moderates the genetic effects on early reading. *Science, 328,* 512–514.
University of Oregon. (2007). DIBELS 2007. Retrieved from http://dibels.uoregon.edu
Woodcock, R. W., McGrew, K. S., & Mather, N. (2001). *Woodcock-Johnson-III Tests of Achievement.* Itasca, IL: Riverside.

# 4
# COMMON CORE TERA
Text Ease and Readability Assessor

*G. Tanner Jackson, Laura K. Allen, and Danielle S. McNamara*

This chapter provides information about the Coh-Metrix Common Core Text Ease and Readability Assessor (TERA[1]), a freely available automated text analysis tool that calculates information about text difficulty at multiple levels of the text. TERA provides a profile of text difficulty encompassing five dimensions: *narrativity (genre), syntax, word concreteness, referential cohesion,* and *deep cohesion*. All five of these dimensions are related to specific aspects of text difficulty. TERA was developed primarily for teachers. It is specifically focused on the analysis of texts assigned to students in kindergarten through early college classes.

In this chapter, we provide an overview of TERA. This overview focuses on the current need for text processing tools, what TERA can potentially do for teachers, how to use TERA, and applications for using TERA to inform and improve educational curricula.

## The Need for TERA

The ability to comprehend texts is a critical skill for success in both school environments and in the workplace. As text becomes a more common medium for communication (e.g., emails, text messages), the importance of developing strong literacy skills has subsequently increased. Unfortunately, the comprehension of texts is not a simple process—indeed, deep comprehension relies on the development of knowledge and skills at multiple levels (e.g., vocabulary knowledge, domain knowledge, self-regulation strategies, etc.). Not surprisingly, then, national assessments consistently demonstrate that students are struggling to develop strong literacy skills (see e.g., https://nces.ed.gov/nationsreportcard/).

One way to improve students' skills in this domain is through deliberate and persistent practice. In other words, students need to be provided with opportunities to read *more* texts across *multiple* domains (Duke & Pearson, 2002). In addition to practicing reading more frequently, students need to read texts that specifically target their own sets of strengths and weaknesses. Texts vary in difficulty across a number of different dimensions (Graesser, McNamara, & Kulikowich, 2011; McNamara, Graesser, & Louwerse, 2012). Thus, students should read texts that have been appropriately matched to their specific knowledge and skills. Aligning text properties to students' abilities and needs allows them to capitalize on their strengths, while also fostering growth in specific comprehension skills.

Consider the following example. Two students, John and Sarah, are in the same class at school and currently read at the same level—a third grade level. The first student, John, has strong vocabulary skills, but has problems integrating information from different places within texts that he is reading. Sarah, on the other hand, is skilled at integrating information and generating inferences; however, she has a fairly limited vocabulary compared to other students in her class. Although both John and Sarah have been classified as "third grade readers," it is likely that the properties of the texts they read will benefit them in different ways. In particular, the difficulty of the words, and the cohesiveness of the text will likely have different effects on John and Sarah's ultimate comprehension and learning due to their varying strengths and weaknesses.

Unfortunately, it is a challenging task for educators to assign individual texts to students based on their prior knowledge and skill levels. In the past, doing so relied primarily on grade level readability estimates (e.g., Lexile, Flesch-Kincaid, etc.) provided by publishers, or intuition and experience garnered across many years of instruction. The latter requires deep knowledge of both the texts and the students, which is both time consuming and subjective. In addition, interpretations and recommendations can vary widely across educators. The former approach (publisher grade level) offers its own set of problems for educators. In particular, text readability and grade level estimates that are commonly available focus solely on challenges stemming from the words (e.g., word frequency) and the sentences, i.e., sentence length (Kincaid, Fishburne, Rogers, & Chissom, 1975).

By contrast, TERA assesses difficulty at multiple levels including challenges from the words and syntax, but also challenges that stem from the genre of the text and the cohesion of the text. This tool leverages the power of automated language processing to provide educators with more information about potential texts to be used, which can help educators align specific texts to student abilities.[2] Specifically, TERA provides educators with a library of preprocessed texts and enables them to submit their own texts for detailed automatic analysis. The remainder of this chapter describes the tool and how it can be of use for educators.

## TERA

TERA is a tool designed to leverage the power of natural language processing and synthesize text analysis into actionable pieces of information. TERA is driven by indices from Coh-Metrix, an automated text analysis tool designed to assess text difficulty (McNamara & Graesser, 2012; McNamara, Graesser, McCarthy, & Cai, 2014). TERA uses these indices to provide information about the "easability" and readability of texts, and to provide educators with actionable information about how these text features potentially relate to students' comprehension of the texts. TERA provides information related to five components of text easability: *narrativity (genre), syntactic simplicity, word concreteness, referential cohesion,* and *deep cohesion*. For a given text, each of these components is associated with an "ease" percentile score, which shows how the text compares to thousands of other texts,[3] and each text within the existing TERA library has a corresponding Common Core grade assignment from human experts.

In general, a text's difficulty is related to a multitude of different linguistic components. For instance, increased cohesion tends to be positively associated with easier reading, and narrative texts tend to be easier to comprehend than expository texts. TERA affords educators the ability to investigate these specific components that contribute to a text's difficulty. Importantly, the features that make texts more or less difficult vary from one text to the next. Therefore, TERA can help to identify the more difficult elements of a particular text and determine whether specific texts are appropriate for different students. Once these components have been identified, educators can work with students to help them recognize and overcome the obstacles that the texts might present. The following sections provide example texts as analyzed by TERA, along with brief descriptions of how the TERA analyses work.

## TERA Components in Action

The TERA components provide a profile of how the linguistic features of a text relate to text readability. The two text excerpts represented in Table 4.1 and Figure 4.1 provide examples of how texts originally designed for similar grade levels can have extremely different linguistic profiles. Importantly, while these two texts are both estimated to be appropriate for students reading at grade levels 4 to 6, that grade estimation may not be appropriate for all students, because each text provides unique challenges to the reader and different pedagogical affordances (see also Figure 4.6 for a comparison of these texts within the TERA interface, where human experts determined both texts are appropriate for grades 4–5).

The two texts presented in Table 4.1 are available within the TERA library and were selected to illustrate the different aspects of the TERA component scores (see Figure 4.1). These texts were originally designed for a similar grade range (4th to 6th grade), but possess very different TERA text profiles. The TERA analyses provide information about how these texts vary in their sources of difficulty and how they may differentially pose difficulties for particular students. Thus, it may not be appropriate to provide texts to students based solely on grade level, but rather, use the TERA component scores as guidelines for selecting texts that match student skills and needs.

TABLE 4.1 Text Excerpts for Similar Grade Levels.

| Title | "Discovering Mars: The Amazing Story of the Red Planet" | "Where the Mountain Meets the Moon" |
|---|---|---|
| **Excerpt** | Mars is very cold and very dry. Scattered across the surface are many giant volcanoes. Lava covers much of the land.<br><br>In Mars' northern half, or hemisphere, is a huge raised area. It is about 2,500 miles wide. Astronomers call this the Great Tharsis Bulge.<br><br>There are four mammoth volcanoes on the Great Tharsis Bulge. The largest one is Mount Olympus, or Olympus Mons. It is the biggest mountain on Mars. Some think it may be the largest mountain in the entire solar system.<br><br>Mount Olympus is 15 miles high. At its peak is a 50 mile wide basin. Its base is 375 miles across. That's nearly as big as the state of Texas!<br><br>Mauna Loa, in Hawaii, is the largest volcano on Earth. Yet, compared to Mount Olympus, Mauna Loa looks like a little hill. The Hawaiian volcano is only 5.5 miles high. Its base, on the bottom of the Pacific Ocean, is just 124 miles wide.<br><br>Each of the three other volcanoes in the Great Tharsis Bulge are over 10 miles high. They are named Arsia Mons, Pavonis Mons, and Ascraeus Mons. | Far away from here, following the Jade River, there was once a black mountain that cut into the sky like a jagged piece of rough metal. The villagers called it Fruitless Mountain because nothing grew on it and birds and animals did not rest there.<br><br>Crowded in the corner of where Fruitless Mountain and the Jade River met was a village that was a shade of faded brown. This was because the land around the village was hard and poor. To coax rice out of the stubborn land, the field had to be flooded with water. The villagers had to tramp in the mud, bending and stooping and planting day after day. Working in the mud so much made it spread everywhere and the hot sun dried it onto their clothes and hair and homes. Over time, everything in the village had become the dull color of dried mud.<br><br>One of the houses in this village was so small that its wood boards, held together by the roof, made one think of a bunch of matches tied with a piece of twine. Inside, there was barely enough room for three people to sit around the table—which was lucky because only three people lived there. One of them was a young girl called Minli. |
| **Flesch Kincaid Grade level** | 5th grade | 6th grade |

Common Core TERA **53**

■ Narrativity ▨ Syntactic Simplicity ▨ Word Concreteness ⦀ Referential Cohesion ≡ Deep Cohesion

*Bar chart showing PERCENTILE SCORE\* for two texts:*

DISCOVERING MARS: 22, 88, 39, 27, 26
MOUNTAIN MEETS THE MOON: 67, 49, 98, 47, 82

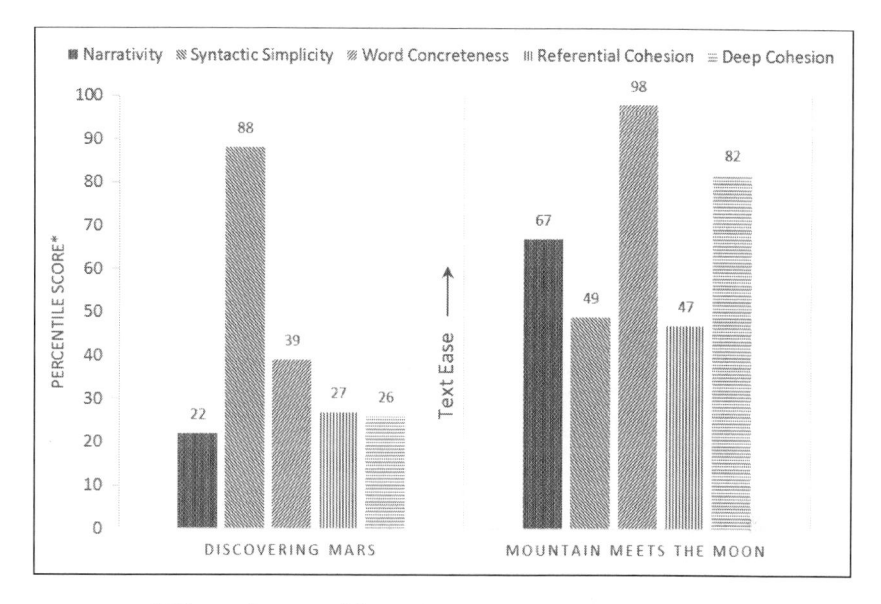

Text Ease →

**FIGURE 4.1** Different Aspects of the TERA Component Scores.

\* Percentile scores were calculated on more than just the text excerpts presented above.

## *Component Scores and Linguistic Analyses*

### *Narrativity (Genre)*

The first component score provided by TERA relates to the genre of a target text. Texts that are more narrative in nature are easier to process, comprehend, and remember (Bruner, 1986; Haberlandt & Graesser, 1985; Schank & Abelson, 1995). In contrast, informational texts are more difficult for readers to parse and understand. The first TERA component score, narrativity, represents this continuum.

Texts that are rated as high in narrativity may contain a relatively high proportion of common words and verbs (e.g., say, join, give, ask, answer, feel), which are easier to understand (Beck, McKeown, & Kucan, 2002; Perfetti, 2007). Verbs convey actions, thoughts, and feelings, all of which make a text more accessible to readers. These kind of narrative text properties allow readers to make connections among action sequences and maintain information about main characters, plot points, and cause-and-effect relationships more effectively (Bruner, 1986; Schank & Abelson, 1995). Additionally, texts high in narrativity may contain more pronouns, which serve to make them more personable and engaging to readers (Cheong & Young, 2006; Vorderer, Wulff, & Friedrichsen, 1996). Conversely, texts that are low in narrativity may contain relatively more complex noun phrases (compared to pronouns) and thus are likely to contain a relatively higher proportion of concepts and information, which can make a text more difficult to read (Biber, Johansson, Leech, Conrad, & Finegan, 1999).

In Figure 4.1, the "Discovering Mars" text received a low narrativity score from TERA (22nd percentile), reflecting the observation that it is less story-like than many texts and contains a relatively small number of common words and verbs. In contrast, the second text, "Where the Mountain Meets the Moon," received a relatively high narrativity score from TERA (67th percentile) due to its inclusion of common words and verbs (e.g., called, working, think, lived, was, cut) and a higher incidence of pronouns (e.g., it, its, their). These different narrativity scores provide a relative comparison between texts and indicate potential linguistic differences that may not be captured by a simple grade level estimation.

## Syntactic Simplicity

The second component score provided by TERA relates to the syntax of a target text. Syntactic simplicity relates to the complexity of the sentences contained in a given text. This measure is calculated based on several indices of syntactic complexity, such as the average number of clauses per sentence, the number of words per sentence, and the number of words before the main verb of the main clause in a sentence. Texts with fewer clauses, fewer words per sentence, and fewer words before the main verb are easier to read and will yield a higher score for syntactic simplicity (McNamara et al., 2014; Pearson, 1974). TERA also measures the similarity of the sentence constructions within each paragraph. Paragraphs that contain sentences with similar structures and verb tenses are typically easier to read.

In Figure 4.1, the syntactic simplicity score for the Mars text was very high (88th percentile) because of the short and similarly structured sentences, whereas the Mountain text received an average score for this same dimension (49th percentile). Thus, while the Mars text was more difficult according to the narrativity component, its sentences are simpler to parse compared to the Mountain text.

## Word Concreteness

The third component score provided by TERA relates to the concreteness of the words in the text. Concrete words (e.g., mask, spoon, forest) are words that refer to things you can see, hear, taste, touch, feel, or smell (Toglia & Battig, 1978). Conversely, abstract words (democracy, appear, success, joy) cannot easily be seen, heard, touched, felt, or smelled. Words that are more concrete tend to be easier to imagine, memorize, and comprehend compared to more abstract words (Paivio, 1991); thus, a text with relatively high numbers of concrete words will be easier to read.

Figure 4.1 reveals that the word concreteness component score was somewhat low for the Mars text (39th percentile), suggesting that this text included more abstract words that were difficult for readers to visualize (e.g., Olympus, astronomers, tharsis, mons). The Mountain text, on the other hand, scored extremely high on the word concreteness dimension (98th percentile), because of its high density of known visualizable words (e.g., bend, brown, mud, mountain, water, houses, roof, people, river).

## Referential Cohesion

Referential cohesion relates to the overlap between words, word stems, or concepts from one sentence to another. When sentences and paragraphs have similar words or conceptual ideas, it is easier for the reader to make connections between those ideas. The repetition of the same words, concepts, or phrases across sentences and paragraphs makes a text higher in referential cohesion.

In Figure 4.1, referential cohesion was low for the Mars text (27th percentile) due to a relatively small amount of word overlap between sentences and ideas. For example, across the first three sentences (*Mars is very cold and very dry. Scattered across the surface are many giant volcanoes. Lava covers much of the land.*), there are no concepts repeated. Clearly, these sentences make sense; however, readers must rely on their world knowledge to make the connections between words such as volcanoes and lava, or surface and land. Similarly, the reader must make the inference that the surface is of Mars. These inferences depend on the reader's prior knowledge as well as active comprehension strategies (see Chapter 7 on iSTART in this volume).

By contrast, the Mountain text has a relatively average amount of referential cohesion (47th percentile). For example, there are several words that are repeated across the text (e.g., village, mountain, mud, land, river). While the sentences are long and likely challenging to parse for some readers, the repetition of words and concepts across the sentences and paragraphs helps the reader to make connections between ideas in the text.

## Deep Cohesion

Deep cohesion measures how well the events, ideas, and information of the whole text are tied together. TERA calculates deep cohesion by measuring the types of words that connect different parts of a text. These words, called connectives, consist of many different categories, including temporal (e.g., after), causal (e.g., because), additive (e.g., furthermore), logical (e.g., as a result), and adversative (e.g., however). All of these connectives help to tie together the events, ideas, and information in the text for the reader.

When there are more connectives and when the text calls for those connectives, the deep cohesion score will be higher. It should be noted though, that in some texts authors might include many of these connectors, because the topic is unfamiliar to students and the relationships are complex. Thus, a high score for deep cohesion is particularly informative for informational texts that are more likely to call for explicit cues about the relationships between ideas.

"Discovering Mars" received a very low deep cohesion score (26th percentile), because it included only one connective ("yet") and did not incorporate many other devices to help make inferences for readers (no causal, temporal, logical, or additive connectives). Because the Mars text is an informational text, the lack of deep cohesion may pose challenges, particularly for low knowledge readers. By contrast, "Where the Mountain meets the Moon" includes several connectives (i.e., two temporal: "over time", "day after day"; and three causal: "because" repeated three times), resulting in a relatively high score for this dimension (82nd percentile). These connectors are likely to facilitate a deeper understanding of the passage.

### Flesch-Kincaid (FK) Grade Level

In addition to the five component scores, TERA provides a comparative estimate of a passage grade level using the original FK Grade Level readability formula (Kincaid, Fishburne, Rogers, & Chissom, 1975). In TERA, the FK Grade Level is computed using a combination of the length of the sentences and the average number of syllables per word. This grade level estimate correlates highly with other common readability formulas (see McNamara et al., 2014), and can serve to augment the component score profile as an additional descriptor for a text. By including the five component scores and the FK grade level, TERA provides educators with a richer set of information to inform integration within assignments or curricula.

### TERA Interface

The TERA website is freely accessible and designed to be used by teachers and educators (see Figure 4.2 for login and account creation page; www.commoncoretera.com).

### Library Tool

The library tool allows users to access an existing database of sample texts from the Common Core that have been analyzed by TERA (see Figure 4.3 for screenshot). The library consists of a variety of genres (e.g., fiction, science, history), grade levels (second grade through higher education), and text sizes (from excerpts to full texts). Although the library includes genres like poetry, automated tools typically provide more accurate analyses of prose text.

The top half of Figure 4.3 is the list of items from the "Text Library" and displays sample text titles designed for grades 4 and 5. Along with the title and estimated grade, the library tool provides the text genre, length, and type (full text or excerpt). The text list is searchable through the fields at the bottom of the "Text Library"

Common Core TERA 57

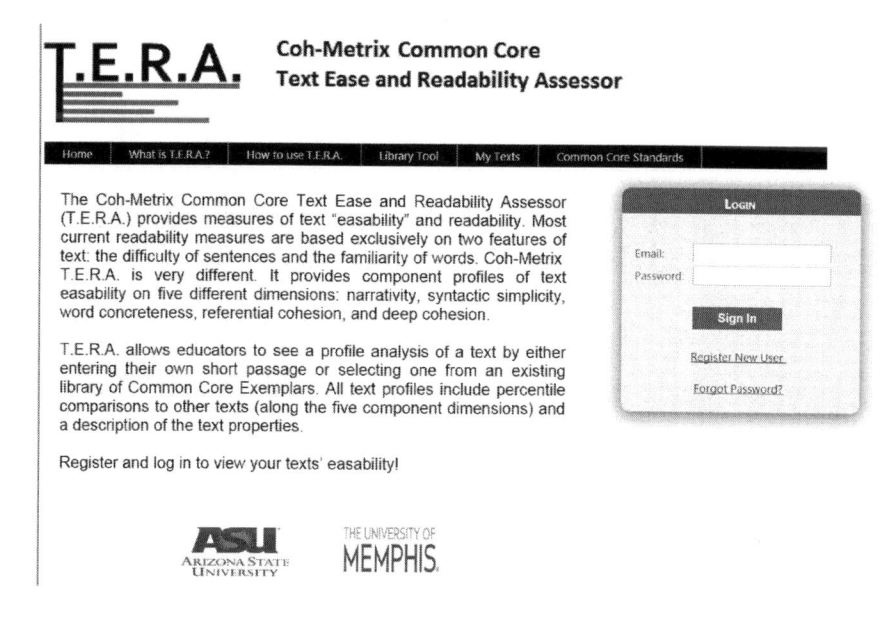

**FIGURE 4.2** Login and Creation Page for TERA Website.

listings. These fields allow the user (e.g., teachers) to search for keywords in the title, particular grades, specific genres, various text lengths, or filter for full texts versus excerpts. These search features allow users to customize the library results being displayed within the table and reduce the full set of available texts to better suit their current needs.

The bottom half of the TERA library tool in Figure 4.3 displays the linguistic results and other information for the current text selected in the list. This information panel provides the title of the selected text, the five linguistic component scores (in percentiles), the estimated FK grade level, an automated description of the percentile scores, and a preview of the text itself. In the bottom left, the five component scores and the estimated grade level represent the values for the currently selected text. The bottom-right area of Figure 4.3 displays the Common Core grade level (as determined by human experts), an automated analysis of the component scores, and an interpretation of the associated percentile scores (based on ranges of each component score). This bottom-right section can also display a "Text Preview" for the currently selected library item.

## My Texts

The "My Texts" page (Figure 4.4) allows users to submit their own texts for analysis (Figure 4.5) and establish their own library of texts. This page provides users with the same layout and features as the pre-existing library tool (i.e., a table

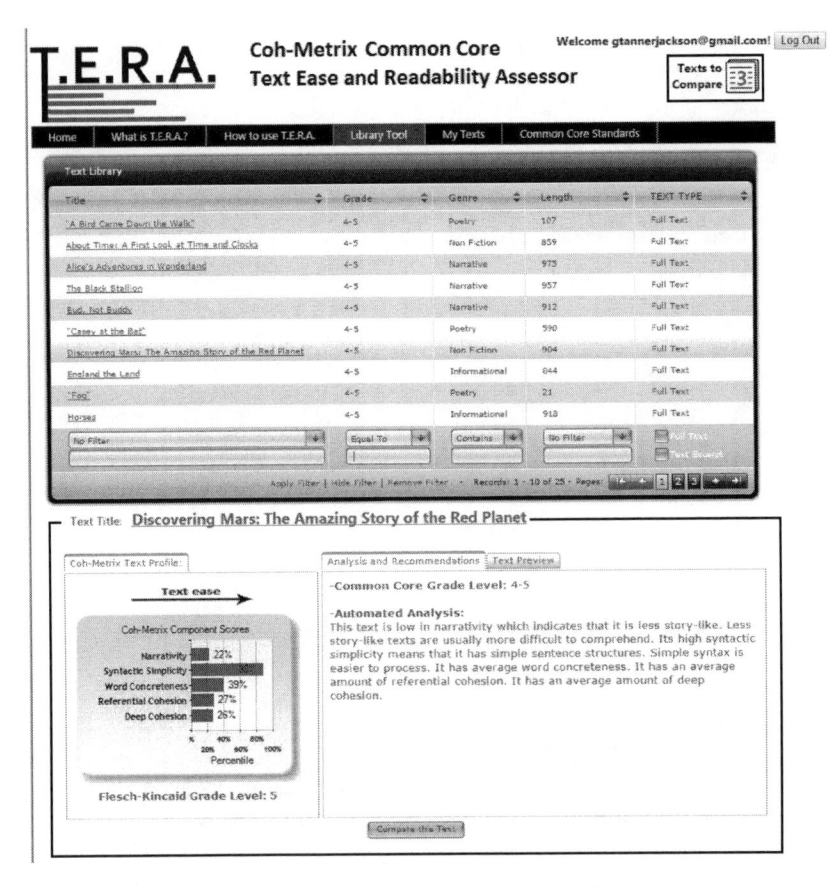

**FIGURE 4.3** Screenshot of Library Tool.

of stored texts, component scores, FK estimated grade level, and an automated analysis of the text). However, all items displayed here are associated with the texts entered by the user through the "input new text" feature (Figure 4.5).

When inputting a new text, TERA prompts users to enter a title, an estimated grade level (determined by the user), a genre for the text (determined by the user), an indication of "full text" or "excerpt," and then to copy/paste the text itself. These parameters facilitate organization of the user's own text entries, but do not affect the linguistic processing of the text or the associated scores. Although there is not a technical limit to the text size for TERA analysis, we recommend restricting texts to approximately 1,000 words in length. The information and text are then sent to the TERA system, a new item is added within the "My Texts" area, and the status is set to pending until the system has had time to receive and process the request (usually only a few minutes depending on the length and complexity of the text).

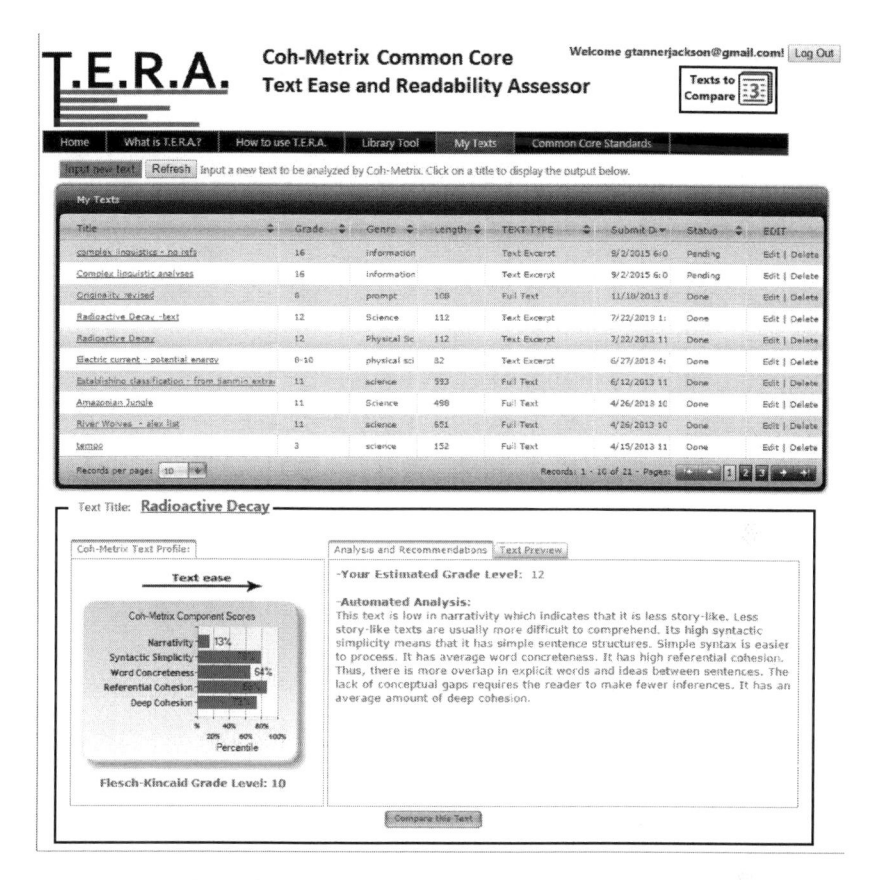

FIGURE 4.4  My Texts Page.

## Text Comparison

TERA also allows users to select texts for comparison (see Figure 4.6 for comparison screenshot). When a text is being displayed on either the Library Tool or My Texts pages, there is an option to "Compare this Text" at the bottom of the screen (see bottom of Figures 4.3 and 4.4 for examples). Once texts are selected to be compared, click on the "Texts to Compare" box in the top right of the screen (see top right of Figures 4.3 and 4.4). Texts selected for comparison will be displayed together vertically (see Figure 4.6 for partial screenshot).

## Leveraging TERA Design

TERA was designed to leverage the power of Coh-Metrix and render it more accessible to educators. Some of the important dimensions include: no download or installation required, web accessibility, an existing library, a personal

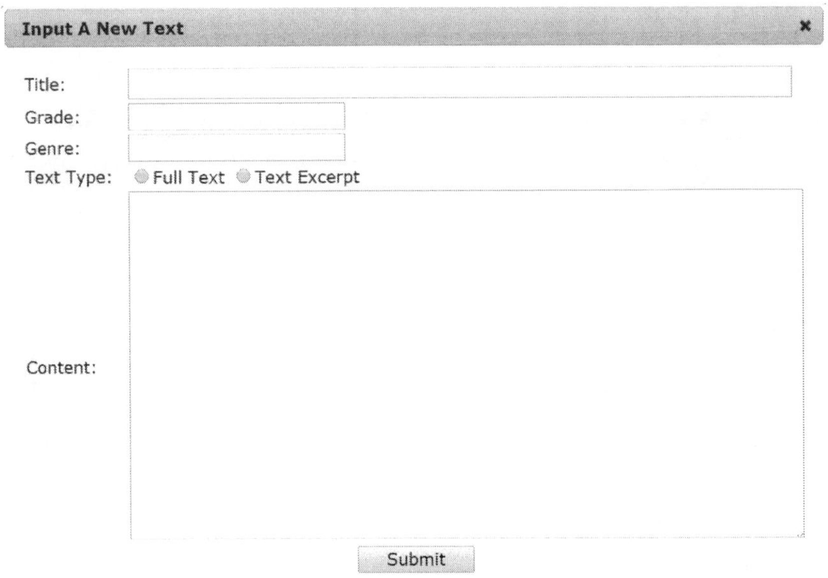

**FIGURE 4.5** Input New Text Feature.

customizable library, and the text comparison feature. Each of these features is designed to help reduce barriers and facilitate application to classroom pedagogy.

TERA requires no installation or download and can be used on any browser. This means that the system can be used on virtually any computer or mobile device that has internet access (users can even input new texts through smart phones). One major benefit of TERA being hosted online (rather than a desktop) is that all texts associated with an account can be accessed from anywhere in the world (i.e., you can upload a new text from home and display its comparison to other texts in front of the class). So whether you are in the classroom, at home, or on the road, the power of TERA is always available, along with all of its resources.

The existing library tool provides educators with a stable repository of documents that have been reviewed by experts and can be leveraged for pedagogical use. These documents were selected and assigned Common Core grade ranges to represent a range of textual features and to facilitate alignment with goals from the Common Core. The library of texts also provides a set of expert-rated samples that can be compared to user-entered texts.

One of the most promising features of TERA is that it allows users to submit their own texts for automated analysis. This allows everyone to have free and quick access to the power and benefits of sophisticated natural language processing that can provide almost instant information about the readability of a given text. Not only does it include an approximate grade level for each text, but TERA

Common Core TERA  61

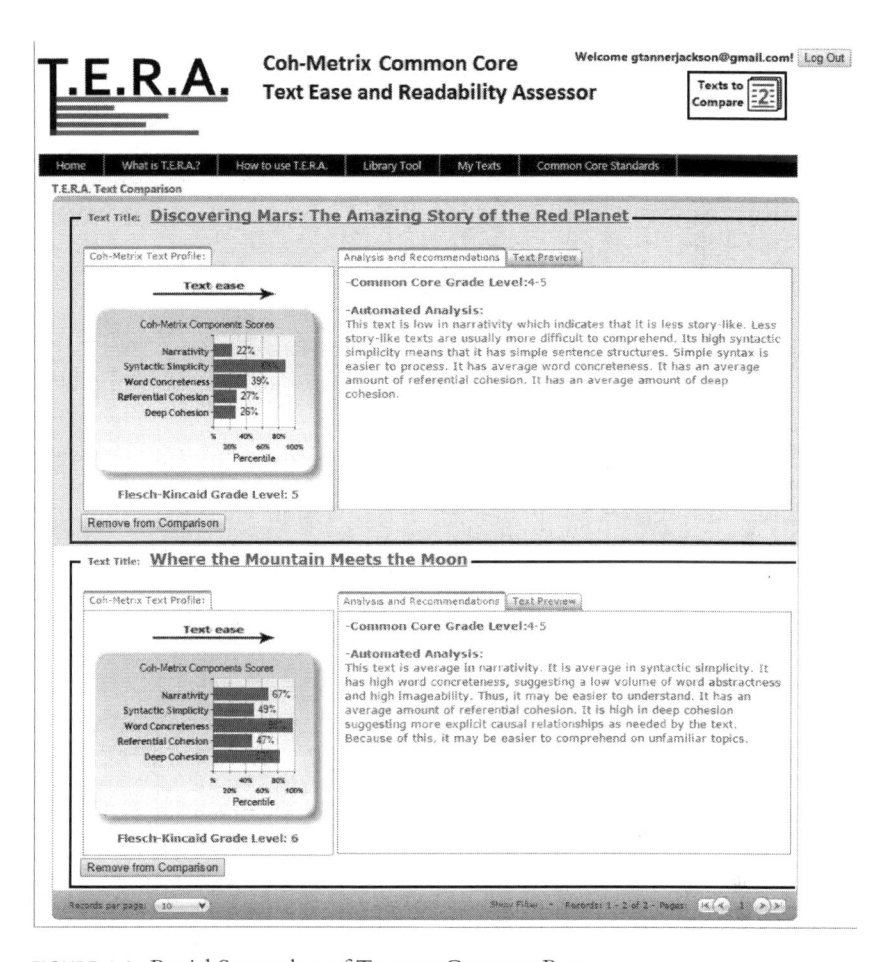

FIGURE 4.6  Partial Screenshot of Texts to Compare Page.

also provides the five component scores, which help to explain why a text may be particularly difficult for certain readers. These component scores can serve as guidelines to allow educators to make more informed pedagogical decisions, which should help to target the needs of students and improve their learning from the selected texts.

## Integrating TERA into the Classroom

TERA is a powerful tool that can help educators personalize instruction for individual students (like John and Sarah from earlier in this chapter). No two complex texts are wholly alike. Similarly, no two students are wholly alike. Thus, TERA is designed to help educators with the challenge of matching specific texts with individual students and groups of students based on their needs. Basic grade level estimates solely indicate whether a typical student (or even a particular student) in a particular grade is well matched to a text. These estimates do not fully characterize the relative ease or pedagogical appropriateness of each text; neither do they indicate why comprehension may fail or flourish, and they do not provide the teacher with any information about why a certain text may or may not align with the readers in the classroom or pedagogical objectives. Because traditional readability measures are unidimensional, they provide little guidance on *how* to modify instruction based on the difficulty of the text. By contrast, teachers who use TERA can use the component scores as guidelines to understand multiple aspects of a text's difficulty, which potentially can guide instruction.

The TERA system can be utilized across subject areas (History, Science, English Language Arts, etc.) and educational activities on a variety of levels, including tasks for an entire classroom or tailoring instruction for individual students. At the classroom level, TERA could be used as part of daily instruction, weekly activities, or even annual planning. On a daily basis, TERA can be used to display text analysis scores for texts that exemplify particular linguistic features. As a weekly assignment, a sample text could be analyzed by TERA and students could each modify that same text in different ways to exemplify changes on a given component dimension (e.g., shorten all sentences to reduce syntactic simplicity). This hands-on student use of TERA may offer additional pedagogical benefits as it requires students to personally manipulate and experience textual properties that can impact text difficulty.

At a curricula development level, educators could use the *library tool* to locate specific types of texts (e.g., a short 9th grade science text, or a general informational text for 4th graders). As part of a curriculum, educators could also use *my texts* to enter their own potential texts and compare multiple versions to determine the appropriate document for use within an assignment (or which versions to recommend to particular students). If a teacher is unable to decide which text to use for a given assignment, the *text comparison* tool can be used to identify text features that afford targeted insights for the class as a whole or to exemplify pedagogical materials in targeted small groups.

There are numerous ways to leverage TERA within a curriculum, and one of the strongest benefits is that TERA can help educators locate and/or analyze texts that are appropriate to address the needs of individual, or groups of, students. For example, previous research has shown that readers with low prior knowledge on a topic benefit from a more coherent text (i.e., high percentile scores), while students with a high prior knowledge can benefit from texts with less cohesion, which require generating inferences while reading (McNamara, Kintsch, Songer, & Kintsch, 1996). Thus the information provided by TERA can be used to align appropriate texts with the skills and knowledge of particular students to improve their overall comprehension and retention. Table 4.2 displays the set of TERA features and examples of how each of them may be used to facilitate educational goals and classroom pedagogy.

**TABLE 4.2** TERA Features and How They May Be Used To Facilitate Educational Goals and Classroom Pedagogy.

| TERA Dimension | Pedagogical Moves |
|---|---|
| Narrativity | • Scaffold knowledge deficits by using high narrative texts<br>• Move readers toward less narrative text when focusing on reading to learn |
| Referential Cohesion | • Use high cohesion text to scaffold low-knowledge readers<br>• Use low cohesion text to push readers to generate inferences |
| Syntactic Simplicity | • Use syntactically simple text to scaffold less skilled readers, particularly when faced with other text challenges such as low narrativity and low cohesion<br>• Move readers toward texts with increasingly complex syntax to build reading skill |
| Word Concreteness | • Use texts with more concrete words to compensate for other challenges in the text<br>• Move readers toward text with increasingly abstract concepts to build reading skill and world knowledge |
| Deep Cohesion | • High deep cohesion is most crucial when the text is low in narrativity and challenging on other dimensions<br>• Texts that are low in deep cohesion can be used to move readers toward making connections between ideas and global inferences |

## Narrativity

Narrative text is easier to read, comprehend, and recall than informational text (Graesser & McNamara, 2011; Haberlandt & Graesser, 1985). If a passage is low in narrativity, students' prior domain knowledge should be considered. If the students have little domain knowledge, teachers may consider texts that help to compensate for these challenges, such as texts that are higher in narrativity, or have fewer sources of challenges on the other dimensions. Nonetheless, transitioning readers toward less narrative text is crucial to reading to learn (Best, Floyd, & McNamara, 2008; Sanacore & Palumbo, 2009). The reader must learn to understand increasingly complex and unfamiliar ideas. If the teacher wishes to move the students toward learning to use their prior knowledge and generating inferences to understand more challenging text, the teacher may consider where the text falls on the spectrum of narrativity in TERA.

## Syntactic Simplicity

More skilled readers are better able to process more complex sentences (e.g., Just & Carpenter, 1992), and, consequently, older readers are typically assigned texts with higher grade levels and more complex syntax. TERA goes beyond typical readability formulas, because it differentiates between texts within grades with finer distinctions. If a text is low in syntactic simplicity, students' low reading skill should be considered, particularly to the extent that other aspects of the text do not compensate for these challenges. For example, the teacher will be able to discern whether a highly narrative text is easier or more challenging in terms of syntax according to the syntactic simplicity component score. Highly narrative texts with challenging syntax may be optimal for tackling the pedagogical goal of learning to parse sentences. By contrast, if a syntactically challenging text is also low in narrativity, then the teacher may wish to consider whether the students' reading skill and prior knowledge are sufficient to tackle that text.

## Word Concreteness

Texts with more concrete words facilitate a wide range of reading processes (Duran, Bellissens, Taylor, & McNamara, 2007; Gee, Nelson, & Krawczyk, 1999). Texts that are low in concreteness may be particularly challenging to students' with knowledge and reading skill deficits, particularly if there are multiple challenges in the texts. For example, if a text is low in concreteness and low in narrativity, this is likely to be a challenging, expository text that covers highly abstract concepts. The teacher might consider the students' domain knowledge and reading skill as well as the degree to which the cohesion of the text scaffolds the reading process or makes it even more challenging.

## Referential and Deep Cohesion

Cohesion is crucial to comprehension, particularly for readers who have low domain knowledge. A low cohesion text should be considered in concert with an understanding of readers' knowledge base. If readers have little knowledge, the text is low in narrativity, and the text is low in cohesion, then comprehension may suffer. For example, our previously mentioned sample student John, may have strong vocabulary skills, but since he has difficulty connecting ideas across texts, then the Mars text in Table 4.1 would likely be fairly difficult for him to understand. In contrast, a student who was skilled at integrating information across low cohesion sentences (like Sarah) may thrive with this same text. Although a student like John may struggle with initial comprehension of the Mars text, with sufficient scaffolding, low referential cohesion can help to push readers to generate inferences to fill in the cohesion gaps (e.g., McNamara, 2004), and thus could be used to help improve his skill in this area.

TERA can be used to identify texts that score low in particular types of cohesion, which can then be provided to students who struggle in that area. A text that is low in deep cohesion could be used to instruct students to make global inferences and pay attention to the locations where comprehension might be breaking down (monitoring their comprehension carefully). It is important for students to recognize these types of connections, because comprehension is more likely to degrade when they fail to process those connectors that provide essential information. Teaching students to recognize sections of the text with conceptual gaps, and how to deal with them, will help them to become better readers (Graesser, McNamara, & Louwerse, 2003).

## Discussion

Understanding complex texts is a daily activity both inside and outside of the classroom. Unfortunately, many students are not currently reading and comprehending at proficient levels. To prepare students for the complex demands of the Common Core, educators need to ensure that students are regularly engaging with high quality and complex texts that have been matched to their specific strengths and weaknesses. In this way, students will gradually come to recognize what makes texts rich and complex and how best to absorb what these texts provide. This outcome can only be achieved with teachers; and TERA is designed to help them accomplish this task.

The development of TERA was motivated by contemporary theories of reading comprehension that suggest that text comprehension occurs at *multiple* levels (e.g., Graesser & McNamara, 2011; Graesser, Millis, & Zwaan, 1997; Kintsch, 1998). In other words, the ability to understand a particular text is not solely reliant on one specific skill, such as decoding words or making inferences; rather, it relies on the development of a wide variety of knowledge and skills, as well as the strategies necessary to successfully regulate these different components (Allen, Snow, Crossley, Jackson, & McNamara, 2014; McNamara & Magliano, 2009). Importantly, successful text comprehension relies both on the characteristics of the individual reader and the multiple levels of the text itself (Graesser & McNamara, 2011; Graesser et al., 2011).

Many studies suggest that text difficulty components vary in their influence on comprehension depending on the knowledge, strategies, and skills available to the person reading the text. McNamara and colleagues (1996), for example, have found that text cohesion primarily benefits students with low knowledge of the text domain, but does not benefit students with high knowledge of the text topic. Students with more knowledge can compensate for cohesion gaps by generating the necessary inferences to comprehend the text (whereas low knowledge readers cannot do so). These findings are important to consider when determining how to teach reading comprehension and provide appropriate content-area texts to students.

TERA was designed to help improve literacy skills by providing educators with the resources necessary to match student skills with appropriate texts. Many years of previous research on reading and text comprehension have been leveraged to develop the TERA dimensions. Future research will continue to improve TERA and provide educators with more accurate, accessible, and formative information to facilitate their educational goals. TERA was designed to provide the information and insights gleaned from research on text comprehension and make them freely available to educators and instructional designers who have such a great impact on student education. This tool has the power to improve personalized student education and help people to understand the complex dimensions of texts and how they can be best aligned with individual sets of knowledge and skills.

## Notes

1 An alternative version of TERA is called TEA (Text Easability Asssessor), which is available at cohmetrix.com. One current difference between the two versions is that TERA provides profiles on a library of Common Core exemplar texts.
2 A system with similar purpose, called TextEvaluator, is also available online (Sheehan, Kostin, Napolitano, & Flor, 2014). For more information, see https://texteval-pilot.ets.org/TextEvaluator/.
3 The TERA component scores were developed using the Touchstone Applied Science Associates, Inc. (TASA) corpus and therefore entail the associated properties of that origin corpus.

## References

Allen, L. K., Snow, E. L., Crossley, S. A., Jackson, G. T., & McNamara, D. S. (2014). Reading comprehension components and their relation to the writing process. *L'année Psychologique/Topics in Cognitive Psychology*, *114*, 663–691.

Beck, I. L., McKeown, M. G., & Kucan, L. (2002). *Bringing Words to Life: Robust Vocabulary Instruction*. New York: Guilford Press.

Best, R. M., Floyd, R. G., & McNamara, D. S. (2008). Differential competencies contributing to children's comprehension of narrative and expository texts. *Reading Psychology*, *29*, 137–164.

Biber, D., Johansson, S., Leech, G., Conrad, S., & Finegan, E. (1999). *The Longman Grammar of Spoken and Written English*. London: Longman.

Bruner, J. (1986). *Actual Minds, Possible Worlds*. Cambridge, MA: Harvard University Press.

Cheong, Y., & Young, R. M. (2006). A computational model of narrative generation for suspense. *Proceedings of the AAAI 2006 Workshop on Computational Aesthetics*, pp. 8–15.

Duke, N., & Pearson, P. D. (2002). Effective practices for developing reading comprehension. In A. E. Farstrup & S. J. Samuels (Eds.), *What Research Has to Say about Reading Instruction* (3rd ed., pp. 205–241). Newark, DE: International Reading Association.

Duran, N., Bellissens, C., Taylor, R., & McNamara, D. (2007). Qualifying text difficulty with automated indices of cohesion and semantics. In D. S. McNamara & G. Trafton (Eds.), *Proceedings of the 29th Annual Meeting of the Cognitive Science Society* (pp. 233–238). Austin, TX: Cognitive Science Society.

Gee, N. R., Nelson D. L., & Krawczyk, D. (1999). Is the concreteness effect a result of underlying network interconnectivity? *Journal of Memory and Language*, *40*, 479–497.

Graesser, A. C., & McNamara, D. S. (2011). Computational analyses of multilevel discourse comprehension. *Topics in Cognitive Science*, *2*, 371–398.

Graesser, A. C., McNamara, D. S., & Kulikowich, J. M. (2011). Coh-Metrix: Providing multilevel analyses of text characteristics. *Educational Researcher, 40*, 223–234.

Graesser, A. C., McNamara, D. S., & Louwerse, M. M. (2003). What do readers need to learn in order to process coherence relations in narrative and expository text. In A. P. Sweet & C. E. Snow (Eds.), *Rethinking Reading Comprehension*. New York, NY: Guilford Publications.

Graesser, A. C., Millis, K. K., & Zwaan, R. A. (1997). Discourse comprehension. *Annual Review of Psychology, 48*, 163–189.

Haberlandt, K., & Graesser, A. C. (1985). Component processes in text comprehension and some of their interactions. *Journal of Experimental Psychology, 114*, 357–374.

Just, M. A., & Carpenter, P. A. (1992). A capacity theory of comprehension: Individual differences in working memory. *Psychological Review, 98*, 122–149.

Kincaid, J., Fishburne, R., Rogers, R., & Chissom, B. (1975). *Derivation of New Readability Formulas for Navy Enlisted Personnel*. Branch Report 8–75. Millington, TN: Chief of Naval Training.

Kintsch, W. (1998). *Comprehension: A Paradigm for Cognition*. Cambridge, UK: Cambridge University Press.

McNamara, D. S. (2004). SERT: Self-explanation reading training. *Discourse Processes, 38*, 1–30.

McNamara, D. S., & Graesser, A. C. (2012). Coh-Metrix: An automated tool for theoretical and applied natural language processing. In P. M. McCarthy & C. Boonthum-Denecke (Eds.), *Applied Natural Language Processing and Content Analysis: Identification, Investigation, and Resolution* (pp. 188–205). Hershey, PA: IGI Global.

McNamara, D. S., & Magliano, J. P. (2009). Toward a comprehensive model of comprehension. In B. Ross (Ed.), *The Psychology of Learning and Motivation*. New York: Elsevier Science.

McNamara, D. S., Graesser, A. C., & Louwerse, M. M. (2012). Sources of text difficulty: Across genres and grades. In J. P. Sabatini, E. Albro, & T. O'Reilly (Eds.), *Measuring Up: Advances in How We Assess Reading Ability* (pp. 89–116). Lanham, MD: R&L Education.

McNamara, D. S., Graesser, A. C., McCarthy, P., & Cai, Z. (2014). *Automated Evaluation of Text and Discourse with Coh-Metrix*. Cambridge, UK: Cambridge University Press.

McNamara, D. S., Kintsch, E., Songer, N. B., & Kintsch, W. (1996). Are good texts always better? Interactions of text coherence, background knowledge, and levels of understanding in learning from text. *Cognition and Instruction, 14*, 1–43.

Paivio, A. (1991). Dual coding theory: Retrospect and current status. *Canadian Journal of Psychology, 45*, 225–287.

Pearson, P. D. (1974). The effects of grammatical complexity on children's comprehension, recall and conception of semantic relations. *Reading Research Quarterly, 10*, 155–192. (Reprinted in H. Singer & R. Ruddell (Eds.), *Theoretical Models and Processes of Reading* (2nd ed.). Newark, DE: International Reading Association, 1976.)

Perfetti, C. A. (2007). Reading ability: Lexical quality to comprehension. *Scientific Studies of Reading, 11*, 357–383.

Sanacore, J., & Palumbo, A. (2009). Understanding the fourth-grade slump: Our point of view. *The Educational Forum, 73*, 67–74.

Schank, R. C., & Abelson, R. P. (1995). Knowledge and memory: The real story. In R. S. Wyer (Ed.), *Knowledge and Memory: The Real Story* (pp. 1–85). Hillsdale, NJ: Lawrence Erlbaum Associates.

Sheehan, K. M., Kostin, I., Napolitano, D., & Flor, M. (2014). The TextEvaluator tool: Helping teachers and test developers select texts for use in instruction and assessment. *The Elementary School Journal, 115*, 184–209.

Toglia, M. P., & Battig, W. (1978). *Handbook of Semantic Norms*. Hillsdale, NJ: Erlbaum.

Vorderer, P., Wulff, H. J., & Friedrichsen, M. (1996). *Suspense: Conceptualizations, Theoretical Analyses, and Empirical Explorations*. Mahwah, NJ: Erlbaum.

# 5

# DYNAMIC SUPPORT OF CONTEXTUAL VOCABULARY ACQUISITION FOR READING (DSCoVAR)

An Intelligent Tutor for Contextual Word Learning

*Gwen A. Frishkoff, Kevyn Collins-Thompson, SungJin Nam, Leslie Hodges, and Scott A. Crossley*

## Introduction

Knowledge of difficult words (e.g., *censure, lithe, epiphany*) is important for success in school, because it has been linked to the development of intermediate and advanced reading (Baumann et al., 2002) and writing (Yonek, 2008). It is also a strong predictor of long-term outcomes, including the likelihood of attaining a college or post-baccalaureate degree (Beck, McKeown, & Kucan, 2013). In current practice, however, vocabulary is given little time in the classroom (Baumann et al., 2002), and it is not usually tailored for individual learners.

In this chapter, we describe an intelligent tutoring system, called DSCoVAR (Dynamic Support of Contextual Vocabulary Acquisition for Reading). DSCoVAR is designed for intermediate-level readers—that is, older children, adolescents, and adults who are proficient spellers and decoders (Beck et al., 2013). DSCoVAR teaches words by presenting them in a series of brief written contexts that are selected to promote individualized, robust learning. This approach should prove an efficient and effective supplement to classroom instruction.

The chapter is organized as follows. First, we explain the need for a computer-based system to teach academic ("Tier 2") words in context. Next, we highlight key features of DSCoVAR and compare alternative computer-based methods for contextual word learning. Finally, we describe how to access the DSCoVAR system.

### The Importance of Tier 2 Word Knowledge

Isabel Beck and colleagues (McKeown, Beck, Omanson, & Pople 1985) have described three word categories or "tiers" that can serve as targets for vocabulary instruction. Tier 1 includes high-frequency words—such as *want* and *happy*—which, for the typically developing child, are learned through everyday conversation. By contrast, Tier 2 words—such as *censure* and *lithe*—occur rarely, if at all, in speech. As young readers transition from "learning to read" to "reading to learn" (Chall, 1983), they encounter more challenging text and discourse, and an increasing number of Tier 2 words (Beck et al., 2013). Because these words are comparatively rare, unless they are explicitly taught, they are unlikely to be learned (Nagy, Anderson, & Herman, 1987). Conversely, if readers do not know these words, they may have difficulty understanding more advanced text and discourse (Stanovich, 1986).

Tier 2 word knowledge may also be important for the development of critical thinking and writing (Yonek, 2008). Tier 2 words often have near synonyms: for example, *garish* has roughly the same meaning as the Tier 1 word, *ugly*. However, the less common word often has a richer set of connotations than its high-frequency synonym: *garish* means not just ugly, but also bright or colorful, and often poor quality or cheap. Thus, readers who have mastered Tier 2 words have a wider range of concepts at their disposal, which should enable more sophisticated thinking and writing (Baumann et al., 2002; Yonek, 2008).

It is also useful to compare Tier 2 and Tier 3 words, which represent different types of lower-frequency vocabulary. Tier 3 words denote specialized meanings (e.g., *hypotenuse*, *ecumenical*) that are best learned within a specific discipline, such as geometry or theology (Beck et al., 2013). By contrast, Tier 2 words denote common meanings, such as objects (*protrusion*), persons (*recluse*), properties of objects (*garish*) and persons (*lithe*), situations (*strife*), mental states (*nostalgia*), actions (*censure*), and events (*languish*). This means that Tier 2 vocabulary instruction can be integrated with the rest of the curriculum. It also suggests that Tier 2 word knowledge can contribute to learning and development across the curriculum. For all of these reasons, reading experts have stressed the importance of Tier 2 word knowledge for reading and academic development (Baumann, Ware, & Edwards, 2007; Beck et al., 2013; Stanovich, 1986).

## *Methods for Efficient and Effective Contextual Word Leaning*

Tier 2 words have subtly different meanings depending on how they are used. For example, *garish* has roughly the same meaning as the Tier 1 word, *ugly*. However, the less common word often has a distinct—and richer—set of connotations than its high-frequency synonym: *garish* means not just ugly, but also bright or colorful, and possibly poor quality or cheap. Thus, to master this word, a learner needs to learn what it means in different contexts (Bolger, Balass, Landen, & Perfetti, 2008).

While reading experts have long recognized the importance of word learning in context, there has been a great deal of debate about the right way to implement it. In general, experts have tended to promote one of two approaches:

*independent reading* or *direct instruction*. These approaches have complementary strengths and weaknesses, as described below. In developing the DSCoVAR system, we sought to combine the best of both methods: namely, multiple high-quality contexts (which an avid reader would get through independent reading), and direct instruction (delivered by a computer avatar), explicit hints, and feedback.

Direct instruction usually refers to teacher-guided learning within a classroom. The teacher selects a small number of words each week, provides student-friendly definitions for these words, and assigns in-class exercises and homework that is explicitly focused on vocabulary (Beck & McKeown, 2004). Such exercises can include using a word in a novel sentence or providing a synonym or definition. When these exercises are carried out within a classroom setting, students can receive immediate and direct support, in the form of teacher feedback and class discussion.

Direct instruction can be highly effective, but it has a major limitation: it may be impractical given the other demands on class time and given the sheer number of words that a child must learn every year just to maintain steady growth in vocabulary (Nagy et al., 1987). For this reason, some reading experts have advocated word learning through *independent reading*. Since Tier 2 words are rarely used in spoken language, the goal here is to motivate students to read actively, independently, and as widely as possible. In theory, this is an excellent solution: independent reading serves a higher goal (e.g., reading for new knowledge or enjoyment) and it does not require class time. However, it also has some risks. Students must have the necessary skills to learn new words in context. For example, they must be able to identify and use context cues, which enable a reader to guess a word's meaning from the surrounding context (Baumann et al., 2002; Beck et al., 2013). In the absence of a teacher or tutor, learning through independent reading may tax higher cognitive skills, such as self-monitoring, which is the ability to think about and control one's actions. Self-monitoring is necessary for a reader to decide when to consult a dictionary or other supplementary source. This ability is particularly important for independent reading, because authentic texts often provide poor, and even misdirective, word meaning cues (Beck, McKeown, & McCaslin, 1983; Frishkoff, Collins-Thompson, Perfetti, & Callan, 2008; Schatz & Baldwin, 1986; Swanborn & De Glopper, 1999). The challenge is that self-monitoring and other skills are still developing in late childhood and adolescence (Cain, Oakhill, & Elbro, 2003; Cain, Oakhill, & Lemmon, 2004), and these skills vary greatly across individuals even into late adolescence and adulthood (Elleman, Lindo, Morphy, & Compton, 2009; Fukkink & De Glopper, 1998). Therefore, it is risky to rely on independent reading if we wish to foster meaningful growth in Tier 2 word knowledge, especially for students who are not necessarily at the top of their class.

To summarize, the two most common existing approaches to teach difficult words in context—independent reading and direct instruction—have not met the need for an effective and efficient approach to vocabulary instruction. Independent reading places fewer demands on class time, and it has the potential for greater gains over the lifespan. However, it also relies on student motivation and higher cognitive skills, such as knowledge and use of context cues and self-monitoring (among others). By contrast, direct instruction is effective, but—given limited class time—it can only teach a fraction of the words that need to be learned. In short, neither approach is sufficient. It is for this reason that we have developed the DSCoVAR system. The goal of this system is to support effective, efficient, and individualized support for learning Tier 2 words.

## The DSCoVAR System

In this section, we describe the main components of the DSCoVAR system and highlight key features of the system. We also describe how to use the web-based interface and Dashboard to access and use the DSCoVAR system.

The DSCoVAR tutor can be used as a stand-alone tool to expand student vocabulary, or it can be integrated with a classroom reading curriculum. For example, teachers may wish to engage students in a larger discussion of what words mean and how they are used in real-world contexts, such as understanding a newspaper article, technical manual, or voter pamphlet (Beck et al., 2013).

### *Strategy Training Module*

Students log in to the system using a web browser, such as Safari, Chrome, Firefox, or Internet Explorer. After log in, students are asked to complete a short (~5 minute) *strategy training module*. The training includes explicit instruction in the use of context cues (e.g., words and phrases that can be used to identify synonymy, antonymy, and cause-effect relations). During strategy training, students watch a short video that introduces the three types of context cues (synonymy, antonymy, and cause-effect relationships) and explains how each can be used to guess the meaning of an unfamiliar word in context. An animated instructor, named Ava, provides spoken explanations throughout the video. After the introduction, Ava summarizes the three types of context cues and talks through multiple examples of each cue type. Figure 5.1 shows some example slides from the strategy training phase.

After the video, there is a short interactive practice session, where students have an opportunity to practice and receive feedback on the use of specific cues to synonymy (e.g., phrases like *that is* or *means that*), antonymy (e.g., phrases like *instead of* or *rather than*), and cause-effect relationships (e.g., *because of* or *due to*). Explicit knowledge of these cues can be used to figure out the meaning of a word within a particular context, and previous work has shown that strategy training may lead

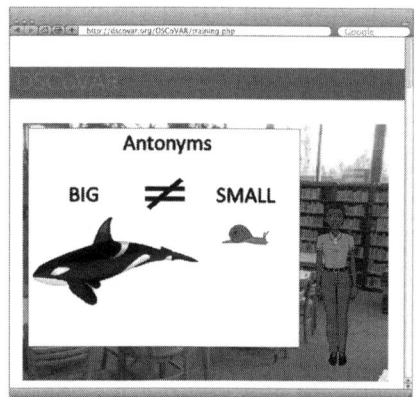

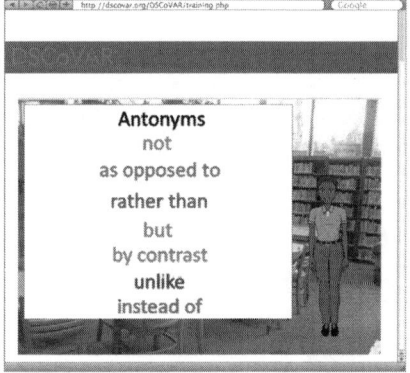

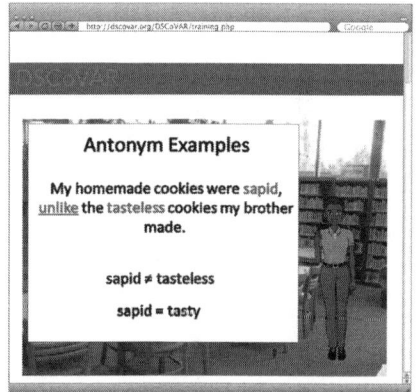

**FIGURE 5.1** Strategy Training Module.

In these example slides, Ava (the avatar) introduces antonyms (top), lists some words and phrases that can be used to identify antonyms within a sentence (bottom left), and illustrates how antonyms can be used to guess the meaning of an unknown word like *sapid* (bottom right).

to improved word learning abilities (Baumann et al., 2002, 2007; Fukkink & De Glopper, 1998), although further research is needed to bolster these claims.

## Contextual Word Learning Module

During contextual word learning, each word is presented in multiple contexts. The student is asked to read each context and then give the meaning of the word that is underlined (Figure 5.2).

Below we discuss important features of the contextual word learning module, including the instructional task, automated assessment of partial word knowledge, and adaptive presentation of contexts, which is designed to optimize learning for each individual student, depending on their current understanding of a particular word in context.

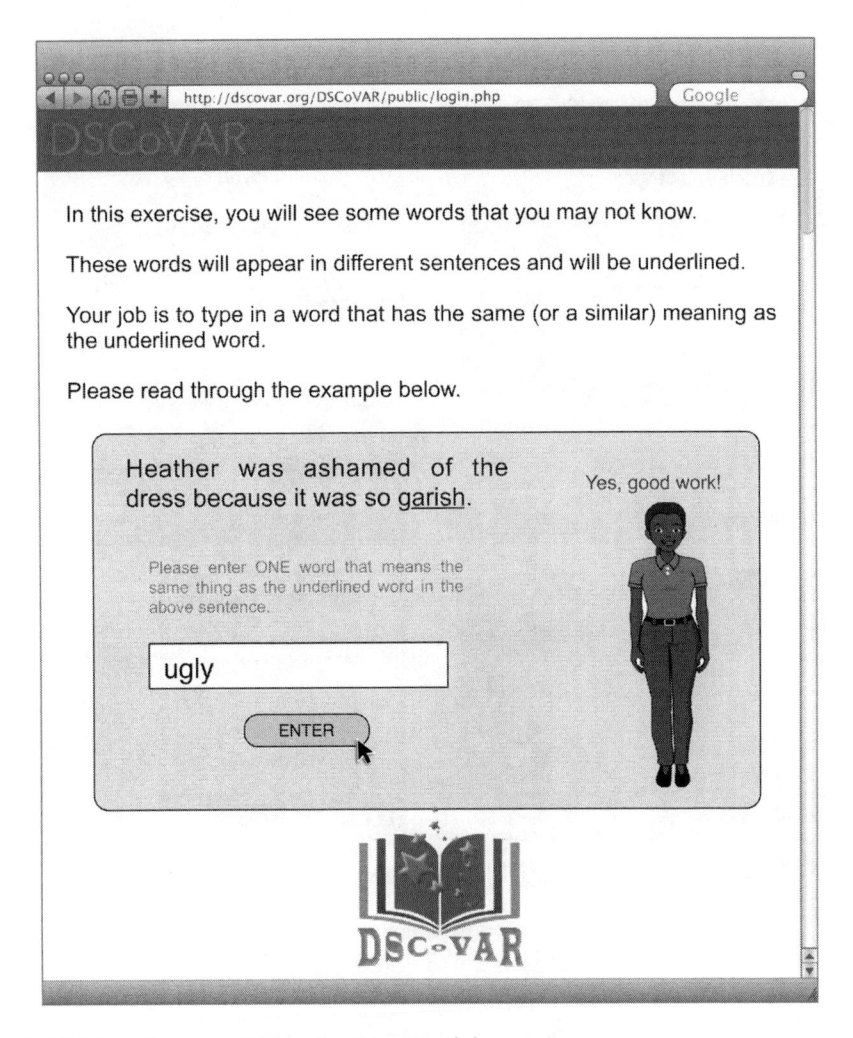

**FIGURE 5.2** Contextual Word Learning Module.

In this example slide, Ava provides feedback on a student's guess about the meaning of the word *garish*.

## Teacher Dashboard

Teachers can monitor student progress using the DSCoVAR Dashboard (Figure 5.3), which is also accessed through a web browser.

The browser has several views. In the Student View (Figure 5.3, left), it displays individual student progress at a coarse-grained level, i.e., how many words a student has been taught, and whether they are performing above or below average. It can also display more fine-grained progress, such as student responses to a word across different sentences. In the Word-Level View (Figure 5.3, right), the

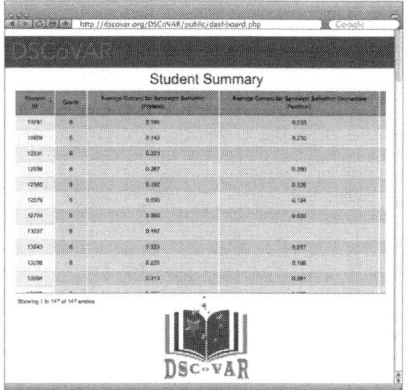

**FIGURE 5.3** Teacher Dashboard.

*Left*, Student Summary shows the average performance for each student before and immediately after training. *Right*, Word-Level Summary displays the words that have been selected for training, together with the average accuracy for the class. In addition to overall accuracy (left-most column), the dashboard shows mean performance before and after training, as well as average gains in accuracy (posttest minus pretest scores).

Dashboard summarizes performance across students for a particular word. This can help teachers to identify words that have been successfully learned and those that may need additional emphasis or examples outside the tutor, for example, through group discussions or homework.

## *Important Features*

The DSCoVAR system has several important features. The first is the *instructional task*, which promotes active engagement throughout the contextual word learning phase. As mentioned previously, students are asked to give the meaning of a word after each example of the word in context. This task encourages users to either infer the meaning of a new word from context or retrieve it from memory on each and every trial. By contrast, other vocabulary learning systems include periodic tests of knowledge that can be completed without actually using contexts to infer the meanings of unknown words. For example, in CAVOCA (Groot, 2000), students are given a series of three contexts for each word. The target word is then given in a new context, and learners are asked to decide whether or not the usage is correct (i.e., whether or not the sentence containing the word makes sense). While this task provides a useful measure of word learning, it can be completed without actually trying to guess the meaning of the target word. As a result, students may acquire good receptive knowledge: that is, they may be able to recognize, at least partially, what a word means if they see it in context. However, they are less likely to develop the kinds of active word skills that are needed to recall the word from memory and use it in novel, self-generated contexts—that is, skills that create capable and confident readers and writers.

A second feature is *automated assessment of partial word knowledge*. DSCoVAR uses computational methods, such as MESA (Collins-Thompson & Callan, 2007; Frishkoff et al., 2008; Frishkoff, Perfetti, & Collins-Thompson, 2010, 2011), to determine whether a student has learned some or all of a word's meaning and to update this assessment throughout learning. This makes it possible for a teacher to track changes in word knowledge throughout learning (e.g., Figure 5.3). Although other systems include multiple measures of word knowledge, DSCoVAR is unique in providing automated assessment of partial semantic knowledge.

Table 5.1 shows some examples of student responses to the Tier 2 word *garish* in easy (high-constraint) and harder (medium- and low-constraint) sentences. Notice that student responses, such as *trustworthy*, which are far from the meaning of *garish*, are scored as incorrect. By contrast, answers that may capture some of the semantic features of the correct response—such as the word *weird*—are scored as partially correct.

Estimates of partial word knowledge enable a third key feature of the DSCoVAR system: *immediate feedback* to students during learning. In particular, users are told whether their guess about a word's meaning is correct, partially correct, or incorrect (Collins-Thompson et al., 2012; Frishkoff et al., in press). Recent studies suggest that immediate feedback of this kind leads to improved word learning: when learners are told that their answer is not correct, they know to look for additional evidence to improve their guess on subsequent trials (Frishkoff et al., in press).

A fourth feature is *adaptive spacing of practice*. Studies of word learning have consistently shown that interleaving (or alternating) practice with different words leads to better learning than seeing the same word repeated several times in a row (e.g., Cepeda, Pashler, Vul, Wixted, & Rohrer, 2006; Pashler, Rohrer, Cepeda, & Carpenter, 2007; Pavlik & Anderson, 2005). DSCoVAR adjusts the spacing of contexts during training to increase the probability that a word will be learned and retained over time. If a student's guess about what a word means is repeatedly wrong, the spacing between examples is reduced. If the guess is right on multiple

**TABLE 5.1** Examples of Student Responses to the Tier 2 Word *Garish*.

| Constraint Category | Sample Context | Sample Response | Feedback Category |
|---|---|---|---|
| Low | Brian was the only one who thought that they were *garish*. | trustworthy | incorrect |
| Medium | Heather was ashamed of the dress because it was so *garish*. | old | partially correct |
| High | Some people think animal prints are pretty, but others think they're *garish*. | ugly | correct |

consecutive trials, the spacing is gradually increased. Increased spacing makes it harder to simply repeat the same answer across trials and increases the reliance on memory or on using the current context to guess the word's meaning. In this way, increased spacing of practice brings about "desirable difficulties" in word learning (Frishkoff et al., 2008).

The fifth feature is *scaffolding of easy and more challenging contexts*. DSCoVAR uses a high-quality corpus of sentences, and each sentence has been extensively normed to determine the level of context constraint: low (no cues as to the specific meaning of the target word), medium (limited cues), or high (strong cues). High-constraint contexts provide strong cues to meaning and are therefore easier: thus, they are important early in learning, when the goal is to promote correct inferences about a target word meaning. Medium- and low-constraint contexts are harder and can thus be useful at later stages of learning when the goal is to encourage learners to recall a word's meaning from memory, rather than relying on cues within the current context. In the following section, we discuss some evidence that scaffolding of easy and hard contexts does indeed support robust word learning.

## Evidence for Effectiveness

The DSCoVAR system is relatively new. Therefore, we are still testing the system across diverse contexts, including high and low socio-economic status (SES) middle school classrooms. In 2016–2017, we will conduct a study with 300 6th to 8th grade students: most of these students (~95 percent) are African-American and attend Title 1 schools in the greater Atlanta area. In this study, we will collect a large amount of information about the learning of Tier 2 words in different types of contexts. We are also assessing memory for trained words over 1-month and 6-month delays to evaluate robust learning and retention of new knowledge.

### *Real-Time Feedback in DSCoVAR*

Frishkoff et al. (in press) tested whether or not real-time feedback within the DSCoVAR system can improve learning and retention of words, beyond word learning gains in the absence of feedback. Adult participants read novel words in multiple contexts, which varied in the strength and types of cues. After each context, participants guessed the word meaning. One group of participants received accuracy feedback based on MESA, which indicated whether the response was completely correct, partially correct, or incorrect. An active control group was exposed to the same input, but did not receive feedback during training. Results indicated that the feedback group outperformed the control group, according to both real-time measures of learning and pretest/posttest measures of learning and retention. This finding shows the added value of including real-time measures of word learning as part of the systems design:

the ability to score performance on a trial-by-trial basis makes it possible to provide real-time feedback to learners. Moreover, this feedback appears to benefit learning, over and above the use of the meaning-generation task and the presentation of multiple supportive contexts.

## Scaffolding of Contextual Constraint

Ideally, practice with sentences that are easy (high-constraint) or harder (medium- or low-constraint) should be sequenced to maximize learning and minimize forgetting, in line with established principles of learning and memory (Koedinger, Corbett, & Perfetti, 2012). However, these principles have not been well tested in contextual word learning. To address this gap, Hodges, Frishkoff, and Collins-Thompson (in press) tested adult learning outcomes using a series of contexts that provided strong initial support and gradually decreased support over time (i.e., scaffolding of support). Scaffolding of support has proven effective in many domains. Our study tested whether this holds true for contextual word learning. We predicted that sustained and highly supportive contexts in training would lead to better immediate learning but worse retention, and that scaffolding would produce optimal outcomes due to fast errorless learning followed by practice retrieving new word meanings from memory. Results confirmed this prediction. Compared to a series of easy contexts (high-constraint condition), using a series of contexts that starts out easy and becomes progressively harder (a scaffolded condition) resulted in lower scores on the immediate posttest, but higher scores on the delayed post-test. These findings suggest that scaffolding may help promote robust gains in Tier 2 word knowledge.

We have recently replicated this pattern of results with a group of children, in 4th to 6th grades (Frishkoff et al., in press). Our preliminary analyses show that children also benefit from the "desirable difficulties" that are associated with scaffolding of context constraint. In particular, there is significantly better retention of words that were learned in a series of scaffolded (easier followed by more challenging) contexts as compared with words that were learned in a series of maximally constraining contexts. It remains to be seen whether these patterns will hold up across diverse populations. This is a question that we aim to address in our next classroom study.

## How to Access DSCoVAR

DSCoVAR is available to educators for non-commercial use. The system is supported by commercial cloud computing services, which enables it to support a large number of simultaneous users: as demand increases, the cloud computing service can allocate more computational resources. This ensures that DSCoVAR can be used in real-world educational settings without compromising the speed or quality of user interactions with the system.

Please contact the authors for permission to try out the system as a user, and for details on how to register new students, so they can access different parts of the system. Further details and links may be found at the main DSCoVAR project site: http://dscovar.org.

## Conclusion

We encourage educators to contact us with questions and comments as they use the DSCoVAR system. Based on our initial studies (summarized above), the probability of learning a new word in DSCoVAR and remembering the meaning of the word after a 1-week delay is ~25–30 percent—which is 4 to 5 times greater than typical gains in word knowledge through contextual word learning (Beck et al., 2013; Fukkink & De Glopper, 1998; Swanborn & De Glopper, 1999). Given these findings, DSCoVAR appears promising as an approach to Tier 2 vocabulary instruction. In addition, we are planning additional improvements to the system in order to address the need for an efficient and effective tool, which is dynamically tuned to support the needs of individual students.

## Acknowledgments

The research reported here was supported by the Institute of Education Sciences, U. S. Department of Education, through Grant R305A140647 to the University of Michigan. The opinions expressed are those of the authors and do not represent the views of the Institute or the U. S. Department of Education. Additional support was provided by an Amazon Web Services in Education Research Grant award.

## References

Baumann, J. F., Ware, D., & Edwards, E. C. (2007). "Bumping into spicy, tasty words that catch your tongue": A formative experiment on vocabulary instruction. *The Reading Teacher, 61*(2), 108–122.
Baumann, J. F., Edwards, E. C., Font, G., Tereshinski, C. A., Kame'enui, E. J., & Olejnik, S. (2002). Teaching morphemic and contextual analysis to fifth-grade students. *Reading Research Quarterly, 37*(2), 150–176.
Beck, I. & McKeown, M. (2004). *Elements of Reading Vocabulary: Teacher's Guide Level A* (Item No. 0-7398-8458-1). Austin, TX.
Beck, I., McKeown, M., & Kucan, L. (2013). *Bringing Words to Life: Robust Vocabulary Instruction*, 2nd ed. New York: Guilford Press.
Beck, I., McKeown, M., & McCaslin, E. (1983). Vocabulary development: All contexts are not created equal. *Elementary School Journal, 83*, 177–181. doi: 10.1086/461307
Bolger, D. J., Balass, M., Landen, E., & Perfetti, C. A. (2008). Effects of contextual variation and definitions in learning the meaning of words. *Discourse Processing, 45*, 122–149.
Cain, K., Oakhill, J. V., & Elbro, C. (2003). The ability to learn new word meanings from context by school-age children with and without language comprehension difficulties. *Journal of Child Language, 30*(3), 681–694.

Cain, K., Oakhill, J., & Lemmon, K. (2004). Individual differences in the inference of word meanings from context: The influence of reading comprehension, vocabulary knowledge, and memory capacity. *Journal of Educational Psychology, 96*(4), 671–681.

Cepeda, N. J., Pashler, H., Vul, E., Wixted, J. T., & Rohrer, D. (2006). Distributed practice in verbal recall tasks: A review and quantitative synthesis. *Psychological Bulletin, 132*(3), 354–80.

Chall, J. S. (1983). *Learning to Read: The Great Debate*. New York: McGraw-Hill.

Collins-Thompson, K., & Callan, J. (2007). Automatic and human scoring of word definition responses. *Proceedings of the North American Association of Computational Linguistics-Human Language Technology.*

Collins-Thompson, K., Frishkoff, G. A., Crossley, S. (2012). Definition response scoring with probabilistic ordinal regression. *Proceedings of the 20th Annual International Conference on Computers in Education.*

Elleman, A. M., Lindo, E., Morphy, P., & Compton, D. L. (2009). The impact of vocabulary instruction on passage-level comprehension of school-age children: A meta-analysis. *Journal of Research on Educational Effectiveness, 2*, 1–44.

Frishkoff, G. A., Perfetti, C. A., & Collins-Thompson, K. (2010). Lexical quality in the brain: ERP evidence for robust word learning from context. *Developmental Neuropsychology, 35*(4), 376–403.

Frishkoff, G. A., Perfetti, C. A., & Collins-Thompson, K. (2011). Predicting robust vocabulary growth from measures of incremental learning. *Scientific Studies of Reading, 15*(1), 71–91.

Frishkoff, G. A., Collins-Thompson, K., Hodges, L. E., & Crossley, S. (in press). Real-time feedback improves word learning from context: Evidence based on measures of partial word knowledge. *Reading & Writing.*

Frishkoff, G. A., Collins-Thompson, K., Perfetti, C. A., & Callan, J. (2008). Measuring incremental changes in word knowledge: Experimental validation and implications for learning and assessment. *Behavioral Research Methods, 40*(4), 907–925.

Fukkink, R. G., & De Glopper, K. (1998). Effects of instruction in deriving word meaning from context: A meta-analysis. *Review of Educational Research, 68*(4), 450–469.

Groot, P. J. (2000). Computer assisted second language vocabulary acquisition. *Language Learning & Technology, 4*(1), 60–81.

Hodges, L., Frishkoff, G., & Collins-Thompson, K. (in press). Desirable Difficulties in Contextual Word Learning: Addressing the "Assistance Dilemma."

Koedinger, K. R., Corbett, A. T., & Perfetti, C. (2012). The knowledge-learning-instruction framework: Bridging the science-practice chasm to enhance robust student learning. *Cognitive Science, 36*(5), 757–798.

McKeown, M. G., Beck, I. L., Omanson, R. C., & Pople, M. (1985). Some effects of the nature and frequency of vocabulary instruction on the knowledge and use of words. *Reading Research Quarterly, 20*(5), 552–535.

Nagy, W. E., Anderson, R. C., & Herman, P. A. (1987). Learning words from context during normal reading. *American Educational Research Journal, 24*(2), 237–270.

Pashler, H., Rohrer, D., Cepeda, N. J., & Carpenter, S. K. (2007). Enhancing learning and retarding forgetting: choices and consequences. *Psychonomic Bulletin & Review, 14*(2), 187–193.

Pavlik, P., & Anderson, J. R. (2005). Practice and forgetting effects on vocabulary memory: An activation-based model of the spacing effect. *Cognitive Science, 29*, 559–586.

Schatz, E. K., & Baldwin, R. S. (1986). Context cues are unreliable predictors of word meanings. *Reading Research Quarterly, 21*(4), 439–453.

Stanovich, K. E. (1986). Matthew effects in reading: Some consequences of individual differences in the acquisition of literacy. *Reading Research Quarterly, 21*, 360–407.

Swanborn, M. S. L., & De Glopper, K. (1999). Incidental word learning while reading: A meta-analysis. *Review of Educational Research, 69*(3), 261–285.

Yonek, L. M. (2008). *The Effects of Rich Vocabulary Instruction on Students' Expository Writing*. Unpublished doctoral dissertation, University of Pittsburgh.

# 6
# INTELLIGENT TUTORING OF THE STRUCTURE STRATEGY
## A Reading Strategy Tutor

*Bonnie J. F. Meyer and Kausalai K. Wijekumar*

This chapter provides an overview of Intelligent Tutoring of the Structure Strategy (ITSS), an automated and adaptive tutoring system that provides instruction for a powerful reading comprehension strategy, the structure strategy. ITSS has been developed at Penn State over the last 15 years (e.g., Meyer et al., 2002; Meyer, Wijekumar, & Lin, 2011; Wijekumar et al., 2014). Current adaptations, extensions, and evaluations of ITSS are collaborations between Texas A&M University and Penn State. Instruction with the structure strategy teaches 4th- to 8th-grade students to a) understand the logical structure of expository and persuasive texts and b) use that structure for selection, encoding, organizing, retrieving, and applying important ideas communicated through nonfiction.

In this chapter, we first discuss text structure strategies in ITSS for increasing reading comprehension. Next we describe the ITSS system. Then we highlight a number of randomized studies demonstrating strong evidence for using ITSS in classrooms. Additionally, we explain how teachers can use and integrate the ITSS system within their classrooms. ITSS is not meant to replace reading or language arts instruction in classrooms; instead, ITSS can help teachers provide their students with a powerful approach to reading nonfiction through adaptive, individualized structure strategy instruction to meet students' particular needs. We close with a short summary of recent adaptations and limitations of the ITSS system.

### Improving Reading Comprehension via the Structure Strategy

Many children in the U.S. have difficulty reading nonfiction texts (e.g., NAEP, 2013). National and State assessments of reading comprehension in our schools point to problems in reading comprehension, with 32 percent of 4th graders reading below basic levels of proficiency (NAEP, 2013). Most language arts curricula at upper elementary levels are designed to prepare students for learning from their reading in content areas. Many instructional programs to improve comprehension focus on background knowledge, vocabulary, summarization, inferences, elaboration, and text structure. With the introduction of the Common Core State Standards to over 40 states, instruction about text structure has received more attention.

The structure strategy is a text structure based comprehension approach that provides a new lens and implementation of text structure that is different from what textbooks are currently using. Specifically, the structure strategy subsumes comprehension strategies, such as summarizing, within the text structure framework allowing children to create coherent and strategic mental representations of the text and to use their memory and text structure to monitor and check their comprehension. The structure strategy based comprehension approach is showcased in a series of videos prepared through recent grant funds for teachers and their students (U.S. Department of Education, Institute of Education Sciences, R305A130327).

Within the structure strategy framework, learners read expository and persuasive texts, identify signaling words, classify text structure (i.e., comparison, problem and solution, cause and effect, sequence, and description), write main ideas (summarize) scaffolded by patterns for each text structure (e.g., comparison scaffold: _____ and _____ (2 or more ideas) were compared on _____, _____, and _____ (1 or more issues)), recall information, check their comprehension, and write as much as they can remember again with the specific text structure as the guide. Within web-based ITSS, students learn all of these comprehension strategies and further learn about authors' intentions to inform or persuade, inferences, and elaborations using text structure.

This approach differs from common classroom comprehension practices where summarization, inferences, elaborations, comprehension monitoring, and writing are independent of the text structure instruction. The structure strategy based comprehension instruction provides a more efficient and integrated approach with important scaffolds for children. When children have difficulty identifying the main idea in a passage, teachers typically instruct them to reread the passage or to find elements that are repeated. This type of instruction for children experiencing difficulties reading often adds to their frustration. In contrast, students are asked to look for who was being compared with whom and on what basis they were being compared when reading a passage with the comparison text structure during structure strategy based instruction. Such direction gives students a strong explicit scaffold that is more powerful than rereading alone.

Knowledge about text structures and how to strategically use them helps students build coherent mental representations. For example, when reading a nonfiction article providing a paragraph about sea lions and followed by a paragraph about seals, it would be helpful to use a comparative structure while creating a mental representation. In ITSS students learn through modeling, explicit instruction, and practice to create a simple main idea for an article that they are reading by using the main idea pattern for the comparison text structure. For this example, a simple main idea is <u>sea lions</u> and <u>seals</u> are compared on <u>weight</u>, <u>mobility on land</u>, and <u>sounds</u>. Next students use their constructed simple main ideas to prepare a thorough main idea (e.g., *Sea lions and seals are compared on weight (660 lbs. vs. 290 lbs.), hind fins (sea lion fins rotate to walk on land vs. seals' fins useless on land), and sounds (noisy barks vs. soft grunts)*). In ITSS, students are taught to use simple and/or thorough main ideas as guides to write about what they understood after reading an article. In writing about this comparative article about sea lions and seals, students would first describe sea lions by presenting characteristics of sea lions for each of the issues (weight, mobility, and sounds) in their main ideas. Next, they would provide a signaling word, such as "In contrast" or "Unlike," to transition from the first paragraph about sea lions to the second paragraph about seals. Then, they would go issue by issue and describe the characteristics of seals. Moving back and forth between the article's creature-by-creature organization and the main idea's issue-by-issue organization can help students to create flexible and useful mental representations using affordances of the comparison text structure.

Many authentic texts use multiple nested text structures and/or ineffective use of signaling. The structure strategy based instruction is useful in those situations as well. The structure strategy also is helpful to learners when they lack relevant prior knowledge and must seek coherence through structural cues in the text without the aid of background knowledge. Learners can impose structure (e.g., comparison, causation) to select important information and encode this information in memory. Such organization will help them remember the information longer and retrieve it for varied applications.

Ray and Meyer (2011) identified text structure awareness as a key individual difference among readers in grades 4–9. Students with list-like mental representations after reading often think that reading comprehension is about remembering a few facts and the general topic of the article, rather than how ideas build upon each other to convey an author's message (Meyer, Brandt, & Bluth, 1980). For example, after fifth-grade students read a newspaper article only 28 percent of them understood that the news article focused on a problem and its solution (Meyer, 2003). Typically fifth graders' retellings do not use the problem and solution structure, but instead a list of loosely related ideas that may mention something about the problem but nothing about the solution. However, after instruction with the structure strategy, students can write a summary with both a problem and a solution part.

Teaching students about text structure and signaling words for expository text structures (e.g., "hazard" for the problem and solution structure) can help readers to see relationships among important ideas in text and subordination of some ideas to others. In order to follow the processing hints provided by signaling words in text, readers need to be able to effectively use the structure strategy.

Readers with poor comprehension skills do not possess the strategies needed to make use of signaling to organize their understanding of nonfiction (Meyer & Rice, 1989). However, most students can learn to use the structure strategy (e.g., Bartlett, 1978; Meyer & Poon, 2001; Meyer & Ray, 2011; Meyer, Young, & Bartlett, 1989; Meyer et al., 2010; Wijekumar et al., 2014; Williams et al., 2005).

## ITSS: A Reading Comprehension Online Tutor

ITSS has been used by over 14,000 students since 2003 and has been refined and updated over that time. The ITSS intervention includes 100+ web-based interactive, structure strategy lessons for students in grades 4 to 8, videos for teacher professional development, and structure strategy laminated "keys" matching expandable keys online. These distinctive keys for each text structure include signaling words, patterns for main ideas and recall, and definitions with an example about the topic of whales. The topic of whales is used for all keys to show students how the same general topic could be organized differently with the five text structures. ITSS also includes a web-based lesson search utility (lessons manual) allowing easy access to all lessons, an administrator tool to generate student status reports, and a fully loaded database with rules and pathways generated for individualizing and adapting ITSS to the learner. The database contains all the rules for interactions with feedback thresholds.

ITSS lessons cover the five text structures in the order of comparison, problem and solution, cause and effect, sequence, and description. There are at least 12 lessons per text structure. In the first lesson for each text structure, an animated tutor named I.T. (Intelligent Tutor) models use of the structure strategy. ITSS includes reviews of text structures studied earlier and instruction about how multiple structures can work together in texts. The lessons use researcher-created sample passages as well as authentic texts from magazines, newspapers, and trade books.

The 150 texts in ITSS lessons cover topics about science (34 percent), social studies (28 percent), animals (23 percent), sports (9 percent), or food (6 percent). Variety in content, style, topic domain, and length (13 to 814 words) was designed to promote transfer of the strategy. Text topics for the first 24 lessons focusing on the comparison, problem, and solution text structures include U.S. Presidents, Benjamin Franklin, colonial times, human and/or animal medical problems and prevention or treatments (e.g., rabies), baseball players, Olympic stars, pets (e.g., characteristics, diet, or training), and differences among the same species of animals living in the same habitat. There are several series of lessons on related content, such as the Pony Express, Newton's 1st law, and the Dust Bowl. For example, there are eight passages of varying lengths, text structures, and complexity related to the Pony Express; these articles range from an authentic advertisement calling for riders to effects of the telegraph on the Pony Express. Students learn how to integrate ideas between different passages with the five basic structures, and how an author's purpose relates to the text structure(s) the author employs.

Students read a text multiple times for three primary tasks in ITSS: identifying signaling words, understanding and using main idea patterns unique to each text structure, and using text structure patterns for recall and previously written main ideas to write what they remember from the targeted text. For the first five or six lessons about each text structure, I.T. reads all texts at least once per lesson with the students (usually once but three times in the first ITSS lesson for modeling the strategy and performance on the three primary tasks). Students read the passages without assistance for the final six or seven lessons per text structure.

The ITSS system has customized scoring of main idea and recall tasks for each text and a rules-engine for providing personalized feedback. For example, the ITSS system scores every recall protocol written in the ITSS lessons on (a) signaling words (1 correct signaling word needed to pass criteria); (b) percent of main ideas possible (50 percent needed to pass criteria for success and moving on in the lessons); and (c) percent of details (40 percent for criteria). Students who have trouble generating 50 percent or more of the main ideas in recalls receive another version of the same lesson, but with different content. If a student's performance is particularly low (less than 25 percent of main ideas), readability of the text will be at the third grade level or below.

To exemplify the power of ITSS to deliver the structure strategy and improve students' understanding of texts, we provide an example from a below-average reader. Dramatic changes in recall were observed for this fifth grader before and after using the first ten ITSS lessons about the comparison text structure (Meyer et al., 2010). Before instruction his recall of a two-paragraph text about two different types of monkeys was, "*The monkeys are the smalls Monkeys weghy Less 4 onces a few in. tall.*"

After 10 lessons working in ITSS 3 times a week for 30 minutes each over about 1 month, the same student wrote a 2-paragraph text contrasting 2 different types of bats. In his recall shown below, he used the signaling word "different" in his first sentence to set up his comparison text structure. Also, he provided the signaling word "smaller" in the first sentence of the second paragraph to transition from one bat to the other bat.

> *There are 2 different kinds of bats. A Black flying fox bat and a leaf-nosed bat. The Black flying fox bat is one of the bigest, they grow up to 6 feet wide and weigh more than 3 pounds. they are jet black.*
>
> *Leaf-noised is smaller than the Black flying bat. the leaf-nois bat is only 1 foot wide. The leaf-nois bats come in different colors and mostley feeds on masquitoes and moths.*

Most of the lessons in ITSS are practice lessons that provide extra scaffolding in early lessons about a specific text structure. Gradually less help is provided for reading texts, generating main ideas, signaling text structure, and scaffolding recall. Next, we highlight key elements of ITSS instruction and practice with pictures.

As displayed in Figure 6.1, I.T. guides and interacts with students through the ITSS program. Students can listen to directions or an article again when this ITSS option is desired and activated for all or some students. Students reread the articles alone without I.T.'s oral reading as they prepare for the main idea and recall tasks.

There are variations in this general design related to reading a new article along with I.T. For example, proficient readers can opt out of listening to I.T. read articles and written instructions (see "Skip Talking" button in Figure 6.2). However, these advanced readers still listen to their specific feedback delivered orally by I.T. about their performance and any instructions that are not available to read on the screen. In several ITSS adaptations to the needs of Spanish native speakers in 4th to 6th grades learning English, students can request to listen to the text and/or instructions in English or Spanish.

In the first ITSS lesson, I.T. models use of the comparison structure to construct a main idea about text comparing George Washington and Abraham Lincoln, and students follow his example (see Figure 6.2). In the second ITSS lesson, I.T. models using the comparison structure to remember ideas about the differences between Presidents Washington and Lincoln and how to organize this recall.

The most frequent questions or types of activities in ITSS include identifying the text structure (see Figure 6.3), clicking on signaling words (see Figure 6.4), writing a main idea with the passage in view (see Figure 6.5), and writing a recall

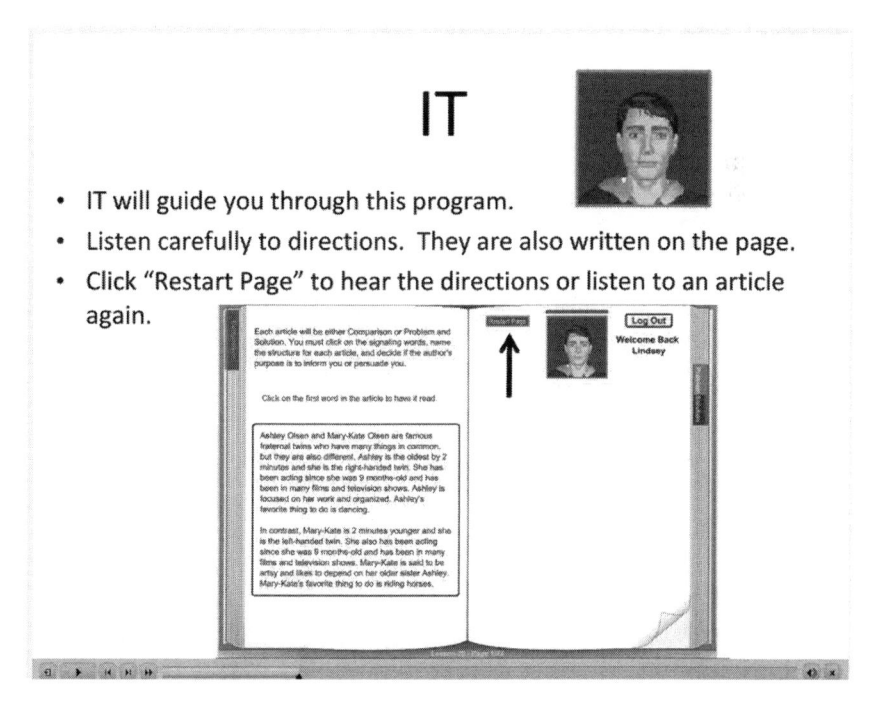

**FIGURE 6.1** Screenshot of I.T. Guidance Page.

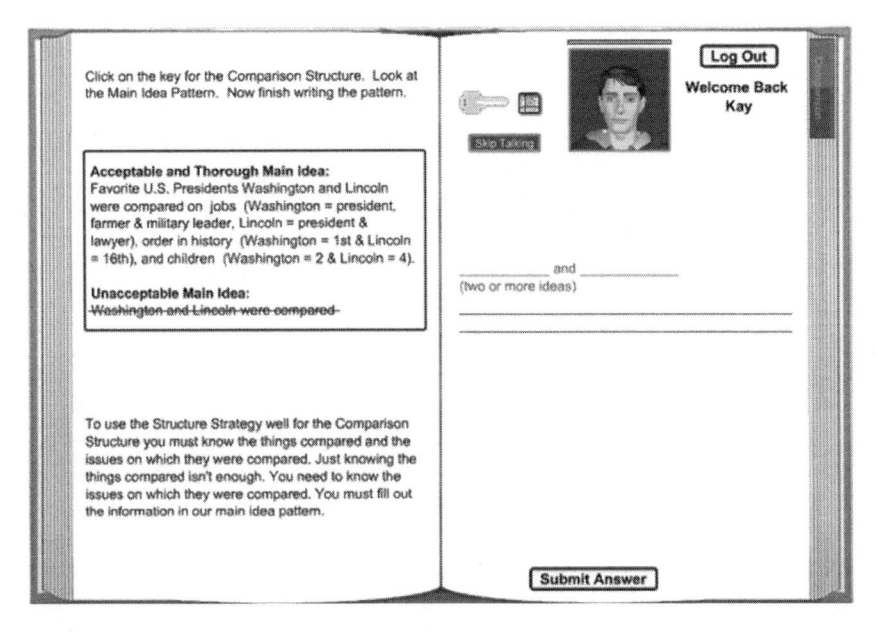

**FIGURE 6.2** Screenshot of I.T. Modeling Use of the Comparison Structure.

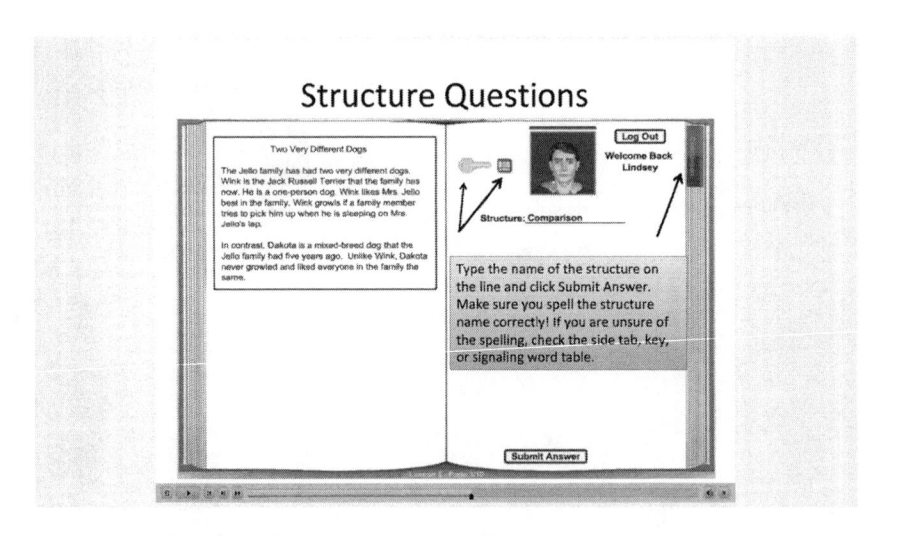

**FIGURE 6.3** Identifying the Text Structure in ITSS.

when the passage is not in view. Each question/activity allows the learner to have numerous attempts. The number of attempts varies among lessons in order to discourage students from "gaming" the system (i.e., doing little work until the computer provides the answer through feedback). Other activities in ITSS include

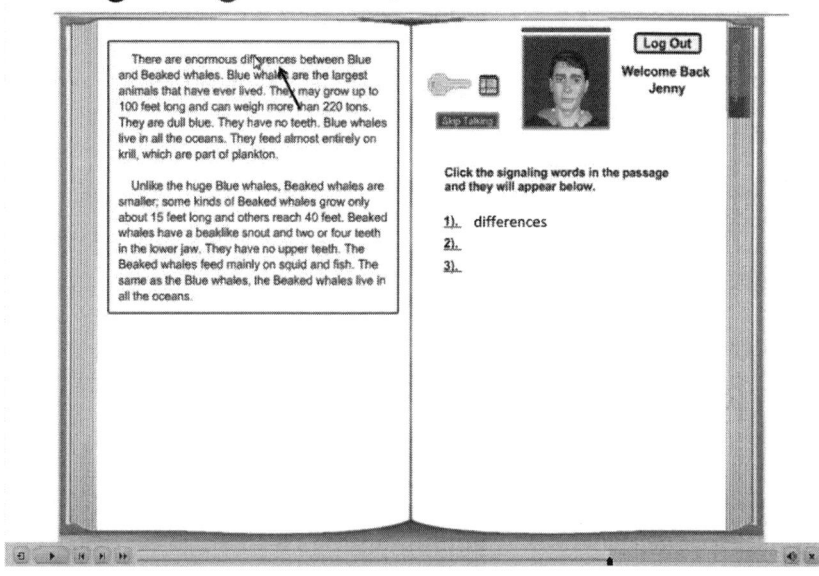

**FIGURE 6.4** Clicking on Signaling Words in ITSS.

**FIGURE 6.5** Writing a Main Idea With the Passage in View in ITSS.

answering multiple-choice questions, evaluating the work of other students, and filling in diagrams of text structures.

Students have access in the lessons to signaling words used in ITSS through the structure key icon available on the screen. Clicking on the small key icon can expand the text structure key (see key icon in Figure 6.5 and expanded key in Figure 6.6). The key, unique to each text structure, contains specific signaling words and patterns for writing with each of the five text structures. Clicking once on the key will turn it over for more information. Double clicking on the key will close it and return it to its original location.

Scaffolding is provided through hints to the student and appears in pop-up boxes during practice tasks. Hints vary from attempt to attempt and type of ITSS activity. After partial success in using the comparison main idea pattern with the passage to consult, a student received the hints and stars displayed in Figure 6.7.

Within ITSS, there are two approaches to generate comparison main ideas. The first requires the student to write a thorough main idea (see Figures 6.2 and 6.6). The second involves a simple main idea that is expanded into a thorough main idea by using a matrix or T-Chart. This approach was designed to reduce some of the typing demands for younger students. For the matrix approach a student generates a simple main idea by providing two or more ideas comparing as well as briefly identifying the issues of comparison. If needed, the student receives hints followed by explicit feedback about the topics and issues compared. Next, a student progresses to the matrix with the topics crossed with the issues

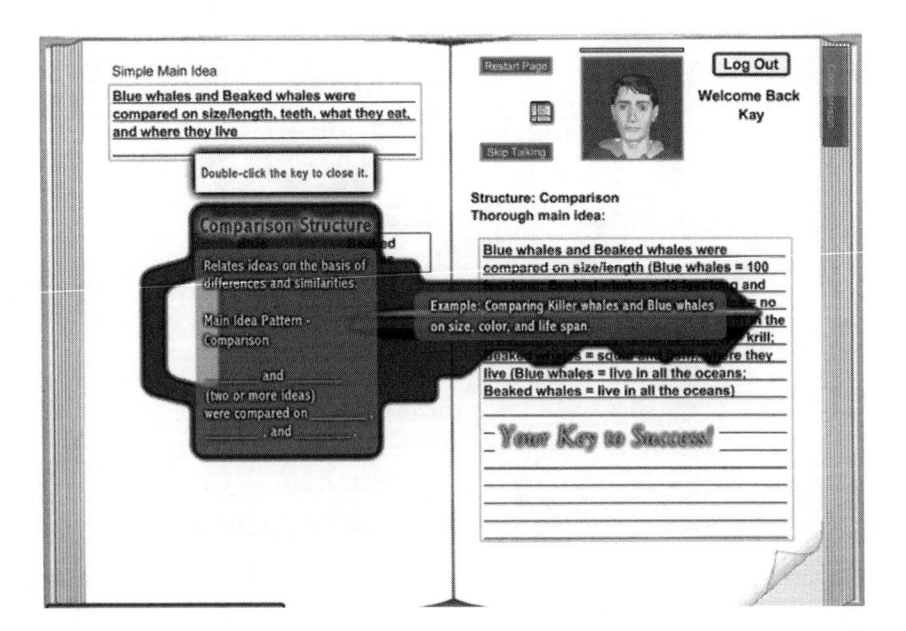

FIGURE 6.6 Expanded Text Structure Key.

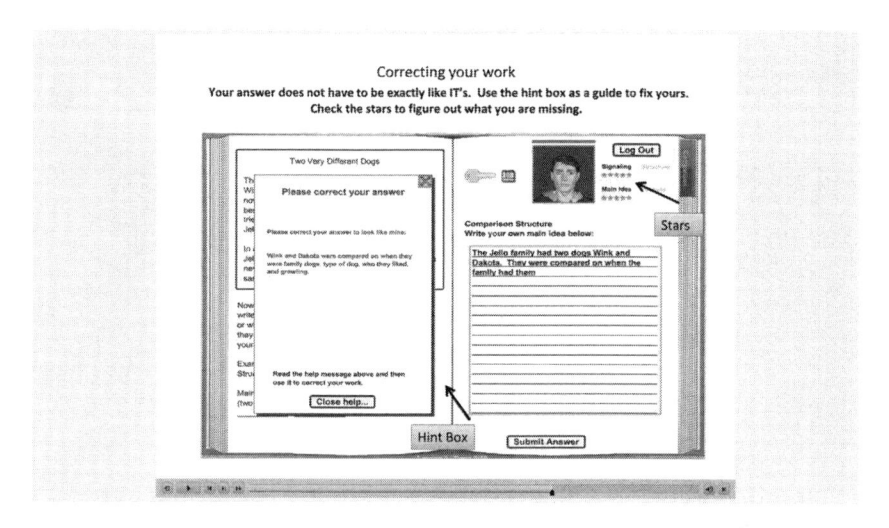

**FIGURE 6.7**  Screenshot on Correcting Your Work.

(see Figure 6.8a). The students click on the cell that they want to fill in the matrix and then click on the appropriate group of words in the article. If a student clicks on the correct information, then the clicked words will appear in that cell of the matrix. After successful completion of a matrix, cell-by-cell, it transforms into the format of a thorough main idea for the student to observe (see Figure 6.8b).

Recall tasks in ITSS involve students composing recalls that include everything they remember about an article as well as using signaling words to cue the overall text structure. In most lessons, students are able to see their own constructed main ideas and use them as guides when writing recalls, as displayed in Figures 6.9a and 6.9b. The work produced by the student in Figure 6.9a is at the criteria level and the student would receive immediate feedback with points/stars along with instructional oral comments from I.T. The recall shown in Figure 6.9b is below criteria; the student required I.T.'s modeled response for help with some details. Figures 6.10a and 6.10b display other types of questions that are less frequently practiced in ITSS than main idea and recall questions.

Additionally, ITSS includes games related to text structure skills (see Figures 6.11 and 6.12). Games primarily serve functions of (a) review for a recently completed group of 12+ lessons on a particular text structure; and (b) fun breaks from careful reading, thinking, and writing in the ITSS lessons. Stars, points, and comments received in ITSS do not influence game activities.

## Development and Efficacy of ITSS

Meyer et al.'s study (2002) on fifth-grade children was the first web-based instruction focusing on the structure strategy. They found that fifth-grade

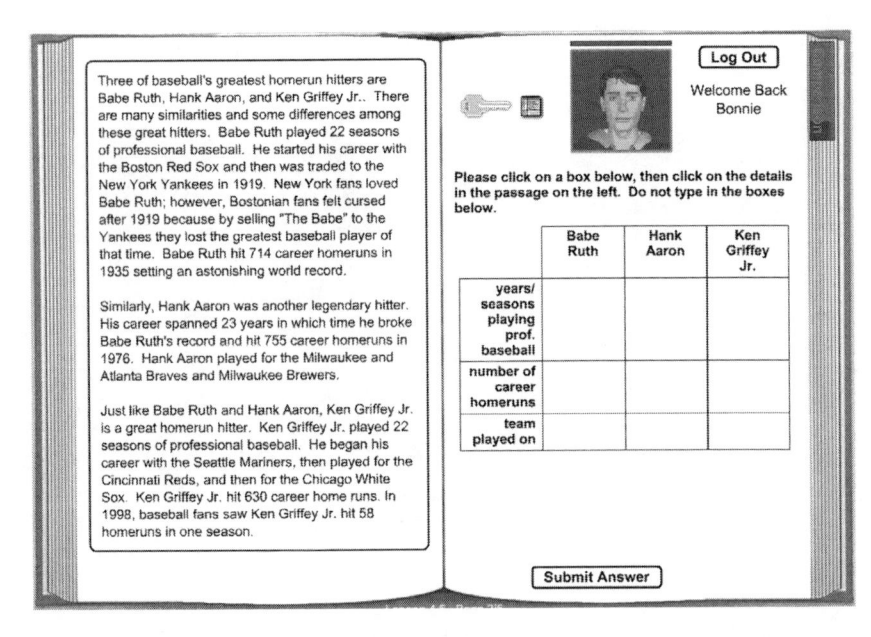

**FIGURE 6.8A** Matrix of Topics Crossed With Issues.

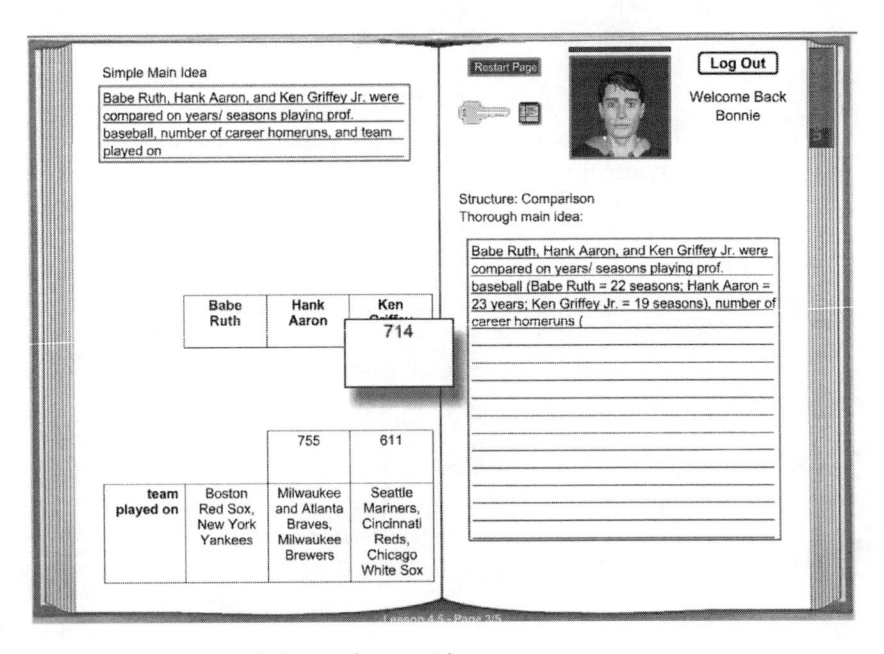

**FIGURE 6.8B** Format of Thorough Main Idea.

Remember to use your main idea to help you remember the details about the article. Check to make sure you have stated the problem. Look to see that you stated what causes the problem (why there is a problem). Be sure you wrote about who the problem affects and how, when, and where the problem affects them. Also, check to be sure you have two solutions that each try to get rid of the cause of the problem.
When you have finished writing, check to make sure you have stated the problem and the solutions with as many details as you can remember. If you remember anything else after checking, then add it.

Structure: Problem/Solution
Signaling Words: solutions, problems, solution

Structure: Problem / Solution

Main Idea: The problem(s) is/are

> Suffering from allergies often means a stuffy nose, red and puffy eyes, itchy throat, sneezing, and coughing. Breathing bits of waste and body parts of house dust mites causes problems for people

and the solution(s) is/are

> One important solution in treating allergies to dust mites is to completely seal up pillows, mattresses, and box springs with special covers that trap bits from dust mites inside. Another solution to be used with these special covers is to wash blankets and sheets every two weeks in water hot enough to kill the live dust mites

---

Log Out

Structure --- Main Idea 50%
Detail 53% Signaling 100%

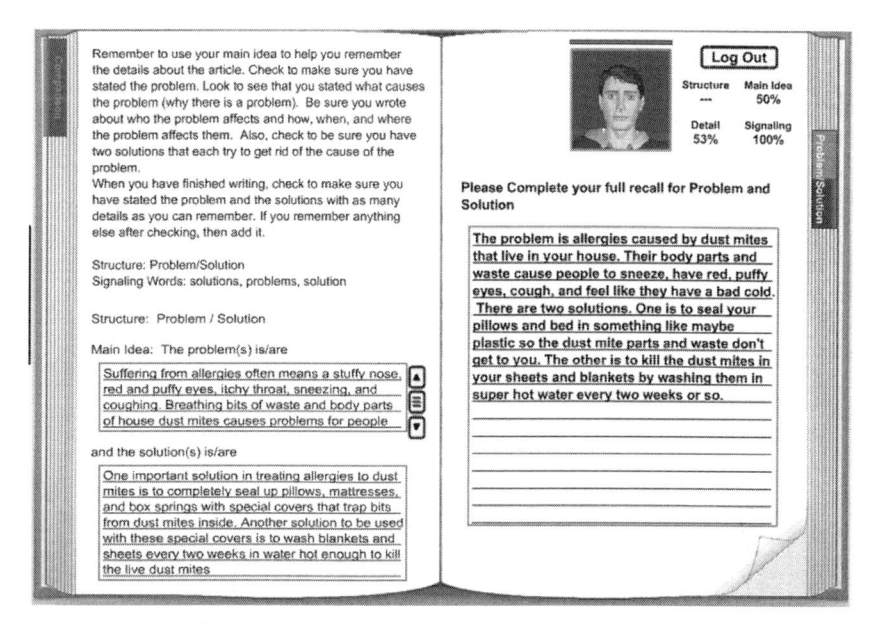

**Please Complete your full recall for Problem and Solution**

> The problem is allergies caused by dust mites that live in your house. Their body parts and waste cause people to sneeze, have red, puffy eyes, cough, and feel like they have a bad cold. There are two solutions. One is to seal your pillows and bed in something like maybe plastic so the dust mite parts and waste don't get to you. The other is to kill the dust mites in your sheets and blankets by washing them in super hot water every two weeks or so.

**FIGURE 6.9A** Students' Constructed Main Ideas to Use as Guides When Writing Recalls.

---

Remember to use one signaling word in your first sentence when you start paragraph 1 about Babe Ruth and [...]

**Please correct your answer**

Please correct your answer to look like mine:

There are many similarities and some differences among three of the greatest homerun hitters in baseball. Babe Ruth played professional baseball for 22 years and hit 714 homeruns during his career. This accomplishment set an astonishing world record like no one had ever seen before. Babe Ruth started his baseball career with the Boston Red Sox, but was later traded to the New York Yankees in 1919. New York fans love Babe Ruth; however, since 1919 Boston fans believe this trade caused the Red Sox to be cursed because Babe Ruth became the greatest baseball player of his time.

Read the help message above and then use it to correct your work.

[ Close help... ]

---

Log Out

Signaling ★★★★★  Structure
Main Idea ★★★★★  Details ★★★★★
Score: 7

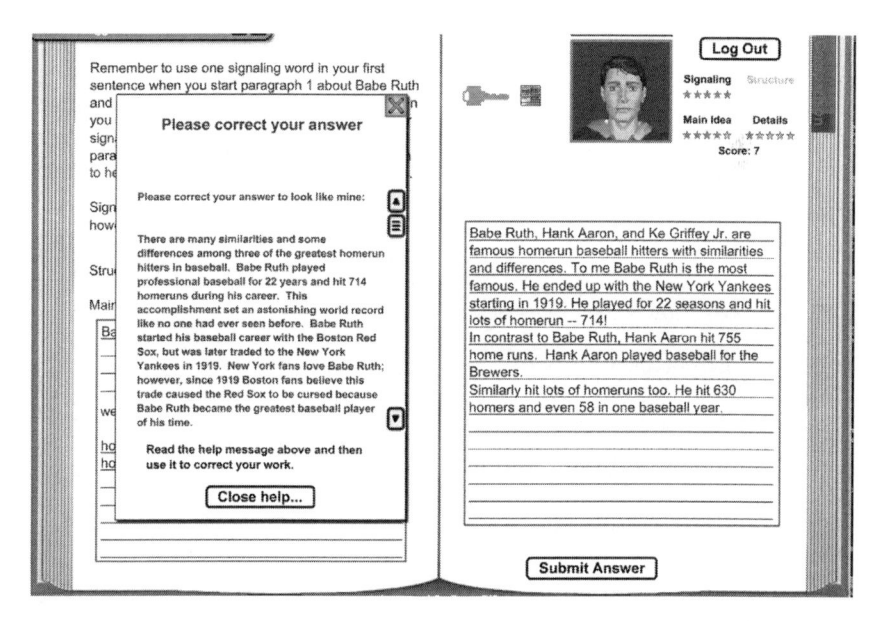

> Babe Ruth, Hank Aaron, and Ke Griffey Jr. are famous homerun baseball hitters with similarities and differences. To me Babe Ruth is the most famous. He ended up with the New York Yankees starting in 1919. He played for 22 seasons and hit lots of homerun -- 714!
> In contrast to Babe Ruth, Hank Aaron hit 755 home runs. Hank Aaron played baseball for the Brewers.
> Similarly hit lots of homeruns too. He hit 630 homers and even 58 in one baseball year.

[ Submit Answer ]

**FIGURE 6.9B** I.T.'s Model Recall to Further Help With Some Missing Ideas About Contrasted Players.

Teachers and tests ask you questions about what you read. For example, what would be a good title for this article? What is the main idea? What's happening in the article? For a Problem and Solution article, you might be asked, What was the problem? What caused the problem? How could the problem affect you? What was the solution to the problem? How did the solution solve the problem?

Try answering some of these Problem and Solution questions about the rabies article. If you need some help click here to see the diagram we made of the structure. Also, you can look at what you recalled from the passage.

IT's Recall:

rabid animal and before the person actually gets sick with rabies. Some pets that can get rabies are dogs, cats, and ferrets.

The solution is to get rabies vaccines and booster shots for animals that live with people. This makes possible bites from pets not dangerous with the threat of rabies. It is a much better solution than killing all pets that could possibly get rabies and bite people.

Log Out

Main Idea
★★★☆☆
Score: 16

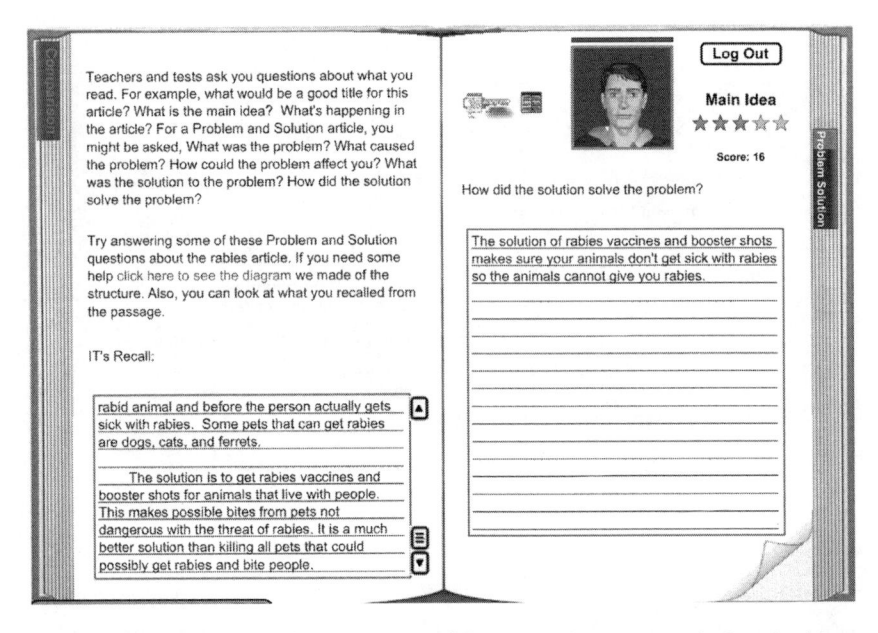

How did the solution solve the problem?

The solution of rabies vaccines and booster shots makes sure your animals don't get sick with rabies so the animals cannot give you rabies.

**FIGURE 6.10A** Examples of Other Types of Questions Less Frequently Practiced in ITSS.

Trouble with Loring's Work

Structure: Comparison

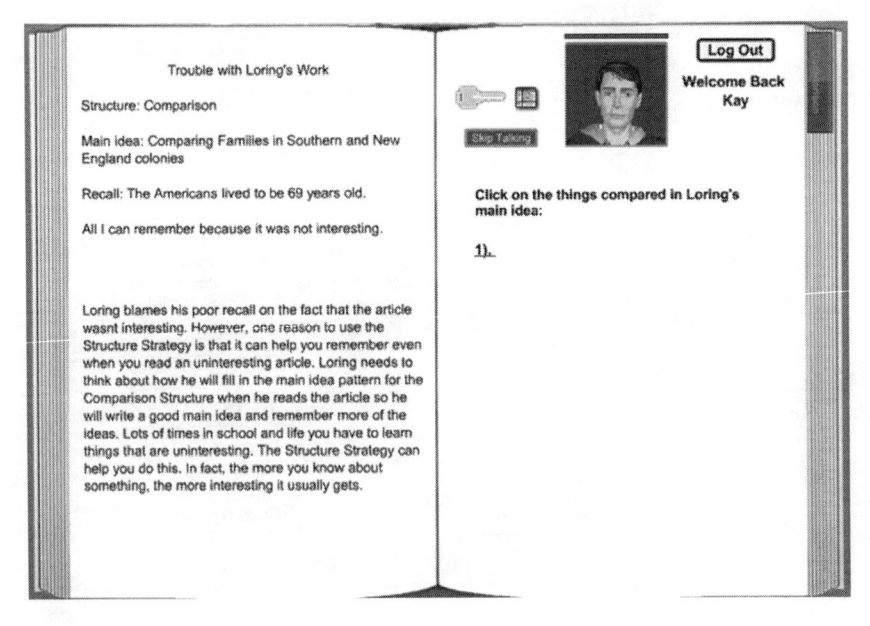

Main idea: Comparing Families in Southern and New England colonies

Recall: The Americans lived to be 69 years old.

All I can remember because it was not interesting.

Loring blames his poor recall on the fact that the article wasnt interesting. However, one reason to use the Structure Strategy is that it can help you remember even when you read an uninteresting article. Loring needs to think about how he will fill in the main idea pattern for the Comparison Structure when he reads the article so he will write a good main idea and remember more of the ideas. Lots of times in school and life you have to learn things that are uninteresting. The Structure Strategy can help you do this. In fact, the more you know about something, the more interesting it usually gets.

Log Out

Welcome Back
Kay

Skip Talking

Click on the things compared in Loring's main idea:

1).

**FIGURE 6.10B** Examples of Other Types of Questions Less Frequently Practiced in ITSS.

**FIGURE 6.11** Games Related to Text Structure Skills.

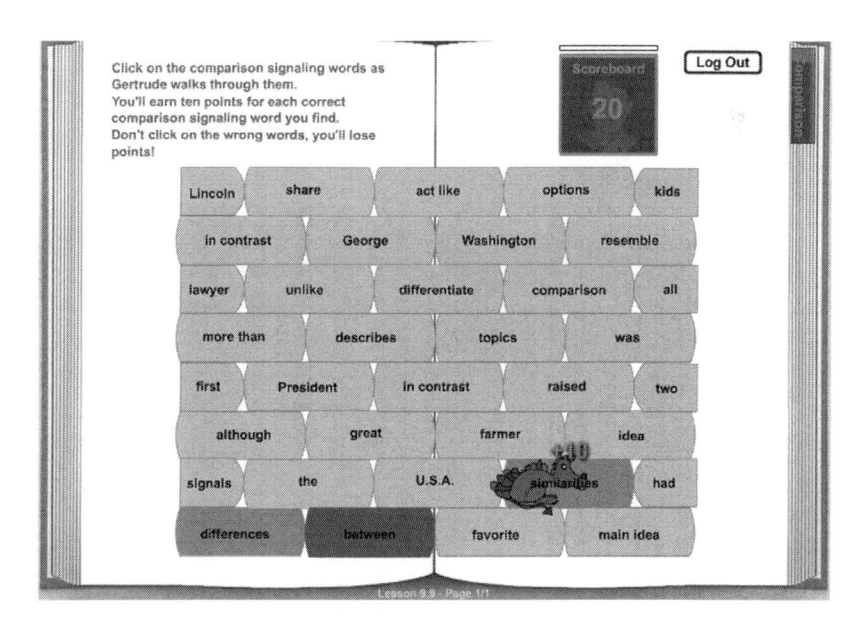

**FIGURE 6.12** Games Related to Text Structure Skills.

students randomly assigned to structure strategy instruction produced better summaries than students randomly assigned to the usual fifth-grade instruction, Accelerated Reader (AR). Students learning the structure strategy worked in the web-based lessons for 20 minutes 3 times a week over 10 weeks. Missing several sessions a week of the usual instruction (AR) to attend structure strategy instruction for over two months did not lower performance on tests covering AR objectives (e.g., STAR tests, AR tests, number of books read in AR program). Additionally, gains in the amount of information remembered from text by the structure strategy group over the control group were found two-and-a-half months after training. The average reader receiving the structure strategy training had a total recall score equal to a reader in the control group who scored at the 81st percentile on the delayed posttest; the effect size ($d$) of .92 was measured by standardized difference, $d$, which is calculated by subtracting the average score of the structure strategy group from the control group and dividing by the standard deviation of the control group. Also, general self-efficacy improved from pre-test to post-test, and positive attitudes toward computers were maintained.

Meyer and Wijekumar (2007) improved the earlier web-based approach to incorporate an animated tutor and immediate online feedback. Meyer et al. (2010) examined the effects of design features varied for ITSS on 5th- and 7th-grade students' reading comprehension (e.g., feedback: simple ("try again") vs. elaborated (after repeated trials with hints a model main idea is provided and I.T. says, "Super work with signaling! Now please read my main idea and improve yours.")) Students who received immediate elaborated feedback performed better on a standardized test of reading comprehension than students who received immediate simple feedback. Increases in reading comprehension after ITSS instruction remained after summer break (four months). In this study, percent correct was displayed, but later only stars were used for visual feedback that accompanied I.T.'s personalized oral feedback (number of gold stars of 5 displayed slots for stars).

Multisite randomized controlled trials in classrooms for grades 4, 5, 7, and 8 in rural and suburban settings clearly showed that a nonhuman, pedagogical agent could teach the structure strategy (Wijekumar, Meyer, & Lei, 2012, 2013). The ITSS tutor successfully addressed the three parts of structure strategy instruction: (a) learning about text structure and signaling words for each text structure; (b) strategically applying knowledge about text structure and main idea patterns, customized for each text structure, to write a good main idea; and (c) increasing reading comprehension as measured by written recall of texts and scores on a standardized reading comprehension test.

In the multisite randomized controlled trial with 5th grade students (Wijekumar et al., 2014), 128 classrooms within 12 school districts participated in the study. Classrooms within each school were randomly assigned to the standard ITSS intervention as substitute for 30 minutes per week of language arts or only the usual language arts curriculum. Students worked in ITSS about 30 minutes once a week for 30 weeks. Reading comprehension was measured using the Gray

Silent Reading Test (GSRT) (Wiederholt & Blalock, 2000), a standardized reading comprehension test with good psychometrics, alternate forms, and multiple-choice questions about main ideas, details, applications, and inferences. Reading comprehension also was measured using experimenter-designed recall and main idea tests about expository texts. ITSS had a positive influence on these reading comprehension measures. ITSS classrooms scored a fifth of a grade level higher on the standardized reading comprehension test than classrooms that did not use ITSS. Additionally, over 70 percent of control classrooms scored below the average ITSS classrooms on comparison main idea quality.

Meyer et al. (2011) provided remediation or enrichment lessons to better match the needs of 5th grade readers in a more individualized version of ITSS. This adaptive and individualized ITSS system has a rules-engine that is able to customize different pathways for ITSS instruction for individual students, rather than following the same sequence of lessons for all students in standard ITSS. Online assessment in a current lesson can be used to select a good match of student and instruction for the next lesson. Alternate versions of lessons include texts with lower readability levels as well as texts with the same text structure and signaling words, but different topics (e.g., problems and solutions for a troublesome dog versus problems and solutions for a troublesome pot-bellied pig). In individualized-adaptive ITSS, the next lesson can then be the next lesson in standard ITSS, a remediation lesson (e.g., repetition of learning objectives of the current lesson with a more familiar topic with readability below grade level), or enrichment lessons (e.g., lessons with texts above grade level or with less familiar topics).

Students who were randomly assigned to the more individualized ITSS instruction had higher learning goals and better work in ITSS lessons than students receiving the standard ITSS instruction. Also, the 5th grade students receiving the more individualized ITSS showed greater improvements with stronger effect sizes on the GSRT ($d = .55$) and signaling words ($d = .78$) than students in standard ITSS.

Fifth graders in individualized-adaptive ITSS did not spend more time in ITSS, work on more lessons, or read more texts than standard ITSS. Instead, individualized-adaptive ITSS better matched the practice lessons a student received to their immediate needs based on the rapid online assessment of the student's work in a current lesson. When the more individualized ITSS detected difficulties in a student's understanding during a current practice lesson, in the subsequent lesson, jumps in complexity were reduced. These smaller jumps in complexity for practice lessons, the greater flexibility in the sequence of lessons, and the reduced difficulty of texts resulted in greater success in the lessons, better reading comprehension, higher learning goals, and more positive attitudes. The superiority of individualized-adaptive ITSS over standard ITSS held similarly across initial reading comprehension levels of students (i.e., high, average, and below grade level readers). Teachers can be particularly assisted by using individualized-adaptive ITSS to meet the needs of individual students so that all students can better participate in classroom applications of the structure strategy.

Further development of ITSS in terms of updating and adapting the software (see Figure 6.13), lessons, and computerized scoring has occurred recently in conjunction with work extending ITSS to English language learners (Wijekumar, Meyer, & Lei, 2014). Our next step is a large efficacy study (2015–2019) using our best adaptations of ITSS in high poverty schools in grades 4 and 5. Here we will apply what we have learned from our design-feature studies about feedback, individualized lessons adapted to learners, ESL adaptations, and professional development.

ITSS can be an efficient vehicle for instructing students in strategic use of text structures. The ITSS technology can provide a tool for teachers to meet the diverse needs of students in a classroom, which is often a drain on the time and resources of classroom teachers. A major strength of web-based reading comprehension instruction is the delivery of individualized timely feedback and individualized lessons to support student learning (e.g., McNamara, O'Reilly, Best, & Ozuru, 2006; Meyer et al., 2011).

## Access and Applications of ITSS for Classroom Teachers

Teachers interested in using ITSS can contact the authors of this chapter for unique usernames and passwords for students along with professional development information for teachers. ITSS can be found on the following internet browsers: Google Chrome, Firefox, Internet Explorer, or Safari at http://itss.psu.edu/it. Once the student logs in, I.T. takes over and guides the learner with modeling, practice tasks, assessment, scaffolding, and feedback. The student can log

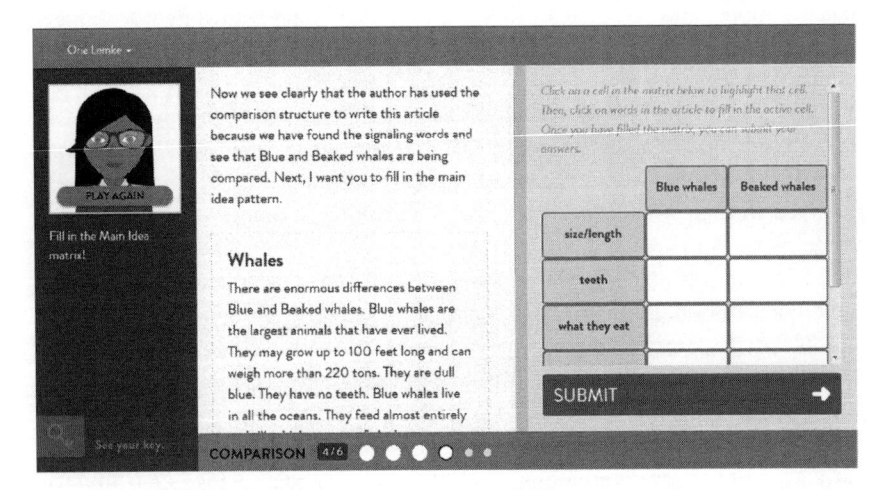

FIGURE 6.13 Example of Further Development of ITSS.

out at any time and the system will save the lesson and page information so that the student can continue at that spot when returning to use ITSS at a future date.

In ITSS classroom teachers can view all student responses and track progress. The menu for the ITSS management and administration tool is displayed in Figure 6.14. Teachers can leave feedback for the team, add students to the system, and view the teacher manual that contains all the reading passages for ITSS. The teacher can generate reports or review online student performance at the classroom level, individual student level, or drill down to see responses and scores for students in a particular lesson.

In ITSS teacher professional development has been revised to accommodate teacher knowledge of text structure and integrating text structure with other classroom reading comprehension practices (e.g., summarizing). Interested teachers are welcome to use the ITSS software with their students, but teachers need some professional development about the approach first in order to make ITSS really powerful. Teachers can view full videos on YouTube about the structure strategy and applications that have been proven efficacious in large-scale studies. The first professional development video is an animated overview of the structure strategy. It includes how and why the structure strategy is powerful, with examples about the comparison text structure (https://www.youtube.com/watch?v=d_ZL0yEeUac). We encourage teachers to show the videos to their students to remind them how to create coherent and strategic memory structures as they read. The next videos provide critical information about the structure strategy's other text structures and how some text structures commonly work together (i.e., problem and solution structure working with the cause and effect structure: https://www.youtube.com/watch?v=gEEXvMPMU2k; sequence working with description: https://www.youtube.com/watch?v=GpD4lcbeSJo). Thinking about these professional development videos may help teachers and

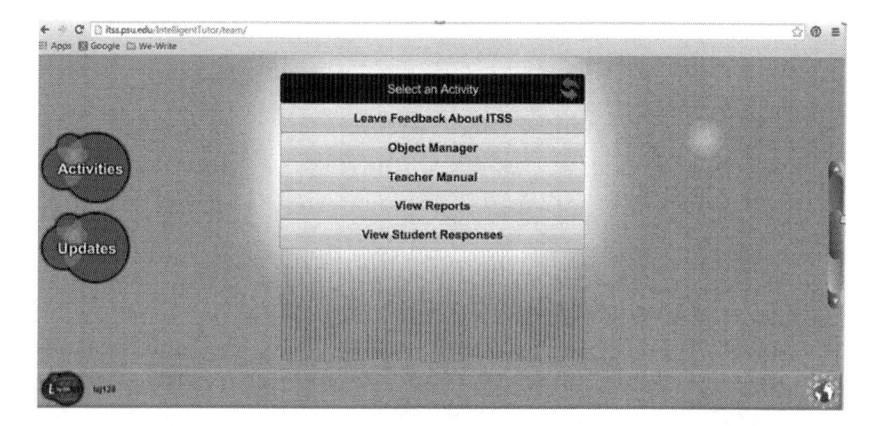

FIGURE 6.14 Menu for the ITSS Management and Administration Tool.

students to focus on the power of text structure to construct organized mental representations of texts.

Additionally, the ITSS research team has prepared lessons to integrate the structure strategy with classroom practices (e.g., T-Charts, Venn diagrams) and can make them available to interested teachers. For example, in response to a recent teacher request for applications to her science unit, we provided available internet sites about volcanoes with texts organized overall with the comparison, sequence, or cause and effect text structures along with suggestions for lessons using online sites (http://pubs.usgs.gov/gip/volc/types.html).

Teachers must actively promote the use of text structure within their classrooms to show students the usefulness of the approach. When teachers do this, the students' results can more than double. Computer time with ITSS should be actively monitored and supported by the teacher, because students tend to think that computer activities are not important as an educational tool when the teacher is not actively engaged during the lab time. Additionally, consistent weekly computer time with practice is an essential component for achieving success in applying the structure strategy. Three 30-minute sessions a week for 6 months is ideal for upper elementary students, but substantial effects in randomized studies resulted from one 30/45-minute session per week for 6 to 7 months as well as several 20-minute sessions per week for 10 weeks.

Teachers can build on ITSS lessons in their content area classes by using matrices, Venn diagrams, and text structure main idea patterns when comparing countries in social studies or types of rocks in science. Also, students can compare an author's solution to a problem with their own solutions and defend their alternate solutions. Meyer, Ireland, and Ray (2013) described classroom applications of the structure strategy to persuasive writing for 8th grade language arts classrooms and provided a detailed lesson plan for teachers with adaptations for different groups of students varying in writing skills. Jennifer Ireland, a collaborator and 8th grade teacher, has developed applications of the structure strategy instruction in ITSS to her classroom and team of 8th grade teachers in language arts, writing, social studies, and science. Their practical work is evident on state assessments of writing and students' superior writing in their subsequent high school science labs.

## Recent Adaptations and Limitations of ITSS

During 15 years of development we have improved the ITSS system. We have made substantial progress in computerized scoring of students' work, individualized feedback, adaptive-individualized paths for lessons, teacher professional development, support of effective use of ITSS in classrooms, and adaptations for English language learners in grades 4 to 6 with Spanish as their native language.

In our early work with ITSS, 80 percent of the students showed active engagement with ITSS instruction and no "gaming" or other off-task behaviors in the lessons. However, a problem was that the other 20 percent of the students submitted

1 to 44 off-task answers in the first 12 ITSS lessons. Meyer and Wijekumar (2014) reported that students with extremely low levels of motivation to read, as measured with the *Motivation to Read* profile (Gambrell, Palmer, Codling, & Mazzoni, 1996), tended to produce off-task responses in ITSS (e.g., "*klllllxx*") rather than work on main ideas or recalls. Also, males in 5th and 7th grades tended to write more off-task responses than females. Low test scores on general self-efficacy and persistence and high work avoidance could account for the gender effect in off-task responses in ITSS. Noteworthy, greater improvements in quality of main ideas produced after ITSS instruction were found for males than females in 4th grade (Wijekumar et al., 2012). Student engagement in ITSS and subsequent strong gains in reading comprehension are also increased with strong support of ITSS by teachers and administrators. Results from an optimal implementation in schools (Wijekumar et al., 2013) showed higher performance by ITSS classrooms compared to their control counterparts with moderate to large effect sizes.

Fortunately, we have reduced students' off-task behaviors in ITSS by (a) varying the number of tries before presenting a model response; (b) individualizing lesson difficulty and sequence; and (c) letting students know that teachers are viewing their work. We continue to monitor and work to intervene early in ITSS with students demonstrating disengagement.

## Conclusion

ITSS focuses on teaching the structure strategy to upper elementary and middle school students through modeling and practice provided by an online intelligent tutor. Work with ITSS can be used to complement classroom reading and content area learning in language arts, science, social sciences, and writing. Continued development, adaptations, and testing of the ITSS system will further increase its efficacy, use by different types of learners, and applications to more content domains.

## Acknowledgments

The research reported here was supported by the Institute of Education Sciences, U.S. Department of Education, through Grants R305G030072, R305A080133, R305A120593, and R305A130327 to The Pennsylvania State University. The opinions expressed are those of the authors and do not represent the views of the Institute or the U.S. Department of Education.

## References

Bartlett, B. J. (1978). *Top-Level Structure as an Organizational Strategy for Recall of Classroom Text.* (Unpublished doctoral dissertation). Arizona State University, Tempe, AZ.

Gambrell, L. B., Palmer, B. M., Codling, R. M., & Mazzoni, S. A. (1996). Assessing motivation to read. *The Reading Teacher, 49,* 518–533.

McNamara, D. S., O'Reilly, T. P., Best, R., M., & Ozuru, Y. (2006). Improving adolescent students' reading comprehension with iSTART. *Journal of Educational Computing Research*, *34*(2), 147–171.

Meyer, B. J. F. (2003). Text coherence and readability. *Topics in Language Disorders*, *23*(3), 204–224.

Meyer, B. J. F., & Poon, L. W. (2001). Effects of structure strategy training and signaling on recall of text. *Journal of Educational Psychology*, *93*(1), 141–159. doi:10.1037/0022-0663.93.1.141

Meyer, B. J. F., & Ray, M. N. (2011). Structure strategy interventions: Increasing reading comprehension of expository text. *International Electronic Journal of Elementary Education*, *4*(1), 127–152.

Meyer, B. J. F., & Rice, G. E. (1989). Prose processing in adulthood: The text, the reader, and the task. In L. W. Poon, D. C. Rubin, & B. A. Wilson (Eds.), *Everyday Cognition in Adulthood and Later Life* (pp. 157–194). New York: Cambridge University Press.

Meyer, B. J. F., & Wijekumar, K. K. (2007). A Web-based tutoring system for the structure strategy: Theoretical background, design, and findings. In D. S. McNamara (Ed.), *Reading Comprehension Strategies: Theories, Interventions, and Technologies* (pp. 347–375). Mahwah, NJ: Lawrence Erlbaum Associates.

Meyer, B. J. F., & Wijekumar, K. K. (2014). Why fifth- and seventh- graders submit off-task responses to a web-based reading comprehension tutor rather than expected learning responses. *Computers & Education*, *75*, 229–252. doi:10.1016/j.compedu.2014.02.013

Meyer, B. J. F., Brandt, D. M., & Bluth, G. J. (1980). Use of the top-level structure in text: Key for reading comprehension of ninth-grade students. *Reading Research Quarterly*, *16*, 72–103. doi:10.2307/747349

Meyer, B. J. F., Ireland, J. J., & Ray, M. N. (2013). Applying the structure strategy to write persuasive texts. In J. C. Richards & C. Lassonde (Eds.), *Writing Strategies for all Students in Grades 4–8: Scaffolding Independent Writing through Differentiated Mini Lessons* (pp. 126–136). Thousand Oaks, CA: Corwin, a SAGE Company.

Meyer, B. J. F., Wijekumar, K. K., & Lin, Y. C. (2011). Individualizing a web-based structure strategy intervention for fifth graders' comprehension of nonfiction. *Journal of Educational Psychology*, *103*(1), 140–168. doi:10.1037/a0021606

Meyer, B. J. F., Young, C. J., & Bartlett, B. J. (1989). *Memory Improved: Enhanced Reading Comprehension and Memory across the Life Span through Strategic Text Structure*. Hillsdale, NJ: Lawrence Erlbaum.

Meyer, B. J. F., Middlemiss, W., Theodorou, E., Brezinski, K. L., McDougall, J., & Bartlett, B. J. (2002). Effects of structure strategy instruction delivered to fifth-grade children using the Internet with and without the aid of older adult tutors. *Journal of Educational Psychology*, *94*(3), 486–519.

Meyer, B. J. F., Wijekumar, K. K., Middlemiss, W., Higley, K., Lei, P., Meier, C., & Spielvogel, J. (2010). Web-based tutoring of the structure strategy with or without elaborated feedback or choice for fifth- and seventh-grade readers. *Reading Research Quarterly*, *45*(1), 62–92. doi:10.1598/PRQ.45.1.4

NAEP. (2013). U.S. Department of Education, Institute of Education Sciences, National Center for Education Statistics, National Assessment of Educational Progress (NAEP), 1992, 2011, and 2013 Reading Assessments.

Ray, M. N., & Meyer, B. J. F. (2011). Individual differences in children's knowledge of expository text structures: A review of literature. *International Electronic Journal of Elementary Education*, *4*(1), 67–82.

Wiederholt, J. L., & Blalock, G. (2000). Gray silent reading tests. Austin, TX: PRO-ED.
Wijekumar, K. K., Meyer, B. J. F., & Lei, P. (2012). Large-scale randomized controlled trial with 4th graders using intelligent tutoring of the structure strategy to improve nonfiction reading comprehension. *Journal of Educational Technology Research and Development*, 60(6), 987–1013. doi:10.1007/s11423–012–9263–4
Wijekumar, K. K., Meyer, B. J. F., & Lei, P. (2013). High-fidelity implementation of web-based intelligent tutoring system improves fourth and fifth graders content area reading comprehension. *Computers & Education*, 68, 366–379. doi:10.1016/j.compedu.2013.05.021
Wijekumar, K. K., Meyer, B. J. F., & Lei, P. (2014). *Improving Content Area Reading Comprehension with 4–6th Grade Spanish ELLs using Web-Based Structure Strategy Instruction.* Paper presented at Internal Conference of Cognition and Exploratory Learning in Digital Age (CELDA). Porto, Portugal.
Wijekumar, K. K., Meyer, B. J. F., Lei, P., Lin, Y. C., Johnson, L.A., Spielvogel, J. A., . . . Cook, M. (2014). Multisite randomized controlled trial examining intelligent tutoring of structure strategy for fifth-grade. *Journal of Research on Educational Effectiveness*, 7(4), 331–357. doi:10.1080/19345747.2013.853333
Williams, J. P., Hall, K. M., deCani, J. S., Lauer, K. D., Stafford, K. B., & DeSisto, L. A. (2005). Expository text comprehension in the primary grade classroom. *Journal of Educational Psychology*, 97(4), 538–550.

# 7

## iSTART-2

### A Reading Comprehension and Strategy Instruction Tutor

*Erica L. Snow, Matthew E. Jacovina, G. Tanner Jackson, and Danielle S. McNamara*

### Introduction

This chapter provides an overview of the Interactive Strategy Tutor for Active Reading and Thinking-2 (iSTART-2). iSTART-2 is a game-based tutoring system designed to improve students' reading comprehension skills. It does so by providing them with instruction on how to self-explain using comprehension strategies. Instruction is provided through lesson videos and practice within a game-based environment. iSTART-2 has demonstrated effectiveness for students in middle school, high school, and college (Jackson & McNamara, 2013; McNamara, Levinstein, & Boonthum, 2004; McNamara, O'Reilly, Best, & Ozuru, 2006; McNamara, O'Reilly, Rowe, Boonthum, & Levinstein, 2007; Snow, Allen, Jacovina, & McNamara, 2015).

In this chapter, we first discuss why reading comprehension is a critical skill and how the iSTART-2 system addresses the development of this skill through the instruction of five comprehension strategies. Second, we provide an overview of the iSTART-2 system and its features. Third, we discuss the need for this reading comprehension technology in the classroom and provide a general overview of how iSTART-2 addresses those needs as well as the Common Core State Standards. Fourth, we describe previous findings from research using the various iterations of the iSTART-2 program. Finally, we describe how iSTART-2 can be accessed by teachers and used within classroom environments.

### Reading Comprehension

Over the last few decades, researchers and educators have worked together to identify ways to improve the development of literacy skills for students in grades

K-12. However, many students still struggle to read at a basic level. In fact, in a recent study it was shown that 25 percent or more of students in the 8th and 12th grades perform below a basic level of reading comprehension (US Department of Education (DOE), 2011). One reason for these comprehension difficulties may be that many students lack the necessary skills and knowledge needed to gain a deep understanding of the content embedded within texts (e.g., O'Reilly & McNamara, 2007).

The iSTART-2 program provides students with instruction on comprehension strategies that help them to overcome gaps in their domain knowledge and achieve deep level comprehension of the material within the text (McNamara, 2004, 2007, 2009, in press). This approach to enhancing reading comprehension skills is theoretically inspired by the Construction-Integration model of comprehension (CI model) (Kintsch, 1998). According to the CI model, readers construct multiple levels of understanding of text and discourse. These levels include a surface level understanding (e.g., understanding individual words and sentences), a textbase understanding (e.g., understanding the meaning of what is explicitly stated), and a situation model understanding (e.g., using prior knowledge to elaborate on text information). Combined, these three levels comprise the reader's mental representation of the text.

Students construct a better understanding of the information found in text when they form a coherent situation model. To do so, they must generate *inferences* that serve as bridges between the information in the text and background knowledge (McNamara & Magliano, 2009). A good deal of research has shown that developing a coherent textbase understanding (i.e., understanding the words in the text) is a first and necessary step toward comprehension. But generating inferences while reading, linking the words in the text to background knowledge, is key to deep comprehension (McNamara & Magliano, 2009).

iSTART-2 provides students with explicit strategy instruction on how to form a coherent textbase and how to generate successful inferences (McNamara, 2004; O'Reilly, Taylor, & McNamara, 2006). The iSTART-2 program aims to foster deeper understanding of information found in text by providing students with strategy training to improve their ability to self-explain text. Self-explanation is the process of explaining information to oneself in their own words using their knowledge of the world and the domain targeted by the text (Chi, de Leeuw, Chiu, & LaVancher, 1994; McNamara, 2004; VanLehn, Jones, & Chi, 1992). These explanations can use information explicitly stated in the text along with other relevant information from the students' own prior knowledge. Research has shown that students who successfully self-explain are more likely to generate inferences, construct coherent mental models, solve problems, and develop a deep understanding of the concepts covered in the text compared to students who do not self-explain or self-explain poorly (Chi et al., 1994; McNamara, 2004). Inferences help students overcome gaps (or breakdowns) in their own understanding of the text, because they aid students in drawing conclusions about information found in text (Bransford, Brown, & Cocking, 2000; Graesser, Leon, & Otero, 2002; Kintsch, 1998).

Importantly, many students do not spontaneously self-explain texts and, when they do, their self-explanations do not enhance their comprehension (Chi et al., 1994). Hence, Self-Explanation Reading Training (SERT) (McNamara, 2004) is a pedagogical intervention designed to provide students with instruction on comprehension strategies to improve their ability to self-explain text. Five comprehension strategies: comprehension monitoring, predicting, paraphrasing, elaborating, and bridging (described in more detail within Table 7.1), were included in SERT based on research demonstrating their effectiveness in enhancing students' comprehension of challenging text (Brown, 1982; Palincsar & Brown, 1984). The process of self-explaining externalizes students' understanding of the text, which helps them more effectively to learn to use the comprehension strategies (McNamara, 2004, 2009). This symbiotic relationship between self-explanation and comprehension strategies enhances students' ability to comprehend challenging text (e.g., McNamara, 2004; O'Reilly et al., 2006) and consequently perform more successfully in their course exams and state standards tests (McNamara,

**TABLE 7.1** The Five Comprehension Strategies in the iSTART-2 Program.

| Strategy Name | Description | Example |
| --- | --- | --- |
| Paraphrasing | When students take information in the text and put it in their own words | "Your chest expands as you take deep breathes" |
| Comprehension Monitoring | When students reflect upon what they have read and assess their understanding of the content | "I understand that muscle contraction causes your chest to expand during a deep breath" |
| Prediction | When students make an inference about what information may come next in the text | "I think that the text will talk about how oxygen fuels the body next" |
| Elaboration | When students make an inference about the text based on their own world knowledge | "When I run, I have to take deep breaths which allows air to move into my lungs and blood stream to fuel my body" |
| Bridging | When students make an inference about the text based on the connections they see between separate clauses, sentences, and paragraphs embedded within the entire text | "Air moves into the lungs when your chest expands and moves your ribs up and out" |

in press; McNamara et al., 2007). The iSTART-2 program leverages the SERT pedagogy to teach the five comprehension strategies mentioned earlier.

Table 7.1 provides brief descriptions of each comprehension strategy, and shows an example self-explanation that might be generated using each type of strategy. The self-explanations in Table 7.1 are generated in response to the following text: the sentence in bold is the *target sentence*, which is the sentence that must be self-explained.

> Breathing is the process of moving air into and out of the lungs. Inspiration is the process of taking air into the lungs. **When you take a deep breath, your chest expands as the muscles contract to move the ribs up and outward.**

## iSTART-2

iSTART-2 is the most recent iteration of the iSTART program.[1] iSTART-2 uses a game-based learning environment designed to enhance students' engagement and persistence during prolonged periods of training (Jackson & McNamara, 2013; Snow et al., 2015). Keeping students interested and engaged during prolonged practice is especially important within classrooms because of the importance of enhancing students' persistence.

iSTART-2 instruction consists of two phases: *training* and *game-based practice*. During the first phase, training, students watch a series of seven videos (lasting a combined total of approximately 35 minutes), which first introduce them to the concept of self-explanation and then provide instruction on each of the five comprehension strategies that students can use to more successfully comprehend challenging content-area texts (e.g., science and history texts). The five strategies covered in iSTART-2 are comprehension monitoring, predicting, paraphrasing, elaborating, and bridging (see Table 7.1). Each training video is narrated by Mr. Evans, a pedagogical agent who defines and explains each reading strategy and gives examples of how students can use the strategy while self-explaining (see Figure 7.1 for screen shot of one of the iSTART-2 strategy training videos). A short quiz follows each video that assesses students' understanding of the specific strategy presented during the lesson video. After completing this initial instructional phase of iSTART-2, students are transitioned to the practice phase within the interactive game-based interface (see Figure 7.2).

Within the interface, students can interact with generative practice games where they read challenging texts (usually science texts) and type self-explanations in response to several target sentences. There are three generative practice environments within iSTART-2: Coached Practice, Showdown, and Map Conquest. These games are designed to maintain students' interest during prolonged generative practice. In Map Conquest, for example, students are asked to compose a self-explanation for numerous target sentences while collecting flags they can use to conquer a map (see Figure 7.3). Students can earn flags in this game by

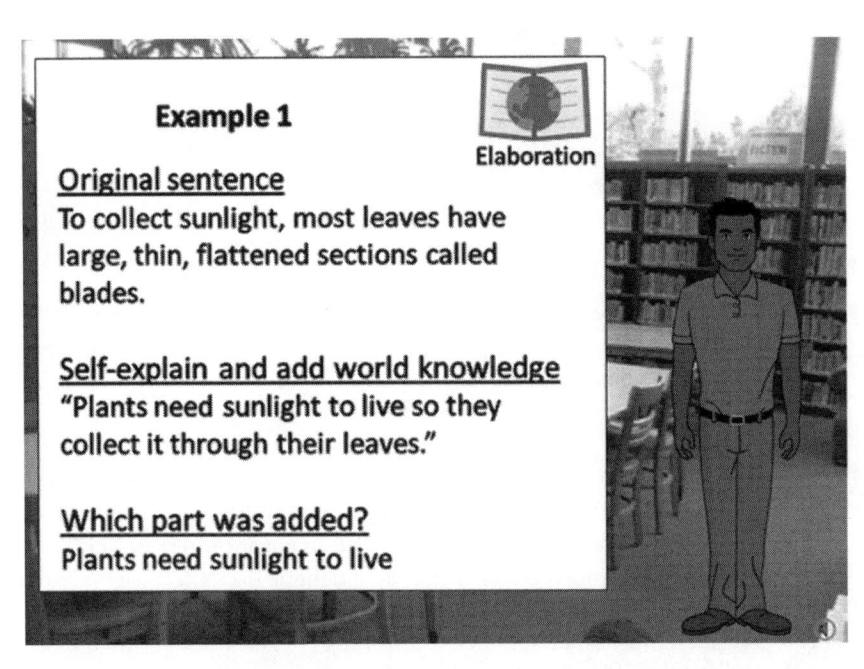

**FIGURE 7.1** Screen Shot of One of the iSTART-2 Strategy Training Videos.

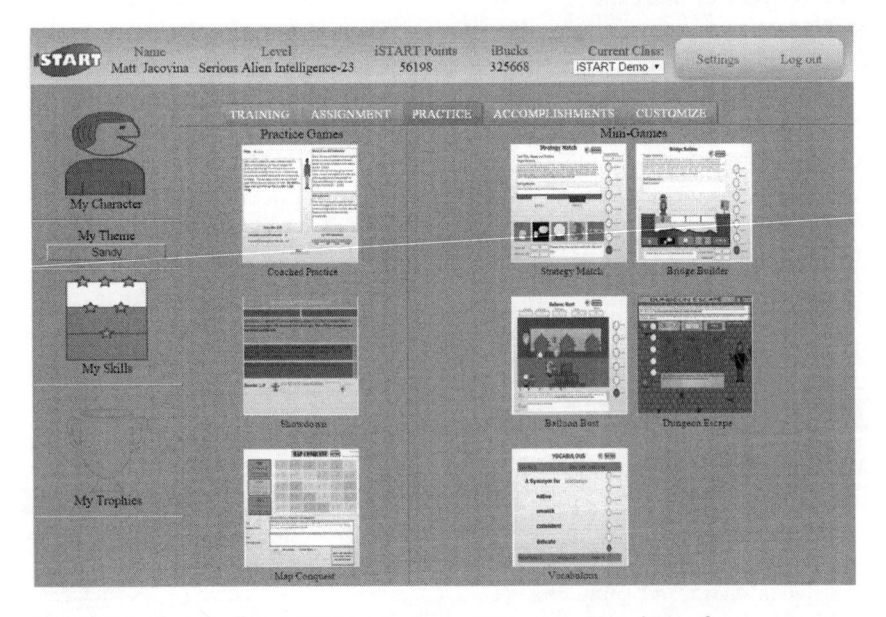

**FIGURE 7.2** Practice Phase Within the Interactive Game-Based Interface.

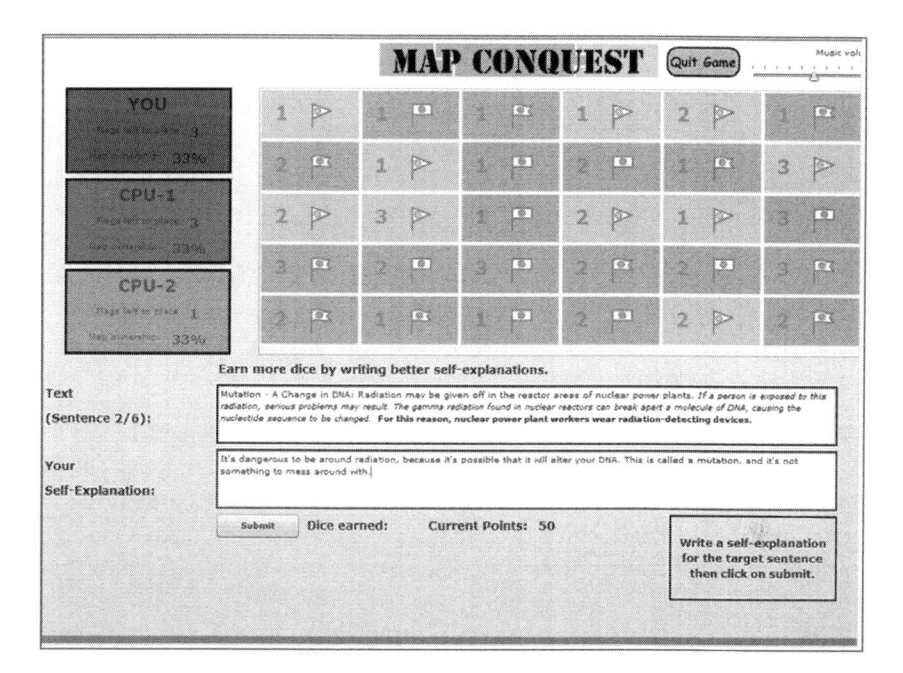

**FIGURE 7.3** Map Conquest.

generating high quality self-explanations. All self-explanations are scored using the iSTART-2 scoring algorithm, which automatically assigns a score between 0 and 3 to each self-explanation. This algorithm uses a combination of computational techniques to automatically assess self-explanation quality (McNamara et al., 2007). Higher scores are assigned to self-explanations that use key words and include language related to the text content (both the target sentence and previously read sentences), whereas lower scores are assigned to unrelated or short responses. The scoring algorithm is designed to reflect how well students have established relevant connections between the target sentence and prior text material and prior knowledge of the content. This algorithm has been shown to be comparable to human-scored self-explanations across a wide variety of texts (Jackson, Guess, & McNamara, 2010).

While playing the games, students can earn iSTART points and *iBucks*. The accumulation of points in the system unlocks new features (e.g., additional games, character accessories, and themes) and determines a student's overall level within the system. iBucks serve as a form of system currency. Students can spend their iBucks personalizing the system interface. Personalizable features include the ability to edit an avatar (e.g., choosing a new hair style or shirt color) and to change the interface's background color. These features are designed to engage students during practice of the strategies and also provide them with a sense of agency over their learning environment (Snow, Allen, Jackson, & McNamara, 2015).

Students can also choose to spend their iBucks on a suite of mini-games designed to provide them with practice identifying the reading strategies covered by iSTART-2. Although mini-games vary in their game mechanics, in each students read a text and a self-explanation and then identify the principal strategy used to generate that self-explanation. For example, Bridge Builder is a mini-game where students are presented with a text and a self-explanation, decide which strategy was used to generate the self-explanation, and drag one of five bricks (each labeled with a different strategy) to an empty slot on a bridge (see Figure 7.4). Students also earn iBucks and iSTART points while playing these mini-games.

## The Need for iSTART-2

The ability to effectively read and comprehend information found in text is essential for both academic and professional success. However, as stated earlier, national assessments of students' reading skills reveal that students often struggle in this area. For example, more than 25 percent of students in grades 8 through 12 within the United States score at or below a basic level of reading comprehension (US DOE, 2011).

One way to improve students' reading comprehension skills is through prolonged and repetitive practice (Anderson, Conrad, & Corbett, 1989; Newell & Rosenbloom, 1981). The original version of iSTART was successful at improving

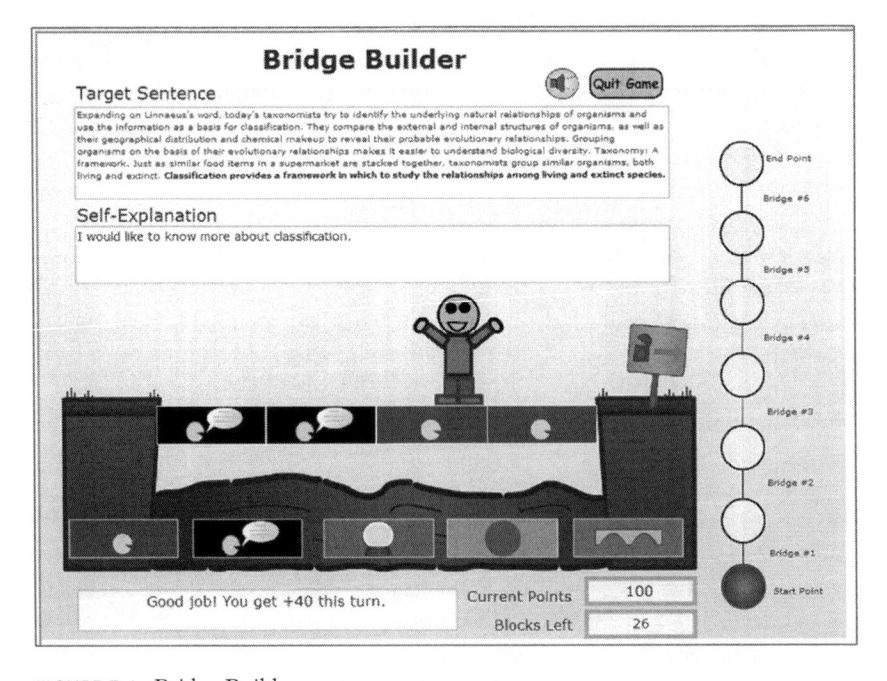

**FIGURE 7.4** Bridge Builder.

students' reading ability over time (Jackson & McNamara, 2013; McNamara et al., 2006, 2007). However, one concern about the prolonged practice was that students became disengaged from the learning task before they reached a desirable level of proficiency (Bell & McNamara, 2007). To address this potential disengagement, game-based elements were incorporated into the system (see the iSTART-2 section for a description of the game features; Jackson & McNamara, 2013; Snow et al., 2015). Thus, the iSTART-2 system provides students with the long-term practice needed to improve literacy skills while also providing game-based practice designed to sustain engagement.

The purpose of iSTART-2 is to supplement teacher instruction within the classroom. In the average-sized classroom, it is unrealistically demanding for teachers to provide individualized feedback on how well students are implementing reading comprehension strategies. iSTART-2 provides each student with real-time feedback and instruction concerning their self-explanations. Thus, each student gets personalized instruction from the system without waiting or disrupting the rest of the classroom.

Finally, iSTART-2 helps students meet the Common Core College and Career Readiness standards for reading. For instance, the new Common Core literacy standards for grades 11 through 12 include the need for students to make logical inferences based on information in text, determine the central idea of a text, analyze the structure of texts, and comprehend complex textual information (National Governors Association Center for Best Practices & Council of Chief State School Officers, 2010). iSTART-2 training is designed to promote each of these principles through self-explanation strategy training (see Table 7.2 for details). Importantly, iSTART-2 focuses on content-area informational texts, which are often difficult for less skilled readers to comprehend.

## Research Support

### Reading Comprehension and Strategy Acquisition

Our research on SERT, the foundation for iSTART-2, has demonstrated the benefits of self-explanation training for a wide range of students, particularly those who have less knowledge about the topic, or low-knowledge readers. Indeed, across a number of studies, the effects of self-explanation and strategy training have been most evident for low-knowledge students. For example, O'Reilly, Best, and McNamara (2004) conducted a study in which 136 inner-city high school students were randomly assigned to receive either no training (control), SERT, or training to preview the text using K-W-L charts (What do you know? What do you want to know? What did you learn?), which was commonly taught in the targeted schools. The effects of these training conditions were examined on students' comprehension of a science text one week after training. There was an overall benefit for SERT, with no benefit of the K-W-L preview condition in comparison to the control condition. This is important, because it demonstrates that

**TABLE 7.2** iSTART-2 and the Common Core Alignment Examples.

| *Common Core Guidelines:* | *iSTART-2 Implementation:* |
|---|---|
| **Key Ideas and Details** Read closely to determine what the text says explicitly and make logical inferences from it; cite specific textual evidence when writing or speaking to support conclusions drawn from the text. Determine central ideas or themes of a text and analyze their development; summarize the key supporting details and ideas. | iSTART-2 provides students with training on multiple comprehension strategies which are used to monitor one's understanding, understand explicit meanings in text, and to derive within-text inferences as well as inferences using prior knowledge. When inferencing in iSTART-2, learners are required to combine ideas from two or more sentences together. Thus, instruction in the bridging strategy assists learners in identifying the main ideas and themes within a text. |
| **Craft and Structure** Analyze the structure of texts, including how specific sentences, paragraphs, and larger portions of the text (e.g., a section, chapter, scene, or stanza) relate to each other and the whole. | The inferencing strategy in iSTART-2 is used to link the current sentence being read to previously read sentences from the text. Successfully applying this strategy involves thinking about how sentences in the text relate to one another. |
| **Range of Reading and Level of Text Complexity** Read and comprehend complex literary and informational texts independently and proficiently. | Within iSTART-2, learners read many texts of varying difficulty and are provided with instruction in the key strategies shown to improve reading comprehension. |
| **Vocabulary Acquisition and Use** Determine or clarify the meaning of unknown and multiple-meaning words and phrases by using context clues, analyzing meaningful word parts, and consulting general and specialized reference materials, as appropriate. Acquire and use accurately a range of general academic and domain-specific words. | iSTART-2 comprehension strategies instruct students on how to use context clues, word deconstruction, world knowledge, or common sense, as well as reference materials to figure out the meanings of unfamiliar words in texts. The texts within iSTART-2 are complex domain specific texts that expose students to diverse general language and scientific terminology. |

SERT training is more effective than instruction to use the K-W-L previewing strategy. The results also indicated that the benefits of SERT were most pronounced for students with less knowledge about science. Importantly, after training, the low-knowledge students who were provided with SERT understood the science text as well as the high-knowledge students.

McNamara (2004) examined the benefits of SERT (compared to a control condition) with undergraduate college students. After training, the students were asked to self-explain a challenging text about cell mitosis. The results again demonstrated an overall benefit for SERT on students' ability to understand challenging text. In addition, this work indicated that SERT's primary role was in helping low-knowledge students use logic and common sense to self-explain the text. SERT helps students with less domain knowledge to more successfully self-explain texts using effective comprehension strategies. Moreover, as found by O'Reilly et al. (2004), the low-knowledge students who received SERT training *caught up to* the high-knowledge students, showing comprehension scores equivalent to the high-knowledge students after training.

In another study, McNamara (in press) demonstrated that college students enrolled in an introductory biology course with low science knowledge scored higher on the course exams if they had completed SERT (compared to a control condition). The advantages of the comprehension strategies included in the iSTART systems can thus have measurable benefits on students' comprehension and long-term performance in challenging content-area courses such as science.

All versions of the iSTART program have maintained the key ingredients of SERT, with benefits for students' comprehension of challenging science text equivalent to that of SERT (O'Reilly, Sinclair, & McNamara, 2004). The benefits of reading strategy training have been demonstrated for a wide range of students, including middle school, high school, and college students. For example, a study by McNamara and colleagues (2006) examined the benefits of reading strategy training for middle school and high school students' comprehension of science text. In this study, students were randomly assigned to iSTART or to a control condition where they were briefly shown how to self-explain, but were given no strategy training. Students who received the iSTART strategy training generated higher quality self-explanations and performed better on challenging comprehension questions than students who did not. Moreover, students of different ability levels benefitted from iSTART, albeit in different ways. For example, the students who were already strategic readers improved on the more difficult comprehension questions. Less strategic students, however, benefitted from iSTART by improving their ability to answer more surface level questions. Thus, iSTART is helpful for students with a range of ability levels.

Another study with high school students showed that using iSTART over the course of eight sessions led to improvements in self-explanation quality, and the less skilled students caught up to the skilled students in terms of the quality of their explanations (Jackson & McNamara, 2013; Snow, Jackson, & McNamara, 2014). This improvement in self-explanation quality persisted a week after completing the training, suggesting that the effects of iSTART training are not short-lived (Jackson & McNamara, 2013).

Finally, several studies have demonstrated that the reading comprehension training provided by iSTART is effective with college student populations. For example, one study showed that students who completed the comprehension strategy training improved in their self-explanation ability, and that both more and less skilled students saw improvements (Magliano et al., 2005). Whereas the less skilled students improved in terms of their ability to understand the basic information in the text (i.e., at the textbase level), the more skilled students improved in their ability to understand the text at deeper levels (i.e., at the situational model level). Hence, a wide range of students benefit from engaging with iSTART, and importantly it helps students to make sense of text, even when they are challenged by less familiar domains.

## Motivation and Engagement

iSTART-2 is a game-based system designed to maintain students' enjoyment and motivation as well as support the development of their reading comprehension skills (Jackson & McNamara, 2013). A study by Jackson and McNamara (2013) compared the impact of both a game-based and non-game-based version of iSTART on students' reading comprehension and strategy acquisition as well as their enjoyment and motivation across time. Results from this work found that while there were no significant differences in learning gains between the two systems (game and non-game versions), students who participated in the game-based version of iSTART reported higher levels of enjoyment and motivation across time. Thus, the features within the game-based version of iSTART decrease the effects of disengagement that are typically associated with prolonged and repetitive practice (Jackson & McNamara, 2013).

## Accessing iSTART-2

iSTART-2 is freely accessible via the web. Teachers can navigate to http://istart.soletlab.com and click on the Teacher Registration link to begin the account creation process (see Figure 7.5). After completing the registration form, a system administrator will approve the account and send additional information about how to begin using the system.

After registering, teachers can log into the system and are transferred to the Teacher Interface (see Figure 7.6). From this interface, teachers can create classrooms, enroll students, assign texts within the system, and view their students' progress. Teachers are also able to view iSTART-2 content through their teacher page, or they are welcome to create a new student account that they can use to test their specific settings.

Creating a classroom is straightforward, only requiring basic information such as the classroom name, a keycode that students can use to join the classroom, and the teacher's school name and location. Teachers can create, view, and organize multiple classrooms within the system. Students can be enrolled into classrooms in multiple ways, for instance, students can create their own accounts and use the

**FIGURE 7.5** Account Creation Process.

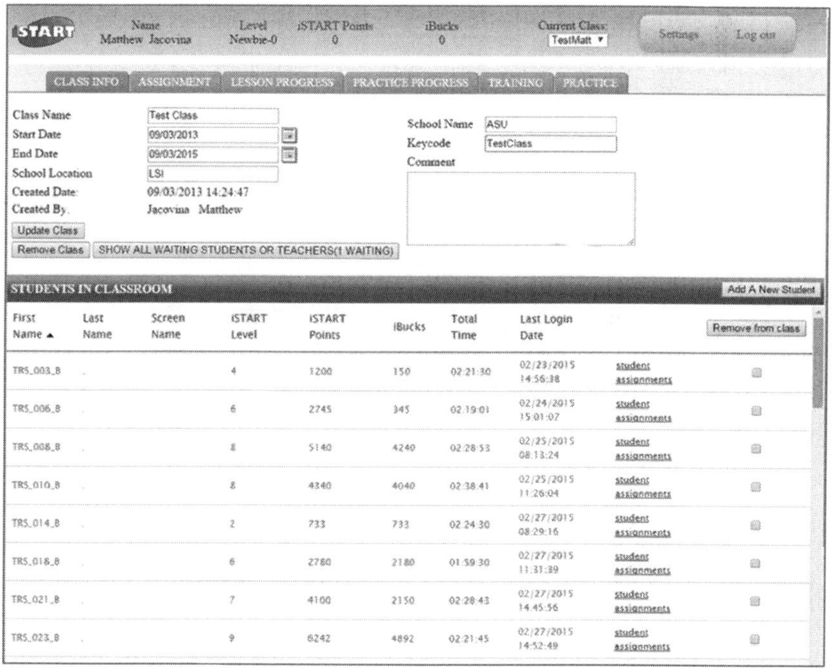

**FIGURE 7.6** Teacher Interface.

class keycode to join a particular iSTART-2 class, teachers can individually add students to their classrooms, or teachers can send a spreadsheet with students' usernames and passwords to the iSTART-2 team to have multiple students added at once. This last option may be most optimal for teachers who have many classrooms and students enrolled within iSTART-2.

The Teacher Interface is also used to assign specific texts for students' practice activities. Within the "Assignment" tab, teachers can select texts related to their course for students to cover in either generative and identification games. Alternatively, teachers may choose to not assign any texts, in which case students can choose their own texts or the texts can be randomly assigned by the system. Teachers may also add new, custom texts to the system and assign those to students from the Assignment tab. To add a new text, teachers click on a link to "Create a New Text" and paste their new text into a prompt. Next, iSTART-2 breaks the text into individual sentences (see Figure 7.7). Finally, teachers select the target sentences, which students will self-explain.

Teachers can monitor students' progress as they interact within the system. The main page of the Teacher Interface displays how long students have been in the system, the last date and time they logged in, and their number of iSTART Points and iBucks (see Figure 7.6). Additional information about students' performance can be found on the Lesson Progress, Practice Progress, and Assignment pages. Lesson Progress displays how many of the lesson videos students have completed, along with the score they obtained on the lesson video checkpoint questions (see Figure 7.8). The Practice Progress and Assignment pages are similar to the Lesson Progress page in that they provide summaries of students' actions. For instance, the Practice Progress page summarizes the performance of each student for each

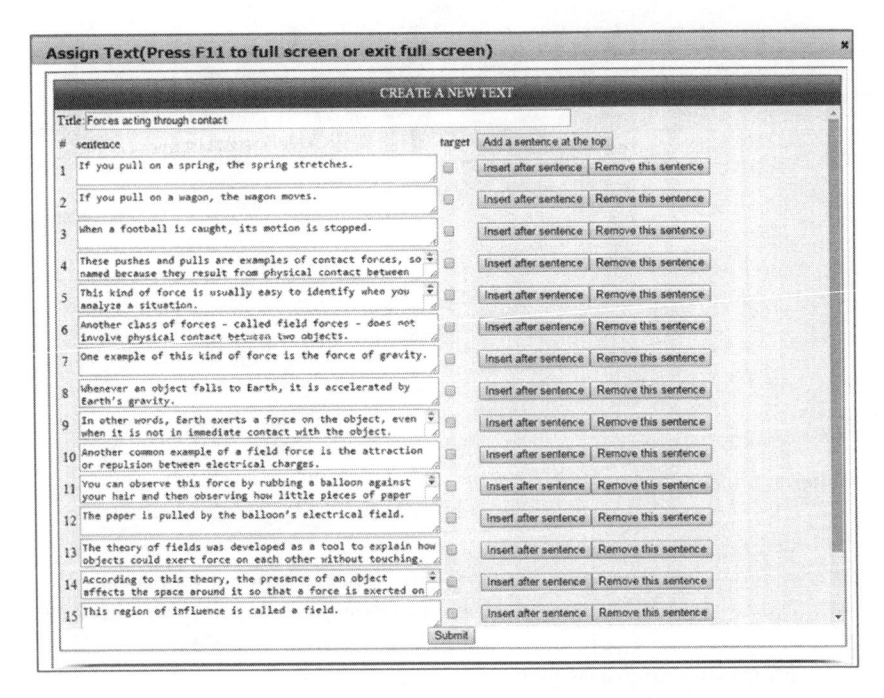

**FIGURE 7.7** Example of iSTART-2 Breaking Text into Individual Sentences.

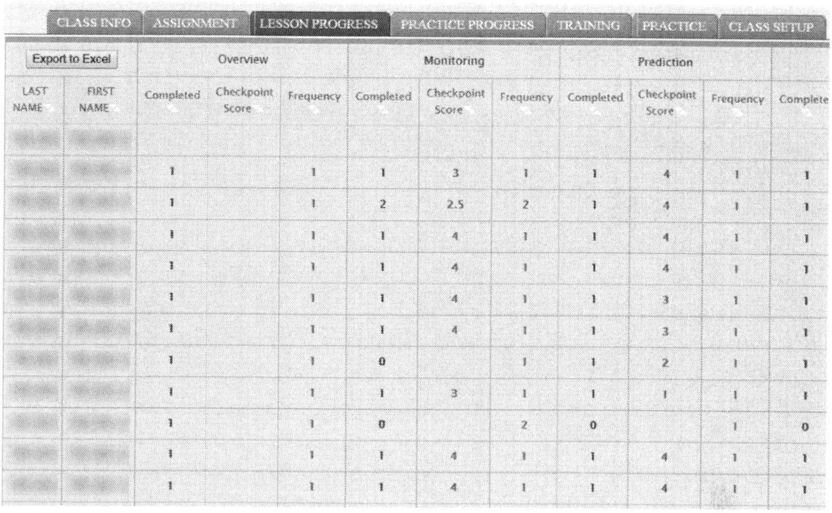

| LAST NAME | FIRST NAME | Overview |  |  | Monitoring |  |  | Prediction |  |  |
|---|---|---|---|---|---|---|---|---|---|---|
|  |  | Completed | Checkpoint Score | Frequency | Completed | Checkpoint Score | Frequency | Completed | Checkpoint Score | Frequency | Complete |
|  |  | 1 | 1 | 1 | 3 | 1 | 1 | 4 | 1 | 1 |
|  |  | 1 | 1 | 2 | 2.5 | 2 | 1 | 4 | 1 | 1 |
|  |  | 1 | 1 | 1 | 4 | 1 | 1 | 4 | 1 | 1 |
|  |  | 1 | 1 | 1 | 4 | 1 | 1 | 4 | 1 | 1 |
|  |  | 1 | 1 | 1 | 4 | 1 | 1 | 3 | 1 | 1 |
|  |  | 1 | 1 | 1 | 4 | 1 | 1 | 3 | 1 | 1 |
|  |  | 1 | 1 | 0 |  | 1 | 1 | 2 | 1 | 1 |
|  |  | 1 | 1 | 1 | 3 | 1 | 1 | 1 | 1 | 1 |
|  |  | 1 | 1 | 0 |  | 2 | 0 |  | 1 | 0 |
|  |  | 1 | 1 | 1 | 4 | 1 | 1 | 4 | 1 | 1 |
|  |  | 1 | 1 | 1 | 4 | 1 | 1 | 4 | 1 | 1 |

**FIGURE 7.8** Lesson Progress Page.

of the individual games, along with a count of how many times the games have been completed. Similarily, the Assignment page presents scores for each text that the teacher has assigned to students in the class.

## *Integrating iSTART-2 in the Classroom*

iSTART-2 is designed to help students become more skilled and strategic readers across a broad range of texts, and teachers can employ the system to support these goals as best suits the needs of their classroom and curriculum. Teachers can be flexible in when practice activities are assigned. For instance, some teachers may find it useful to assign iSTART-2 practice during class time while others may prefer to use the system as a homework device or prescriptively when students show signs of struggling with comprehending difficult texts.

We encourage teachers to talk about and practice using self-explanation and the comprehension strategies in the classroom. iSTART-2, like all educational technologies, is more effective when it is integrated into classroom activities. A teacher can implement SERT strategies by explaining and demonstrating self-explanation, and encouraging students to use the comprehension strategies. For example, the teacher can have the students self-explain as a class—calling on students to begin or continue self-explanations and asking students to write out self-explanations for selected sentences in text. Students can also be placed in pairs and asked to take turns self-explaining a portion of the textbook. This is particularly effective if one student self-explains a paragraph and then the other summarizes the paragraph. These simple exercises have important added benefits, particularly for the struggling students.

Teachers' ability to input their own texts further encourages students to practice self-explaining while reading about particularly difficult (but relevant) course content. If teachers would like students to read from course material, we suggest targeting the most challenging sections. The teacher can select (and potentially modify) approximately 20 to 30 excerpts from the textbook that include 16 to 30 sentences, and then choose 8 to 10 sentences from each for the students to self-explain.

However, we do not recommend using iSTART-2 as the sole delivery method for new course content, because iSTART-2 is not designed to provide students with content specific feedback. iSTART-2 improves students' comprehension of challenging course material, in particular science. iSTART-2 also combats misconceptions of science content (Allen, McNamara, & McCrudden, 2015). However, iSTART-2 does not provide direct feedback on potential misconceptions. The scores that students receive during practice are solely indicative of students' use of self-explanation strategies and the depth of comprehension, rather than the accuracy of their understanding. Hence, while the pedagogy of the iSTART-2 program helps students better to understand the material and helps students to learn how to comprehend challenging course material, more is needed for mastery of the material.

### Optimal Length of Practice

How much practice do students need? Although the optimal length of practice depends on a variety of factors (e.g., students' prior reading ability, age level, prior knowledge of the domain), in general, after students have completed the 7 instructional videos (~35 minutes) we recommend they engage in about 8 to 10 hours of practice. Spreading this practice across time can also be beneficial, because students would have more opportunities to recognize challenges that they may encounter in their everyday experiences and to recognize when and why self-explanation and the use of comprehension strategies could be helpful.

## Conclusion

iSTART-2 provides students with instruction and game-based practice for five self-explanation strategies. These strategies are designed to improve students' reading comprehension skills, particularly for complex texts. The instruction and practice embedded within iSTART-2 complement classroom instruction and provide students with opportunities for extended practice within a game-based environment. These game-based elements have been shown to maintain students' interest as well as increase their motivation over time.

An important element of iSTART-2 is that it provides teachers with multiple ways to use the system. This flexibility allows iSTART-2 to be easily adapted for a variety of age groups and course topics. For instance, the amount of time and practice required for iSTART-2 training is flexible. This eliminates the need for teachers to spend valuable classroom time assigning texts and complete practice activities. iSTART-2 also affords teachers the ability to choose the content of texts with which students interact or enter their own texts that are a part of their established curriculum. iSTART-2 practice is also adaptive and personalizable; thus, practice activities and meaningful feedback can be adjusted based on students' ability levels.

iSTART-2 is appropriate for a wide range of ability levels, because the strategies target different levels of understanding, and students improve at their proximal level of comprehension ability. The ability for teachers to enter in their own texts affords the opportunity to customize and select texts that match student needs and reading levels. In addition, iSTART-2 is currently being expanded to include strategy instruction in summarization and question asking, strategies shown to be effective for younger readers (e.g., Rosenshine, Meister, & Chapman, 1996; Wade-Stein & Kintsch, 2004). A Spanish version of iSTART-2 is also currently available.

Finally, iSTART-2 is aligned with many of the Common Core College and Career Readiness standards for reading, as well as any number of individual state standards. iSTART-2 provides an individualized and engaging practice environment that promotes mastery of effective comprehension strategies, helps students to recognize the importance of generating logical inferences, determine the central idea of texts, analyze the structure of texts, and comprehend complex textual information. In combination with teacher instruction, iSTART-2 assists in the development of these crucial skills with the goal of helping students achieve both academic and professional success.

## Acknowledgments

The research reported here was supported by the Institute of Education Sciences (IES R305G020018–02, R305G040046, R305A080589, R305A130124), the National Science Foundation (NSF REC0241144, IIS-0735682), and the Office of Naval Research (ONR N000141410343). We are grateful to many students and faculty who have contributed to iSTART research over the years. We would also like to thank Jenna Snow for her insightful comments and suggestions. The opinions expressed are those of the authors and do not represent the views of the Institute or the U.S. Department of Education, NSF, or ONR.

## Note

1 iSTART-2 is the third iteration of the iSTART program. While features and mechanics may vary across iterations, each one builds upon the pedagogical techniques in SERT. For more information concerning the various iterations of iSTART, please see Jackson, Boonthum, & McNamara, 2010; Jackson & McNamara, 2013; McNamara, in press; McNamara et al., 2007.

## References

Allen, L. K., McNamara, D. S., & McCrudden, M. T. (2015). Change your mind: Investigating the effects of self-explanation in the resolution of misconceptions. In D. C. Noelle, R. Dale, A. S. Warlaumont, J. Yoshimi, T. Matlock, C. D. Jennings, & P. Maglio (Eds.), *Proceedings of the 37th Annual Cognitive Science Society Meeting* (Cog Sci 2015). Pasadena, CA.

Anderson, J. R., Conrad, F. G., & Corbett, A. T. (1989). Skill acquisition and the LISP tutor. *Cognitive Science, 1*, 467–505.

Bell, C., & McNamara, D. S. (2007). Integrating iSTART into a high school curriculum. In D. S. McNamara & G. Trafton (Eds.), *Proceedings of the 29th Annual Meeting of the Cognitive Science Society, Nashville, Tennessee, August 1–4, 2007* (pp. 809–814). Austin, TX: Cognitive Science Society.

Bransford, J. D., Brown, A. L., & Cocking, R. R. (Eds.). (2000). How people learn: Brain, mind, experience, and school. Washington, DC: National Academy Press.

Brown, A. (1982). Learning how to learn from reading. In J. A. Langer & M. T. Smith-Burke (Eds.), *Reader Meets Author: Bridging the Gap* (pp. 26–54). Newark, DE: International Reading Association.

Chi, M. T. H., De Leeuw, N., Chiu, M., & LaVancher, C. (1994). Eliciting self-explanations improves understanding. *Cognitive Science, 18*, 439–477.

Graesser, A. C., Leon, J. A., & Otero, J. C. (2002). Introduction to the psychology of science text comprehension. In J. Otero, J. A. Leon, & A. C. Graesser (Eds.), *The Psychology Of Science Text Comprehension* (pp. 1–5). Mahwah, NJ: Erlbaum.

Jackson, G. T., & McNamara, D. S. (2013). Motivation and performance in a game-based intelligent tutoring system. *Journal of Educational Psychology, 105*, 1036–1049.

Jackson, G. T., Boonthum, C., & McNamara, D. S. (2010). The efficacy of iSTART extended practice: Low ability students catch up. In J. Kay & V. Aleven (Eds.), *Proceedings of the 10th International Conference on Intelligent Tutoring Systems* (pp. 349–351). Berlin: Springer.

Jackson, G. T., Guess, R. H., & McNamara, D. S. (2010). Assessing cognitively complex strategy use in an untrained domain. *Topics in Cognitive Science, 2*, 127–137.

Kintsch, W. (1998). *Comprehension: A Paradigm for Cognition*. New York: Cambridge University Press.

Magliano, J. P., Todaro, S. Millis, K., Wiemer-Hastings, K., Kim, H. J., & McNamara, D. S. (2005). Changes in reading strategies as a function of reading training: A comparison of live and computerized training. *Journal of Educational Computing Research, 32*, 185–208.

McNamara, D. S. (2004). SERT: Self-explanation reading training. *Discourse Processes, 38*, 1–30.

McNamara, D. S. (ed.). (2007). *Reading Comprehension Strategies: Theory, Interventions, and Technologies*. Mahwah, NJ: Erlbaum.

McNamara, D. S. (2009). The importance of teaching reading strategies. *Perspectives on Language and Literacy, 35*, 34–40.

McNamara, D. S. (in press). Self-Explanation and Reading Strategy Training (SERT) improves low-knowledge students' science course performance. *Discourse Processes*.

McNamara, D. S., & Magliano, J. (2009). Toward a comprehensive model of comprehension. *Psychology of Learning and Motivation, 51*, 297–384.

McNamara, D. S., Levinstein, I. B., & Boonthum, C. (2004). iSTART: Interactive strategy trainer for active reading and thinking. *Behavior Research Methods, Instruments, & Computers, 36*, 222–233.

McNamara, D. S., O'Reilly, T., Best, R., & Ozuru, Y. (2006). Improving adolescent students' reading comprehension with iSTART. *Journal of Educational Computing Research, 34,* 147–171

McNamara, D. S., O'Reilly, T., Rowe, M., Boonthum, C., & Levinstein, I. B. (2007). iSTART: A web-based tutor that teaches self-explanation and metacognitive reading strategies. In D. S. McNamara (ed.), *Reading Comprehension Strategies: Theories, Interventions, and Technologies* (pp. 397–420). Mahwah, NJ: Erlbaum.

National Governors Association Center for Best Practices & Council of Chief State School Officers. (2010). *Common Core State Standards.* Washington, DC: Authors.

Newell, A., & Rosenbloom, P. (1981). Mechanisms of skill acquisition and the law of practice. In J. R. Anderson (Ed.), *Cognitive Skills and Their Acquisition* (pp. 1–55). Hillsdale, NJ.

O'Reilly, T. P., & McNamara, D. S. (2007). The impact of science knowledge, reading skill, and reading strategy knowledge on more traditional "high-stakes" measures of high school students' science achievement. *American Educational Research Journal, 44*(1), 161–196.

O'Reilly, T. P., Best, R., & McNamara, D. S. (2004). Self-explanation reading training: Effects for low-knowledge readers. In K. Forbus, D. Gentner, & T. Regier (Eds.), *Proceedings of the 26th Annual Cognitive Science Society* (pp. 1053–1058). Mahwah, NJ: Erlbaum.

O'Reilly, T. P., Sinclair, G. P., & McNamara, D. S. (2004). Reading strategy training: Automated versus live. In K. Forbus, D. Gentner & T. Regier (Eds.), *Proceedings of the 26th Annual Cognitive Science Society* (pp. 1059–1064). Mahwah, NJ: Erlbaum.

O'Reilly, T. P., Taylor, R. S., & McNamara, D. S. (2006). Classroom based reading strategy training: Self-explanation vs. reading control. *Proceedings of the 28th Annual Meeting of the Cognitive Science Society* (pp. 1887–1892). Austin, TX: Cognitive Science Society.

Palincsar, A. S., & Brown, A. L. (1984). Reciprocal teaching of comprehension-fostering and monitoring activities. *Cognition and Instruction, 2,* 117–175.

Rosenshine, B., Meister, C., & Chapman, S. (1996). Teaching students to generate questions: A review of the intervention studies. *Review of Educational Research, 66,* 181–221.

Snow, E. L., Jackson, G. T., & McNamara, D. S. (2014). Emergent behaviors in computer-based learning environments: Computational signals of catching up. *Computers in Human Behavior, 41,* 62–70.

Snow, E. L., Allen, L. K., Jackson, G. T., & McNamara, D. S. (2015). Spendency: Students' propensity to use system currency. *International Journal of Artificial Intelligence in Education, 25,* 1–21.

Snow, E. L., Allen, L. K., Jacovina, M. E., & McNamara, D. S. (2015). Does agency matter?: Exploring the impact of controlled behaviors within a game-based environment. *Computers & Education, 26,* 378–392.

U.S. Department of Education. (2011). *Reading 2011: National Assessment of Educational Progress at Grades 4 and 8.* (NCES 2012–455). Washington, DC: National Center for Education Statistics.

VanLehn, K., Jones, R. M., & Chi, M. T. H. (1992). A model of the self-explanation effect. *Journal of the Learning Sciences, 2,* 1–60.

Wade-Stein, D., & Kintsch, E. (2004). Summary Street: Interactive computer support for writing. *Cognition and Instruction, 22,* 333–362.

# 8

# TuinLEC

## An Intelligent Tutoring System to Teach Task-Oriented Reading Skills to Young Adolescents

*Eduardo Vidal-Abarca, Maria-Ángeles Serrano, Luis Ramos, Laura Gil, and Antonio Ferrer*

### Introduction

This chapter presents an intelligent tutoring system called TuinLEC designed to teach basic task-oriented reading skills to young adolescents following the framework developed by the Program for International Students Assessment (PISA) to assess reading literacy skills. TuinLEC is based on recent approaches of reading that emphasize the use of documents for applied purposes. It includes explicit teaching and deliberate practice of task-oriented reading skills with adaptive feedback in a game-like environment. Task-oriented reading activities include any activity in which a reader uses an available text with a specific purpose (e.g., finding information, writing a summary of the text, or using the text as a source for writing an essay on a topic, among many other possibilities). However, our focus here is on answering comprehension questions with the text available. TuinLEC targets Spanish-speaking students and was thus designed to teach reading in Spanish to Spanish speakers.

In this chapter, we first explain the PISA framework of reading literacy to clarify what we mean by task-oriented reading skills. The core of task-oriented reading is making decisions on the part of the reader that guide their behavior throughout the whole process of reading. The need for a technology capable of recording all these decisions and providing appropriate feedback will be explained in the following section. Then, we give a general overview of TuinLEC, provide some evidence of TuinLEC's effectiveness, and describe how it can be integrated into the classroom. We finish the chapter with a short section on the current limitations and future directions of the system.

### Task-Oriented Reading Skills

An important goal for schools is to prepare students to acquire the skills needed to perform the huge variety of task-oriented reading activities that people execute in ordinary life (White, Chen, & Forsyth, 2010). Thus, for example, people want to be informed (e.g., newspapers), to learn (e.g., encyclopedia, textbooks), to gather information (e.g., product descriptions), to be entertained (e.g., magazines, novels) or to perform a concrete task (e.g., to cook a recipe). The importance and versatility of skilled task-oriented reading is acknowledged in large-scale surveys as the OECD's PISA study (OECD, 2008). The PISA framework and other theoretically grounded approaches (Rouet, 2006; McCrudden & Schraw, 2007) have inspired the development of TuinLEC. Thus, we will use this framework to explain the structure of TuinLEC and the reading situations it includes.

In a typical task-oriented reading situation, a reader is presented with a text and a set of questions with the specific instruction of answering the questions using the information in the text. The reader has the text available for the whole task, and is thus able to go back and forth from the text to the question at will. Furthermore, the reader has to make constant decisions on *what* to read to answer the questions, *when* to read, and *how* to read (e.g., how much text information to read initially before start to answer the questions, and how carefully to perform that initial reading). According to the PISA framework, questions are of three types and cover a broad range of cognitive operations representative of activities that people perform with written texts:

- retrieving information tasks, which focus the reader on separate pieces of information;
- forming a broad understanding and developing and interpretating tasks, which focus the reader on relationships within the text (e. g., cause and effect, global ideas);
- reflecting on the content (e.g., if a claim is true or reasonable) and the form of the text (e.g., if the text is clear or appropriate for the audience), both of which require the reader to draw on knowledge outside the text and relate it to what is being read.

Texts are of different formats. In TuinLEC we retained from PISA the distinction between continuous texts, which are composed of sentences organized into paragraphs, and non-continuous texts (e.g., tables, diagrams, graphs, charts, maps). These two kinds of texts have different organizations and are read differently. A different categorization of texts is by text type (e.g., description, narration, exposition, argumentation, instruction). TuinLEC includes a variety of text types, although we emphasize the fact that the texts and questions are interesting and challenging. In fact, we developed almost triple the number of texts and questions that we needed, and we asked a large group of students to read the texts, answer the questions, and score the materials according to their interest, prior background knowledge, and how challenging they found all of them. Then, we selected those texts scored as more interesting, challenging, and less familiar.

It should be noted that task-oriented reading activities in TuinLEC require understanding on the part of the reader, but the focus of these activities is not comprehension processes *while* reading the text, but the *use* of text information for specific purposes. This is an important issue, since using a text to answer comprehension questions requires that the reader make important decisions (Rouet, 2006). For instance, how much and how deeply should I read the text initially? Should I search the text to answer a question? If I decide to search, how should I do it? When should I stop searching? These decisions are highly strategic and, as a result, they can be trained. Furthermore, many students have trouble applying these strategies. For example, in a seminal study, Cataldo and Oakhill (2000) found that less-skilled 5th graders displayed ineffective strategies when searching a text to look for information appropriate to answer a question (e. g., they started to read the text again from the beginning after every question instead of going directly to the right point, as good comprehenders did). Rouet and Coutelet (2008) studied how the ability to search for information in an encyclopedia develops from ages 9 to 13 years old. They found that older students were significantly faster at searching longer texts, and they used more effective structural text organizers, such as the table of contents and the index. Vidal-Abarca, Mañá, and Gil (2010) found that the decision to search the text to answer a question, which is a sort of metacognitive decision, is relatively independent of reading skills, but has an impact on performance. That is, the more often students decide to search, the better they score on a comprehension test. Gil, Martínez and Vidal-Abarca (2015) also found that the amount of text initially read before moving to questions is predictive of performance.

To summarize, using a text to answer comprehension questions requires the reader to make decisions based on strategic knowledge, which can be trained. TuinLEC has been developed after careful analysis of this strategic knowledge and how it can inform strategic decisions (see Table 8.1).

Task-oriented reading skills can be trained at very different levels. That is, it is not the same to train these skills at 5th grade as it is to train at 10th grade. TuinLEC was designed to be implemented with 6th graders or students at a grade equivalent. The main reason is that 6th grade is the last grade of primary school in the Spanish school system and in most European countries. Teachers' goals at this level are for students to learn how to read whereas in upper grades their goal is for students to read in order to learn in different content areas. Furthermore, the main activity for reading comprehension instruction in primary school is question answering (Ness, 2011). That is, teachers routinely ask students to answer questions as a comprehension strategy. Then, students independently search for answers in the text and the teacher provides feedback on the correctness of the students' responses. Thus, TuinLEC takes advantages of this frequent instructional activity to introduce students to basic strategies around this activity.

**TABLE 8.1** Strategy Content of Modules Used in TuinLEC.

| Strategic Knowledge | Strategic Decisions |
| --- | --- |
| How to form a good representation of the text | How to read the text initially |
| How to build a good representation of the task | How to read the question |
| How to search the text | How to match the mental representations of the text and the task |
| How to self-regulate the need of searching information | How to monitor the search decision |

## The Need for Task-Oriented Reading Technology

As mentioned above, task-oriented activities involve reading literacy skills that go beyond classical reading comprehension skills, such as making inferences or macrostructure formation (e.g., Graesser, Singer, & Trabasso, 1994; Kintsch, 1998), as they demand that the reader self-regulate their reading strategies to make decisions about what and how to read the text to fulfill the requirements of a specific task (Rouet, 2006). As will be explained later, these strategic decisions are trained in TuinLEC through explicit instruction and sustained practice combined with computer-generated adaptive feedback based on students' performance (i.e., summative feedback providing information about the correctness of their answers), and their strategic decisions (i.e., formative feedback providing suggestions about how to increase their performance through the use of a particular reading literacy skill).

Thus, while students are practicing with TuinLEC, they read texts and answer different types of questions by making different decisions (e.g., how to read the text initially, how to read the question, or how to search the text) and immediately receive summative and formative feedback, which allows them to compare their current performance with some desired standard of performance (i.e., Hattie & Timperley, 2007; Shute, 2008). In general, formative feedback has been considered significantly more effective when it provides details of how to improve the answer (i.e., Narciss, 2004; Shute, 2008). In task-oriented reading, this additional information should focus on strategic decisions about how to self-regulate the need for searching information and how to search the text (Llorens, Cerdán, & Vidal-Abarca, 2014). Furthermore, this formative feedback should adapt to the students' initial reading strategies (i.e., Hattie & Timperley, 2007).

Providing this kind of adaptive and immediate feedback to students requires the use of a technology capable of recording the reading behavior online while answering questions, transforming this behavior into indexes of strategic behavior, computing these indexes to assess the level of readers' strategies, and, finally, generating adaptive feedback messages. In TuinLEC, this complex process is possible thanks to a new computer-based technology based on Read&Answer (Vidal-Abarca et al., 2011). It records every reading action the students undertake, the order of these activities, and the durations of each activity. Using this information, the software automatically displays formative feedback messages based on the connection between the students' performance and their strategic decisions. For instance, the student would receive a feedback message informing them about the connection between their current performance and search decisions (e.g., "You did it wrong! When you searched the text, you did not reread information which is necessary to answer"), as well as a specific recommendation on how to proceed in subsequent questions (e.g., "In the following questions, rereading the necessary information will help you to correctly answer").

Read&Answer is a variation of the moving window technique (e.g., Duggan & Payne, 2009; Kaakinen & Hyönä, 2005). The main innovation is the online registration of self-regulatory variables related to the process of task-oriented reading (see Vidal-Abarca et al., 2011, for a detailed explanation of this technology). It has been used in several experiments designed to investigate good and poor strategies in task-oriented reading situations (Vidal-Abarca et al., 2010), whose results have been the basis of the algorithms that generate the feedback messages provided by TuinLEC. For instance, Mañá, Vidal-Abarca, Domínguez, Gil, & Cerdán (2009) found that specific indexes of search effectiveness, such as the number of visits to relevant information and the use of relevant information, explained a significant portion of variance in answering questions from a text beyond general comprehension skills, and Cerdán, Vidal-Abarca, Martínez, Gilabert, and Gil (2009) demonstrated that reading the whole text initially before reading the questions, produces better understanding of the text, as well as better selection and subsequent processing of the relevant information to answer questions.

Read&Answer has also been used recently to develop a computer-based test to assess students' strategic reading literacy skills (Gil et al., 2015), which provides self-regulation and reading behavior indices predictive of performance. The reliability and validity of these indices support their use for the students' assessment in e-learning contexts such as TuinLEC. Finally, and directly related to the use of Read&Answer in TuinLEC, the effectiveness of this technology to boost strategic search decisions and performance in task-oriented reading situations has been demonstrated in several studies performed by Llorens and colleagues (e.g., Llorens et al., 2014).

## TuinLEC

We have developed two versions of TuinLEC. The first one was a desktop application (a description of this version can be seen in Vidal-Abarca et al., 2014), whereas the second one is a web-based version in which a number of changes have been implemented as a result of our experience and the suggestions made by students and teachers. We describe the web-based version in this chapter.

TuinLEC provides instruction on task-oriented reading strategies and enables deliberate practice of these strategies. It consists of eight modules divided into two phases, one for explicit teaching and guided practice (i.e., instructional phase), and another one for practice (i.e., practice phase).

## *TuinLEC Instructional Modules*

Strategy instruction is provided to TuinLEC's users through four modules. The modules correspond to the main stages of a task-oriented reading process and provide strategies to optimize students' execution in every stage of the process. These modules cover: (a) how to read continuous and non-continuous texts; (b) how to understand and respond to questions; (c) how to search the text; and (d) when to decide to search the text to answer the questions (see Table 8.2 for an overview).

The strategy instruction is conducted through explicit teaching, modeling, and guided practice via dialogs between two animated agents: Ramiro, the teacher, and Lue, the student (see Figures 8.1a and 8.1b for screenshots of instructional modules screens). The agents' dialogs are controlled by the user by pressing the *next* button. The *back* button is also available to reread previous explanations, allowing students to self-regulate their own learning pace.

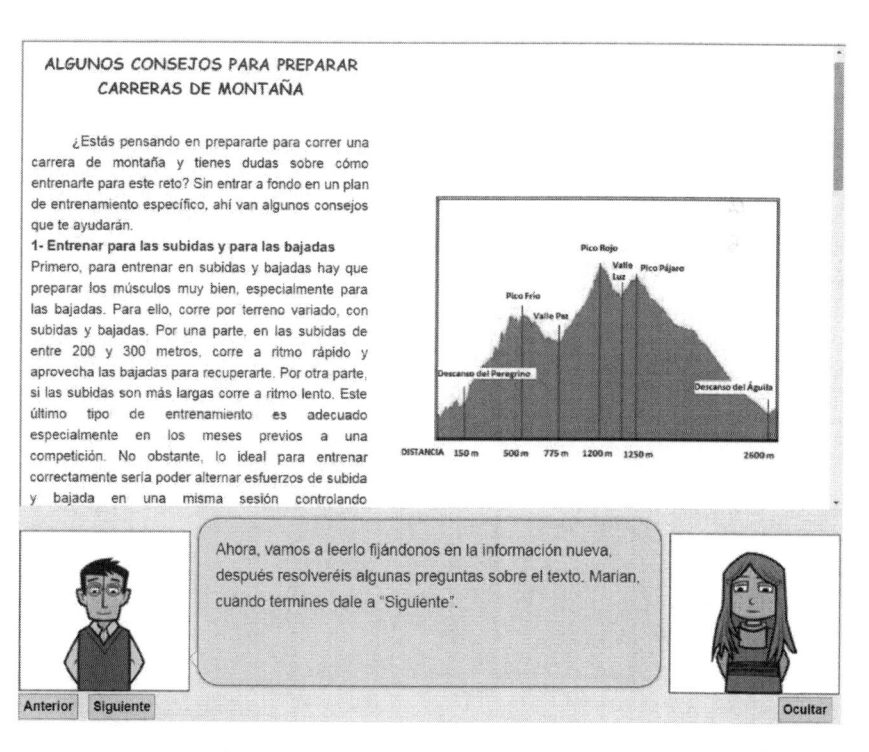

**FIGURE 8.1A** Screenshot of Instructional Modules Screen.

**TABLE 8.2** Overview of Modules Used in TuinLEC.

| Module | Task-Oriented Reading Stages | Strategy Content |
|---|---|---|
| Introductory Module | – | Objective, instructions, contents and structure, animated characters, feedback, points, and rewards. |
| **Instructional Phase** | | |
| Module 1 | Reading the text initially | Strategies for building a mental scheme of the text contents: noticing text organization, identifying ideas of each paragraph, and recognizing text structure organizers. |
| Module 2 | Examining question demands | Strategies for examining the question demands: identifying the nucleus of the question and the process required to retrieve the information and answer it. |
| Module 3 | Searching the text | Strategies for self-regulating the search process: locating relevant information depending on task demands and process required, discarding distracting information, and avoiding word-matching. |
| Module 4 | Self-regulating search decisions | Strategies for self-regulating the search decision: monitoring the need for external information, deciding to search the text depending on the monitoring result, and checking the answer with the text. |
| **Practice Phase** | | |
| Introductory Module to Practice | – | Reviews all strategies learned and introduces TuinLEC Practice Phase: objective, instructions, aids, selecting tool, and feedback. |
| Modules 5–8 | All stages | All strategies. |

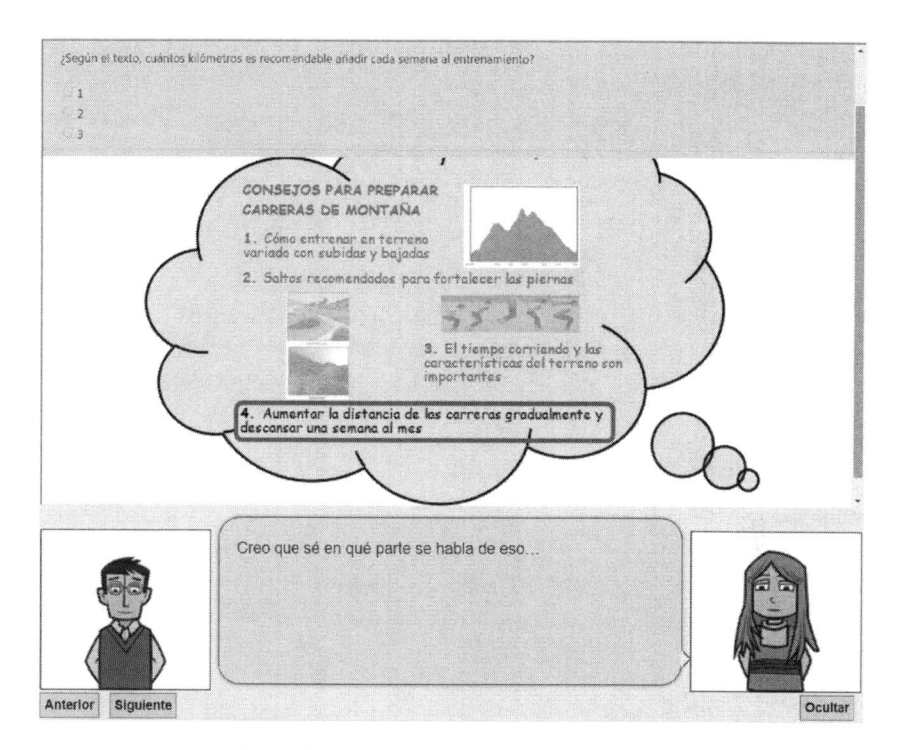

**FIGURE 8.1B** Screenshot of Instructional Modules Screen.

Each module is introduced by Ramiro, who explains what is going to be taught in that module and what is it for. The strategies are introduced and explained throughout the module by Ramiro, and supported by the student avatar, who acts as a model. This modeling performed by Lue is not only a demonstration of appropriate strategies but also incorrect strategies, allowing Ramiro to correct her in order to teach and warn the real student. The virtual agents also introduce the students to the use of three help utilities available for the students in the practice phase.

The student is actively involved throughout the module by answering questions and performing a variety of tasks. Both real and virtual students work together to find solutions to tasks by implementing the strategy learned. However, at the end of every module, the students' active participation increases, because they practice the strategies more independently.

In each module, the strategies are taught and practiced using 1 or 2 texts and between 14 and 21 activities. The texts are of different formats, both continuous and non-continuous. For the activities, TuinLEC displays multiple-choice questions, pairing tasks, selecting key-words, and selecting textual information. Multiple-choice questions are of the three types explained above: access-retrieve, integrate-interpret information, and reflect-evaluate upon the content or the form of the text. For simplicity, questions are referred to as locating, deducting, and reflecting. In addition, each type of question is identified with a different icon (see Figures 8.2a and 8.2b).

Throughout the entire module, Ramiro provides feedback not only referring to the right or wrong answer but also to the strategy involved in the answering process. Thus, the feedback usually includes explanations for correct and incorrect answers, information about the type of error based on the strategy involved, and hints about effective strategies.

Each module includes a conclusion in which the strategies learned in that module are reviewed. In addition, at the beginning of every new module, the agents review the strategies learned previously, so the user can easily link the new strategy with the previous one.

### TuinLEC Practice Modules

After the explicit teaching phase, students are trained through extensive practice of the strategies learned during the four modules. Each practice module consists of two texts, one continuous and one non-continuous text, and seven multiple-choice questions per text.

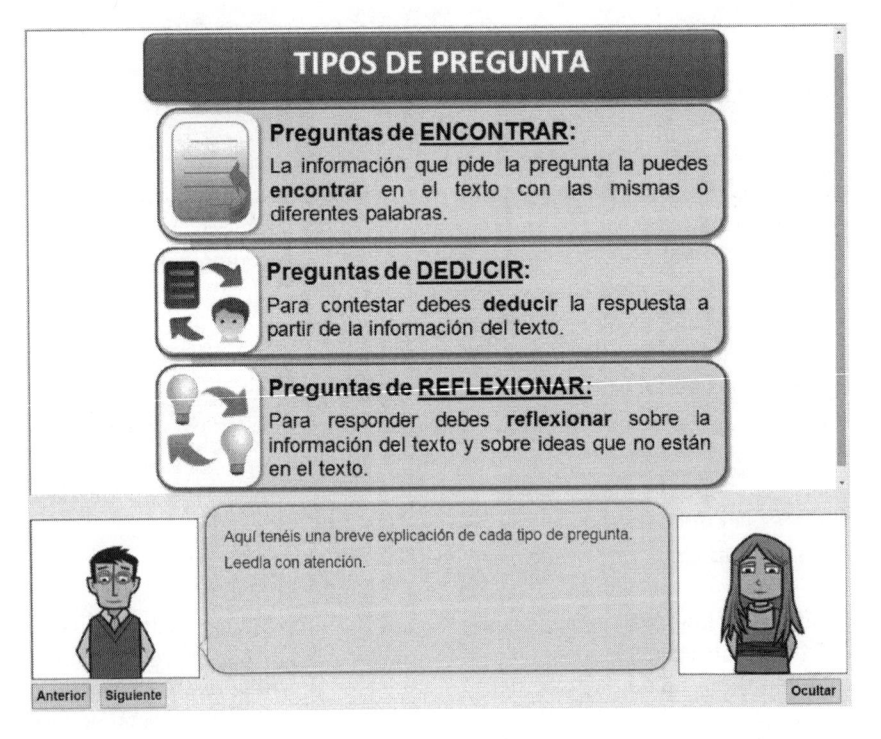

**TIPOS DE PREGUNTA**

**Preguntas de ENCONTRAR:**
La información que pide la pregunta la puedes **encontrar** en el texto con las mismas o diferentes palabras.

**Preguntas de DEDUCIR:**
Para contestar debes **deducir** la respuesta a partir de la información del texto.

**Preguntas de REFLEXIONAR:**
Para responder debes **reflexionar** sobre la información del texto y sobre ideas que no están en el texto.

Aquí tenéis una breve explicación de cada tipo de pregunta. Leedla con atención.

**FIGURE 8.2A** Identification of Different Types of Questions.

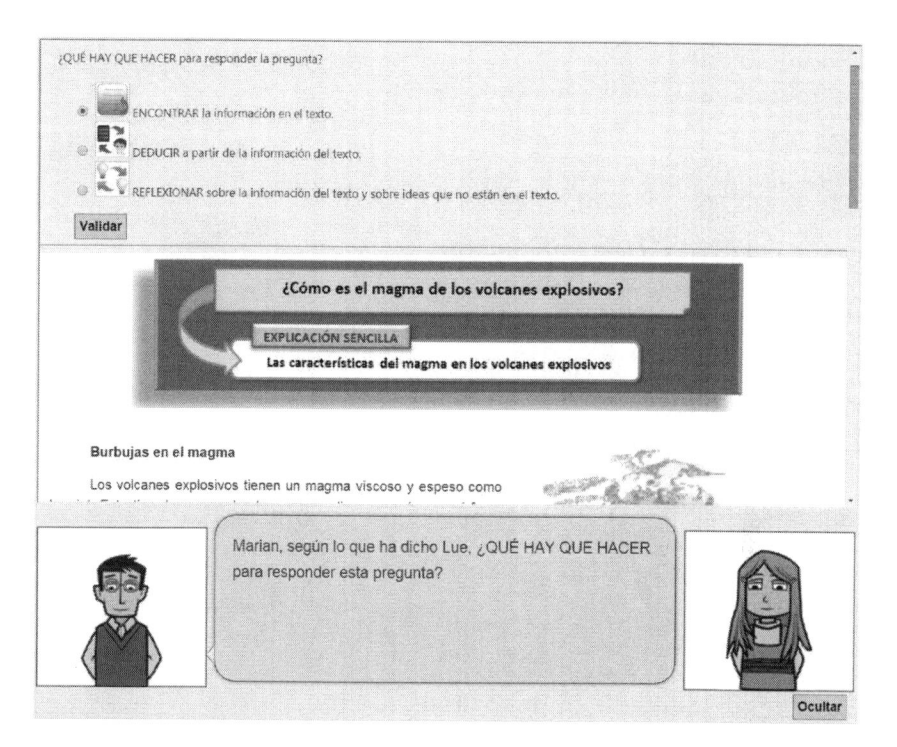

**FIGURE 8.2B** Identification of Different Types of Questions.

In these practice modules, virtual agents are absent and the interface is somewhat different (see Figure 8.3 for a screenshot of a practice module screen). Instead, students have three help tools available throughout this phase. The lifebuoy help is aimed at helping students to identify the task demands and the process required to answer the questions, whereas the other two are intended to assist students with the search process. The binoculars help and the magnifying glass help indicate the paragraphs and sentences, respectively, where relevant information to answer the questions may be found (see Figure 8.4 for a screenshot of the binoculars help used in a question). Using help tools is free, but it has a cost in points. Therefore, it demands self-regulation on the part of the student. The use of these tools is taught through the instructional phase and reviewed in the introductory module to practice. In addition, the selection task is included in this phase as a failure-dependent supportive tool, so that it launches only when the student accumulates a certain percentage of incorrect answers. It consists of forcing students to select the information they consider relevant to the question as a way of thinking carefully about which information could help them to answer the question correctly. After that, students receive feedback about the accuracy of their selection (Llorens, Vidal-Abarca, & Cerdán, in press).

**132**   Eduardo Vidal-Abarca et al.

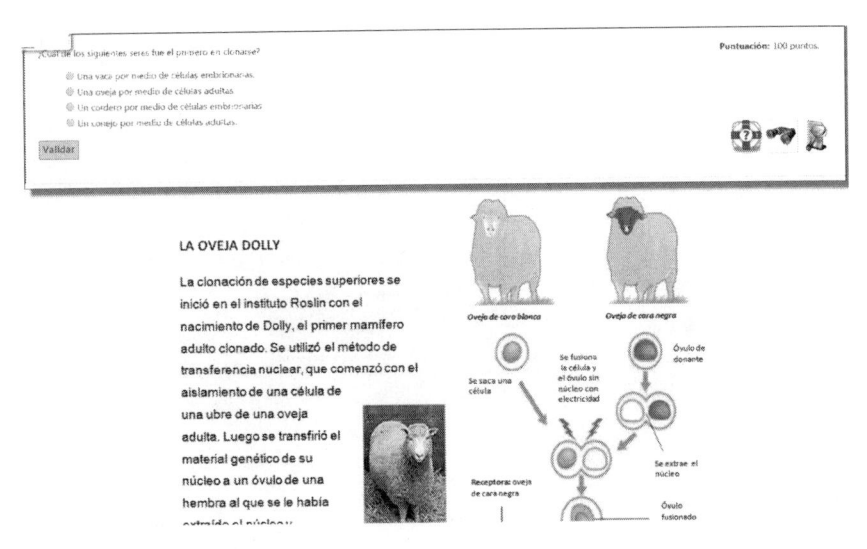

**FIGURE 8.3**   Screenshot of a Practice Module Screen.

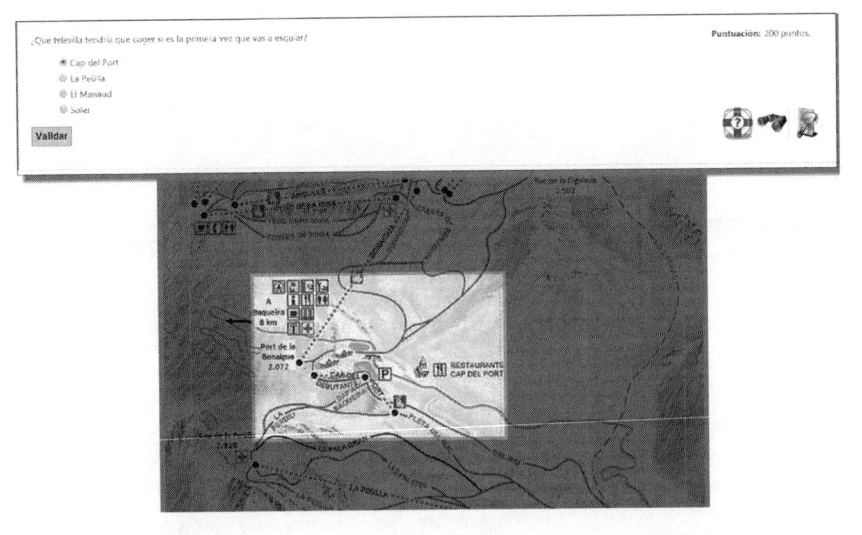

**FIGURE 8.4**   Screenshot of the Binoculars Help Used in a Question.

After answering each question, students receive different types of feedback presented in distinct modes (see Figure 8.5). First, the correct option of the question is indicated by a green tick, while the remaining options are marked by a red cross. Thus, the students can compare their choice with the correct one. Second, the relevant information for the question is highlighted in the text. This feedback focuses students' attention on the part of the text containing relevant information to

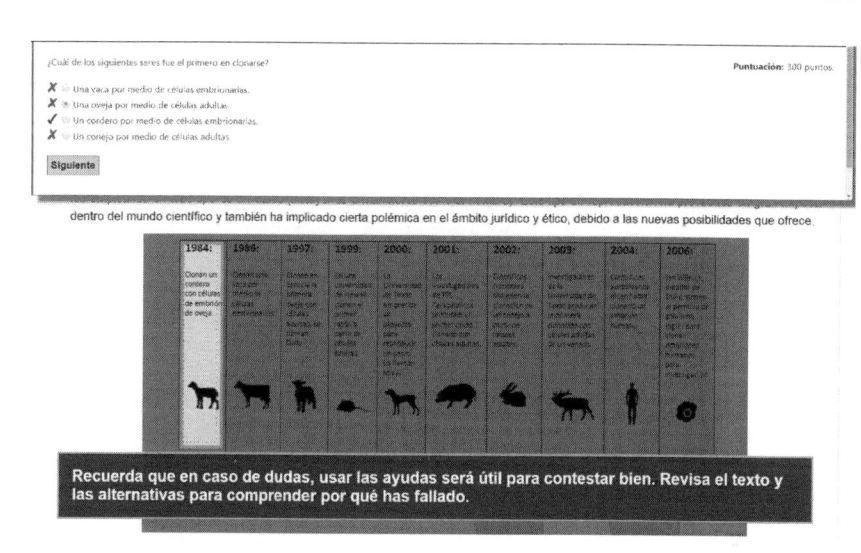

**FIGURE 8.5** Different Types of Feedback Presented in Distinct Modes.

answer the question, which seeks fostering self-assessment and reflection. It can be especially useful for students who struggle in the search process. Finally, TuinLEC delivers adaptive feedback depending on the students' performance, their strategic decisions (e.g., searching the text), and their use of help tools. It is presented in written form and may include some advice on how to proceed in the following questions, encouraging them to use the strategies learned. It also has a motivational function, such as reinforcing right strategies or encouraging effort and persistence.

This adaptive feedback is based on a series of threshold algorithms that depend on different indicators: right or wrong answer, searching decision, use of help tools, and decision of checking the relevant information after answering the question. Therefore, the feedback content does not always include information about all the indicators, rather only about those for which the parameters are above a triggering threshold. Thus, the student who fails repeatedly after searching the text will not receive the same feedback messages as the one who repeatedly fails but does not search the text or the one who never fails and uses some help tools. In addition, in order to maintain the feedback effectiveness, students receive different messages depending on the number of times the same content was shown in previous feedback messages. For instance, a student who never searches for information and fails every question will not receive the same feedback message repeatedly, but it will change as the student progress through the module (e.g., the first feedback message would be "Don't forget that searching the text will help you to answer correctly"; but after several questions, the feedback message could be "Again, a little effort searching the text will help you to answer correctly"). The combination of all these variables results in the generation of about 300 different feedback messages that are designed to meet the individual needs of each student.

## TuinLEC Game-Like Elements

TuinLEC is set up as a game-like environment. Thus, in both instructional and practice phases students earn points with every correct answer. These points are turned into stars (from one to four) at the end of each module. As student progress in the modules, they can view the stars obtained in the different modules from a module chart in the student interface (see Figure 8.6). This seeks to maintain motivation and commitment to the task.

## Studies on TuinLEC's Effectiveness

We have tested TuinLEC's usability and its effectiveness to increase students' skills and motivation. In this section, we summarize our results regarding these studies as well as the specific questions addressed, which are also relevant for practitioners. These questions include identifying the appropriate target age for TuinLEC and whether it is more effective for less-skilled comprehenders than for skilled comprehenders. The effectiveness on usability, motivation, and self-efficacy were measured with questionnaires where students ranked their opinions on a Likert scale from totally disagree to totally agree, whereas the effectiveness on learning skills was measured with independent task-oriented reading tests immediately after training and a short period of delay.

## Usability of TuinLEC

Most of the students (76 percent) agreed that TuinLEC was easy to use and that the interface was easy to understand. Students enjoyed the aesthetic design of TuinLEC during the practice phase (73 percent) more than they did during the phase of explicit teaching (59 percent). When asked about the messages of the virtual agents, students declared that they were clear and easy to understand

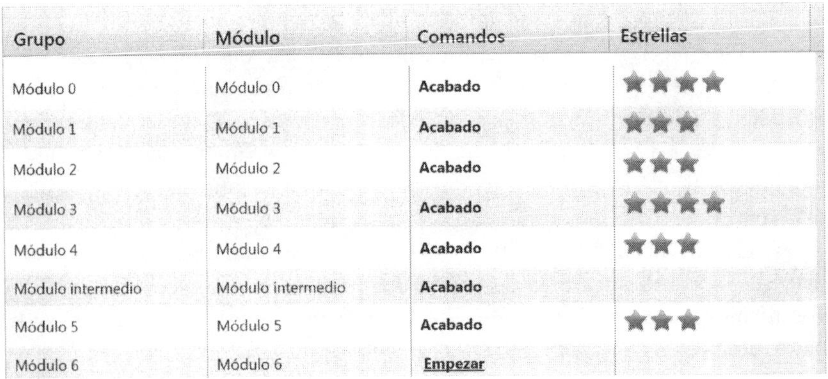

| Grupo | Módulo | Comandos | Estrellas |
|---|---|---|---|
| Módulo 0 | Módulo 0 | Acabado | ★★★★ |
| Módulo 1 | Módulo 1 | Acabado | ★★★ |
| Módulo 2 | Módulo 2 | Acabado | ★★★ |
| Módulo 3 | Módulo 3 | Acabado | ★★★★ |
| Módulo 4 | Módulo 4 | Acabado | ★★★ |
| Módulo intermedio | Módulo intermedio | Acabado | |
| Módulo 5 | Módulo 5 | Acabado | ★★★ |
| Módulo 6 | Módulo 6 | Empezar | |

**FIGURE 8.6** A Module Chart in the Student Interface.

(85 percent), although only 68 percent thought that they were helpful or very helpful. With regards to the utility of the three help tools (i.e., the lifebuoy, the binoculars, and the magnifying glass), 61 percent of students on average agreed that these tools were useful. Overall, students perceived TuinLEC as easy to use, understandable and quite helpful.

After each study we had informal interviews with participant teachers about their beliefs and attitudes toward TuinLEC. Teachers perceive TuinLEC as easy to use, engaging, and motivating for students. They emphasize the motivational role played by technology, the immediacy of feedback, and TuinLEC's game-like environment as crucial elements.

## Skill Acquisition

The main goal of TuinLEC is to teach task-oriented reading skills to students. We first tested this goal in a study where half of a group of 25 6th graders were trained with TuinLEC out of school hours, whereas the other half performed general activities on their own (e.g., reading books in the school library). The two groups were tested before and after training. The trained group increased their reading literacy skills over the non-trained group (Vidal-Abarca et al., 2014).

In a second study, we wanted to know if the success of TuinLEC could be attributed to the explicit teaching of the four strategies included in the program by means of the virtual agents, their modeling and explanations, or to the deliberate practice plus feedback that TuinLEC includes. To this end, we developed a version of TuinLEC in which the virtual agents and the explicit teaching were removed. So, this version was identical to that described for the second part of TuinLEC in the previous section; that is, it included texts and questions with adapted feedback, plus the help tools. We only included very short instructions for students to understand the goal and structure of the lessons, as well as how to use the help tools. We called this version TuinLEC-Practice. Approximately, one-third of a total group of 114 6th graders were trained with TuinLEC, another third was trained with TuinLEC-Practice, whereas the control group received no training. We found that the two versions of TuinLEC were equally effective (Ramos, 2014), though students trained with the complete version of TuinLEC showed behavior strategies during training more consistent with the training. For instance, students trained with the complete version of TuinLEC read a higher percentage of text initially before moving to questions, and they decided to search the text more often than students that were trained with TuinLEC-Practice. The two trained groups performed better on a reading literacy test in comparison to the control group. Therefore, it seems that practice plus adapted feedback are the key elements to explain the success of TuinLEC. Nonetheless, informal conversations with the students led to further revisions of the agent dialogs, the explanations provided by the virtual teacher, and other elements, leading to the version of TuinLEC used in the following study.

Our third study (Serrano et al., 2015) was aimed at checking if TuinLEC would be more effective for less-skilled comprehenders than for skilled ones, since they need more assistance in their learning due to specific difficulties in task-oriented reading (Cerdán, Gilabert, & Vidal-Abarca, 2011; Vidal-Abarca et al., 2010). Sixty-one 6th and 7th graders were trained with TuinLEC and assessed three times in task-oriented reading: a pretest before being instructed with TuinLEC, a post-test after training with TuinLEC, and a follow-up, two weeks after post-test. We found that students in the posttest improved their scores with regards to the pretest, although the increase did not maintain for the follow-up test. However, we found that less-skilled comprehenders' scores increased in the follow-up test in comparison to the pretest whereas skilled comprehenders showed no gains from pretest to the follow-up test. Therefore, TuinLEC appeared to be particularly effective long term for less-skilled comprehenders.

## Accessing TuinLEC

TuinLEC is web-based and freely available for teachers who wish to use it in their classrooms. To begin using TuinLEC, teachers must register an account and send an email to the Administrator.

To register an account, teachers access http://lectura.uv.es/tuinlec. Once on the welcome screen, teachers click on the registration link (see Figure 8.7) and fill in the registration form. The user (nombre de usuario) and password (contraseña) will be necessary to login later. It should be noted that, since the registration form is the same for students, teachers have to identify their account as a teacher-account by selecting the option *teacher* (*docente*) in the dropdown field *type of account* (*tipo de cuenta*) (see Figure 8.8).

Teachers should then send an email to tuinlec@gmail.com with the subject *TuinLEC user* to receive a comprehensive user's manual. In the body of the message, teachers need to add their TuinLEC user's name and the country where TuinLEC will be used.

All teachers who have a TuinLEC account will have access to the TuinLEC teacher interface. It allows teachers to view their students' progress and interactions within the system's elements, both online and offline. Teachers can find this interface within *monitoring* (*seguimiento*) in the main menu.

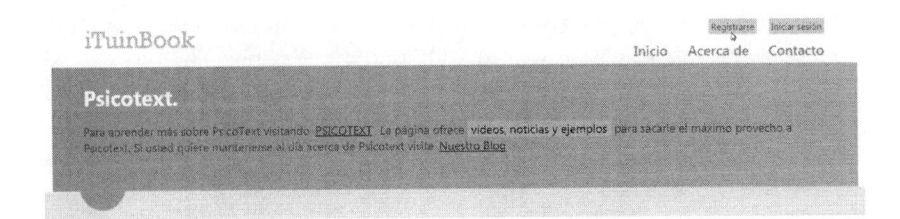

**FIGURE 8.7** Welcome Screen.

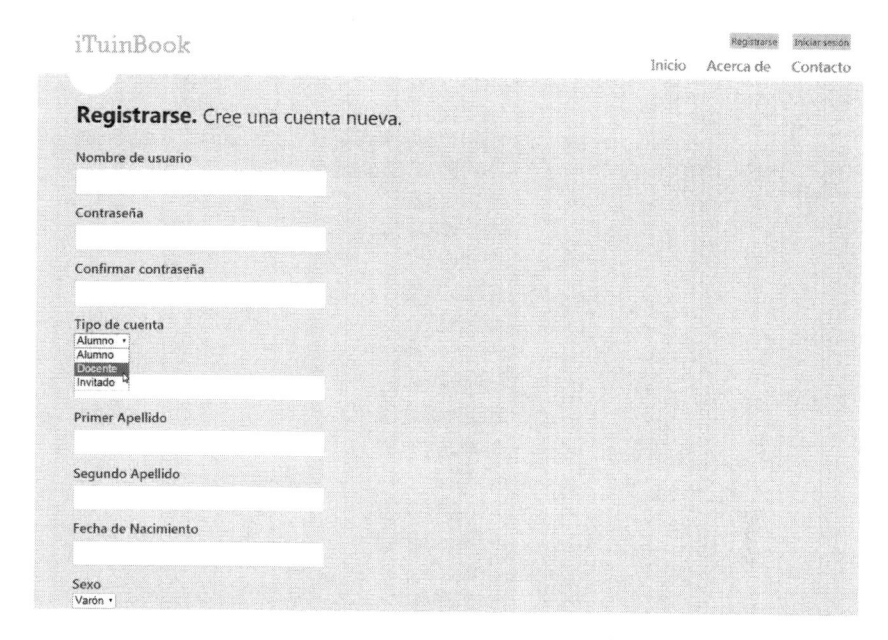

**FIGURE 8.8** Registration Form Showing Dropdown Field "Type of Account".

In the instructional modules, students' progress can be monitored while interacting with the system (see Figure 8.9). This interface provides online information about the percentage of the current module that has been completed, and launches warnings depending on two variables: the time the student spent in every slide or activity, and the number of failures. When the student is interacting with TuinLEC too quickly, the system shows a rocket; whereas a red cross is shown when the student is making lots of mistakes.

The teacher interface also allows teachers to view offline information when a module is completed by the student. The monitoring table of each instructional module shows students' scores, their last login, and the total time spent in the current module. In the practice modules, the monitoring table also shows how many questions were answered after searching the text, after using any help tool, and how many times the student checked the relevant information highlighted in the text after answering a question (see Figure 8.10).

Finally, teachers can view individual detailed information about students' performance on each question in a module. This interface includes the indicators described below (searching decision, using help tools, checking relevant information) as well as the quality of selected information on those questions that required it, and time spent on every question. In addition, the main indicators are displayed in a graphic, which compares the student with the group (see Figure 8.11). All of this information is fully described in the user's manual of TuinLEC.

**FIGURE 8.9** Monitoring Students' Progress.

## Integrating TuinLEC into the Classroom

TuinLEC has been designed to complement not replace the teachers' reading literacy instruction in the last grade of primary school. The first four modules, including the explicit teaching of the four reading literacy strategies, were designed as a supplement to the teacher explicit instruction of these strategies in the classroom, which can lead to a more effective and varied reading literacy instruction. On the other hand, the last four modules, where the students practice the four strategies all together independently, could be used by the teacher as a repository of task-oriented reading activities and as a tool for providing adaptive and formative reading feedback to all students.

Teachers can decide how to integrate TuinLEC in their classrooms; however they may consider a number of recommendations for its implementation. First, the explicit instruction modules must be presented in the same order they appear in the program. The reason for that is that each module includes virtual agents' dialogs that build upon each other. Furthermore, the fourth module includes a summary of all of the content included in the previous modules. Second, each phase must start with its introductory module, which includes specific instructions on the use of the interface that are necessary to ensure a correct understanding of the functioning of the system.

**Menú**

Alumnos
Módulos
Grupos
Feedback
Seguimientos

**Seguimientos - (Ver Todos)**

| Nombre | Usuario | Puntos | Inicio | Tiempo | BUSCA | AYUDA | REVISA | Resp. Bi |
|---|---|---|---|---|---|---|---|---|
| Ainara | CAL6A14 | 1400 | 05/05/2014 10:06:32 | 396,903 | 1 | 0 | 0 | 14 |
| María | CAL6A13 | 1200 | 05/05/2014 10:08:22 | 785,327 | 10 | 0 | 1 | 12 |
| Nerea | CAL6A15 | 1400 | 05/05/2014 10:08:31 | 814,547 | 3 | 0 | 4 | 14 |
| Ester | CAL6A12 | 800 | 05/05/2014 10:08:42 | 878,78 | 13 | 3 | 2 | 8 |
| Elvira | CAL6A22 | 800 | 05/05/2014 10:09:46 | 856,103 | 12 | 0 | 1 | 8 |
| Ferran | CAL6A24 | 1000 | 05/05/2014 10:09:50 | 1008,813 | 12 | 2 | 2 | 10 |
| Alex | CAL6A21 | 900 | 05/05/2014 10:09:56 | 901,26 | 13 | 0 | 4 | 9 |
| Sergi | CAL6A02 | 1100 | 05/05/2014 10:11:33 | 794,087 | 5 | 0 | 7 | 11 |
| Iván | CAL6A08 | 800 | 05/05/2014 10:12:26 | 509,763 | 12 | 0 | 9 | 8 |
| Natalia | CAL6A06 | 1200 | 05/05/2014 10:13:05 | 351,92 | 1 | 0 | 2 | 12 |
| Pau | CAL6A09 | 1100 | 05/05/2014 | 845,52 | 13 | 4 | 0 | 11 |

**FIGURE 8.10** Monitoring Table.

**Menú**

Alumnos
Módulos
Grupos
Feedback
Seguimientos

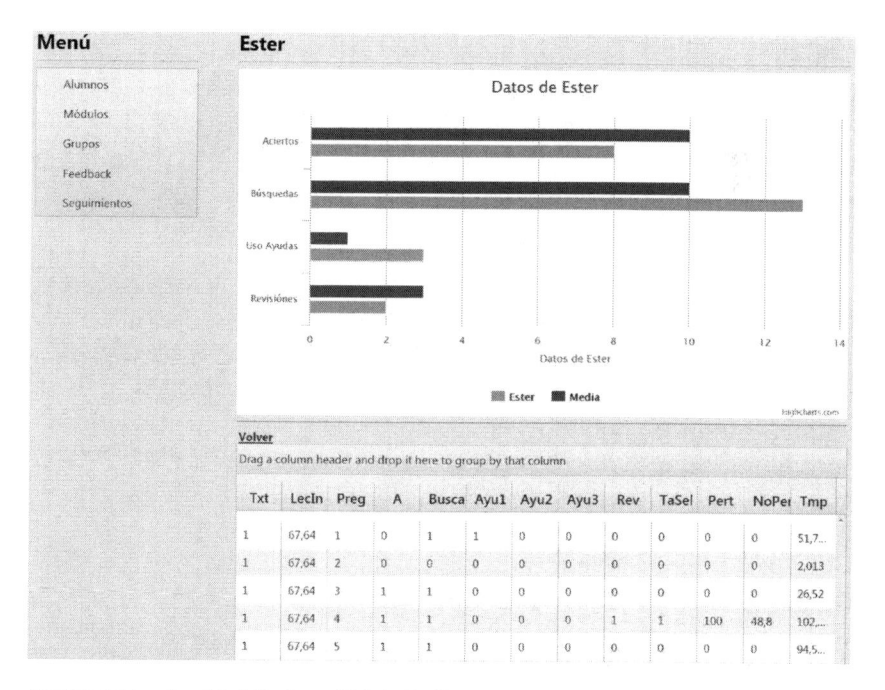

**Ester**

Datos de Ester

(bar chart with categories: Aciertos, Búsquedas, Uso Ayudas, Revisiones; series: Ester, Media; x-axis: Datos de Ester 0–14)

Volver

Drag a column header and drop it here to group by that column

| Txt | LecIn | Preg | A | Busca | Ayu1 | Ayu2 | Ayu3 | Rev | TaSel | Pert | NoPer | Tmp |
|---|---|---|---|---|---|---|---|---|---|---|---|---|
| 1 | 67,64 | 1 | 0 | 1 | 1 | 0 | 0 | 0 | 0 | 0 | 0 | 51,7... |
| 1 | 67,64 | 2 | 0 | 0 | 0 | 0 | 0 | 0 | 0 | 0 | 0 | 2,013 |
| 1 | 67,64 | 3 | 1 | 1 | 0 | 0 | 0 | 0 | 0 | 0 | 0 | 26,52 |
| 1 | 67,64 | 4 | 1 | 1 | 0 | 0 | 0 | 1 | 1 | 100 | 48,8 | 102,... |
| 1 | 67,64 | 5 | 1 | 1 | 0 | 0 | 0 | 0 | 0 | 0 | 0 | 94,5... |

**FIGURE 8.11** Graphic Display of Main Indicators.

The amount of time students should spend in TuinLEC largely depends on the instructional phase. During the explicit instructional phase, where they have to attend to the virtual agents' dialogs and perform several types of tasks, they need about 40 to 50 minutes to complete each module. However, the modules of independent practice usually take less time, being completed in approximately 30 minutes. Obviously, the total amount of time required to complete TuinLEC depends on both the students' pace and the teacher's use of the system. In that sense, the structure of TuinLEC allows teachers to decide either to implement the entire system or to assign specific modules to students based on their specific needs. Finally, as explained above, teachers could decide to either use or not use the teacher interface to follow the progress of each student, obtaining individual information about their performance and reading skills. With this information, they could decide to interact directly with the student at a given moment of the learning process. For instance, they could help the student during the process of answering a set of questions presented in TuinLEC, or they could provide additional explanation or instruction.

## Limitations

One limitation of TuinLEC is that it targets Spanish-speaking students from Spain. Therefore, it is not clear to what extent cultural differences implicit in the text topics, the vocabulary used, the way questions are formulated, the way feedback is provided or the dialogs between the virtual agents are shared and understood by Spanish-speaking students from other countries. TuinLEC has also been designed for students who speak Spanish as a first language. Thus, it is an open question if TuinLEC could also be used for students learning Spanish as a second language.

Another important limitation is the age and skills level for which TuinLEC has been developed, which is related to the general goal of TuinLEC. As we stated previously, TuinLEC was developed as an introductory training to general task-oriented reading skills for students at the end of primary school, but it does not train students in very specific skills (e.g., evaluating sources of conflicting information in a text). A third limitation of the current version of TuinLEC is that it does not incorporate open-ended questions due to the difficulty of automatically scoring these kinds of questions. However, future versions may incorporate an algorithm that we have already successfully implemented in an automatic assessment task-oriented reading test called CompLEC (Gil et al., 2015).

## Conclusions

TuinLEC takes advantage of the common practice of teachers asking students to read texts and answer questions in the classroom. It includes this common practice within a theoretically well-grounded framework providing students with systematic strategies to deal with this global task. At the same time, it expands the kind of texts that students use, including a great variety of continuous and non-continuous texts. Systematic and adaptive feedback and a game environment that helps to sustain motivation and engagement with the task are two additional key features of TuinLEC. The end goal is to increase the students' self-regulation skills in everyday reading activities where students have to use texts with the purpose of understanding and reflection. TuinLEC is just a first step on the way to becoming a skilled reader. Teachers' use of instructional procedures in their classrooms similar to those implemented in TuinLEC can help students to achieve this goal.

## Acknowledgments

The research reported in this chapter has been supported by funding from the Spanish Ministry of Science and Innovation (Grant EDU2011–27091) and Generalitat Valenciana (Grant PROMETEO/2013/081). The opinions expressed are those of the authors and do not represent the views of the funding agencies.

## References

Cataldo, M., & Oakhill, J. (2000). Why are poor comprehenders inefficient searchers? An investigation into the effects of text representation and spatial memory on the ability to locate information in text. *Journal of Educational Psychology, 92*(4), 791–799.

Cerdán R., Gilabert R., & Vidal-Abarca E. (2011). Selecting information to answer questions: Strategic individual differences when searching texts. *Learning and Individual Differences, 21*, 201–205.

Cerdán, R., Vidal-Abarca, E., Martínez, T., Gilabert, R., & Gil. L. (2009). Impact of question-answering tasks on search processes and reading comprehension. *Learning and Instruction, 19*, 13–27.

Duggan, G. B., & Payne, S. J. (2009). Text skimming: the process and effectiveness of foraging through text under time pressure. *Journal of Experimental Psychology: Applied, 15*, 228–242.

Gil, L., Martínez, T., & Vidal-Abarca, E. (2015). On-line assessment of strategic reading literacy skills. *Computers & Education, 82*, 50–59.

Graesser, A. C., Singer, M., & Trabasso, T. (1994). Constructing inferences during narrative text comprehension. *Psychological Review, 101*(3), 371–395.

Hattie, J., & Timperley, H. (2007). The power of feedback. *Review of Educational Research, 77*(1), 81–112.

Kaakinen, J. K., & Hyönä, J. (2005). Perspective effects on expository text comprehension: Evidence from think-aloud protocols, eye-tracking, and recall. *Discourse Processes, 40*(3), 239–257.

Kintsch, W. (1998). *Comprehension: A Paradigm for Cognition*. New York: Cambridge University Press.

Llorens, A. C., Cerdán, R., & Vidal-Abarca, E. (2014). Adaptive formative feedback to improve strategic search decisions in task-oriented reading. *Journal of Computer Assisted Learning, 30*, 233–251.

Llorens A. C., Vidal-Abarca, E., & Cerdán, R. (in press). Formative feedback to transfer self-regulation of task-oriented reading strategies. *Journal of Computer Assisted Learning*.

Mañá, A., Vidal-Abarca, E., Domínguez, C., Gil, L., & Cerdán, R. (2009). Papel de los procesos metacognitivos en una tarea de pregunta-respuesta con textos escritos. The role of metacognitive processes in a question-answering task with written texts. *Infancia y Aprendizaje, 32*(4), 553–565.

McCrudden, M. T., & Schraw, G. (2007). Relevance and goal-focusing in text processing. *Educational Psychology Review, 19*, 113–139.

Narciss, S. (2004). The impact of informative tutoring feedback and self-efficacy on motivation and achievement in concept learning. *Experimental Psychology, 51*(3), 214–228.

Ness, M. (2011). Explicit reading comprehension instruction in elementary classrooms: Teacher use of reading comprehension strategies. *Journal of Research in Childhood Education, 25*(1), 98–117.

OECD (2008). *PISA 2009 Assessment framework: Key competencies in reading, mathematics and science*. Retrieved from http://www.oecd.org/

Ramos, L. (2014) Enseñanza y aprendizaje de la competencia lectora en grados medios mediante el tutor inteligente TuinLEC (Teaching and learning of reading literacy in middle school grades with the Intelligent Tutoring System TuinLEC). (Unpublished doctoral dissertation). University of Valencia, Spain.

Rouet, J. F. (2006). *The Skills of Document Use: From Text Comprehension to Web-Based Learning*. Mahwah, NJ: Lawrence Erlbaum.

Rouet, J. F., & Coutelet, B. (2008). The acquisition of document search strategies in grade school students. *Applied Cognitive Psychology, 22*(3), 389–406.

Serrano, M. A., Vidal-Abarca, E., Máñez, I., Mañá, A., Gil, L., Gilabert, R., & Ávila, V. (2015, July). *Effects of an Intervention with TuinLECweb on Reading Literacy Skills in Good and Poor Comprehenders*. Poster presented at the 16th Biannual EARLI Conference for Research on Learning and Instruction, Limassol, Cyprus.

Shute, V. J. (2008). Focus on formative feedback. *Review of Educational Research, 78*(1), 153–189.

Vidal-Abarca, E., Mañá, A., & Gil, L. (2010). Individual differences for self-regulating task-oriented reading activities. *Journal of Educational Psychology, 102*(4), 817–826.

Vidal-Abarca, E., Martínez, T., Salmerón, L., Cerdán, R., Gilabert, R., Gil, L., Ferris, R. (2011). Recording on-line processes in task-oriented reading with Read&Answer. *Behavior Research Methods, 43*, 179–192.

Vidal-Abarca, E., Gilabert, R., Ferrer, A., Ávila, V., Martínez, T., Mañá, A., . . . Serrano, M. A. (2014). TuinLEC, an intelligent tutoring system to improve reading literacy skills. *Infancia y Aprendizaje, 37*(1), 25–56.

White, S., Chen, J., & Forsyth, B. (2010). Reading-related literacy activities of American adults: Time spent, task types, and cognitive skills used. *Journal of Literacy Research, 42*(3), 276–307.

# PART II
# Writing Technologies for the Classroom

This part contains chapters that focus on providing students with deliberate practice, individualized feedback, and strategy instruction for writing. The purpose of these chapters is to inform the reader of what type of writing instruction tools exist and how they can be used to improve students' writing quality. There are many systems in the commercial sector that provide students with writing practice and feedback. Hence, this part begins with a chapter that provides an overview of many of the available commercialized systems. Each of the chapters that follow describes systems that differ in their specific functionalities, but also share some form of writing practice, scoring, and feedback. The feedback can vary widely between systems, ranging from more basic feedback regarding spelling and grammar to more complex feedback on higher-level components of language and style. The independent functionalities of each system include scaffolded instruction and practice, opportunities for revision, conventions for specific writing tasks, as well as opportunities to facilitate peer review.

# 9
# COMMERCIALIZED WRITING SYSTEMS

*Laura K. Allen and Cecile A. Perret*

This chapter provides an overview of the most common computer-based writing instruction systems that are currently commercially available. These systems vary considerably in their specific properties, but share a few key components. All of these systems utilize automated essay scoring (AES) engines to assign scores to essays, and all of them provide students with some form of feedback on their writing. This feedback can range from the detection of lower-level spelling and grammar errors to higher-level components related to rhetorical language use.

In the chapter, we briefly discuss the primary skills targeted by these systems, as well as the need for computer-based writing technologies in the classroom. We then provide an overview of the key components of these systems, as well as the accuracy and reliability of the scoring systems. The majority of the chapter is devoted to descriptions of the systems. These descriptions provide information about the general components of the systems and describe where teachers can go to obtain access to the systems. Finally, the chapter closes with a brief section on the future directions of these computer-based writing systems.

## The Need for Computer-Based Writing Instruction

An important aspect of contemporary education is students' development of strong writing skills (Powell, 2009). Critically, the production of high-quality writing requires students to have mastered a complex array of skills, the success of which primarily depends on the instruction and feedback that is provided to students. Past writing research indicates that this proficiency is best promoted via deliberate practice and individualized feedback (Ericsson, Krampe, & Tesch-Römer, 1993; Johnstone, Ashbaugh, & Warfield, 2002; Kellogg & Raulerson, 2007). Unfortunately, however, the curricula developed to meet these goals are exceedingly challenging to implement within classrooms due to the time required from teachers, particularly regarding reading and providing individualized feedback on students' essays. Teachers today are faced with larger class sizes than ever before and, therefore, do not have the time that is necessary to read and process large quantities of student essays (National Commission on Writing, 2004).

Computer-based systems for writing assessment and instruction have been developed to help ease some of the burden on teachers, while providing students with opportunities for deliberate writing practice (Allen, Jacovina, & McNamara, 2015; Shermis & Burstein, 2003, 2013). The purposes and specific features of these systems vary considerably, from simply providing automated scores of students' essays to assigning strategy-based formative feedback (Dikli, 2006; Graesser & McNamara, 2012; Roscoe, Allen, Weston, Crossley, & McNamara, 2014; Weigle, 2013; Xi, 2010). The majority of research conducted on these computer-based writing systems has focused on the assessment of the *accuracy* of the automated scores assigned to students' essays. However, researchers and system developers have recently begun to investigate the efficacy of these systems to provide students with formative feedback and explicit instruction on the writing process (Roscoe & McNamara, 2013; Roscoe et al., 2011).

## AES Systems

The most commonly used computer-based writing tools are AES systems. These technologies are the engines that calculate automated scores for students' essays (McNamara et al., 2015; Shermis & Barrera, 2002; Shermis & Burstein, 2003, 2013). These systems have been largely successful at calculating accurate essay scores, and have therefore enabled writing teachers to assign deliberate writing practice to students more frequently without increasing their own workload (Dikli, 2006; Page, 2003; Shermis & Burstein, 2003; 2013). Additionally, large-scale testing services frequently utilize these AES systems to help score the writing components of high-stakes standardized assessments (e.g., the GRE). Notably, these systems do not provide students with any sort of formative feedback, neither do they contain any explicit writing instruction. The singular purpose of these systems is to assign valid and reliable scores to essays in a cost- and time-effective manner (Bereiter, 2003; Myers, 2003; Page, 2003).

## Automated Writing Evaluation Systems

Automated writing evaluation (AWE) systems have been developed as extensions of typical AES systems and provide students with feedback on their writing (Crossley, Varner, Roscoe, & McNamara, 2013; Grimes & Warschauer, 2010; see Allen et al., 2015 for an overview). These systems are most notably beneficial to students, because they provide opportunities for *deliberate practice* along with *formative feedback*—all without any input from the instructor. The AES elements of these computer-based writing systems calculate the scores on the essays; however, the AWE elements extend these engines by providing instruction and feedback to students, as well as classroom management features for teachers (e.g., downloadable reports).

AWE systems promote deliberate practice and formative feedback in order to provide students with opportunities to improve their writing and better understand *why* they receive the essay scores that they do. Unfortunately, teachers do not have the time to provide individualized, formative feedback to each student on multiple writing assignments. Thus, computer-based writing systems have been expanded to provide supplements to traditional classroom instruction (Roscoe et al., 2014). In the case of these AWE systems, students have the ability to practice essay writing and receive feedback that is specific to many of the problems displayed in their essays (Foltz, Rosenstein, Dronen, & Dooley, 2014). Further, students can then take this immediate feedback and revise their essays without having to wait for feedback from their teachers (Roscoe et al., 2011; Roscoe, Varner, Crossley, & McNamara, 2013; Shute, 2008).

One of the most beneficial characteristics of these AWE systems is that they have the ability to provide accurate and *formative* feedback on students' essays (Foltz et al., 2014). Due to the considerable effort required from teachers to provide helpful essay feedback and direct students to helpful practice activities based on this feedback, AWE systems can be extremely beneficial supplements in the classroom. In fact, a recent meta-analysis by Graham, Hebert, and Harris (in press) revealed positive benefits of computer-based writing assessments on students' writing performance. Specifically, this analysis examined the benefit of formative assessments that were directly tied to information taught in the classroom. The study revealed that the delivery of feedback to students from computers significantly enhanced the quality of their writing, yielding an average weighted effect size of 0.38. Overall, these findings indicate that computer-based writing systems have the capacity to help foster improvements in students' writing, given that they can provide formative feedback that is directly tied to instruction.

A key benefit of these computer-based writing instruction systems is the automation of the feedback delivery. Receiving immediate feedback from a computer system can help students more readily to identify their strengths and weaknesses in writing, while keeping them more engaged in the writing process (Gikandi, Morrow, & Davis, 2011). In the classroom, students typically receive feedback on a longer delay, often once they have already moved on to new assignments. As a result, they are less likely to be engaged and attentive to the contents of the feedback (Frey & Fisher, 2013).

There are a number of AWE systems that have been developed for use within writing classrooms. Some of these systems have been developed by writing researchers and are freely available (see Chapters 10-14 in this book for examples), whereas others have been developed by not-for-profit and for-profit companies and are available for a fee. In the remainder of this chapter, we will focus on those computer-based systems that are commercially available for writing instruction and feedback. In other words, we will discuss the systems that were specifically developed by companies that are *for-profit*. For information on the systems that are developed by researchers and other not-for-profit companies (e.g., the Criterion system developed by ETS, see Chapter 10), see the more through descriptions in the chapters contained in this book (Chapters 10-14). We will provide brief overviews of the systems and describe both the student and teacher features implemented within these systems.

## Commercialized Writing Systems

### MyAccess!

MyAccess! (https://www.myaccess.com/myaccess/do/log) is a web-based writing instruction program that was developed by Vantage Learning to provide students in grade 4 through college with opportunities for deliberate writing practice. Specifically, this program aims to improve the quality of students' narrative, persuasive, informative, literary, and expository essays by providing automated feedback, along with support for multiple phases of the writing process. The feedback provided by MyAccess! includes both holistic and analytical essay scores. The analytic essay scores cover six distinct features related to essay quality: focus and meaning, content and development, organization, language, use and style, mechanics and conventions (Vantage Learning, 2007). Within MyAccess!, students are also able to receive essay feedback in Spanish or Chinese if permitted by the teacher (Dikli, 2006; Vantage Learning, 2007).

The automated scores provided by MyAccess! are driven by the IntelliMetric scoring engine (Rudner, Garcia, & Welch, 2006). IntelliMetric employs a blend of artificial intelligence, natural language processing (NLP), and statistical techniques to assign holistic and analytical scores to students' essays across a variety of different writing prompts (Dikli, 2006; Elliot, 2003; Shermis & Barrera, 2002; Vantage Learning, 2000, 2003). At the high school level, IntelliMetric's scoring engine has an exact agreement with human raters, ranging from 69 percent to 85 percent of the time, and adjacent agreement (i.e., scores are within one point of each other) 100 percent of the time. These exact agreement scores are similar for the upper elementary school level (69 percent to 83 percent), middle school level (62 percent to 86 percent), and higher education level (63 percent to 90 percent). Across a wide variety of different prompts included in the MyAccess! system, IntelliMetric achieves an average exact agreement of 76 percent (Vantage Learning, 2006).

### Student system features

The student version of MyAccess! provides students with access to pre-writing activities, as well as sample essays that students can use to guide their own writing. The purpose of these activities and materials is to give students clear objectives and criteria for how to succeed on particular writing assignments (Vantage Learning, 2007). Additionally, during the writing process, students have access to a number of different tools, including: a writer's checklist, scoring rubric for self-assessment, grammatical advice and corrections, word counter, word bank, spell checker, and pre-writing tools (e.g., Venn diagrams) to help with idea organization.

In addition to these writing supports, students receive automated feedback on their essays immediately after submitting their essay or a revision of a previous essay (Vantage Learning, 2007). Finally, MyAccess! provides students with access to an online portfolio of their writing practice. These portfolios contain their essay drafts, the scores they have received, their revisions, teacher comments, journal entries, and feedback.

## Teacher system features

The teacher version of MyAccess! allows teachers to create essay assignments for their students and to access their students' writing portfolios. When creating assignments, teachers can choose the prompts, tools, and scores that will be available to their students. They have access to over 700 prompts, which cover a multitude of topics in areas of science, math, and social studies and include narrative, persuasive, informative, literary, and expository genres. Teachers are also given the freedom to create their own prompts if they choose. Teachers additionally have access to students' writing portfolios in MyAccess! (Vantage Learning, 2007). These portfolios allow teachers to view students' average essay scores, as well as how these scores have changed over time and specific essay components that individual students are struggling with.

## System effectiveness

Previous research with MyAccess! suggests that the system can help to improve the essay scores of students across a range of grade levels. In one study, Grimes and Warschauer (2010) examined the use of the system in middle schools across three school years. The teachers reported that the students who used the system wrote essays more often, demonstrated more independence in their development of writing skills, and were more motivated to persist in practice.

## WriteToLearn

WriteToLearn (http://www.writetolearn.net/) is a web-based literacy tutor developed by the educational company, Pearson, to enhance both the reading comprehension and writing skills of students in grades 4 to 12. Specifically, WriteToLearn contains a reading comprehension component (Summary Street) and an essay practice component (Intelligent Essay Assessor), which both provide students with automated feedback on their practice, as well as opportunities to revise their work (Landauer, Lochbaum, & Dooley, 2009).

Summary Street helps students to improve their reading comprehension skills by teaching them summarization techniques. In this system, students read texts and are asked to produce summaries of what they have read. Once students have completed their summaries, they receive automated feedback on the quality of their summaries in relation to the text they have read. This feedback is based on the students' use of correct grammar, as well as the relevance of the summary to the original text.

The Intelligent Essay Assessor helps students to improve their writing skills by providing them with opportunities to engage in deliberate writing practice. Once students have submitted an essay to the system, they are provided with a holistic score on their writing, and specific scores on six common aspects of essay writing: ideas, organization, conventions, sentence fluency, word choice, and voice. Additionally, students are provided with feedback on their spelling and grammar accuracy, as well as whether they were being repetitive in their language (Pearson Education, 2011). This system uses the Knowledge Analysis Technology (KAT) engine to evaluate the meaning, coherence, and relevance of texts, in addition to the correctness of the spelling and grammar (Pearson Education, 2009).

## Student system features

The student version of WriteToLearn contains opportunities for students to write essays and text summaries. Within this interface, students can write essays and summaries, receive automated feedback, and engage in revision activities (Landauer et al., 2009). Importantly, within the system, students are provided with advice and hints for producing better essays. Additionally, the system offers personalized vocabulary instruction that relates to domain-specific and academic language use to scaffold students through the reading comprehension and writing processes.

## Teacher system features

In the teacher version of WriteToLearn, teachers have the opportunity to select texts for their students to read from topics in science, social studies and history. Additionally, teachers have access to the essays and summaries produced by their students, along with their feedback and progress over multiple sessions. Teachers can then use this information to provide different assignments to students at different proficiency levels. Teachers also have the capability to modify scoring thresholds, expected response lengths, and spelling and grammar check options. Within this interface, teachers receive graphical reports that detail the progress of individual students, as well as for complete classes (Landauer et al., 2009).

## System effectiveness

Previous research with WriteToLearn suggests that the system can help to improve the reading comprehension and writing skills of students (Landauer et al., 2009). The results of one study (Franzke, Kintsch, Caccamise, Johnson, & Dooley, 2005), for instance, revealed that students in the 50th percentile on their writing skills were able to increase their essays scores to reflect the scores of students in the 82nd percentile (Caccamise, Franzke, Eckhoff, Kintsch & Kintsch, 2007; Franzke et al., 2005). Additionally, Landauer and colleauges (2009) revealed that students' reading comprehension and writing skills increased after only two weeks of practice with the WriteToLearn system.

## Prentice Hall Writing Coach

The Prentice Hall Writing Coach (http://www.pearsonschool.com/index.cfm?locator=PSZpO2) is an adaptive writing curriculum developed by Pearson to provide students in grades 6 to 12 with practice and instruction on argumentative, informative, and narrative writing. This system specifically provides instruction on writing and grammar and contains four different types of writing prompts for practice: progress monitoring prompts, feature assignment prompts, writing for assessment prompts, and teacher-entered prompts. Importantly, the system provides students with personalized coaching and feedback at the paragraph and essay levels. Feedback in the Prentice Hall Writing Coach includes strategy information, as well as grammar instruction and remediation. Importantly, the Writing Coach is also sold in multiple formats (i.e., text, online, or a combination of the two). However, the interactive instruction and assessment are only available through the online version of the system.

## Student system features

Within the student version of the Prentice Hall Writing Coach, students have the opportunity to produce essays and receive feedback on these essays at both the essay and paragraph level. The system provides ratings for three specific aspects of the essay paragraphs: topic focus, topic development, and organization. In addition to this paragraph-level feedback, students also receive feedback on the sentence variety within their essays (length, structure, etc.), word choice (e.g., vague adjectives, repeated words), and mechanics (spelling and grammar). The holistic essay feedback in the system is provided on either a 4 or 6 point scale (decided by the teacher) and students receive feedback scores on six components of their essay: ideas, organization, conventions, sentence fluency, word choice, and voice. The Writing Coach gives students tips on how they can specifically improve these six components of their essays. In addition to the automated feedback, the Writing Coach also contains a number of writing supports to help students during the writing process, such as personalized instructional modules and game-based grammar practice.

### Teacher system features

The teacher version of the Writing Coach allows teachers to plan writing assignments and assign personalized practice to their students. Specifically, the system contains features that allow teachers to set individual learner levels that can be automatically updated based on the students' performance within the system. Additionally, the system contains components that help teachers to customize lesson plans and assessments based on the performance of students in their classes. Finally, the teacher version of the system contains graphical reports that allow teachers to view results and track the progress of the students within their classes.

### System effectiveness

There is currently no publically available information on the effectiveness of this system.

## Writing Roadmap

The Writing Roadmap (https://www.writingroadmap.com/) is a web-based writing tool that was developed to provide students in grades 3 and above (through adult language learners) with the opportunity to engage in deliberate practice on their persuasive, informative, expository, narrative, and argumentative writing. Writing Roadmap prompts students to write essays based on short essay assignments and reading passages that have been validated in previous studies. These assignments cover five separate genres; additionally, teachers have the ability to create their own writing prompts for students to respond to (White, Hixson, & Whisman, 2011).

The scores assigned to students' essays in Writing Roadmap are calculated using the Mosaic™ AES engine that has been developed to assign essay scores that correspond to students' specific grade levels. These scores are reported automatically and the system provides students with guidelines for improving their essays based on these scores. Additionally, the system provides teachers with information about their students' writing performance in order to benefit their instruction. Prior studies have indicated that the scores assigned by the Writing Roadmap match essay scores assigned by expert human raters (Li, 2014).

### Student system features

Within the student version of the Writing Roadmap system, students have the ability to write and receive feedback on their essays. Specifically, students can

Commercialized Writing Systems **153**

receive two different forms of feedback on their writing. The Writing Narrative report calculates essay quality on a three-point scale and provides information about five writing traits: organization, development, sentence structure, word choice/grammar use, and mechanics. The second report is the Writing Traits report, which is a color-coded chart that shows students' scores on each writing dimension and provides a narrative explanation of the score based on the scoring rubric. Within this report, students can see the word count of their essays, as well as the assigned holistic and analytic scores for their essays.

## Teacher system features

The teacher version of Writing Roadmap allows teachers to select specific writing assignments based on a large library of writing prompts and reading passages (n = 111). These prompts cover five separate writing genres (i.e., persuasive, informative, expository, narrative, and argumentative). Teachers also have the option of generating their own writing prompts. In addition to creating assignments, teachers have the ability to generate reports based on their students' performance. These reports can be customized by the teacher to include a variety of different types of information about students' writing performance based on the automated scores. Teachers can also customize the interface of the Writing Roadmap. For instance, they can determine whether students have predetermined sections of their essays (e.g., title, introduction section) or have one response section. Additionally, teachers can determine whether their students have access to specific instructional tools, such as hints or the thesaurus. Finally, the teacher interface allows teachers to review, rescore, or provide comments on students' essays.

## System effectiveness

Previous research suggests that the Writing Roadmap system is effective at increasing students' writing skills. Specifically, studies have shown that students who interacted with the system had increased average scores on the state summative writing test in West Virginia. Further, this system was shown to be more effective for students with lower writing skills. Finally, studies have shown that teachers who have used the Writing Roadmap typically rate that they are highly satisfied with the system (average satisfaction rating of 82 percent; Rich, Harrington, Kim, & West, 2008).

## Project Essay Grade (PEG)

The PEG system (http://www.pegwriting.com) is a web-based writing program that was developed to enable students in grades 3 to 12 to improve their writing skills at their own pace. Specifically, this program provides writing practice for three genres: narrative, informative, and argumentative writing. Within the PEG online system, users have access to writing prompts, writing organizers, writing portfolios, and interactive tutorials, along with automated scoring and feedback on their work (see http://pegwriting.com/about for more information).

The automated scores in the PEG online system are driven by the PEG AES engine. PEG was the first AES scoring engine developed (Shermis, Burstein, Higgins, & Zechner, 2010), and uses correlational analyses to model the holistic quality of submitted essays (Chung & O'Neil, 1997; Dikli, 2006; Kukich, 2000; Rudner & Gagne, 2001). Previous research with the PEG scoring engine has revealed that the automated scores calculated by PEG are similar to essay scores assigned by expert human raters (Chung & O'Neil, 1997). The primary focus of PEG is on surface-level features of essays (as opposed to semantic or rhetorical language features); therefore, the system does not provide instructional feedback to students (Chung & O'Neil, 1997; Kukich, 2000).

## Student system features

The student version of PEG contains writing prompts, supports for the writing process, automated feedback, instructional materials, as well as a peer review component. The prompts in PEG are categorized as narrative, informative, or argumentative and relate to a diversity of stimulus materials, including videos, images, and news articles. Additionally, each science prompt conforms to "next generation" science standards. Some of the prompts are also accompanied by additional reading passages, web links, and videos that students can reference within their essays. In addition to these writing prompts, PEG provides students with access to graphic organizers to help them with the pre-writing process. Once students have written their essays, they receive feedback on their overall writing quality, as well as the essay quality along six dimensions: organization, development, language/style, conventions, word choice, and sentence structure. They then also have the option of engaging with multiple tutorials and training activities that are related to the feedback they have received. Finally, student users of PEG can request a peer review at any time during the revision process from other members of their group. The essay reviewers then read and assess the essay using a "Two Stars and a Wish" method, which requires reviewers to comment on two areas of strength for the essay and one area that could use improvement.

## Teacher system features

The teacher version of PEG allows teachers to add their own writing prompts to the system, provide specific feedback on students' essays, and view student progress reports and writing portfolios. Teachers can create multiple types of assignments for their students, such as tests, assignments, essays, or team research projects.

Additionally, they have control over multiple features related to these assignments, including the number of revisions allowed, the availability of spelling and grammar feedback, and essay time limits. In addition to creating individual assignments for their students, teachers can also organize peer review assignments. In this system module, teachers first organize groups of students by either specifying which students should belong in each group, or through a "randomize" option. They can then monitor their students' reviews and edit the comments as needed. This feature allows multiple teachers to provide feedback on students' essays, which allows them to work together to teach the curriculum content.

Finally, teachers have the option of viewing students' progress in the form of portfolios that contain system content and progress reports. The essays that students generate in the system, along with any system, teacher, and peer feedback are recorded and compiled to form a portfolio that teachers and students can review. Specifically, the portfolios include: a list of completed essays, a list of all messages exchanged between the teacher and student, a holistic and an analytical score for each essay, a monthly average report, and a progress report in the form of a bar graph. This progress report illustrates students' monthly performance averages and a lesson activity report reveals how much time students have spent on lessons, exercises, and pre-writing activities.

## *System effectiveness*

There are few research studies investigating PEG as an effective instructional tool. However, the efficacy of the PEG essay scoring engine (the AES system) has been supported by a number of research studies (Page, 2003; Page & Peterson, 1995; Shermis, Mzumara, Lillig, Brown, 1997). In one of the first studies investigating the efficacy of AES engines, Page and Peterson (1995) identified a high correlation between the scores produced by the PEG scoring engine and the scores assigned by expert human raters. Additionally, researchers have investigated the PEG system's performance with respect to assigning accurate grades and feedback. In these studies, they have found that PEG scores are comparable to human raters and the system provides feedback similar to other AES engines (Shermis & Burstein, 2003).

## *LightSide Revision Assistant*

The LightSide Revision Assistant (RA) is a web-based computer program that provides automatic writing support to middle and high school students (https://www.revisionassistant.com/#/). This system was specifically developed to target writing improvements on the following genres: narrative, persuasive, informative, literary, and expository. The primary emphasis of this system is on the delivery of *formative feedback* (as opposed to grammar and spelling feedback) that can prompt better discussions between students and teachers. Within the LightSide

RA system, students have the ability to request feedback on their writing *during* the writing process, as well as once it has been completed. Importantly, the feedback provided by this system was developed to model the behavior of real writing teachers and provides personalized feedback that includes both positive and constructive comments.

The LightSide RA feedback is powered by the LightSide scoring engine. This system employs machine-learning approaches to analyze essays in a *prompt-specific* manner. This means that the system cannot assess essays that are unrelated to prompts that have been previously entered into the system. The rationale behind this feature of the LightSide RA system is that the system can place an emphasis on the content and objectives of the essay, rather than simply linguistic markers of strong writing. Thus, rather than primarily providing surface-level feedback (e.g., spelling or grammar), LightSide RA can report on rhetorical and content-level features of students' essays (Latifi et al., 2013).

## Student system features

In the student version of LightSide RA, students can write essays and receive both holistic and localized feedback on these essays. The holistic feedback provided to students is sorted into four primary components: clarity, evidence, language, and development. These feedback categories are visualized as "Wi-Fi" signals, and students are assigned a rating on a four-point scale that corresponds to the "Wi-Fi" signal. Thus, concurrent with Wi-Fi signals, the more signals that students receive on each component, the higher their score on that essay component. In addition to these holistic ratings, students' essays are also highlighted in key areas, and the system provides comments along the side of the essay. Specifically, LightSide RA highlights sentences that contain particularly strong examples of writing (illustrated by a green checkmark in the comments) or weak examples of writing (indicated by a red flag in the comments).

## Teacher system features

Within the teacher version of the LightSide RA system, teachers are able to create assignments and view their students' writing progress. The system contains a library of prompts that teachers can choose to assign to their students. These prompts cover topics related to the persuasive, narrative, and expository genres. Some of the prompts require source-based evidence, and others follow more typical standardized test format. Teachers can also review their students' essay drafts, as well as their final submissions to the system. Along with these essay submissions, teachers can view each student's feedback, as well as any requests for feedback that have been made. Finally, teachers have the ability to comment on students' essays, download grade reports for groups of students, as well as for individual students.

## System effectiveness

Previous research studies have demonstrated the reliability and validity of the LightSide system to score student essays. For instance, in a previous research study, Mayfield and Rose (2013) revealed that the agreement between the LightSide system and a human rater exceeded the agreement of eight other commercially available writing systems (Mayfield & Rose, 2013). Additionally, the system was highly accurate at predicting human scores, and the agreement between LightSide and an individual human rater tended to be higher than two human raters together.

## Discussion

Writing is a complex skill that is often extremely difficult for students to master. Previous research suggests that the best method for developing these writing skills is for students to engage in repeated deliberate practice along with formative feedback (Kellogg & Raulerson, 2007). Unfortunately, teachers often do not have the time to provide individualized feedback on all of their students' writing assignments. Therefore, computer-based writing systems have been developed to supplement writing instruction in the classroom. In this chapter, we have provided an overview of the types of systems available for classroom use, including AES engines and AWE systems. Additionally, we have provided overviews for the most common commercially available computer-based writing systems. Importantly, all of the described systems are currently available for classroom use and include supplementary information to help teachers get started using the systems.

One important point to note about these systems is that they are not intended to replace classroom instructors. It has never been the case that the feedback or instructional materials provided by these systems were intended to take the place of teacher feedback or writing instruction from within the classroom. Rather, these systems are intended to provide supplementary help for students and teachers, because the skills required to produce high-quality writing often necessitate repeated practice to master. Indeed, previous studies have shown that the feedback provided by these computer-based writing systems is most effective when directly tied to classroom instruction (Graham et al., in press). Thus, our overall aim in this chapter is to provide teachers with an overview of the aims of these systems, as well as multiple options for systems that can be easily adopted in the classroom, with the hope that these systems will be able to provide much needed support for the teaching of writing skills.

A final note is that, despite their significant benefits, computer-based writing systems are not without their limitations. Specifically, there are a couple of primary issues that should be discussed and considered before implementing these systems within a classroom. The first issue relates to problems with *access* to the systems.

Computer-based writing systems are typically web-based and, by definition, always delivered on computers. Although access to computers and the internet is becoming more prevalent, it should not be taken as a given fact that students will have access to computers at their homes. In those circumstances where students do not have their own computers, teachers may have to set aside time after school when students have access to computers, so that they can complete their homework assignments. Additionally, if a teacher wants to have students access the systems during classroom time, they may have to reserve the computer lab at school, or request to borrow laptops. Although many of these access issues can be solved quite easily, they are still important to consider when developing curriculum and considering how the systems will be integrated into the classroom environment.

An additional limitation and consideration of these commercialized writing systems is that they are typically developed with a very specific audience in mind. For instance, many of the systems have been designed for a particular grade band (e.g., grades 9 to 12) or for students with specific language skills (e.g., native speakers of English). As a result, widespread implementation of these systems in school districts can sometimes be difficult. Teachers must keep in mind that these systems may not be effective for particular audiences and, in these cases, they may need to provide students with additional support and scaffolding.

Finally, given the availability and effectiveness of these other systems, an important consideration and limitation of commercialized instructional systems relates to their cost. In contrast to most systems developed in academic settings (see systems described in Chapters 10-14 of this book), commercial writing systems require a fee to be used in the classroom. Typically, this fee is associated with the fact that these systems have a higher likelihood of being maintained over a longer period of time (as opposed to grant-funded research systems). Thus, for some teachers, this fee may be an acceptable option. Depending on the resources of a particular school or district, however, these fees may present significant issues. In these cases, teachers may wish to work with an academic research team to implement open-source instructional tools in their classrooms. For example, the Writing Pal is an intelligent tutoring system that was developed by researchers to provide explicit writing strategy instruction and practice (see Chapter 12). Because this system is still in its testing phase, it is freely available for schools to use. Additionally, teachers have the opportunity to provide critical feedback on the system that can be used to inform future system developments. Overall, although these systems may still be in the earlier development phases, the teachers will have access to the system that is free of cost and, in many cases, they will have the ability to request changes to the systems and be actively engaged in the development process.

## Conclusion

Overall, automated writing systems can have a positive impact on classroom effectiveness by providing students with additional opportunities to receive writing instruction and engage in deliberate practice. In this chapter, we have provided brief overviews of the most commonly used *commercialized* writing systems, which have been developed by "for-profit" companies and, thus, require a fee to use. Throughout the rest of this book, there are a number of chapters (see Chapters 10-14) that describe automated writing systems developed by researchers and "not-for-profit" companies. For instance, Criterion is one of the most widely used AWE systems currently available and was developed by Educational Testing Services (ETS; see Chapter X) to provide students with computerized writing instruction and practice. Additionally, the Writing Pal provides strategy-based writing instruction, as well as writing practice with summative and formative feedback (see Chapter 12).

## References

Allen, L. K., Jacovina, M. E., & McNamara, D. S. (2015). Computer-based writing instruction. In C. A. MacArthur, S. Graham, & J. Fitzgerald (Eds.), *Handbook of Writing Research* (pp. 316–329). New York: The Guilford Press.

Bereiter, C. (2003). Automated essay scoring's coming-of-age. In M. D. Shermis & J. Burstein (Eds.), *Automated Essay Scoring: A Cross-Disciplinary Approach*. Mahwah, NJ: Lawrence Erlbaum Associates.

Caccamise, D., Franzke, M., Eckhoff, A., Kintsch, E., & Kintsch, W. (2007). Guided practice in technology-based summary writing. In D. S. McNamara (Ed.), *Reading Comprehension Strategies: Theories, Interventions, and Technologies* (pp. 375–396). Mahwah, NJ: Erlbaum.

Chung, K. W. K. & O'Neil, H. F. (1997). Methodological approaches to online scoring of essays (ERIC reproduction service no ED 418 101).

Crossley, S. A., Varner, L. K., Roscoe, R. D., & McNamara, D. S. (2013). Using automated cohesion indices as a measure of writing growth in intelligent tutoring systems and automated essay writing systems. In K. Yacef et al. (Eds.), *Proceedings of the 16th International Conference on Artificial Intelligence in Education (AIED)*, (pp. 269–278). Berlin and Heidelberg, Germany: Springer.

Dikli, S. (2006). An overview of automated scoring of essays. *Journal of Technology, Learning, and Assessment, 5*, 3–35.

Elliot, S. (2003). IntelliMetricTM: From here to validity. In M. D. Shermis & J. C. Burstein (Eds.), *Automated Essay Scoring: A Cross-Disciplinary Perspective* (pp. 71–86). Mahwah, NJ: Lawrence Erlbaum.

Ericsson, K. A., Krampe, R. T., & Tesch-Römer, C. (1993). The role of deliberate practice in the acquisition of expert performance. *Psychological Review, 100*, 363–406.

Foltz, P. W., Rosenstein, M., Dronen, N., & Dooley, S. (2014, March). *Automated Feedback in a Large-Scale Implementation of a Formative Writing System: Implications for Improving Student Writing*. Paper presented at the 2014 meeting of the American Educational Research Association.

Franzke, M., Kintsch, E., Caccamise, D., Johnson, N., & Dooley, S. (2005). Summary Street®: Computer support for comprehension and writing. *Journal of Educational Computing Research, 33*, 53–80.

Frey, N., & Fisher, D. (2013). A formative assessment system for writing improvement. *English Journal, 103*, 66–71.

Gikandi, J. W., Morrow, D., & Davis, N. E. (2011). Online formative assessment in higher education: A review of the literature. *Computers & Education, 57*, 2333–2351.

Graesser, A. C., & McNamara, D. S. (2012). Reading instruction: Technology-based supports for classroom instruction. In C. Dede & J. Richards (Eds.), *Digital Teaching Platforms: Customizing Classroom Learning for Each Student* (pp. 71–87). New York: Teachers College Press.

Graham, S., Hebert, M., & Harris, K. R. (in press). Formative assessment and writing: A meta-analysis. *The Elementary School Journal.*

Grimes, D., & Warschauer, M. (2010). Utility in a fallible tool: A multi-site case study of automated writing evaluation. *The Journal of Technology, Learning and Assessment, 8*(6). Retrieved from www.jta.org.

Johnstone, K. M., Ashbaugh, H., & Warfield, T. D. (2002). Effects of repeated practice and contextual-writing experiences on college students' writing skills. *Journal of Educational Psychology, 94*(2), 305–315.

Kellogg, R. T., & Raulerson, B. (2007). Improving the writing skills of college students. *Psychonomic Bulletin & Review, 14*, 237–242.

Kukich, K. (2000, September/October). Beyond automated essay scoring. In M. A. Hearst (Ed.), *The Debate on Automated Essay Grading.* IEEE Intelligent systems (pp. 27–31). Retrieved from http://citeseerx.ist.psu.edu/viewdoc/download?doi=10.1.1.92.5600&rep=rep1&type=pdf

Landauer, T. K., Lochbaum, K. E., & Dooley, S. (2009). A new formative assessment technology for reading and writing. *Theory into Practice, 48,* 44–52. http://dx.doi.org/10.1080/00405840802577593.

Latifi, S. M. F., Guo, Q., Gierl, M. J., Mousavi, A., Fung, K., & Lacroix, D. (2013, June). Towards automated scoring using open-source technologies. *In Annual Meeting of the Canadian Society for the Study of Education Victoria* (pp. 13–14).

Li, L. (2014). Experimental Study on the Validity of AES Systems in the College EFL Classroom. *In 2nd International Conference on Teaching and Computational Science.* Shenzhen, China: Atlantis Press.

Mayfield, E., & Rose, C. P. (2013). LightSIDE: Open source machine learning for text. In M. D. Shermis & J. C. Burstein (Eds.), *Handbook of Automated Essay Evaluation: Current Application and New Directions* (pp. 124–135). New York: Psychology Press.

McNamara, D. S., Crossley, S. A., Roscoe, R. D., Allen, L. K., & Dai, J. (2015). Hierarchical classification approach to automated essay scoring. *Assessing Writing, 23,* 35–59.

Myers, M. (2003). What can computers contribute to a K-12 writing program? In M. D. Shermis & J. Burstein (Eds.), *Automated Essay Scoring: A Cross-Disciplinary Approach* (pp. 3–20). Mahwah, NJ: Lawrence Erlbaum Associates, Inc.

The National Commission on Writing. (2004). *Writing: A ticket to Work. Or a Ticket Out.* College Board.

Page, E. B. (2003). Project Essay Grade: PEG. In M. D. Shermis & J. Burstein (Eds.), *Automated Essay Scoring: A Cross-Disciplinary Perspective* (pp. 43–54). Mahwah, NJ: Lawrence Erlbaum Associates.

Page, E. B., & Peterson, N. S. (1995). The computer moves into essay grading: Updating the ancient test. *Phi Delta Kappan, 76*(7), 561.

Pearson Education (2009). General overview of WriteToLearn and its components. Retrieved from http://www.writetolearn.net/downloads/WTLOverview-040609.pdf

Pearson Education (2011). WriteToLearn efficacy report: Demonstrating reading & writing performance gains. Retrieved from http://www.writetolearn.net/downloads/WTL_EfficacyReport.pdf

Powell, P. (2009). Retention and writing instruction: Implications for access and pedagogy. *College Composition and Communication, 60,* 664–682.

Rich, C. S., Harrington, H., Kim, J., & West, B. (2008, March). *Automated Essay Scoring in State Formative and Summative Writing Assessment.* Paper presented at the Annual Meeting of the American Educational Research Association, New York City, NY.

Roscoe, R. D., & McNamara, D. S. (2013). Writing Pal: Feasibility of an intelligent writing strategy tutor in the high school classroom. *Journal of Educational Psychology, 105,* 1010–1025.

Roscoe, R. D., Varner, L. K., Crossley, S. A., & McNamara, D. S. (2013). Developing pedagogically-guided algorithms for intelligent writing feedback. *International Journal of Learning Technology, 8,* 362–381.

Roscoe, R. D., Allen, L. K., Weston, J. L., Crossley, S. A., & McNamara, D. S. (2014). The Writing Pal intelligent tutoring system: Usability testing and development. *Computers and Composition, 34,* 39–59.

Roscoe, R. D., Varner, L. K., Cai, Z., Weston, J. L., Crossley, S. A., & McNamara, D. S. (2011). Internal usability testing of automated essay feedback in an intelligent writing tutor. In R. C. Murray & P. M. McCarthy (Eds.), *Proceedings of the 24th International Florida Artificial Intelligence Research Society (FLAIRS) Conference* (pp. 543–548). Menlo Park, CA: AAAI Press.

Rudner, L. M., & Gagne, P. (2001). *An Overview of Three Approaches to Scoring Written Essays by Computer* (ERIC Digest number ED 458 290).

Rudner, L. M., Garcia, V., & Welch, C. (2006). An evaluation of the IntelliMetric™ essay scoring system. *Journal of Technology, Learning, and Assessment, 4*(4).

Shermis, M. D., & Barrera, F. D. (2002). Automated essay scoring for electronic portfolios. *Assessment Update, 14,* 1–5.

Shermis, M. D., & Burstein, J. (Eds.). (2003). *Automated Essay Scoring: A Cross-Disciplinary Perspective.* Mahwah, NJ: Erlbaum.

Shermis, M. D., & Burstein, J. (Eds.). (2013). *Handbook of Automated Essay Evaluation: Current Applications and Future Directions.* New York: Routledge.

Shermis, M. D., Burstein, J., Higgins, D., & Zechner, K. (2010). Automated essay scoring: Writing assessment and instruction. *International Encyclopedia of Education, 4,* 20–26.

Shermis, M. D., Mzumara, H. R., Lillig, C. & Brown, M. (1997, August) *Computerized Adaptive Testing through the World Wide Web.* Paper presented at the annual meeting of the American Psychological Association, Chicago, IL.

Shute, V. J. (2008). Focus on formative feedback. *Review of Educational Research, 78,* 153–189.

Vantage Learning. (2000). *A True Score Study of IntelliMetric Accuracy for Holistic and Dimensional Scoring of College Entry-Level Writing Program* (RB-407). Newtown, PA: Vantage Learning.

Vantage Learning. (2003). *A True Score Study of 11th Grade Student Writing Responses Using IntelliMetric Version 9.0* (RB-786). Newtown, PA: Vantage Learning.

Vantage Learning (2006). Research summary: IntelliMetricTM scoring accuracy across genres and grade levels. Retrieved from http://www.vantagelearning.com/docs/intellimetric/IM_ReseachSummary_IntelliMetric_Accuracy_Across_Genre_and_Grade_Levels.pdf

Vantage Learning. (2007). MY Access! Efficacy Report. Newtown, PA: Vantage Learning. Retrieved from http://www.vantagelearning.com/docs/resources/MY_Access!_Efficacy_Report_August_2006_1.pdf

Weigle, S. C. (2013). English language learners and automated scoring of essays: Critical considerations. *Assessing Writing, 1*, 85–99.

White, L. J., Hixson, N. K., & Whisman, S. A. (2011). *Writing Roadmap Usage and Additional Predictors of WESTEST 2 Online Writing scores.* Charleston, WV: West Virginia Department of Education, Division of Curriculum and Instructional Services, Office of Research.

Xi, X. (2010). Automated scoring and feedback systems: Where are we and where are we heading? *Language Testing, 27*, 291–300.

# 10
# THE *CRITERION®* ONLINE WRITING EVALUATION SERVICE

*Chaitanya Ramineni and Paul Deane*

## Introduction

This chapter surveys the *Criterion®* Online Writing Evaluation Service,[1] an online instructional writing tool that supports easy collection of writing samples, efficient scoring of writing, and immediate feedback using the *e-rater®* automated essay scoring (AES) engine (Burstein, Chodorow, & Leacock, 2004; Burstein, Tetreault, & Madnani, 2013). It is one of the earliest instructional writing products for classroom use backed by automated evaluation and scoring, and is available for use across grades 4 to 12 and in higher education institutions, domestically as well as internationally.

The *Criterion* service has recently been revised to emphasize features designed to help students learn how to manage an extended writing process (planning, drafting, editing, and revising) in which they actively engage with the teacher and peers. Within this larger context, the automated scoring and feedback component is designed to support frequent essay writing, which can in turn support increased composition fluency and language control. The tool also supports teacher management (creating assignments, assigning peer groups, providing feedback) and student interaction (e.g., peer review). These features are designed to facilitate development of multiple writing skills including planning, peer review, and discussion.

In this chapter, we discuss the growth of digital writing technologies, place the *Criterion* service within that context, and identify the primary skills targeted by the service's automated scoring and feedback capabilities (discourse structure, fluency, and adherence to language conventions). The body of the chapter provides an overview of the *Criterion* service as a pedagogical writing environment, discusses potential impacts of automated writing evaluation (AWE) technology on classroom learning and instruction, summarizes key efficacy studies, and outlines how teachers can access the *Criterion* service and integrate it with classroom practice. Finally, we discuss current limitations of the service and future directions for enhancement.

## The Need for Writing Technology

With the increasing popularity of digital environments as platforms for communication and social interaction, digital writing has become one of the most important literacy skills of the present age (Barton & Lee, 2013; National Assessment Governing Board, 2011; National Writing Project, DeVoss, Eidman-Aadahl, & Hicks, 2010).

Best practice recommends that teachers provide students with many different opportunities to practice and support multiple rounds of revision with feedback between drafts (Graham & Harris, 2013). Immediate, specific, detailed feedback can be effective in motivating students to edit, revise, and improve their writing (Beach & Friedrich, 2006; Ferris, 2003). But reviewing student work often requires substantial amounts of time that may lead teachers to limit the number of writing assignments (Grimes & Warschauer, 2010). Also, teachers may find themselves responding to recurring problems including large amounts of editing errors.

AWE technology can play a critical role in writing pedagogy by automating some forms of feedback while supporting more efficient classroom processes. In particular, the use of AWE can provide students with increased opportunities for practicing writing in digital environments, while freeing up teachers' time for more targeted feedback and classroom management activities (Myers, 2003; Warschauer & Grimes, 2008). When placed in the context of online writing environments like the *Criterion* service that creates a digital space under the teacher's control, AWE technology can potentially facilitate learning both inside and outside the classroom.

## How AWE Can Support Development of Writing Skills

Composition fluency is critical to long-term success as a writer (see Deane, 2011, 2013; McCutchen, 2006). Skilled writers are able to efficiently generate and express ideas on a wide range of topics in text form. Language control is closely connected to fluency, in that dysfluency leads to various forms of surface or form errors such as subject-verb agreement and ill-formed verbs. Writers need to develop the ability to monitor their writing for such errors, and develop editing and proofreading skills to correct them (Ferris, 2011; Saddler, 2013).

AWE systems support the revision and screening of student responses by providing immediate holistic scores and feedback. The holistic scores can be used as preliminary indicators of the quality of a draft, thus prompting the need for revision. The detailed feedback can help students take a more systematic approach during the editing and proofreading stages of writing, particularly English as second language learners.

*Criterion*[2] (including the underlying *e-rater* scoring engine) supports development of composition fluency in a variety of ways. Most critically, *Criterion* gives students the opportunity to plan and create multiple drafts and receive automated feedback on preliminary drafts. There are templates available for students to create plans (such as outlines and idea trees), which can then be used to craft a full response. Automated evaluation and feedback are available across multiple drafts to support revisions prior to finalizing the response for the teacher's review.

Feedback on language control is targeted by several natural language processing (NLP) components focusing on grammar, usage, mechanics, stylistic elements, and discourse elements (e.g., organization). Additional feedback is also available through instructor comments and peer-review options, which are designed to facilitate the collaborative writing practices. These features are designed to foster a higher level of engagement in which students are motivated to develop their writing more extensively; internalize the necessary strategies and processes; and thereby increase their composition fluency. But composition fluency and language control do not cover all the critical aspects of writing skill (Council of Writing Program Administrators, National Council of Teachers of English, & National Writing Project, 2011; National Governors Association Center for Best Practices & Council of Chief State School Officers, 2010). Hence, digital tools such as *Criterion* function most effectively when they are embedded in an environment in which the teacher and peers provide student writers with effective support that encourages them to develop all targeted skills.

## An Overview of the *Criterion* Online Writing Evaluation Service

*Criterion* (http://www.ets.org/criterion/) supports the easy collection of writing samples and provides scoring and feedback services via the *e-rater* automated scoring engine. It has several features designed to support students' improvement in writing. These include planning templates to encourage a structured approach to writing, feedback screens, and review tools to encourage students to improve their essays by undertaking multiple revisions of an initial draft. It also includes resources, such as sample scored essays, a writer's handbook, a spell checker, and a thesaurus. Figure 10.1 presents the general theory of action underlying *Criterion* specifying how classroom implementation of the product may lead to positive educational outcomes.

### *Prompt Library*

*Criterion* has a large library of essay prompts suitable for student writing practice and class writing assignments in grades 4 to 12 and at the college level. The writing

**Criterion Components**

**Tools for Students**
*Criterion* provides tools for:
Planning and Writing
- 8 planning templates, with the ability for students to edit their plan during assignments
- Writer Samples, examples of well-written essays by grade level

Revising and Editing
- Opportunities for revision and resubmission
- Diagnostic feedback on grammar, usage, mechanics, style, and organization & development
- A score with an associated rubric and a Trait Score Level (Basic, Proficient, or Advanced)
- An online writer's handbook
- An online thesaurus

Communication and Access
- Tools to facilitate dialogue
- Opportunities to develop online portfolios
- Ability to access from school, home, and other locations (e.g., library)

**Tools for Teachers**
*Criterion* offers time-saving tools:
- A large library of essay topics aligned to Common Core State Standards
- Options within assignments
- Instant diagnostic feedback and score reports
- Online tracking of student portfolios
- Access from school, home, and other locations

Teachers can further customize instruction by:
- Enabling prewriting tools for student planning, with the ability to designate a specific planning template
- Selecting level-appropriate writing resources and feedback
- Tailoring assignments to target specific skills
- Creating their own essay topics
- Using summary class reports to analyze progress and patterns of errors
- Commenting on student work through different modalities, including Peer Review
- Offering bilingual resources and writer's handbook

**Student and Teacher Outcomes**

- More prewriting activities completed
- Increased time drafting and composing essays
- More revisions made to essays
- More writing tasks assigned, with increased opportunities to practice writing
- More time for teachers to support students in learning the higher-order aspects of writing
- More opportunities for effective interactions between teachers and students

→ **Improved student writing**

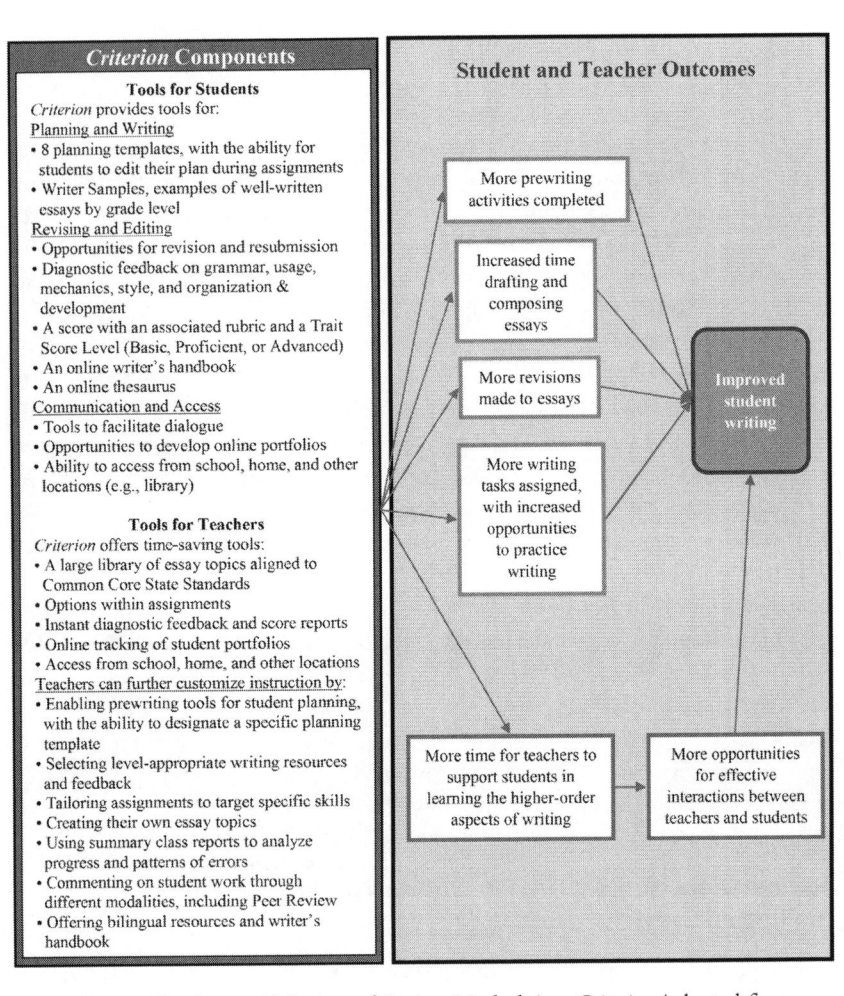

**FIGURE 10.1** The General Theory of Action Underlying *Criterion* (adapted from Leahy, Leusner, Lyon, King, & Ridolfi, 2014).

prompts are a collection of items from various ETS tests and client programs such as NAEP. The prompts are designed to elicit responses in multiple genres such as persuasive, expository, narrative, and argumentative, and are scored using a four- or six-point scoring guide for writing quality. Instructors can modify and adapt an existing prompt or write a completely new prompt to align with their classroom instruction for which students can receive automated feedback. When instructors create prompts that are parallel to those in the existing library, students can also receive automated holistic scores. Instructions for creating prompts with the options of automated scores and/or feedback are provided in the instructor's guide. Some of the prompts in the library have been aligned to the Common Core Standards for English Language Arts.

*Criterion* inherently supports automated scoring of writing quality for essay-type writing completed under timed conditions. Hence, the prompts in the library are all essay prompts associated with rubrics for assessing writing quality. However, instructors can attach reading and/or source texts for existing prompts as well as create prompts that elicit non-essay type writing (such as summaries and research papers). Only automated feedback for writing quality is available for such prompts, and the evaluation of skills, such as the use of sources, must be completed by the teacher for feedback and scoring.

## Planning tools

Eight different planning templates along with space to enter notes, print, save, or paste into the writing screen are available to encourage planning and pre-writing. These include outlines, an idea web, an idea tree, a compare/contrast planner, a cause/effect planner, a free write, a list, and a persuasive outlining template. The instructor can assign a specific plan or let students select the template. Students can copy and paste text from the plan into the main response, as well as simultaneously update the plan during writing. Figure 10.2 provides an example of the planning template for cause/effect.

## AWE Scoring and Feedback

The holistic scoring and feedback provided by *Criterion* is supported by the *e-rater* automated scoring engine. Built-in scoring models are provided, based on a representative sample of student responses written under high-stakes testing conditions and scored by trained human raters. Each model has been evaluated on an

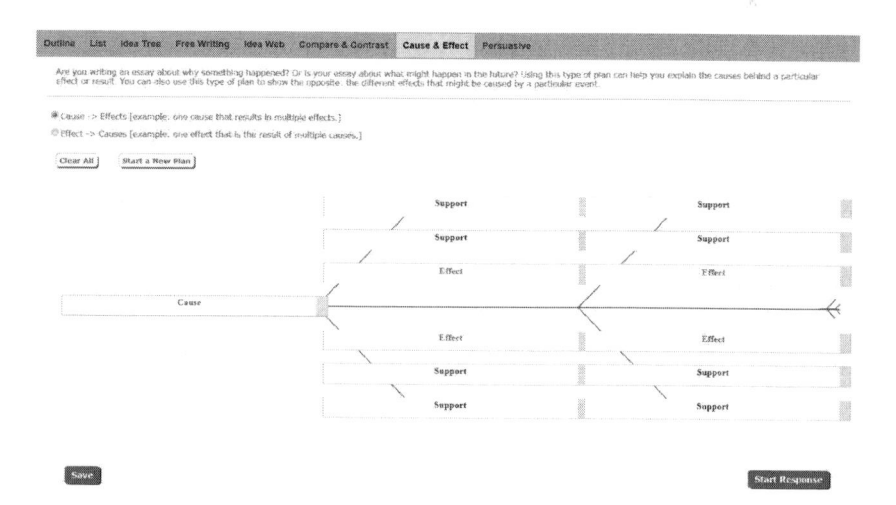

**FIGURE 10.2** Example of the Planning Template for Cause/Effect.

independent testing sample to confirm that there is close agreement between the automated and human scores. The majority of prompts for a grade level (including instructor-created topics parallel to those present in the topic library) are scored by a single generic scoring model trained on responses to many different writing prompts. For a few of the prompts, separate models are trained and used to evaluate the presence and quality of prompt-specific content (for further description of *e-rater* scoring models, see Ramineni & Williamson, 2013).

Table 10.1 lists the features included in the *e-rater* scoring model,[3] grouped by construct dimension (see Attali and Powers, 2008). For further descriptions of the features, see Deane, 2013 and Burstein et al., 2013. The features for which feedback is available (indicated in italics in Table 10.1) include grammar, usage, mechanics, style elements, and organization and development. The style feature is currently used just for feedback. Other features in Table 10.1 (those not placed in italics) are currently used only for scoring purposes, though ongoing research may lead to corresponding feedback in future versions of *Criterion*.

The Scoring model, *e-rater*, assigns scores to responses that are at least 25 words in length and under 1,000 words. These word limits mimic the characteristics of essays written under testing conditions. However, instructors can create prompts to elicit short (one paragraph or less) and long (research papers) responses, which receive automated feedback, but not a holistic score. Holistic scores are accompanied by descriptors (developing, proficient, and advanced) for performance on three specific traits (i.e., categories) of features: fluency, word choice, and language conventions (see Figure 10.3; for a description of the traits, see Attali & Powers, 2008). Additionally, a detailed feedback analysis based

**TABLE 10.1** Features Included in the *e-rater* Scoring Model Grouped by Construct Dimension.

| Construct Dimension | Features |
| --- | --- |
| Fluency | Organization |
|  | Development |
|  | Sentence variety |
| Language Conventions | *Grammar errors* |
|  | *Usage errors* |
|  | *Mechanics errors* |
|  | *Style elements* |
|  | Correct usage of collocations and prepositions |
| Vocabulary | Word frequency |
|  | Average word length |
| Content* | Similarity to the highest scoring essays |
|  | Similarity to essays at each score level |

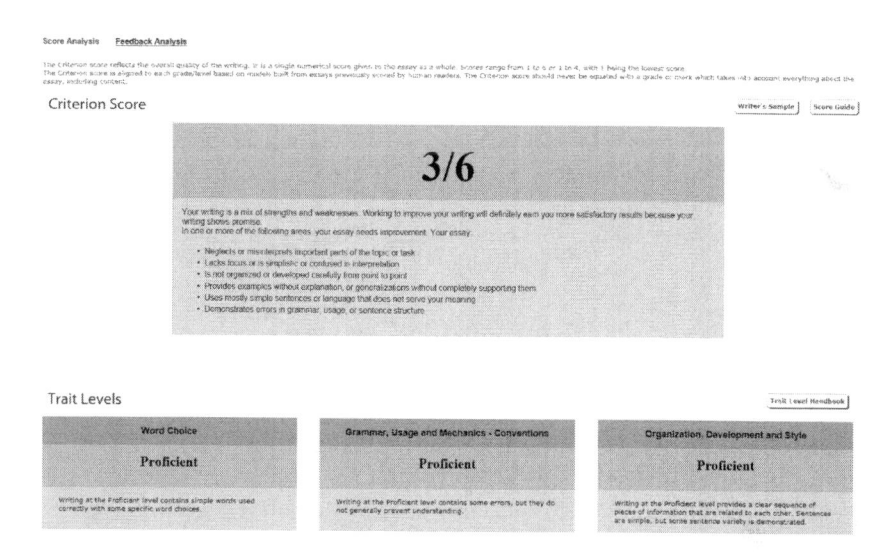

FIGURE 10.3 Descriptors for Performance.

on NLP techniques is provided for specific elements, such as the presence or absence of discourse elements (introduction, thesis, etc.), style elements (passive voice, repetition of words, etc.), and errors in grammar, usage, and mechanics categories (see Table 10.2). *Criterion* also provides error detection and feedback for specific language errors more common in L2 writing such as *article* and *preposition errors* (Han, Chodorow, & Leacock, 2006; Tetreault & Chodorow, 2008).

*Criterion/e-rater* is not currently configured to detect cheating or plagiarism, however, warnings (called advisories) are issued when responses appear to be atypical (such as too long, too short, off-topic), in which case they may be excluded from scoring by the *e-rater* engine and directed to the instructor for review, or submitted to the instructor with a warning. Advisories therefore serve as one mechanism to monitor and prevent gaming attempts against the scoring engine.

Underlying all of *e-rater*'s features and advisories are NLP algorithms trained on human annotated data. These algorithms are evaluated on how well they perform to identify errors in an annotated corpus of student essays. For individual *e-rater* features, a minimal threshold for accuracy is set at 80 percent (Burstein, 2012). Accuracy refers to ensuring that at least 80 percent of the errors that are found by *Criterion/e-rater* are correctly identified as errors, to ensure that students will be able to model and improve their writing based upon feedback that is correct. In order to achieve the desired rate of accuracy, conservative NLP rules are implemented to minimize the chances that an aspect of student writing is marked as incorrect when it is actually grammatically and stylistically correct. This strategy leads to *Criterion* providing students with feedback on some errors while leaving some errors for them to find on their own.

**TABLE 10.2** Examples of Detailed Feedback Analysis Based on NLP Techniques.

| Error Type | Brief Description | Example |
|---|---|---|
| Subject-verb agreement | A singular noun with a plural verb or a plural noun with a singular verb | "A uniform represent the school." |
| Ill-formed verb | A mismatch between the tense of a verb and the local syntactic environment; also, use of *for have*, as in *could of* | "We need the freedom to chose what we want to wear." |
| Pronoun error | An objective case pronoun where nominative pronoun is required, or vice versa | "Us students want to express ourselves." |
| Possessive error | A plural noun where a possessive noun should be; usually the result of omitting an apostrophe | "They stayed at my parents house." |
| Wrong word form | A verb used in place of a noun | "The choose is not an easy one." |

All scores and feedback are available for viewing by both students and their instructors. The feedback is displayed using easily interpretable graphic descriptors (see Figure 10.4), which provide counts of errors by type. In addition to the graphs, there is an annotated feedback screen for each error type, which highlights the location of errors and provides comments that explain each error and suggest possible revisions (see Figures 10.5 and 10.6). Similar screens provide information regarding the location of stylistic and discourse elements.

Since the automated feedback focuses primarily on error patterns and discourse elements, it should be used to supplement a rich pedagogy provided by the instructor, including extensive feedback and support on additional writing skills (Warschauer & Ware, 2006). Ideally, feedback from *Criterion* will help students build the habits of mind necessary to produce well-edited texts; that is, a willingness to produce multiple drafts, and the ability to monitor the results, and edit and revise drafts as needed.

## *Supporting Resources*

The annotated feedback feature is designed to help students who are struggling with language conventions (i.e. grammar, mechanics, and style). *Criterion* also supplies a number of other resources for student writers. There is a writer's handbook that defines each error and provides examples of correct and incorrect use. Different handbook versions are available for elementary, middle, and high school/college students, as well as for English language learners. There are also

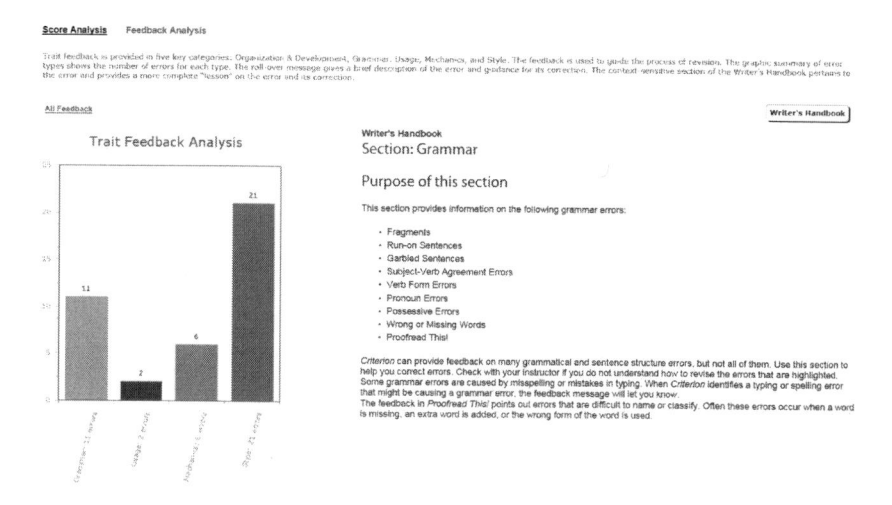

**FIGURE 10.4** Graphic Descriptors.

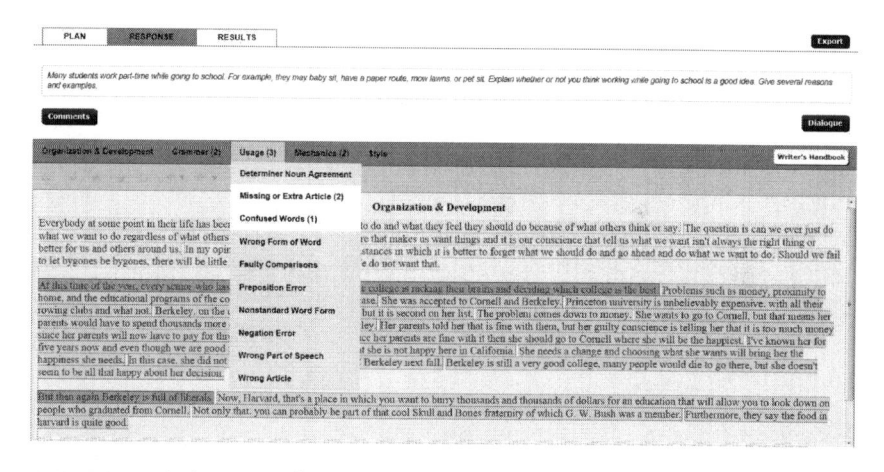

**FIGURE 10.5** Assistance with Errors.

four bilingual versions in Japanese/English, Korean/English, Spanish/English, and Simplified Chinese/English. Additionally, the spell checker is supported by either an American or British dictionary, a thesaurus for editing, a sample of good writing at the particular grade level for reference, and support for peer and teacher dialogue and comments. The planning templates support students as they learn how to structure their essays, and the sample essays provide models of good writing. There is also a portfolio component in *Criterion* to allow teachers and students to review the entire body of work completed during the course.

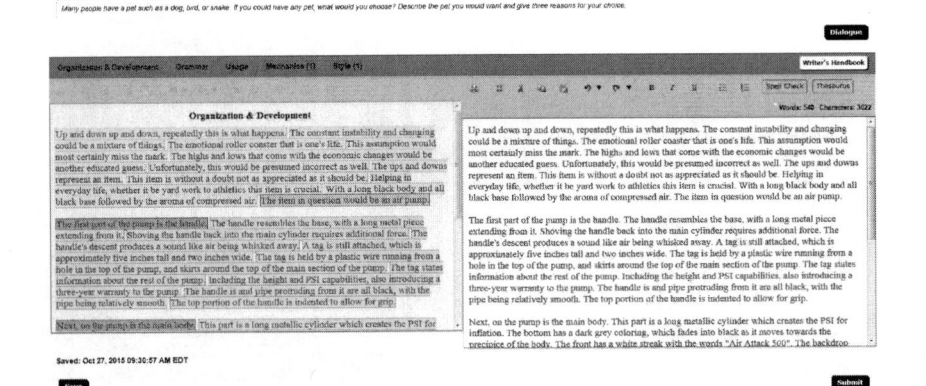

FIGURE 10.6  Assistance with Errors.

## Efficacy Studies

In this section, we summarize findings from research studies on the efficacy of *Criterion* to support student learning and facilitate improvement in writing (see Stevenson & Phakiti, 2013 for a critical review of studies in this area). These studies were conducted at primarily middle school and college levels, and target both native and non-native speakers of English. There are both quantitative studies (focusing on holistic scores, response length, and errors) and qualitative studies (focusing on classroom observations, interviews, and surveys). These include: (1) studies on the perceived utility of the system; (2) studies designed to measure improvement in writing when *Criterion* is used; and (3) studies reviewing the accuracy of the feedback.

### Utility of the System

Multiple studies using student and teacher surveys and classroom observations have reported positive perceptions of *Criterion* for classroom use (Choi, 2010; Dikli & Bleyle, 2014; Huang, 2014; Kim, 2014; Li, Link, Hegelheimer, 2015; Li, Link, Ma, Yang, & Hegelheimer, 2014; Schroeder, Grohe, & Pogue, 2008; Warschauer & Grimes, 2008). The number of students and teachers varied across the studies with a maximum of 172 students and 4 instructors. User surveys emphasized the ability of *Criterion* to implement an extended writing process that included planning, revising, and editing, supported by automated feedback.

Attali (2004) and Ramineni, Calico, and Li (2015) analyzed student activity across multiple grades and for 8th graders respectively, using the data generated by *Criterion*. They reported that out of the thousands of students using *Criterion* over the school year, 30 to 50 percent of them worked on multiple assignments and completed multiple revision activities interleaved with AWE feedback. Based on the high frequency of writing and revising practices among a large percentage of the students exposed to *Criterion*, they concluded that the system was useful in providing students with multiple opportunities to write and revise.

The use of *Criterion* has also been evaluated for institutional assessments for placement and remediation (Klobucar, Elliot, Deess, Rudniy, & Joshi, 2013; Ramineni, 2013). The *Criterion* placement test was found to be a better predictor of students' end-of-year performances compared to off-the-shelf placement tests and standardized writing admissions tests, which do not provide diagnostic information on student writing. As such, Klobucar and colleagues have developed a placement and diagnostic assessment framework for first-year composition courses at their four-year research university using the *Criterion* system. There, *Criterion* is used as a writing placement tool and is leveraged to provide early diagnostics to support remediation strategies and help instructors modify instruction. The application of *Criterion* in this context supports construct-specific program goals (such as improving student writing skills) as well as larger institutional goals (such as increasing student retention and the proportion of students who complete a four-year degree).

## *Improvement in Writing*

Empirical studies to evaluate the effectiveness of AWE feedback can be hard to set up due to several factors, such as the technological competence of the participants, pedagogical choices that provide the context, self-revision skills of the participants, and logistics of including a control group. Nonetheless, many studies have been completed on the effectiveness of the feedback provided by *Criterion* for improving writing. The sample sizes for these studies vary widely ranging from 45 to 2,017 students. Harris (2013) and Kellogg, Whiteford and Quinlan (2010) found positive association between greater numbers of submissions/revisions and higher holistic scores. Multiple studies reported increases in text-production skills (greater fluency and fewer errors) and holistic scores (Chodorow, Gamon, & Tetreault, 2010; Choi, 2010; Harris, 2013; Kim, 2014; Li et al., 2015; Rock, 2007; Schroeder et al., 2008; Shermis, Burstein, & Bliss, 2004; Shermis, Garvan, & Diao, 2008; Wang, 2013). In addition, Kim (2014) reported a gain in mean holistic scores for students' class writing assignments in both the low and the high English proficiency groups.

## *Accuracy of Feedback*

Since *Criterion* (and most other AWE tools) focuses heavily on detecting language-use errors as part of the automated feedback, there have been several studies reviewing the accuracy and completeness of the error detection (Chapelle, Cotos, & Lee, 2015; Chen, Chiu, & Liao, 2009; Dikli & Bleyle, 2014; Long, 2013; Otoshi, 2005). All of these studies were conducted using non-native writers of English enrolled in college writing courses. Except for Chen et al., (2009) who studied a sample of approximately 250 students, the remaining studies had 50 or fewer students. While these studies highlight differences between the errors identified by human raters versus *e-rater* and emphasize the presence of a percentage of false positives in automated feedback, their results are consistent with the design of the underlying technology, which seeks to achieve an accuracy of at least 80 percent on identified errors. *Criterion*'s automated feedback is designed to provide useful triggers that prompt students to monitor and review their work. *Criterion* feedback identifies potential errors and suggests possible solutions, while prompting students to train themselves to exercise editorial judgment.

Overall, despite concerns from writing instructors that AWE feedback focuses heavily on surface errors (Cheville, 2004; Hagerman, 2011; Herrington & Stanley, 2008; Ware, 2011), studies using *Criterion* suggest a different interpretation. In many of these studies, students and teachers indicate that AWE feedback is helpful in motivating students to write and revise more. Many of the studies also indicate that the targeted feedback and multiple revision opportunities provided by the tool can lead to improvement in student writing by increasing fluency, reducing errors, and increasing writing scores. Overall, it can be concluded that AWE feedback can have positive effects on student learning when coupled with rich pedagogy that includes teacher evaluation and peer feedback (Chen & Cheng, 2008; Choi, 2010; Warschauer & Grimes, 2008).

## Accessing *Criterion*[4]

*Criterion* is a web-based instructional tool available for purchase by institutions or individual instructors with several subscription options designed to fit their needs. These paid subscriptions provide unlimited access to the tool anywhere and anytime. *Criterion* is supported by all browsers and platforms, including the iPad tablet with iOS 5.1 or higher.

Teachers can register and create accounts to access *Criterion*. Once registered, they can create classes, add students to the classes, create assignments, and review class rosters, student activity, and student/class performance reports. The instructor's home page provides access to additional resources, including a quick access guide and tutorials providing information on how to create classes, monitor student and class activity reports, and create assignments (see Figure 10.7).

When creating assignments, instructors can choose the grade level of the prompt and its discourse mode, and set a variety of parameters, such as the types of planning tools available, time limits, the number of attempts that students are allowed to make for a single assignment (with a maximum default of ten), the kinds of feedback to be provided (including scores, automated feedback, and teacher comments), and whether students are able or required to participate in peer reviews (see Figures 10.8a and 10.8b).

There are tools for tracking student activity and various reports that support easy viewing and monitoring of student performance. Teachers can track student

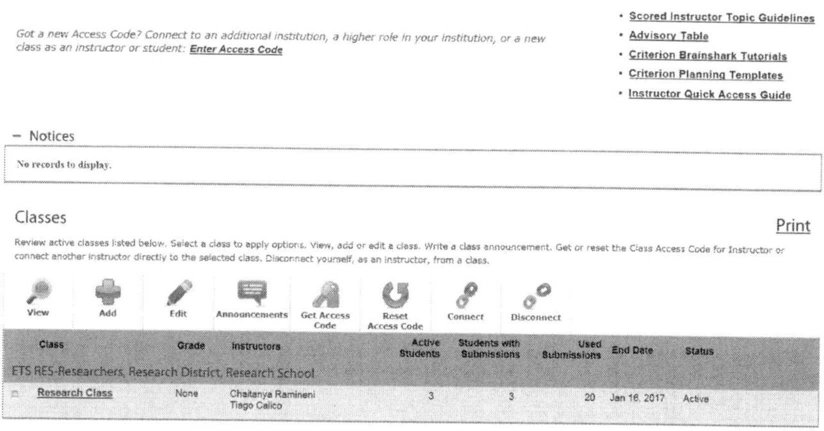

**FIGURE 10.7** Instructor's Home Page.

revision behaviors (for the percentage of attempts, see Figure 10.9) and can view student scores and error reports (see Figures 10.9 and 10.10). Teachers can also view student performances for the entire body of work completed during a course via a portfolio report (see Figure 10.11).

In addition, *Criterion* provides an interface for teachers to annotate student writing and provide summary comments. Teacher comments can be stored in a comments library, allowing them to provide quick feedback for recurring problems. *Criterion* also supports synchronous communication through a dialogue (or chat) window, between both the teacher and student as well as between students assigned to the same peer-review group.

*Criterion* includes reports that provide teachers with information about individual students as well as those that provide summary information at the class level, which can be used to inform changes in a teacher's curriculum or instruction. *Criterion*'s AWE functionality makes it possible for teachers to view patterns of student performance across multiple assignments. By tracking performance using automated features, teachers can examine the extent to which students have significantly revised and improved their work over the course of the writing process, without having to examine and respond to every single intermediate draft.

## Integrating *Criterion* into the Classroom

Pedagogical approaches can influence the effective use of AWE in the classroom context. *Criterion* can be integrated into the classroom in multiple ways. Instructors have the autonomy to choose an implementation model that fits their pedagogical approach. Some teachers may prefer to use it in the early stages of writing while others may prefer to use the machine evaluation to support students during final editing and proofreading. Instructors can choose

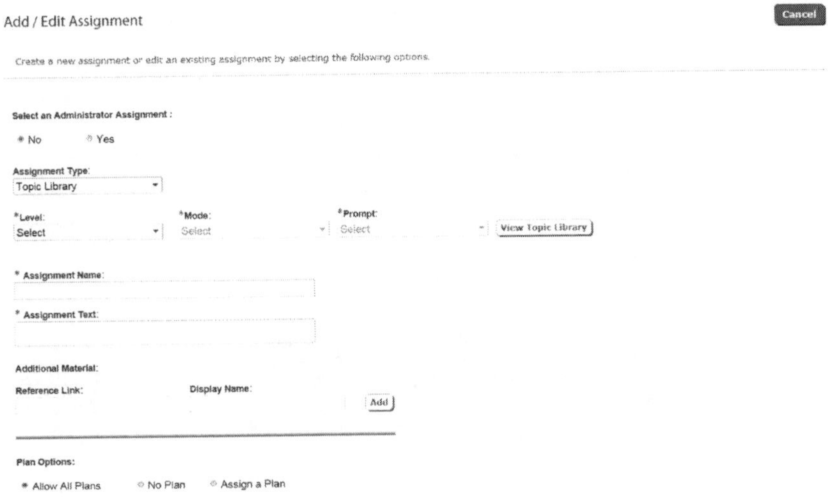

**FIGURE 10.8A** Creating Assignments.

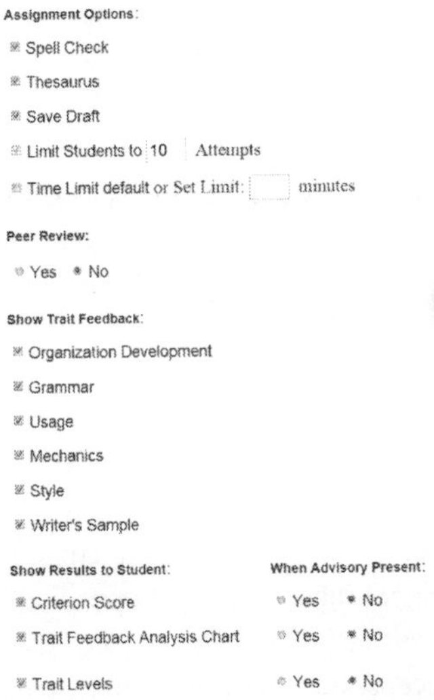

**FIGURE 10.8B** Creating Assignments.

the number, frequency, and topics for the writing assignments; and the scoring guide, the number of revisions, and other assignment conditions (whether to score essays, time them, or provide automated feedback).

*Criterion*'s prompt library is designed to allow teachers to easily assign certain standard types of writing assignments (e.g., expository and persuasive essays). It also offers a flexible platform for instructors to assign writing in different genres

**Criterion Score by Student**
Instructor: Chaitanya Ramineni
Instructor Report Accessed: October 27, 2015 9:46 AM US/Eastern

Student: All Students
Assignment Creator: All
Assignment Type: All Topics
Standard: All Standards
Mode: All Modes
Prompt: All Prompts
Assignment: All Assignments
Criterion Scale: 6
Criterion Scores: All Scores
Number of Attempts Made: Any Number
Student Saved a Plan: Disregard Plan
Assignments With Time Limits: With and without
Advisories: Scores with and without Advisories

Export

Print

| Student Name | Criterion Score | Number of Attempts | Average Score | Percent of Attempts | Advisories |
|---|---|---|---|---|---|
| Calico, Tiago A | Advisory (3/6) | 2 | | 10.5% | 2 |
| Calico, Tiago A | Advisory (1/6) | 1 | | 5.3% | 1 |
| Calico, Tiago A | (6/6) | 1 | | 5.3% | 0 |
| Calico, Tiago A | (5/6) | 3 | | 15.8% | 0 |
| Ramineni, Chaitanya | Advisory (6/6) | 3 | | 15.8% | 3 |
| Ramineni, Chaitanya | Advisory (4/6) | 1 | | 5.3% | 1 |
| Ramineni, Chaitanya | Advisory | 2 | | 10.5% | 2 |
| Ramineni, Chaitanya | (1/6) | 1 | | 5.3% | 0 |
| VanWinkle, Waverely | Advisory (2/6) | 1 | | 5.3% | 1 |
| **Class Total:** | | 15 | 3.5 | | 10 |

**FIGURE 10.9** *Criterion* Score by Student—Revision Attempts.

**Trait Errors by Student**
Instructor: Chaitanya Ramineni
Instructor Report Accessed: October 27, 2015 9:50 AM US/Eastern

Dates: October 06, 2006 - October 28, 2015
Student: All Students
Assignment: All Assignments
Errors: All Errors

Export

Print

| Category | Error Type | Attempts | Errors | Attempts with Errors # | Attempts with Errors % |
|---|---|---|---|---|---|
| Grammar | Fragment or Missing Comma | | 24 | 7 | 35% |
| | Run-On Sentences | | | | |
| | Garbled Sentences | | | | |
| | Subject-Verb Agreement | | 2 | 1 | 5% |
| | Ill-formed Verbs | | 10 | 7 | 35% |
| | Pronoun Errors | | 1 | 1 | 5% |
| | Possessive Errors | | 1 | 1 | 5% |
| | Wrong or Missing Word | | 1 | 1 | 5% |
| | Proofread This! | | | | |
| **Grammar Total:** | | 20 | 39 | 7 | 35% |
| Usage | Determiner Noun Agreement | | | | |
| | Missing or Extra Article | | 13 | 9 | 45% |
| | Confused Words | | 14 | 8 | 40% |
| | Wrong Form of Word | | | | |
| | Faulty Comparisons | | | | |
| | Preposition Error | | | | |
| | Nonstandard Word Form | | 1 | 1 | 5% |

**FIGURE 10.10** Student Scores.

178  Chaitanya Ramineni and Paul Deane

**Portfolio Report**
Instructor: Chaitanya Ramineni
Instructor Report Accessed: October 27, 2015 9:57 A

Student: Ramineni, Chaitanya
Assignment: All Assignments
Attempt: 1st and Most Recent Attempt

[Export]

Print

| Class | Student | Assignment Name | Attempt Date | Criterion Score | Number of Grammar Errors | Number of Usage Errors | Number of Mechanic Errors | Number of Style Errors | Trait Level for Word Choice | Trait Level for Conventions | Trait Level for Fluency/Organization | Attempt Number |
|---|---|---|---|---|---|---|---|---|---|---|---|---|
| Research Class | Ramineni, Chaitanya | Demo Elementary | Apr 30, 2014 10:50:04 AM EDT | Advisory | 0 | 2 | 9 | 2 | | Proficient | Developing | 1 |
| Research Class | Ramineni, Chaitanya | Demo Elementary | Mar 24, 2015 11:16:57 PM EDT | Advisory (6/6) | 0 | 0 | 1 | 1 | Proficient | Proficient | Advanced | 8 |
| Research Class | Ramineni, Chaitanya | Test Assignment (disregard) | Nov 12, 2014 12:40:50 PM EST | (4/4) | 0 | 5 | 3 | 0 | Proficient | Proficient | Advanced | 1 |

**FIGURE 10.11**  Error Reports.

(e.g., longer forms of writing using sources); however, in such cases, instructor evaluations should supplement the automated evaluation of student writing for aspects such as how effectively the student has used materials drawn from a source. *Criterion* is an instructional tool for teachers and students, and as such, its efficacy depends on the way in which it is deployed in the classroom. While it offers considerable flexibility, it is specifically designed to support a multi-step writing process in which the teacher, other students, and the AWE system play complementary roles. In an ideal implementation, an instructor would:

- structure assignments for students to understand the need to prewrite and plan and as part of that process, have students learn how to make effective use of the planning tools;
- assign some tasks that link to external sources and require students to write about them;
- assign other tasks that require students to generate their own ideas;
- have students write multiple drafts, with appropriate teacher feedback and support;
- have students evaluate their own and other students' work using *Criterion*'s peer-review functionality;
- leverage *Criterion*'s feedback to encourage students to revise their work independent of the teacher (in the early stages) and edit and proofread their work without waiting for the teacher's feedback (when the essay is ready for a final draft).

The literature on writing instruction suggests that these are practices that make for effective writing instruction in any context (cf. Graham & Harris, 2013). A digital writing environment like *Criterion* can facilitate these practices; however, any tool can be misused. For example, it should not be used for assigning tasks without the use of teacher or peer feedback, or using *e-rater* scoring for final grades without any serious engagement with the student can yield less positive outcomes. However, given the relatively limited number of studies currently available, it would be premature to provide more detailed implementation guidelines in this context. Effectiveness and utility are best judged by the instructor, depending on the local curriculum and student needs.

## Limitations of *Criterion*

Since the mid-2000s, the landscape of the writing curriculum and writing in the classroom have evolved to include multiple genres of writing and an increased emphasis on writing processes and rhetorical strategies. Periodic upgrades are made in *Criterion*—to the features, advisories, the scoring models, and the learning resources—but there are still some limitations consistent with its focus on composition fluency and accuracy of language. Many of these limitations are connected with the current state-of-the-art in NLP. In particular:

1. The error detection algorithms in *Criterion* (like those in a wide range of existing grammar-checking programs) are associated with a certain percentage of false positives that require human judgments. Instructors should train students (especially ELL/ESL students) to use AWE feedback as an opportunity to learn and improve their own judgment, not as a mechanical list of corrections to be relied upon without thought.
2. The feedback in *Criterion* is limited to the elements of writing related to composition fluency and the accuracy of language, including organization, grammar, and mechanics, and should not be treated as a substitute for teacher feedback, particularly with respect to rhetorical effectiveness and the quality of text content.
3. The *e-rater* scoring engine in *Criterion* is currently best suited for evaluating essay-type responses written under testing conditions. Teachers can still use *Criterion* to assign writing tasks of any length, from short responses (less than a paragraph) up to full research papers; however, more teacher involvement and feedback will be necessary for the best results in these situations.
4. The Common Core State Standards place an increased emphasis on argumentative and literary analysis tasks that make extensive use of source texts. While *Criterion* can easily be used to assign tasks of this type through instructor-created topics, they are not yet integrated in the standard prompt library and scoring guides. As noted previously, the current version of the *e-rater* scoring engine does not yet incorporate features that address the distinctive features of these forms of writing; therefore, the evaluation of skills beyond writing quality specifically elicited by such tasks should be completed by teachers.
5. In its current form, the *e-rater* scoring engine in *Criterion* contains features designed to identify certain common errors for non-native speakers of English, such as errors in articles and prepositions, and the performance of all features is evaluated on non-native text before any changes or upgrades are made to the underlying *e-rater* scoring engine. However, teachers should be

aware that different language groups might have different characteristic error patterns, some of which may not currently be detected by *e-rater*.

These limitations are not specific to *Criterion* or *e-rater*; instead, they reflect general limitations in the kinds of analysis currently supported by state-of-the-art NLP. There is ongoing research at ETS to address many of these limitations, including research into error patterns of English learners, research intended to develop features to score specific genres of writing such as the narrative and argumentation genres, and research intended to measure the use of material from external sources. While many of these limitations may be overcome in the next generation of AWE systems, it is important to recognize that no AWE system can substitute for an effective, engaged teacher. Rather, AWE feedback is an important tool that—when used appropriately—can help teachers create effective digital learning environments.

## Conclusion

*Criterion* was one of the earliest applications of AWE technology to writing pedagogy. It combines automated scoring and feedback with digital tools for managing an online writing environment. It therefore embodies an approach in which AWE systems are treated as part of a larger toolkit that can support effective instruction. We believe that AWE systems should neither be demonized nor treated as a panacea; instead, they should be integrated with other writing tools and used in a manner in which they will be most effective.

The power of a digital writing environment is that AWE methods can be integrated with other practices that support effective writing practices. The literature on writing instruction strongly favors writing pedagogies that teach students to implement an extended writing process, which incorporates feedback from peers and experts, in a collaborative space in which students are able to exercise agency. AWE feedback—in particular, the kind of AWE feedback provided by *Criterion*—can play an important role in this process, by making it easier for teachers to allow students to work independently, using AWE feedback as an intermediate indicator of their progress in developing compositional fluency and language control.

## Acknowledgments

We would like to thank the *Criterion* service program representatives as well as multiple reviewers for their comments on the manuscript.

## Notes

1 Educational Testing Service is a not-for-profit corporation whose mission is to help advance fair and valid assessments, research, and related services. The *Criterion* writing service is a commercial product of ETS designed to support this mission.

2 Henceforth, for the sake of efficiency, the *Criterion* service or system will be referred to as *Criterion* and the *e-rater* scoring engine will be referred to as *e-rater*.
3 The current version was deployed in 2014; the *e-rater* scoring engine is continuously updated to include new and enhanced NLP features.
4 The data and names have been fabricated in all of the Figures in this section.

## References

Attali, Y. (2004, April). *Exploring the Feedback and Revision Features of Criterion*. Paper presented at the annual meeting of the National Council on Measurement in Education, San Diego, CA.

Attali, Y., & Powers, D. (2008). *A Developmental Writing Scale* (ETS Research Rep. No. RR-08-19). Princeton, NJ: Educational Testing Service.

Barton, D., & Lee, C (2013). *Language Online: Investigating Digital Texts and Practices*. New York: Routledge.

Beach, R. & Friedrich, T. (2006). Response to writing. In MacArthur, C. A., Graham, S., & Fitzgerald, J. (Eds.), *Handbook of Writing Research* (pp. 222–234). New York: Guilford Press.

Burstein, J. (2012). Fostering best practices in writing assessment and instruction with e-rater®. In N. Elliot & L. Perelman (Eds.), *Writing Assessment in the 21st Century: Essays in Honor of Edward M. White* (pp. 203–217). New York: Hampton Press.

Burstein, J., Chodorow, M., & Leacock, C. (2004). Automated essay evaluation: The Criterion Online writing service. *AI Magazine, 35*, 27–36.

Burstein, J., Tetreault, J., & Madnani, N. (2013). The e-rater automated essay scoring system. In M. D. Shermis & J. Burstein (Eds.), *Handbook of Automated Essay Evaluation: Current Applications and New Directions* (pp. 55–67). New York: Routledge Academic.

Chapelle, C., Cotos, E., & Lee, J. (2015). Validity arguments for diagnostic assessment using automated writing evaluation. *Language Testing, 32*(3), 385–405. doi: 10.1177/0265532214565386.

Chen, C. E., & Cheng, W. E. (2008). Beyond the design of Automated Writing Evaluation: Pedagogical practices and perceived learning effectiveness in EFL writing classes. *Language Learning & Technology, 12*(2), 94–112.

Chen, H. J., Chiu, T. L., & Liao, P. (2009). Analyzing the grammar feedback of two automated writing evaluation systems: My Access and Criterion. *English Teaching and Learning, 33*(2), 1–43.

Cheville, J. (2004). Automated scoring technologies and the rising influence of error. *The English Journal, 93*(4), 47–52.

Chodorow, M., Gamon, M., & Tetreault, J. (2010). The utility of article and preposition error correction systems for English language learners: Feedback and assessment. *Language Testing, 27*(3), 419–436.

Choi, J. (2010). *The Impact of Automated Essay Scoring for Improving English Language Learners' Essay Writing* (Unpublished doctoral dissertation). University of Virginia, Charlottesville, VA.

Council of Writing Program Administrators, National Council of Teachers of English, and National Writing Project. (2011). *Framework for Success in Postsecondary Writing*. Retrieved from Council of Writing Program Administrators website: http://wpacouncil.org/files/framework-for-success-postsecondary-writing.pdf.

Deane, P. (2011). *Writing Assessment and Cognition* (ETS Research Rep. No. RR-11-14). Princeton, NJ: Educational Testing Service.

Deane, P. (2013). On the relation between automated essay scoring and modern views of the writing construct. *Assessing Writing, 18*(1), 7–24. doi:10.1016/j.asw.2012.10.002.

Dikli, S., & Bleyle, S. (2014). Automated essay scoring feedback for second language writers: How does it compare to instructor feedback? *Assessing Writing, 22*, 1–17.

Ferris, D. R. (2003). *Response to Student Writing: Implications for Second Language Students.* Mahwah, NJ: Lawrence Erlbaum Associates

Ferris, D. R. (2011). *Treatment of Error in Second Language Writing* (2nd ed.). Ann Arbor, MI: University of Michigan Press.

Graham, S., & Harris, K. (2013). Designing an effective writing program. In S. Graham, C. A. MacArthur, & J. Fitzgerald (Eds.), *Best Practices in Writing Instruction* (pp. 1–26). New York: Guilford Press.

Grimes, D., & Warschauer, M. (2010). Utility in a fallible tool: A multi-site case study of automated writing evaluation. *Journal of Technology, Language, and Assessment, 8*(6), 1–43.

Hagerman, C. (2011). An evaluation of automated writing assessment. *The JALT CALL Journal, 7*(3), 271–292.

Han, C., Chodorow, M., & Leacock, C. (2006). Detecting errors in English article usage by non-native speakers. *Natural Language Engineering, 12*(2), 115–129.

Harris, C. (2013). *Criterion(RTM) online writing evaluation service program's impact on eighth grade writing skills* (doctoral dissertation). Retrieved from ProQuest Dissertations & Theses Global. (3603784).

Herrington, A., & Stanley, S. (2008, March). *CriterionSM: Promoting the Standard.* Paper presented at the annual meeting of the Conference on College Composition and Communication, San Francisco, CA.

Huang, S. J. (2014). Automated versus human scoring: A case study in an EFL context. *Electronic Journal of Foreign Language Teaching, 11*(1), 149–164.

Kellogg, R. T., Whiteford, A. P., & Quinlan, T. (2010). Does automated feedback help students learn to write? *Journal of Educational Computing Research, 42*(2), 173–196.

Kim, J. E. (2014). The effectiveness of automated essay scoring in an EFL college classroom. *Multimedia-Assisted Language Learning, 17*(3), 11–36.

Klobucar, A., Elliot, N., Deess, P., Rudniy, A., & Joshi, K. (2013). Automated scoring in context: Rapid assessment for placed. *Assessing Writing, 18*(1), 62–84. http://dx.doi.org/10.1016/j.asw.2012.10.002.

Leahy, S., Leusner, D., Lyon, C., King, T., & Ridolfi, L. (2014). *Product Efficacy Argument for the Criterion® Online Writing Evaluation Service Third Edition* (PEAr-14–01). Princeton, NJ: Educational Testing Service.

Li, Z., Link, S., & Hegelheimer, V. (2015). Rethinking the role of automated writing evaluation feedback in ESL writing instruction. *Journal of Second Language Writing, 27*, 1–18. doi: 10.1016/j.system.2014.02.007.

Li, Z., Link, S., Ma, H., Yang, H., & Hegelheimer, V. (2014). The role of automated writing evaluation holistic scores in the ESL classroom. *System, 44*(1), 66–78. doi: 10.1016/j.system.2014.02.007.

Long, R. (2013). A review of ETS' Criterion online writing program for student compositions. *The Language Teacher, 37*(3), 11–16.

McCutchen, D. (2006). Cognitive factors in the development of children's writing. In C.A. MacArthur, S. Graham, & J. Fitzgerald (Eds.). *Handbook of Writing Research* (pp. 115–130). New York: Guilford Press.

Myers, M. (2003). What can computers and AES contribute to a K-12 writing program? In M. D. Shermis & J. Burstein (Eds.), *Automated Essay Scoring: A Cross-Disciplinary Perspective* (pp. 3–20). Mahwah, NJ: Lawrence Erlbaum Associates.

National Assessment Governing Board. (2011). *Writing Framework for the 2011 National Assessment of Education Progress* (ERIC No. 512552). Retrieved from http://files.eric.ed.gov/fulltext/ED512552.pdf.

National Governors Association Center for Best Practices, and Council of Chief State School Officers. (2010). *Common Core State Standards initiative*. Washington, DC: NGA and CCSSO.

National Writing Project, DeVoss, D. N., Eidman-Aadahl, E., & Hicks, T. (2010). *Because Digital Writing Matters: Improving Student Writing in Online and Multimedia Environments*. San Francisco, CA: Wiley.

Otoshi, J. (2005). An analysis of the use of Criterion in a writing classroom in Japan. *The JALT CALL Journal, 1*(1), 30–38.

Ramineni, C. (2013). Validating automated essay scoring for online writing placement. *Assessing Writing, 18*(1), 40–61. doi:10.1016/j.asw.2012.10.005.

Ramineni, C., & Williamson, D. M. (2013). Automated essay scoring: Psychometric guidelines and practices. *Assessing Writing, 18*(1), 40–61. doi: 0.1016/j.asw.2012.10.004.

Ramineni, C., Calico, T., & Li, C. (2015). Integrating product and process data in an online automated writing evaluation system. In O. C. Santos, J. G. Boticario, C. Romero, M. Pechenizkiy, A. Merceron, P. Mitros, . . . M. Desmarais (Eds.), *Proceedings of the 8th International Conference on Educational Data Mining* (pp. 626–627). Madrid, Spain.

Rock, J. (2007). *The Impact of Short-Term Use of Criterion on Writing Skills in Ninth Grade* (ETS Research Rep. No. RR-07-07). Princeton, NJ: Educational Testing Service.

Saddler, B. (2013). Best practices in sentence construction skills. In S. Graham, C. A. MacArthur, & J. Fitzgerald (Eds.). *Best Practices in Writing Instruction* (pp. 238–256). New York: Guilford Press.

Schroeder, J., Grohe, B., & Pogue, R. (2008). The impact of Criterion writing evaluation technology on criminal justice student writing skills. *Journal of Criminal Justice Education, 19*(3), 432–445.

Shermis, M. D., Burstein, J. C., & Bliss, L. (2004, April). *The Impact of Automated Essay Scoring on High Stakes Writing Assessments*. Paper presented at the annual meeting of the National Council on Measurement in Education, San Diego, CA.

Shermis, M. D., Garvan, C. W., & Diao, Y. (2008, March). *The Impact of Automated Essay Scoring on Writing Outcomes*. Paper presented at the annual meeting of the National Council on Measurement in Education, New York.

Stevenson, M., & Phakiti, A. (2013). The effects of computer-generated feedback on the quality of writing. *Assessing Writing, 19*, 51–65.

Tetreault, J., & Chodorow, M. (2008). Native judgments of nonnative usage: Experiments in preposition error detection. In R. Artstein, G. Boleda, F. Keller, & S. Schulte im Walde, (Chairs), *Proceedings of the Workshop on Human Judgments in Computational Linguistics* (pp. 24–32). Stroudsburg, PA; Association for Computation Linguistics.

Wang, P. (2013). Can automated writing evaluation programs help students improve their English writing? *International Journal of Applied Linguistics and English Literature, 2*(1), 6–12.

Ware, P. (2011). Computer-generated feedback on student writing. *TESOL Quarterly, 45*(4), 769–774. doi: 10.5054/tq.2011.272525.

Warschauer, M., & Grimes, D. (2008). Automated writing assessment in the classroom. *Pedagogies: An International Journal, 3*, 22–36.

Warschauer, M., & Ware, P. (2006). Automated writing evaluation: Defining the classroom research agenda. *Language Teaching Research, 10*(2), 1–24.

# 11

# WE-WRITE

## A Web-Based Intelligent Tutor for Supporting Elementary Classroom Teachers in Persuasive Writing Instruction

*Kausalai K. Wijekumar, Karen R. Harris, Steve Graham, and Bonnie J. F. Meyer*

### Introduction

In this chapter, we provide an overview of We-Write, a system integrating teacher-led instruction and a web-based intelligent tutor for developing persuasive writing abilities and self-efficacy for writing among upper elementary school children (i.e., Grades 4 and 5). We-Write focuses on:

- persuasive writing with and without source texts;
- POWerful strategies to guide the writing process (Pick your ideas, Organize your notes, Write and say more):
  a. reviewing the prompt (Topic-Audience-Purpose = TAP);
  b. note-taking for elements (Topic, Reason(s), Explanation(s), Ending = TREE) and characteristics of this genre (write to this target audience, clear organization, catchy opening, good ending, good word choice, etc.);
  c. writing (incorporating all of the above);
  d. self-assessment (of elements and/or quality of writing);
  e. peer and/or teacher-assessment (of elements and/or quality of writing);
  f. revision (e.g., improve on reasons, explanations, and/or organization, revise for more effective opening or ending, sentence combining, etc.).
- POWerful strategies to manage the writing process: goal setting, self-instructions, self-assessment over time, and self-reinforcement;
- developing self-efficacy for writing.

We-Write uses the self-regulated strategies development (SRSD) instructional approach to develop persuasive writing and self-regulation strategies as well as motivation and self-efficacy for writing. For over 30 years, research on SRSD for writing instruction has shown strong research results across multiple outcomes when teachers deliver instruction, which has most commonly been done in small groups. Recent research, however, indicates that when SRSD for writing is used with whole classes rather than small groups, significant and meaningful improvements are also found. Teachers, however, find meeting the diverse needs of the wide range of writers in their classrooms a challenge and have expressed the need for support at the whole class level (Festas et al., 2015; Harris, Graham, & Adkins, 2015; Harris et al., 2012).

We-Write is the first implementation of SRSD where teachers are supported by web-based interactive lessons, scoring of some student activities, a teacher dashboard from which they can customize learning pathways, review reports of student performance, and extend learning through web-based practice lessons. We-Write further supports the development of source-based persuasive writing abilities by weaving text structure (e.g., problem and solution) into reading, selecting, note-taking, planning, and encoding tasks that are part of writing. The use of text structure-based reading comprehension strategies (see Chapter 6) promotes careful selection of information for writing, encoding of information in strategic memory structures, and organizing and signaling the persuasive essay.

The We-Write system choreographs teacher-led components seamlessly with computer supported learning modules that extend and enhance learning throughout SRSD instruction for writing. We-Write learning modules include teacher-led and computer supported modeling, practice tasks, assessment, feedback, and scaffolding. Children progress through the six flexible and recursive stages of the SRSD approach (see Table 11.1) beginning with reading and discussing model persuasive essays to note the essential parts of persuasive essays

**TABLE 11.1** The Six Stages of the SRSD Approach.

*SRSD Instruction\**

1. *Develop and Activate Knowledge Needed for Writing and Self-Regulation*
    - Read and discuss works in the genre being addressed (persuasive essays, reports, etc.), to develop declarative, procedural, and conditional knowledge (e.g., *What is an opinion?; What does it mean to persuade?; Why is it important to think about your readers?; What are the parts of a persuasive essay, are they all here?; How do you think the author came up with this idea, what would you do?; What might the author have done to organize the ideas?; What might the author have done when he/she got tired or frustrated?;* and so on), appreciation of characteristics of effective writing (e.g., *How did the writer grab your interest?*), and other knowledge and understandings targeted for instruction. Continue development through the Model It stage as needed until all key knowledge and understandings are clear
    - Discuss and explore both writing and self-regulation strategies to be learned (we typically begin development of self-regulation, introducing goal setting and the goals we will be working on)

*(continued)*

**TABLE 11.1** *(continued)*

*SRSD Instruction\**

2. *Discuss It – Discourse is Critical!*
   o Discuss students' current writing and self-regulation abilities, their attitudes and beliefs about writing, what they are saying to themselves as they write, and how these factors might help or hinder them as writers; emphasize role of both effort and powerful strategies in becoming a better writer (begin development of attributions to knowing the "tricks" of writing and to effort in order to strengthen motivation and self-efficacy for writing)
   o Graph number of genre specific essay elements and other goals targeted included in pretest or prior essays; this assists with goal setting and tracking progress in writing (graphing prior writing can be skipped if students are likely to react negatively)
   o Further discuss writing and self-regulation strategies to be learned: purpose, benefits, how and when they can be used or might be inappropriate (this assists with generalization as well as initial learning)
   o Introduce graphic organizer for the writing genre and task being addressed
   o Analyze good, grade appropriate model papers (we often have to write these essays ourselves or collect them from peers, as text found in the classroom is typically above many or most students' writing levels)
   o Take notes from these papers on a graphic organizer to assist students in learning to make notes (we find that many students need practice and support in learning to make notes rather than writing full sentences on graphic organizers)
   o With the teacher, analyze poor essay(s), make notes for a better essay on a graphic organizer, and write this essay collaboratively
   o Establish students' commitment to learn strategies and act as collaborative partners; further establish role of student effort and strategy use in becoming an effective writer
   o Give students copies of the appropriate mnemonic chart and graphic organizer when appropriate in Stages 1 and 2 for their writing files (these are used throughout stages 3–5 as supports for memory and performance and are gradually faded; see following stages)

3. *Model It*
   o Teacher modeling and/or interactive, collaborative modeling of writing and self-regulation strategies, including self-statements, goal-setting, self-assessment, and self-reinforcement; teacher refers to the mnemonic chart and graphic organizer during the writing process (it is not necessary for teachers to model alone while students watch and listen, many teachers prefer interactive, collaborative modeling while maintaining control of the writing process and modeled elements)
   o Analyze and discuss strategies and model's performance; make changes as needed; discuss how students will use or modify aspects of the model's performance
   o Students develop and record personal self-statements to assist them throughout the writing process and use of the writing and self-regulation statements (these are now kept in students' writing files and used as another support through Stage 5)

- Model self-assessment and self-recording through graphing of collaboratively written compositions
- Promote student development of self-regulation and writing strategies across other tasks and situations; discuss use in other settings (continue generalization support)

4. *Memorize It*
   - Although begun in earlier stages, require and confirm memorization of strategies, meaning and importance of each step in each strategy, mnemonic(s), and self-instructions as appropriate
   - Continue to confirm and support memorization in following stages, make sure students have memorized the mnemonics, what they mean, and the importance of each step before Independent Performance (as one student told us, "Of course you can't use it if you can't remember it!")

5. *Support It*
   - Teachers and students use writing and self-regulation strategies collaboratively as needed to meet all of the goals identified for composing in this genre while using the visual supports in students' writing folders (the mnemonic strategy chart, graphic organizer, personal self-statements sheets, and targeted words lists such as linking words or "million dollar words"/effective vocabulary
   - Challenging initial goals for genre elements and characteristics of writing established collaboratively with students and individualized as needed; criterion levels increased gradually until final goals met
   - Graphic organizer replaced with student creating mnemonic-based organizer on scratch paper (this makes use of the strategy "portable" and not reliant on the physical graphic organizer)
   - Prompts, guidance, and collaboration faded individually until the student can compose successfully alone
   - Self-regulation components (goal setting, self-instructions, self-monitoring, and self-reinforcement) are all being used by this stage; additional forms of self-regulation, such as managing the writing environment, use of imagery, and so on may be introduced
   - Discuss plans for maintenance, continue support of generalization

6. *Independent Performance*
   - Students able to use writing and self-regulation strategies independently; teachers monitor and support/enhance as needed
   - Fading of overt self-regulation may begin (graphing may be discontinued, self-statements sheets may not be out during writing, and so on)
   - Plans for maintenance and generalization continue to be discussed and implemented

---

\* A "stage" of instruction is not equivalent to a single lesson; Stages 1 and 2 are often combined in instruction; a stage or combination of stages may take several lessons to complete; Stages 3 and 5 typically take the most time in instruction; instruction is often recursive across stages; students should progress across stages as they meet criteria for doing so. This table was adapted from Harris, Graham, Chambers, & Houston, (2014).

written at their writing level. They also develop vocabulary and understanding necessary for effective persuasive writing. During the next stages students learn how to address the topic, audience, the purpose for writing, take short notes, and write a draft of the essay using the TREE mnemonic as a guide. After writing, the children can review the essay to make sure they have all the parts, and revise the essay (e.g., add million dollar words, combine sentences). The We-Write system supports and extends teacher-led lessons by allowing students to plan, draft, revise, and reflect on persuasive writing tasks using a web-based tutor.

We-Write supports self, peer, teacher, and/or computerized assessment and feedback with a repository of all student writing samples for reflection. The computerized assessment uses some natural language processing approaches to check student responses to specific questions (e.g., checking for keywords and number of words). We-Write relies on the teacher to provide tailored, constructive feedback on the elements of the composition, given that natural language processors have not yet been developed to provide this level of formative feedback in We-Write (cf. Chapter 1). The system targets upper elementary (i.e., Grades 4 and 5) or middle grade writers, but can be easily extended for higher grade levels.

In this chapter, we present the persuasive writing skills targeted by the We-Write system for upper elementary students. We then describe the use of technology in concert with the teacher to develop strong persuasive writing skills. We also present supporting evidence on the SRSD-based persuasive writing approach as well as iterative design studies on We-Write. Finally, we present information on future studies and planned extensions.

## The Targeted Skill—Persuasive Writing Skills with Upper Elementary Grade Children

Good writing is essential to success in school and effective schooling. Teachers ask students to write in order to assess students' learning of subject-matter material and important concepts (e.g., written tests and assignments) (National Council of Teachers of English, 2004). Additionally, writing about material read or presented in class enhances students' learning (Bangert-Drowns, Hurley, & Wilkinson, 2004; Graham & Hebert, 2010). Beyond the school years, good writing is also critical, as over 90 percent of white-collar workers and 80 percent of blue-collar workers report that writing is important to job success (National Commission on Writing, 2004, 2005, 2006).

Skilled writing is complex, requiring extensive self-regulation of a flexible, goal-directed problem-solving activity. In addition to basic skills, students must also develop knowledge about the writing process, genre knowledge, and strategies for writing and self-regulating the writing process. Students who struggle with writing produce text that is less polished, expansive, coherent, and effective than that of their peers (Harris, Graham, Brindle, & Sandmel, 2009). Harris and Graham (2009) report that less skilled writers often:

- lack critical knowledge of the writing process, writing strategies, and self-regulation of the writing process;
- do not understand the social aspects of writing, such as readers' needs and perspectives, and communication between author and reader;
- have difficulty generating ideas and selecting topics;
- do little to no advance planning;
- engage in knowledge telling (e.g., simply restating text or listing ideas);
- lack important strategies for planning, producing, organizing, and revising text;
- emphasize mechanics over content when making revisions;
- frequently overestimate their writing abilities.

Further adding to this picture, research indicates the majority of teachers report inadequate pre- and in-service preparation in writing instruction, and often do not have easy access to good professional development and evidence-based interventions. Upper elementary grade children need the following abilities to become skilled writers:

- planning, drafting, and revising effectively;
- effectively managing the complex writing process;
- focusing attention on important elements and characteristics in writing;
- generating good ideas for writing;
- organizing ideas;
- presenting ideas effectively to the audience;
- adhering to the language rules and writing conventions;
- maintaining persistence and motivation to write.

Unfortunately, the majority of students in the U. S. are not good writers; this may be due to the complexity of writing, the lack of sufficient focus on writing development in our schools, and the need for more evidence-based approaches to writing instruction (Harris et al., 2009). On the National Assessment of Educational Progress (NAEP, 2005; Salahu-Din, Persky, & Miller, 2008), only 33 percent of grade 8 and 24 percent of grade 12 students performed at or above the "proficient" level (defined as solid academic performance) in writing. Further, 55 percent of grade 8 and 58 percent of grade 12 students scored at or below the "basic" level, denoting only partial mastery of the writing skills needed at these grade levels. Poor writing abilities make it difficult for students to use writing effectively as a tool for learning, communication, and self-expression.

## The Need for the Technology

We-Write is designed to address these needs of learners by developing a web-based tutoring tool to work in concert with the teacher in applying the SRSD approach to instruction in writing. SRSD for writing has had the strongest impact of any strategies instruction approach in writing and has been deemed an evidence-based practice (cf. Baker, Chard, Ketterlin-Geller, Apichatabutra, & Doabler, 2009; Graham & Perrin, 2007). Initially developed and continuously revised since the early 1980s, SRSD integrates multiple lines of research from multiple theoretical perspectives in order to develop powerful interventions for students who face significant academic challenges and their normally achieving peers (Harris & Graham, 2009).

SRSD instruction includes interactive, explicit learning of powerful strategies for writing both across and within genres, the knowledge (including vocabulary and background knowledge) needed to use these strategies, and strategies for self-regulating use of these writing strategies throughout the writing process (e.g., goal setting, self-assessment, self-instructions, and self-reinforcement). Discourse is critical in this development of knowledge and understandings. Equally important, SRSD enhances engagement and purposively develops self-efficacy for writing, attributions to strategy knowledge and effort, and motivation for writing. Instruction takes places across six flexible, recursive, and highly interactive stages, with gradual release of responsibility for writing to students (Harris et al., 2009). Instruction proceeds based on students' progress; students are given the time they need to make these strategies their own. Procedures for maintaining what has been learned and determining how to use this knowledge across writing tasks when appropriate are included as well.

The structure strategy provides the We-Write framework for source-based persuasion where children are required to read information, select, encode, gather, and organize evidence in support of their writing. The structure strategy is based on the strategic mental representation that readers are able to generate based on five text structures: comparison, problem and solution, cause and effect, sequence, and description (Meyer, 1975; Meyer & Poon, 2001; Meyer, Young, & Bartlett, 1989; Wijekumar, Meyer, & Lei, 2012). The We-Write platform integrates the problem and solution text structure within the information gathering and writing stages to support persuasive writing. It is important to note that the comparison text structure also provides a powerful framework to compare alternatives or solutions in support of persuasion and will be integrated in the near future.

In summary, the We-Write system integrates teacher-led and computer supporting modeling, practice, assessment, scaffolding, feedback, and reflection for upper elementary school children so that they may become proficient, confident, and efficacious writers. Learners develop cognitive and metacognitive skills through the six stages of SRSD modules led by the teacher and supported by the computer software. Examples of how the SRSD approach is implemented within We-Write are presented in Table 11.2.

## The Need for We-Write and Integration with Teacher Components

We-Write addresses four practical problems faced in schools today. First, as noted previously, the majority of students in this country are not good writers despite

TABLE 11.2 Samples of Operationalization of SRSD in We-Write.

| SRSD Stage and Approach | Example of Implementation in We-Write Software | Example of Implementation in Teacher-Led Session |
| --- | --- | --- |
| Develop and Activate Knowledge Needed for Writing and Self-Regulation | We-Write presents videos on important elements about writing (e.g., Pick your ideas, Organize your notes, Write and say more—POW) | Discourse focuses on aspects such as fact vs. opinion, how knowing who your reader is influences what is written, etc. (see Table 11.1) |
| Discuss It—Discourse is Critical! | Students identify the topic sentence, reasons, explanations, and end with system-provided model sample essays | Teacher and students develop important elements of note-taking using the TREE graphic organizer |
| Model It | Children enter their own self-statements into We-Write for use whenever they need them to support themselves in the writing process | Teachers do the same asking the children to write their self-statement on their folder. Teacher engages in cognitive modeling while planning and writing with help and support from students |
| Memorize It | We-Write quizzes the children on POW, TAP, and TREE mnemonics | Teacher does brief memory activity in class as needed to assess and support memorization of the mnemonic and the meaning and importance of each part |
| Support It | Students assess collaborative and independent essays for number of persuasive genre elements and graph their performance | Teacher and students first plan and write collaboratively with gradual transfer to students as appropriate |
| Independent Performance | Students compose independent essays in the system and self-assess | Teacher monitors students' writing and provides feedback |

the importance of writing. Second, national concern about poor writing skills is reflected in the new grade-level expectations for writing in the Common Core State Standards Initiative (CCSSI) (Gewertz, 2011). These standards have been adopted by 44 states and the District of Columbia and provide a road map for the writing skills students need to be ready for college and work. A prominent emphasis in the standards is learning how to write logical, coherent, and compelling arguments, with opinion writing (a basic form of persuasive writing) emphasized in the elementary grades. Writing persuasively is also critical to both college

(Clark, 2005) and work success (National Commission on Writing, 2004, 2005, 2006). CCSSI specifies that grade 5 students need to be able to write persuasive essays, based on either given topics or about texts read, that support a clearly presented opinion with logically ordered and linked reasons. These reasons should be backed by facts and details, and the essay should end with an effective conclusion (standard W.5.1).

Third, focusing attention only on improving students' writing is not sufficient to improve the practical problems facing our students today. Students need to understand how reading and writing work together, as learning to write and writing to learn are used across the school years and beyond (Newell, Beach, Smith, & Van Der Heide, 2011). Reading comprehension using text structure is an integral part of gathering the necessary content information to write (based on previous work by Meyer et al., 2010). Planning, drafting, evaluating, and revising a persuasive essay requires both powerful general and persuasive writing strategies, as well as important strategies for self-regulating the writing process and maintaining motivation (Graham, Harris, & Mason, 2005; Harris, Graham, & Mason, 2006; Harris, Graham, Mason, & Friedlander, 2008).

Finally, there is a need to exploit all the available technologies in schools to improve writing. Web-based software provides a powerful platform for learners through the consistency of delivery, valuable individualized extensions and adaptations for practice tasks, immediate assessment and feedback, scaffolding and guidance, and a repository that can support reflection (Wijekumar et al., 2012).

We-Write focuses on persuasive writing at upper elementary grades to address these challenges. Further, the system integrates the text structure-based approach to further cement the foundational skills related to information seeking, encoding, gathering, and writing.

## Description of the We-Write Framework and Technology

We-Write uses a unique approach in integrating the teachers' role with the technology support thereby maintaining the teacher as the instructional leader in the classroom and allowing the teacher to maintain control of the learning environment. Writing is a complex task and early experiences with writing are critical.

Within the We-Write framework teacher-led lessons are followed by web-based lessons to extend the learning with videos, practice tasks, assessment, and feedback. The teacher has a dashboard from which they can review the students' performance and move students to advanced practice or to review the lessons. We-Write uses some indices to provide simple formative feedback to the learner. Advanced feedback designed to scaffold the learner relies on a teacher scoring tool where teachers can read the responses, record audio feedback, and/or provide feedback related to the quality of ideas, organization of ideas, topic sentence(s), reason(s), explanation(s), a strong ending, sentence structure, addressing the audience, grabbing the attention of the reader, and overall quality of writing. Our approach uses the latest technologies available for natural language processing and data mining to monitor student interactions on the system.

We have opted to let the teachers do what they do best and the computer, or intelligent tutor, serve as a critical support in writing development and in meeting the needs of all students in diverse classrooms. The computer tutor acts as an advanced writing tool (to support learning powerful writing and self-regulation strategies as well as the planning, drafting, evaluating, and revising of the persuasive essay. Details about the operationalization of the SRSD in We-Write are presented in Table 11.2.

The software system serves as a writing environment that has expert models to guide the learner interactions (Koedinger & Corbett, 2006). Expert writing tutors were observed and interaction models were created for the We-Write framework. Each lesson unit was designed to feature the teacher-led lessons followed by modeling, practice, and feedback on the web-based tutor. Sample lessons for the teacher contain scripts from expert tutors as a guide (we encourage teachers to use these only as a guide). The observed expert tutor interactions also serve as the design guide for the web-based modeling, practice activities, and feedback. The system also reduces the need to remember many aspects of the writing process by providing note-taking windows, reminders about self-assessments, and on-demand help about planning, writing, and revising. The system also allows easy sharing of writing samples for peer reviews as well as feedback from teachers. Students' writing throughout instruction is stored in the electronic portfolio, allowing students to track and reflect on their progress, and gain increased confidence to write (self-efficacy) based on their observed improvements.

## Evidence on the Effectiveness of the Technology

Over 100 studies of SRSD in multiple countries (including true-experiments, quasi-experiments, and single-subject design studies) have been conducted across grades 2 to 12 and with adults (Graham, Harris, & McKeown, 2013). These studies provide convincing evidence that SRSD is an effective method for teaching writing strategies to students who represent the full range of writing ability in a typical class, as well as struggling writers and students with writing and other disabilities. SRSD has been used effectively with whole classes, small groups, and individual students. Meta-analyses have shown that SRSD achieves significantly higher effect sizes than other instructional approaches (e.g., Writers Workshop) in writing (Graham & Perrin, 2007). SRSD for writing was deemed an evidence-based practice in the U. S. Institute for Education Sciences Practice Guide: Teaching Elementary School Students to Be Effective Writers (June, 2012) and by a panel of independent researchers (Baker et al., 2009). SRSD was identified as having the strongest impact of any strategies instruction approach in writing in a large study commissioned by the Carnegie Corporation (Graham & Perrin, 2007; Graham, Harris, & Hebert, 2011).

Similar to SRSD, the structure strategy based reading comprehension approach has been tested extensively in experimental studies and shown to be efficacious in large-scale randomized controlled trials in grades 4 and 5 (Wijekumar et al., 2012, 2013, 2014). The *structure strategy* has a strong theoretical foundation and empirical support (e.g., Armbruster, Anderson, & Ostertag, 1987; Bartlett, 1978; Carrell, 1985; Cook & Mayer, 1988; Meyer, 1975; Meyer, Brandt, & Bluth, 1980; Meyer & Poon, 2001; Meyer et al., 1989, 2002, 2010, 2011; Wijekumar et al., 2012, 2013; Williams, Hall, & Lauer, 2004; Williams, Stafford, Lauer, Hall, & Pollini, 2009). Structure strategy instruction increases how well students can write main ideas, remember what they read, organize their ideas from texts about science or social studies, and score on a standardized reading comprehension test (e.g., Meyer et al., 2002, 2010, 2011; Wijekumar et al., 2012, 2013, 2014). Combining both approaches into the We-Write platform builds on the success of both approaches.

Recent research studies have also shown positive results when trained teachers managed the We-Write intervention delivery and seamlessly transitioned students to the web-based platform for further practice and instruction. Teachers presented materials to the learners in the classroom setting and followed each session with practice on the computer. When students had completed the computer lessons, the teacher reviewed the student performance and made instructional choices about the next lessons for each child.

Design studies were conducted in 2012–13 and 2013–14 with 11 classrooms in Pennsylvania each year. The number of children completing the tests were 286 for pre- and 246 for post-tests. Results from two pretest-posttest design studies showed that 5th grade children using the We-Write approach made significant improvements in their planning, persuasive writing, and efficacy for writing. Fidelity observations of classrooms showed that all teachers attended to the implementation factors within the SRSD framework and carefully managed their instructional time to support each child to make progress on writing strategy, process, and efficacy.

From pretest to post-test, the planning improved significantly. At pretest, 10 percent of children utilized the planning page of the test and most wrote full essay type of planning responses. At post-test, over 80 percent of the children planned and wrote focused notes using the TREE graphic organizer. Teachers noted that the students also exhibited these skills when they were completing the end of year assessments administered by the State of Pennsylvania. Overall, the We-Write teacher and computer modules are well integrated and have shown positive findings that can translate into making an impact for all children.

## How to Access We-Write

The software is available at no cost for schools at http://wewrite.fasct.org (Figure 11.1). However, it is very important to note that teachers are an integral part of the We-Write approach and based on our experience should complete approximately two days of professional development prior to using the software and at least one additional day of in-school coaching during implementation. Professional development focuses on the stages of the SRSD approach, guidelines for customizing learning for the learners, milestones for reviewing progress, and practice on using the We-Write lessons and teacher dashboard, During professional development, teachers receive a complete set of lesson plans for use in the classroom, learn how to adapt the lessons to their students' strengths and needs as well as the local classroom context, review the roadmap showing the alternating pattern of teacher-led and computer supported lessons, learn how to use the We-Write dashboard to monitor the student progress and/or assess student responses, learn how to group students and move them to appropriate next lessons in the We-Write learning pathways, and enhance We-Write with their own lessons and writing prompts to promote transfer.

Once the accounts are setup, the user can upload their classroom rosters into the system. All children on the roster will be provided with a username and password to access the software.

Ideally, teachers should use the We-Write sequence of lessons for approximately 45 minutes once or twice a week with the teacher-led lessons preceding the computer supported lessons. The series of lessons are organized around the SRSD stages, and the goal is to reduce scaffolding as students become proficient

FIGURE 11.1  Teacher Dashboard.

writers and gain confidence. Because each student will develop strategies and skills at their own pace, the teacher has the ability to carefully support each child by noting any abilities that need further development prior to moving to the next stage. In most classrooms, it is likely that some students will proceed through SRSD instruction at a faster pace and can work on advanced writing skills. Teachers can use the teacher dashboard to transfer these students to enrichment activities available in the We-Write platform (e.g., sentence combining, improving vocabulary using million dollar words).

Figure 11.2 presents a sample roadmap for teachers presented during the professional development sessions. This is intended as a guide to successful implementation and is not designed to be a restrictive flowchart to be followed without thought to the needs of the learner and local context. Teachers have reported ease of use, because of the roadmap and the explicit lessons preparing children for the computer time. Further, the teacher dashboard shown in Figures 11.1, 11.3 to 11.4 allows teachers to control the pace of instruction, place children into lessons for further development as needed, or move children forward where they can access enrichment lessons. The teacher is also notified when there are essays that require grading. The teacher is able to provide feedback in audio, text, or in a simple TREE rubric for the children. Finally, teachers can customize the We-Write lessons with prompts and activities that are relevant to their local context, as shown in Figure 11.4. This allows them to customize the learning to suit the profile of learners in their classrooms or create new prompts that are more challenging or less challenging for their students.

We-Write computer lessons allow students to follow the SRSD stages beginning with a "Get Set" stage of developing background knowledge, followed by activities that support learning and scaffold the learner through all the stages. Upper elementary grade children learn three mnemonics through the We-Write platform:

POW = **P**ick your ideas, **O**rganize your notes, **W**rite and say more

TAP = **T**opic, **A**udience, **P**urpose

TREE = **T**opic, **R**easons (3 or more), **E**xplanations (1 or more for each reason), **E**nding

With the intelligent tutor's guidance, learners can view videos where the self-regulation and writing strategies are modeled, test their understanding of each step in the writing strategies, identify the parts of model essays (pick out TREE shown in Figure 11.5), identify problems with poor essays, improve their abilities in note-making, plan and write their own essays, self-assess their essays, revise and submit essays for teacher grading, and reflect on their progress by checking their writing progress on the portfolio. Students are also able to revise their essays using

## We-Write 197

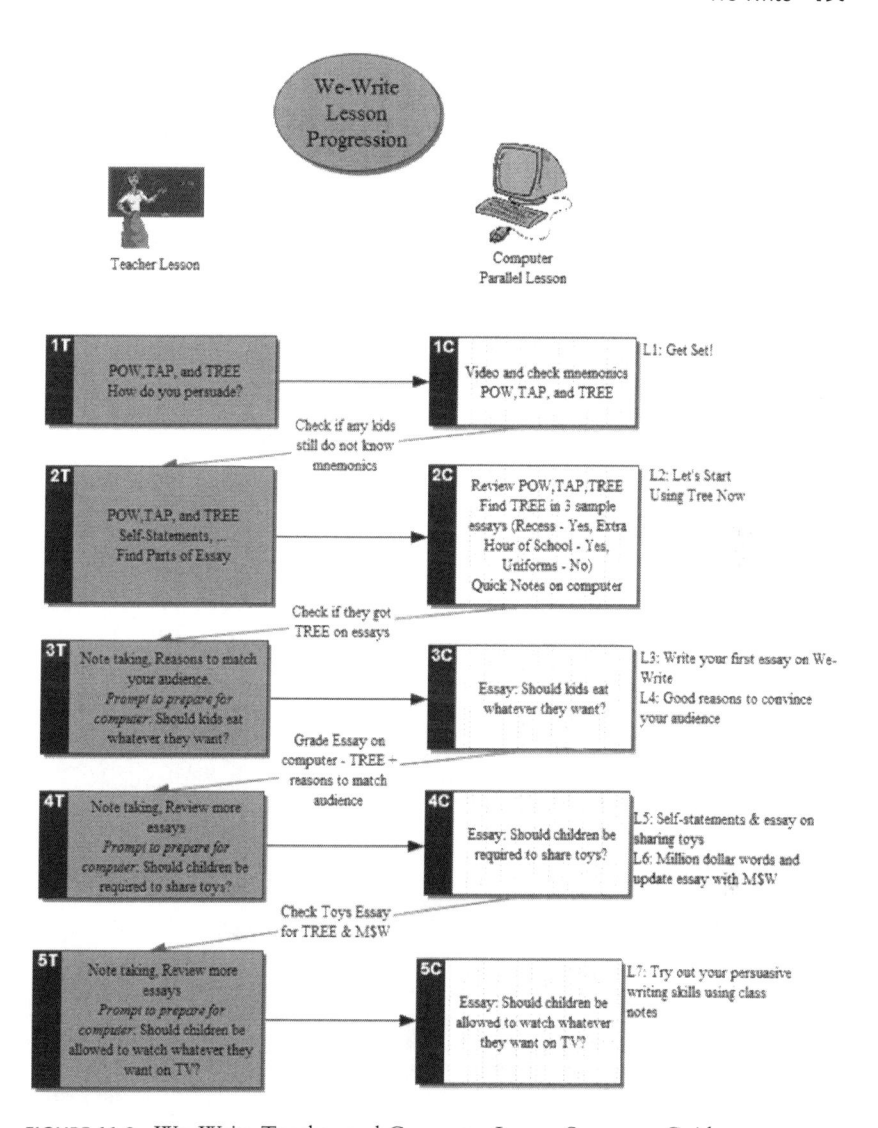

**FIGURE 11.2** We-Write Teacher and Computer Lesson Sequence Guide.

effective vocabulary, sentence combining, and other approaches as appropriate. Finally, children are able to learn about the problem and solution text structure, and plan and organize their reading and writing using the text structure. Using the text structure also supports the children in using sophisticated linking words that signal the problem and solution text structure when writing their persuasive essay. All student activities are preceded by teacher-led classroom lessons to prepare students for the web-based activities.

**FIGURE 11.3** Creating Custom Lessons.

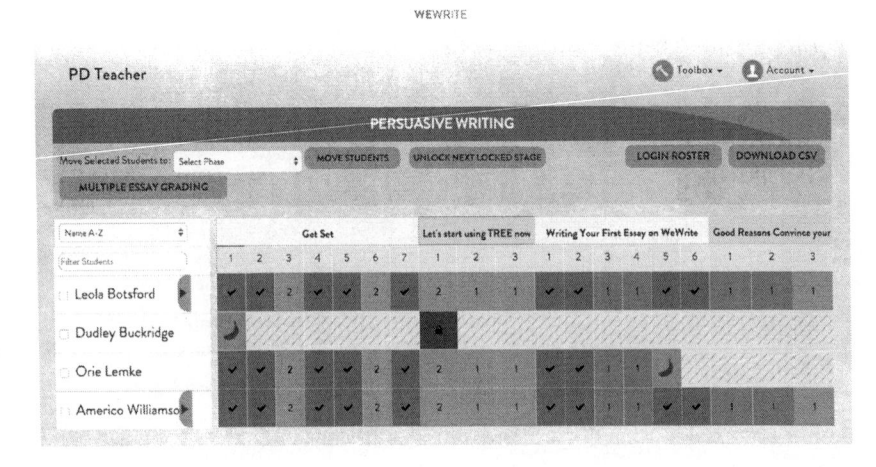

**FIGURE 11.4** Tracking Student Progress.

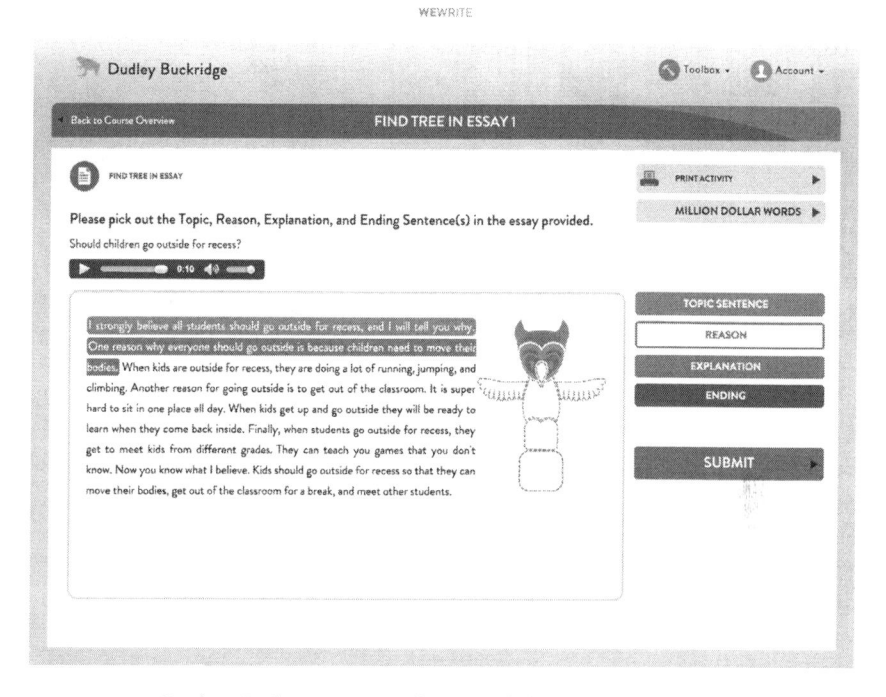

FIGURE 11.5 Student Picks out TREE from Model Essay in Early SRSD Stage.

## Teacher Experiences and Notes

The We-Write system has been carefully designed to maintain the teacher as the instructional leader in the classroom and allow the computer to support the development of persuasive writing skills for students in upper elementary school. Teachers collaborating with the design and development team have echoed sentiments from previous research studies:

1. Teachers received little to no preparation in teaching writing. We-Write professional development provided a solid foundation for teachers in teaching writing and efficacy for teaching writing.
2. Language arts time during the school day focuses mostly on reading with little time devoted to writing instruction. We-Write allows the teacher to control writing instruction and is supported by computer tools that promote and support students' learning.
3. SRSD-based writing instruction is a systematic, elegant, and powerful approach to developing control of the writing process, critical writing strategies, and self-efficacy for writing. We-Write implementation led by the teacher captures the ebb and flow of the SRSD stages, allowing practice and

further development for children who need it and enrichment for those who are ready to move on.
4. Text structure-based reading allows learners to select information carefully from source materials in preparation for writing. Text structure also provides a powerful means to approach and organize persuasive essays and enhances vocabulary related to persuading the reader.
5. Teachers have expressed some concern about the need to provide feedback on the We-Write platform. The teacher administrative interface has been re-designed to allow teachers to group essays with similar characteristics to minimize the need for individual feedback. Additionally, teachers can use the audio feedback capability within We-Write to alleviate the need for extensive written feedback to the learners.

The We-Write platform currently is being expanded to include persuasive writing with the comparison text structure and informational writing for upper elementary school children. These extensions were created because teachers expressed strong interest in these genres. By combining the teacher-led and web-based lessons, we have provided support for the teachers and students with modeling, practice, assessment, and feedback. Recent research studies show that the system functions very well. Thus the We-Write framework provides a sound approach to improving the writing skills of children in upper elementary grades.

## Acknowledgments

The research reported here was supported by the Institute of Education Sciences, U. S. Department of Education, through Grants R305A1300705 to Texas A&M University. The opinions expressed are those of the authors and do not represent the views of the Institute or the U. S. Department of Education.

## References

Armbruster, B., Anderson, T., & Ostertag, J. (1987). Does text structure/summarization instruction facilitate learning from expository text? *Reading Research Quarterly, 22*, 331–346.

Baker, S. K., Chard, D. J., Ketterlin-Geller, L. R., Apichatabutra, C., & Doabler, C. (2009). Teaching writing to at-risk students: The quality of evidence for self-regulated strategy development. *Exceptional Children, 75*, 303–318.

Bangert-Drowns, R. L., Hurley, M. M., & Wilkinson, B. (2004). The effects of school-based writing-to-learn interventions on academic achievement: A meta-analysis. *Review of Educational Research, 74*, 29–58.

Bartlett, B. J. (1978). *Top-Level Structure as an Organizational Strategy For Recall of Classroom Text*. Unpublished doctoral dissertation, Arizona State University.

Carrell, P. L. (1985). Facilitating ESL reading by teaching text structure. *TESOL Quarterly, 19*, 727–752.

Clark, H. (2015). *Building a Common Language for Career Readiness and Success: A Foundational Competency Framework for Employers and Educators*. ACT Working Paper Series. Retrieved from http://www.act.org/content/dam/act/unsecured/documents/WP-2015-02-Building-a-Common-Language-for-Career-Readiness-and-Success.pdf.

Cook, L. K., & Mayer, R. E. (1988). Teaching readers about the structure of scientific text. *Journal of Educational Psychology, 80*, 448–456.

Festas, I., Oliveira, A., Rebelo, J., Damião, M., Harris, K. R., & Graham, S. (2015). The effects of self-regulated strategy development (SRSD) on the writing performance of eighth grade Portuguese students. *Contemporary Educational Psychology, 40*, 17–27.

Gewertz, C. (2011). Common-assessment consortia add resources to plans. *Education Week, 30*, 8.

Graham, S., & Hebert, M. (2010). *Writing to Reading: Evidence for How Writing Can Improve Reading*. Washington, DC: Alliance for Excellence in Education.

Graham, S., & Perrin, D. (2007). *Writing Next: Effective Strategies to Improve Writing of Adolescent Middle and High School*. Washington, DC: Alliance for Excellence in Education.

Graham, S., Harris, K. R., & Hebert, M. (2011). *Informing Writing: The Benefits of Formative Assessment*. Washington, DC: Alliance for Excellence in Education. (Commissioned by the Carnegie Corp. of New York.)

Graham, S., Harris, K. R., & Mason, L. (2005). Improving the writing performance, knowledge, and motivation of struggling young writers: The effects of self-regulated strategy development. *Contemporary Educational Psychology, 30*, 207–241.

Graham, S., Harris, K. R., & McKeown, D. (2013). The writing of students with LD and a meta-analysis of SRSD writing intervention studies: Redux. In L. Swanson, K. R. Harris, & S. Graham (Eds.), *Handbook of Learning Disabilities* (2nd ed., pp. 405–438). New York: Guilford Press.

Harris, K. R., & Graham, S. (2009). Self-regulated strategy development in writing: Premises, evolution, and the future. *British Journal of Educational Psychology* (monograph series), *6*, 113–135.

Harris, K. R., Graham, S., & Adkins, M. (2015). Practice-based professional development and self-regulated strategy development for Tier 2, at-risk writers in second grade. *Contemporary Educational Psychology, 40*, 5–16.

Harris, K. R., Graham, S., & Mason, L. (2006). Improving the writing, knowledge, and motivation of struggling young writers: Effects of Self-Regulated Strategy development with and without peer support. *American Educational Research Journal, 43*, 295–340.

Harris, K. R., Graham, S., Brindle, M., & Sandmel, K. (2009). Metacognition and children's writing. In D. Hacker, J. Dunlosky, & A. Graesser (Eds.), *Handbook of Metacognition in Education* (pp. 131–153). Mahwah, NJ: Erlbaum.

Harris, K. R., Graham, S., Mason, L. H., & Friedlander, B. (2008). *Powerful Writing Strategies for All Students*. Baltimore, MD: Brookes.

Harris, K. R., Lane, K. L., Graham, S., Driscoll, S., Sandmel, K., Brindle, M., & Schatschneider, C. (2012). Practice-based professional development for self-regulated strategies development in writing: A randomized controlled study. *Journal of Teacher Education, 63*(2), 103–119.

Koedinger, K., & Corbett, A. T. (2006) Cognitive tutors: Technology bringing learning science to the classroom. In Sawyer, R. K. (ed.), *The Cambridge Handbook of the Learning Sciences*, (pp. 61–78). New York: Cambridge University Press.

Meyer, B. J. F. (1975). *The Organization of Prose and its Effects on Memory*. Amsterdam, Netherlands: North-Holland.

Meyer, B. J. F., & Poon, L. W. (2001). Effects of structure strategy training and signaling on recall of text. *Journal of Educational Psychology, 93,* 141–159. Cambridge, MA: MIT Press.

Meyer, B. J. F., Brandt, D. M., & Bluth, G. J. (1980). Use of the top-level structure in text: Key for reading comprehension of ninth-grade students. *Reading Research Quarterly, 16,* 72–103. http://dx.doi.org/10.2307/747349.

Meyer, B. J. F., Wijekumar, K. K., & Lin, Y. (2011). Individualizing a web-based structure strategy intervention for fifth graders' comprehension of nonfiction. *Journal of Educational Psychology, 103*(1), 140.

Meyer, B. J. F., Young, C. J., & Bartlett, B. J. (1989). *Memory Improved: Reading and Memory Enhancement across the Life Span through Strategic Text Structures.* Hillsdale, NJ: Lawrence Erlbaum.

Meyer, B. J. F., Middlemiss, W., Theodorou, E., Brezinski, K. L., McDougall, J., & Bartlett, B. J. (2002). Effects of structure strategy instruction delivered to fifth-grade children using the Internet with and without the aid of older adult tutors. *Journal of Educational Psychology, 94,* 486–519.

Meyer, B. J. F., Wijekumar, K., Middlemiss, W., Higley, K., Lei, P., Meier, C., & Spielvogel, J. (2010). Web-based tutoring of the structure strategy with or without elaborated feedback or choice for fifth- and seventh-grade readers. *Reading Research Quarterly, 41,* 62–92.

National Assessment of Educational Progress. (2005). *The Nation's Report Card.* Washington, DC: U. S. Department of Education, Institute of Education Sciences, National Center for Education Statistics. National Center.

National Council of Teachers of English. (2004). *NCTE Beliefs about the Teaching of Writing.* Retrieved from http://www.ncte.org/print.asp?id= 118876&node=367.

National Commission on Writing in America's Schools. (2004). *Writing: A Ticket to Work . . . Or a Ticket out.* New York: College Board.

National Commission on Writing in America's Schools. (2005). *Writing: A Powerful Message from State Government.* New York: College Board.

National Commission on Writing in America's Schools. (2006). *Writing and School Reform.* New York: College Board.

Newell, G., Beach, R., Smith, J., & Van Der Heide, J. (2011). Teaching and learning argumentative reading and writing: A review of research. *Reading Research Quarterly, 46*(3), 273–304.

Salahu-Din, D., Persky, H., & Miller, J. (2008). *The Nation's Report Card™: Writing 2007. National Assessment of Educational Progress at Grades 8 and 12. National, State, and Trial Urban District Results.* (NCES 2008–468). National Center for Education Statistics, Institute of Education Sciences, U. S. Department of Education, Washington, D. C. Retrieved from http://search.proquest.com.ezaccess.libraries.psu.edu/docview/61971023?accountid=13158.

Wijekumar, K. K., Meyer, B. J. F., & Lei, P. (2012). Large-scale randomized controlled trial with 4th graders using intelligent tutoring of the structure strategy to improve nonfiction reading comprehension. *Journal of Educational Technology Research and Development, 60,* 987–1013.

Wijekumar, K. K., Meyer, B. J. F., & Lei, P. (2013). High-fidelity implementation of web-based Intelligent tutoring system improves fourth and fifth graders content area reading comprehension. *Computers & Education, 68,* 366–379.

Wijekumar, K. K., Meyer, B. J. F., Lei, P.-W, Lin, Y., Johnson, L. A., Shurmatz, K., . . . Cook, M. (2014). Improving reading comprehension for 5th grade readers in rural and suburban schools using web-based intelligent tutoring systems. *Journal of Research in Educational Effectiveness, 7*(4), 331–357, doi: 10.1080/19345747.2013.853333.

Williams, J. P., Hall, K. M., & Lauer, K. D. (2004) Teaching expository text structure to young at-risk learners: Building the basics of comprehension instruction. *Exceptionality, 12*(3), 129–144.

Williams, J. P., Stafford, K. B., Lauer, K. D., Hall, K. M., & Pollini, S. (2009). Embedding reading comprehension training in content-area instruction. *Journal of Educational Psychology, 101,* 1–20.

# 12

# THE WRITING PAL

## A Writing Strategy Tutor

*Scott A. Crossley, Laura K. Allen, and Danielle S. McNamara*

This chapter provides an overview of the Writing Pal (W-Pal), an automated tutoring system that provides instruction on writing strategies through lessons and game-based practice on these strategies: essay writing practice, automated essay scoring, and practical feedback for essay revision. The system targets adolescent writers, but can be used effectively from middle school to first-year college classes.

In this chapter, we first discuss the primary skills targeted by W-Pal, namely writing and revising persuasive essays. We also discuss the need for writing technology in the classroom and provide a general overview of the W-Pal system. We describe a number of studies that provide evidence for the strengths of using W-Pal in the classroom and explain how teachers can access W-Pal and integrate the system within their own classrooms. We close with a short section on the current limitations and future directions of the system.

## Writing Skills

When developing an automated tutoring system, it is important to have a strong understanding of the basic constructs that underlie the skills that will be taught. In the case of W-Pal, this is the construct of writing or the way in which writing is understood and valued in a given community (Elliot et al., 2013). The most widely accepted framework for the construct of writing comes from the Framework for Success in Postsecondary Writing (FSPW) released by the Council of Writing Program Administrators, National Council of Teachers of English, and the National Writing Project in 2011. The framework lists a number of skills that can specifically be fostered through students' reading and writing experiences:

- rhetorical knowledge (understanding audience, purposes, and contexts of writing);
- critical thinking in text analysis;
- knowledge of the writing process (the strategies used in the writing process);
- knowledge of conventions (the formal rules of writing);
- the ability to write texts for a variety of environments.

Beyond the FSPW, a number of writing researchers have also helped to define the writing construct and define the skills that successful writers use. For instance, researchers have found that *knowledge* is a critical component of the writing process. Specifically, when students have a greater knowledge of the language in which they are writing (e.g., strong vocabulary and grammar knowledge), of the topic of the writing assignment, as well as of the cultural and rhetorical purposes of writing (e.g., addressing different audiences in specific ways), they are more likely to generate effective and high-quality texts (Condon, 2013; Deane, 2013). Given the wide variety of knowledge types that are required to produce texts, students must develop skills and strategies that can help them to successfully *coordinate* these different aspects of the text (Elliot & Klobucar, 2013). Accordingly, successful writers are generally better at successfully using strategies during complex writing tasks, and have stronger reading, analytical, and social skills (McCutchen, 2006).

To improve students' performance on writing tasks, it is critical that students are taught the components of the writing process (i.e., the process of prewriting, writing, and revising), as well as strategies that can help them to engage in these processes. Strategies are effortful and purposeful procedures that are enacted in order to achieve a goal or accomplish a task (Alexander, Graham, & Harris, 1998; Healy, Schneider, & Bourne, 2012). Instruction on the use of strategies can benefit students by providing them with concrete information and heuristics (Alexander et al., 1998) that allow them to break up complex tasks into more manageable pieces (Healy et al., 2012). For instance, the Writing Pal system teaches students the FAST (*F*igure out the prompt, *A*sk and answer questions, *S*upport arguments with evidence, *T*hink about the other side) mnemonic to help them engage in freewriting. This mnemonic provides students with manageable tasks that can help them to generate ideas quickly during the prewriting process. This type of strategy instruction has been shown to be extremely effective at improving students' performance on writing tasks (Graham & Perin, 2007). It is particularly effective for less-skilled students (Graham, Harris, & Mason, 2005), because these strategies can help students to overcome deficiencies that they may have in related areas (e.g., in their vocabulary or domain knowledge).

The most effective form of writing strategy instruction is explicit and provides students with background knowledge about the processes and goals of a particular writing task (Graham & Perin, 2007). To help to cement newly learned strategies, students need to be provided with opportunities for sustained and deliberate writing practice (Kellogg, 2008), which can also help them understand how and when to use strategies appropriately (Plant, Ericcson, Hill, & Asberg, 2005). Individualized feedback is another important element of learning to write, because it can help students select when to use learned strategies more effectively and appropriately (Shute, 2008). In addition, such feedback can assist learners in gauging performance and provide guidance to writers during the writing process (Roscoe, Brandon, Snow, & McNamara, 2013a). Overall, sustained and deliberate practice mixed with individualized feedback are important components for developing writing strategy use, because learned strategies can be forgotten or misapplied and, during the initial stages of learning, the strategies may be applied slowly or incorrectly (Rohrer & Pashler, 2010).

## The Need for Writing Technology

The ability to read and write is essential for communication in contemporary societies. As the prevalence of electronic messaging increases, the development of strong literacy skills is more important than ever before. As described in the prior section, it is widely accepted that the best way to improve literacy skills is through sustained practice that includes both summative feedback (i.e., an overall score) and formative feedback (i.e., suggestions on how to revise portions of a text to improve it). However, providing both summative and formative feedback is difficult in terms of time and cost (Higgins, Xi, Zechner, & Williamson, 2011) and, with average elementary class sizes of 24 students and lower secondary class size averages of 23 students (Snyder & Dillow, 2012), providing frequent individualized writing feedback to all students becomes exceedingly difficult especially when teachers have five classes a day.

One solution to the time and cost constraints associated with providing opportunities for students to receive writing feedback is the use of automatic essay scoring (AES) systems and automatic writing evaluation (AWE) systems. AES systems use computer algorithms to predict human ratings of essay quality. These systems can be helpful in both classroom settings and in high stakes testing by increasing the reliability of essay scores and decreasing the time and cost normally associated with essay scoring (Higgins et al., 2011). In the classroom, AES systems can provide students with opportunities for evaluated writing practice in addition to the evaluation opportunities that a teacher gives (Dikli, 2006; Warschauer & Grimes, 2008). In high stakes testing, AES is used for assessments such as the Graduate Record Exam (GRE) and the Test of English as a Foreign Language internet-Based Test (TOEFL iBT) to provide cost-effective and reliable scores on performance assessments (Dikli, 2006). AWE systems are generally built upon AES technology, but go beyond simply providing an overall score of essay quality by providing formative feedback to students about their writing.

A number of prominent AES and AWE systems are currently in use, including e-rater (Burstein, Chodorow, & Leacock, 2004), Intellimetric (Rudner, Garcia, &

Welch, 2005, 2006), Intelligent Essay Assessor (IEA) (Landauer, Laham, & Foltz, 2003), and the AWE system in W-Pal (W-Pal) (McNamara, Crossley, & Roscoe, 2013). Although the details of these scoring models vary, they are created using the same general method. The first step is to collect a large number of writing samples that have been given scores by human raters. Researchers then identify certain properties of those writing samples that are of theoretical interest to the construct(s) being assessed and that can be reliably identified by a computer program (e.g., the use of accurate grammar rules, the use of difficult or rare words, the production of complex or long sentence structures, and the use of rhetorical features related to argumentation and text organization). These textual features are then calculated for each essay, and statistical models are created that use the features to predict human scores.

High levels of agreement have been reported in a number of studies between AES systems and human raters. The level of agreement between AES systems and human raters is similar to the level of agreement between two human raters (Landauer et al., 2003; Warschauer & Ware, 2006). Some studies have even reported higher levels of agreement between an AES system and a human rater than between two human raters. However, both AES and AWE systems have their detractors who criticize the systems for not scoring essays in the same manner as human raters. Such criticisms are based on the notion that the systems are not able to attend to essential aspects of writing such as rhetorical effectiveness, argumentation, purpose, or audience (Condon, 2013; Deane, 2013). Thus, critics tend to be concerned about the form of the writing tasks that AES and AWE systems are typically developed to score. The effectiveness of AES models has generally been limited to shorter essay types, such as those found on standardized tests; they have not yet been found to be effective in scoring more authentic writing assessments (e.g., portfolios; Condon, 2013). Additional concerns relate to the notion that students using AWE systems are less likely to trust the system than a teacher, which may limit AWE effectiveness (Grimes & Warschauer, 2010). Finally, many AWE systems are still focused more on summative than formative feedback (Roscoe, Varner, Crossley, & McNamara, 2013b).

## *Writing Pal*

W-Pal provides writing strategy instruction to students who are learning to write persuasive essays. This includes students who are in middle school up through students entering college, but most typically students who are in high school and preparing for college entry exams. W-Pal is not a traditional AWE system in that the primary focus of W-Pal is on strategy instruction. This strategy instruction is strengthened through game-based practice and later through deliberate writing practice. It is during the writing practice that students receive automatic feedback from the W-Pal AWE. Thus, W-Pal is principally a tutoring system that focuses on writing instruction, but has the capacity to include automatic summative and formative feedback.

## Writing Pal Modules

Strategy instruction is provided to W-Pal users via nine writing strategy modules. The content for these modules was developed based on research on writing strategy instruction (e.g., Graham & Perin, 2007) and extensive input from expert writing educators (Roscoe, Allen, Weston, Crossley, & McNamara, in press). The modules each focus on particular strategies that correspond to one of the three phases of the writing process: prewriting, drafting, and revising. training modules are provided for strategies that facilitate each phase of writing. Prewriting modules include (a) freewriting; and (b) planning. Drafting strategies include (a) introduction building; (b) body building; and (c) conclusion building. The revising strategies include (a) paraphrasing; (b) cohesion building; and (c) polishing of the text (see Table 12.1 for an overview).

The content within the W-Pal modules is based on English Composition curricula and is designed to provide the users with writing strategies that will help them compose persuasive essays as well as basic strategies needed for any writing task. The strategies are discussed by three animated agents via lesson videos that vary between 5 and 10 minutes each. The scripts for the interactions were developed through a collaborative process between composition experts and learning scientists. Each module contains approximately five short lesson videos. While watching the videos, students also have the option to record information they learn in the video using a "notepad" feature.

Each of the videos in W-Pal is presented by one pedagogical agent in one of three locations: Mr. Evans is a teacher in a classroom; Sheila is a student in her computer room at home; and Mike is a businessman in his work office. In these videos, the agents describe and provide examples of particular writing strategies (see Figure 12.1 for a screenshot of one of the W-Pal lesson videos). For many of the lessons, strategies are presented using mnemonic devices, which can facilitate students' recall and use of writing strategies (De La Paz & Graham, 2002). Quiz and game-like checkpoints are embedded after each lesson to reinforce the content and check for students' understanding of the information. All modules are accessible from a "Lessons Tab" in the W-Pal interface (see Figure 12.2), which allows users to progress through the modules in a flexible order.

## Writing Pal Game-based Practice

A key component of W-Pal is game-based practice. Housed within W-Pal is a suite of educational games. There has been a good deal of research showing that the engaging properties of games increase both students' motivation toward a particular task (Shank & Neaman, 2001), persistence throughout training (Barab, Gresalfi, & Arici, 2009), and the learning of information during these tasks (Rowe, Shores, Mott, & Lester, 2011). In addition, the use of game-based features such as narrative or competition can increase students' enjoyment of and engagement in a task (Craig et al., 2004; McNamara, Jackson, & Graesser, 2010),

TABLE 12.1 Summary of Writing Strategy Module Content and Practice Games.

| Module Name | Strategy Content | Practice Games |
|---|---|---|
| Prologue | Introduces W-Pal, the animated characters, and discusses the importance of writing | |
| **Prewriting Phase** | | |
| Freewriting (FW) | Covers freewriting strategies for quickly generating essay ideas, arguments, and evidence prior to writing *(FAST mnemonic)* | Freewrite Flash |
| Planning (PL) | Covers outlining and graphic organizer strategies for organizing arguments and evidence in an essay | Mastermind Outline Planning Passage |
| **Drafting Phase** | | |
| Introduction Building (IB) | Covers strategies for writing introduction paragraph thesis statements, argument previews, and attention-grabbing techniques *(TAG mnemonic)* | Essay Launcher Dungeon Escape Fix It |
| Body Building (BB) | Covers strategies for writing topic sentences and providing objective supporting evidence *(CASE mnemonic)* | RoBoCo Fix It |
| Conclusion Building (CB) | Covers strategies for restating the thesis, summarizing arguments, closing an essay, and maintaining reader interest in conclusion paragraphs *(RECAP mnemonic)* | Lockdown Dungeon Escape Fix It |
| **Revising Phase** | | |
| Paraphrasing (PA) | Covers strategies for expressing ideas with more precise and varied wording, sentence structure, splitting run-ons, and condensing choppy sentences | Adventurer's Loot Map Conquest |
| Cohesion Building (CH) | Covers strategies for adding cohesive cues to text, such as connective phrases, clarifying undefined referents, and threading ideas throughout the text | CON-Artist Undefined & Mined |
| Polishing (PO) | Covers strategies for reviewing an essay for completeness and clarity, and strategies for how to improve an essay by adding, removing, moving, or substituting ideas *(ARMS mnemonic)* | Speech Writer |

**210**  Scott A. Crossley, L.K. Allen, and D.S. McNamara

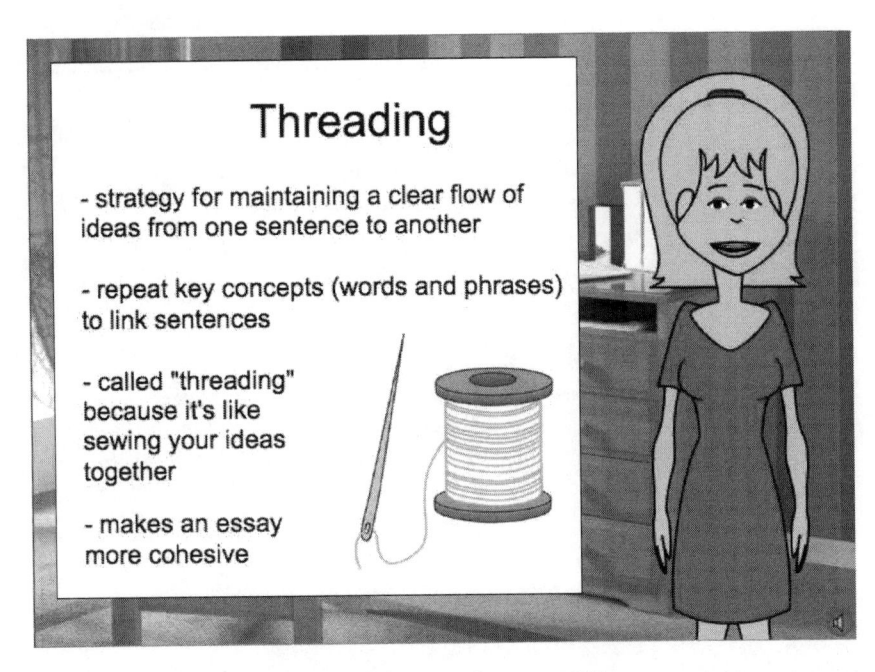

**FIGURE 12.1**  Screenshot of One of the W-Pal Lesson Videos.

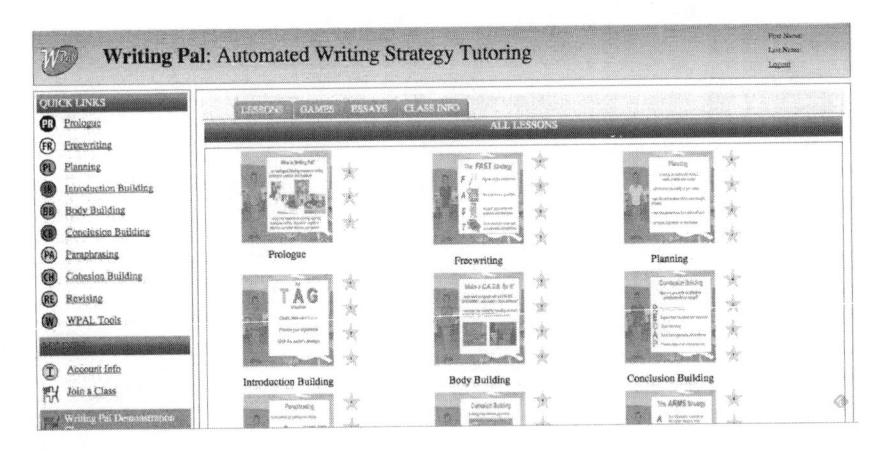

**FIGURE 12.2**  "Lessons Tab" in the W-Pal Interface.

increase positive affect and cognitive skills (Wilson et al., 2009), and decrease disinterest (Boekaerts, Pintrich, & Zeidner, 2000; D'Mello & Graesser, 2006; D'Mello, Taylor, & Graesser, 2007).

In W-Pal, students use games to practice a given skill or strategy for the purpose of learning the material and improving their understanding of a topic.

Each writing strategy module is associated with one or more practice games that students can "unlock" by completing the lesson videos (see Table 12.2). As of 2015, W-Pal offers 15 unique games developed by selecting key strategies found in the modules and then constructing generative or identification practice tasks (see Figure 12.3 for a screenshot of a W-Pal game). In generative practice, students write short texts (e.g., a conclusion paragraph) while applying one or more of the strategies taught in W-Pal. In identification practice, students examine text excerpts, label the strategies used, or identify how strategies can be used to improve the text. These practice tasks are then embedded within game-based environments that contain a variety of narratives and game mechanics such that students feel they are playing substantially different games, rather than repeatedly playing the same game with minor shifts in content. Feedback in the practice games is game-based and includes incentives, such as winning or losing, earning points, consuming fuel, or obtaining treasure. In some cases, formative feedback is also offered, such as tips for succeeding in the game by using certain strategies or mnemonics. As students progress in the games, they can begin to judge whether their application of particular strategies is effective.

Overall, the educational games found in W-Pal help students practice the writing strategies learned in the lesson videos in order to increase strategy acquisition (Allen, Crossley, Snow, & McNamara, 2014). The educational games are seen as a middle path between learning and acquiring. So, instead of immediately requiring students to implement new strategies within essay writing, the games allow students to practice strategies in isolation first. The game-based nature of this practice is intended to offset potential obstacles stemming from attitudes and emotions, and motivate more deliberate and sustained practice.

**FIGURE 12.3** Screenshot of a W-Pal Game.

**TABLE 12.2** Brief Descriptions of Writing Pal Practice Games.

| Game | Description |
| --- | --- |
| Freewrite Flash | Fill the Idea Meter and earn Idea Flash Cards by freewriting on a prompt. |
| Mastermind Outline | Repair the Mastermind Mainframe by assembling an outline from given argument and evidence statements. |
| Planning Passage | Travel to various destinations and earn souvenirs by selecting appropriate arguments and evidence. |
| Dungeon Escape | Escape by avoiding the guard and rising waters. Select doors by labeling attention-grabbing techniques. |
| Essay Launcher | Rescue spaceships by selecting thesis statements and attention-grabbers for sample introduction paragraphs. |
| Fix It | Evaluate paragraphs for missing key elements, such as thesis statements and evidence. Fix the broken circuit board. |
| RoBoCo | Build robots by writing topic and evidence sentences for a given thesis. |
| Lockdown | Stop computer hackers by writing conclusions based on a given outline. |
| Adventurer's Loot | Explore different locations and obtain treasure by correctly identifying use of paraphrasing strategies. |
| Map Conquest | Earn flags by identifying paraphrasing strategies, and then use those flags to conquer the game board. |
| Undefined & Mined | Disarm mines by identifying undefined referents in short texts. |
| CON-Artist | Catch a thief by following clues. The clues are solved by selecting transition words to link given sentences. |
| Speech Writer | Help a friend on the debate team revise a *speech*. Identify the major problems and then edit the speech to improve it. |

## *Writing Pal Essay Practice and Feedback*

After students have had the opportunity to practice the strategies they learned in the videos through game-based practice, they are given the opportunity to use these strategies in essay writing. Specifically, W-Pal gives students the chance to practice writing timed, persuasive essays that use SAT-style prompts. These prompts require no specialized background knowledge on the part of the student, but do require the student to synthesize information and apply the strategies covered in the W-Pal modules. Students or teachers can select the prompts and set the time limits for each practice essay. Essays are written using a simple word processor interface that includes a scratch pad for prewriting activities.

Once a student has completed an essay, it is submitted to the W-Pal AWE system. The AWE system is powered by a number of text analysis tools that assess the student's essay for content, rhetorical style, text cohesion, and language sophistication (McNamara et al., 2013). Essays submitted to the W-Pal AWE initially received a holistic rating from poor to great on a six-point scale. Writers also receive formative feedback that addresses particular writing goals and strategy-based solutions (see Figure 12.4). The feedback is based on a series of scaffolded and thresholded algorithms that provide information on different linguistic properties and categories including legitimacy (e.g., proportion of nonwords), length (e.g., number of words), relevance (e.g., occurrence of key words), and structure (e.g., number of paragraphs). The feedback given to students is based on relevant modules and games found in W-Pal and delivered based on the lowest threshold failed in a series of categories. Thus, students who struggle to produce enough text may not be ready to implement feedback about cohesion. Instead, these students may gain more from freewriting or planning. Depending on the quality of individual sections in the submitted essay, more targeted formative feedback may be provided for introduction body and/or conclusion building strategies. If an essay passes all basic thresholds, they receive feedback encouraging overall revision.

## Writing Pal Efficacy Studies

A number of studies have been conducted to test whether interactions with the W-Pal system lead to beneficial outcomes for students. These studies have examined the usability of the system (i.e., is the system easy to use?) and the perceptions of the feedback given (i.e., is the feedback appropriate and usable?), as well as whether the system helps students acquire the writing strategies, whether the system leads to gains in writing proficiency, and whether the system leads

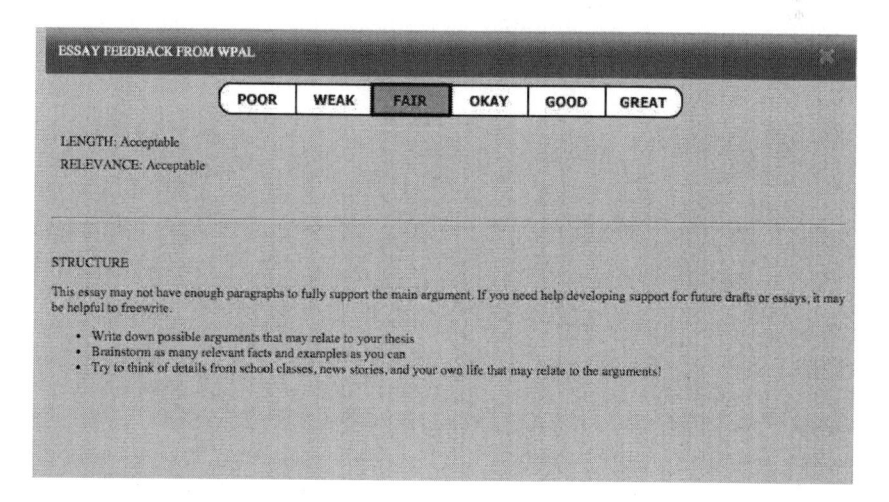

FIGURE 12.4 Formative Feedback.

to increased engagement, motivation, and perceived writing success. Overall, the results have been quite positive: W-Pal participants report that the system is user-friendly and that the feedback algorithms are helpful. In addition, the studies show that students learn writing strategies and show gains in writing proficiency, engagement, motivation, and perceived success. Each of these items is discussed in more depth below.

## Writing Pal Usability

Students who have used W-Pal provide positive reviews and judge the majority of W-Pal components to be beneficial. The components valued most positively by students relate to writing instruction, practice (both game-based and writing), and writing feedback. Overall, students perceive W-Pal to be a worthwhile addition to the writing classroom (Roscoe & McNamara, 2013; Roscoe et al., in press).

More specifically, students have reported that the mnemonic strategies taught in W-Pal were the most helpful and that the general strategies taught in W-Pal helped them to better understand and enact the writing process. Across sampled games, a large majority (80 percent) of students rate the games as somewhat helpful or very helpful for practicing the writing strategies covered in the modules. Similarly, well over half of students interviewed (66 percent) rate the games as somewhat enjoyable or very enjoyable to play. Most students (82 percent) rate the essay writing tools as easy or very easy to use and half of students report that they received an appropriate amount of feedback (50 percent) while a large percentage report that they received not enough (39 percent) or too much (12 percent) feedback. From a practical perspective, most students rate the feedback as understandable (61 percent) and most students (79 percent) report that the feedback is useful overall (Roscoe et al., in press).

## Strategy Acquisition

An important component of the W-Pal system is the teaching of writing strategies. Thus, knowing whether W-Pal users learn strategies is an important research question. In one recent study, 65 high school students participated in a summer program using W-Pal. The students who interacted with the full W-Pal system (i.e., animated strategy lessons, game-based practice, and essay-based practice with feedback) were better able to articulate and apply new writing strategies than students who only used the W-Pal AWE system. Although strategy acquisition for W-Pal users was almost certainly supported by the direct instruction provided by the lessons, performance within several educational games was also a strong predictor of strategy acquisition, indicating that it is probably not direct instruction alone that leads to successful learning (Roscoe et al., 2013a).

## Writing Development

A number of studies have found that W-Pal leads to increases in essay scores (whether judged by human or by AES systems) as well as to increases in certain characteristics of essays that are associated with writing quality. For instance, Roscoe et al. (2011) used the feedback provided by W-Pal to revise a number of essays. This feedback included topics, such as the need for idea elaboration, the need for essay structure, and the need for stronger arguments. After the revisions were made, the quality of the revised essays was compared to that of the original essays. The results of this comparison indicated that the scores on the revised essays were significantly higher than the original essays.

A second study examined writing growth over the course of using the W-Pal system. Students were placed into two groups. The first group interacted with the complete W-Pal system and the second group interacted with W-Pal AWE only, but wrote twice as many essays. Student essays from the beginning to the end of the study were compared. Both groups produced higher essay scores after interacting with the systems. The gains for users in both systems were stronger for lower proficiency writers than for higher proficiency writers, indicating the systems work best for less-skilled writers. Lastly, the study found that the percentage of students who demonstrated writing gains was greater for the group that experienced the complete W-Pal system as compared to the practice-only group.

In addition to overall essay scores, both groups also showed gains in the sophistication of the language that they produced. For instance, writers in both groups wrote longer essays that had a greater number of paragraphs. The writers also showed changes in the use of cohesion (e.g., they used more conjuncts, such as *although*, in their essays), the complexity of their sentences (e.g., they had a greater number of relative clauses in their essays), the number of rhetorical features (e.g., they used more conclusion statements), and the sophistication of their words (e.g., they produced more nominalizations). This finding indicates that instruction, game play, writing practice, and feedback can be just as effective as writing practice mixed with feedback alone (Crossley, Roscoe, & McNamara, 2013).

One important aspect of these findings is that the students in the practice-only group composed and revised 16 essays, whereas those in the W-Pal group wrote 8 essays and had a greater variety of tasks as well as games. We assume that motivating students to repeatedly write essays may be challenging in real-world classroom contexts and, hence, the lessons and game-based practice in W-Pal are designed to help motivate students to persist in the learning process.

## Engagement, Motivation, Perceived Performance

Previous research has demonstrated that educational games, like those found in W-Pal, can increase a student's engagement and motivation (Barab et al., 2009).

A recent study tested this assumption with first language and second language writers in the W-Pal system (Allen et al., 2014). This study revealed that for all students (both first and second language), training with the W-Pal system led to increased performance on writing tasks, as well as positive attitudes toward the system (i.e., engagement, motivation, and perceived performance). We also found that the difficulty of the W-Pal games predicted boredom for the first language students. They reported more boredom while engaging with W-Pal when they had also perceived the games to be easier, and less boredom when the games were more difficult, indicating that participants enjoyed the challenge. Conversely, for the second language students, game *enjoyment* predicted both motivation and perceived improvement in writing. They were more motivated when they enjoyed the games. In general, this study suggested that students' enjoyment of strategy practice (in the form of games) was strongly related to their general feelings of engagement, motivation, and perceived learning. Hence, the game-based practice in W-Pal serves as an engaging alternative to repetitive strategy training sessions, such as practice drills.

## Accessing Writing Pal

W-Pal is web-based and freely available for teachers who are interested in using it in their classrooms. To begin using W-Pal, teachers simply need to create and register an account, which will then need to be approved by a Writing Pal system administrator. The account creation page for W-Pal is available at http://wpal.soletlab.com. Once on the *Welcome* screen for the W-Pal system (see Figure 12.5), teachers click on the *Teacher Registration* link and begin the registration process. A confirmation email is sent to the provided email address, along with a copy of the W-Pal manual, which describes the registration process and the system in more detail.

All teachers who have an approved W-Pal account will have access to the W-Pal *Teacher Interface* (see Figure 12.6 below). This interface allows teachers to

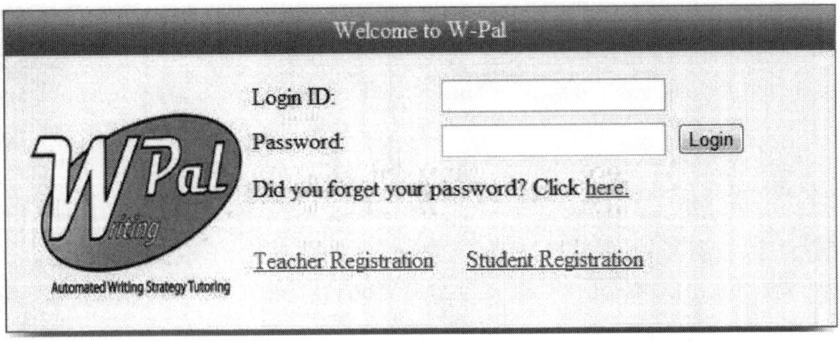

**FIGURE 12.5** Welcome Screen for the W-Pal System.

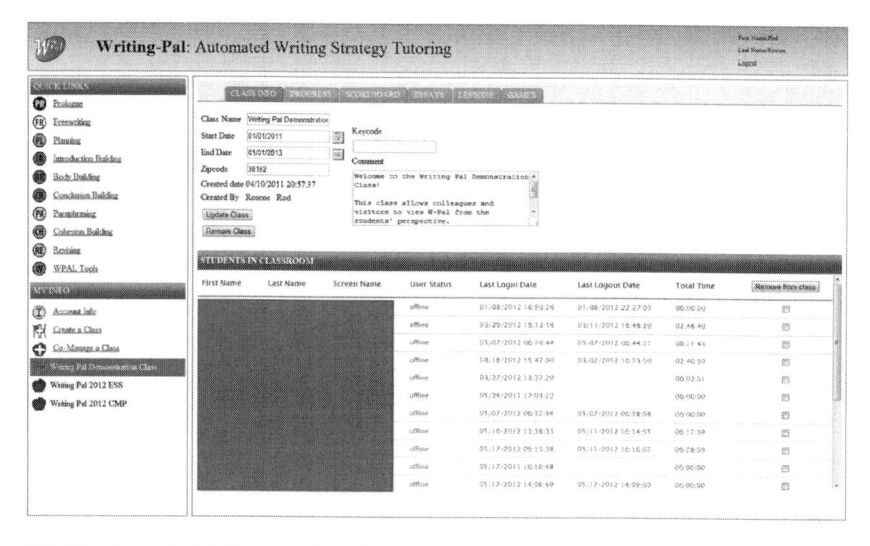

**FIGURE 12.6** W-Pal Teacher Interface.

view their students' progress, interactions with the system, and completed assignments, as well as manage their own account, classes, and assignments. Teachers also have the ability to access the system from a student's perspective, which can be helpful when designing classroom lessons and projects.

From the main interface, teachers can update their account information within *My Info*, use the *Quick Links* to access the W-Pal modules, and use Class Info to view their current class roster. In the *Class Info* tab, teachers can also view their students' User Status (i.e., "online" or "offline"), their last login and logout dates, and their total time spent in W-Pal.

Students' progress in the W-Pal system can be monitored with the *Progress*, *Scoreboard* and *Essays* tabs, which provide information about students' interactions within the system, including the frequency of their game play, their scores on essays and game practice, as well as the number of lessons they have watched (see Figure 12.7 for a screenshot of the *Scoreboard* tab). In addition to serving as a measure of progress, the *Essays* tab allows teachers to create essay assignments and view students' completed assignments and practice essays. When creating an essay assignment, teachers have the option of selecting a specific topic and time limit for the practice essay, as well as specifying whether students should revise the essay based on the W-Pal feedback (see Figure 12.8 for a screenshot of the Assignment Creation window).

Finally, W-Pal contains two tabs that allow teachers to view the system from a student's perspective. In particular, the *Lessons* and *Games* tabs function just like the *Student Interface* version of these tabs (see Figure 12.9 for a screenshot of the Lessons tab). Having this functionality within the *Teacher Interface* benefits

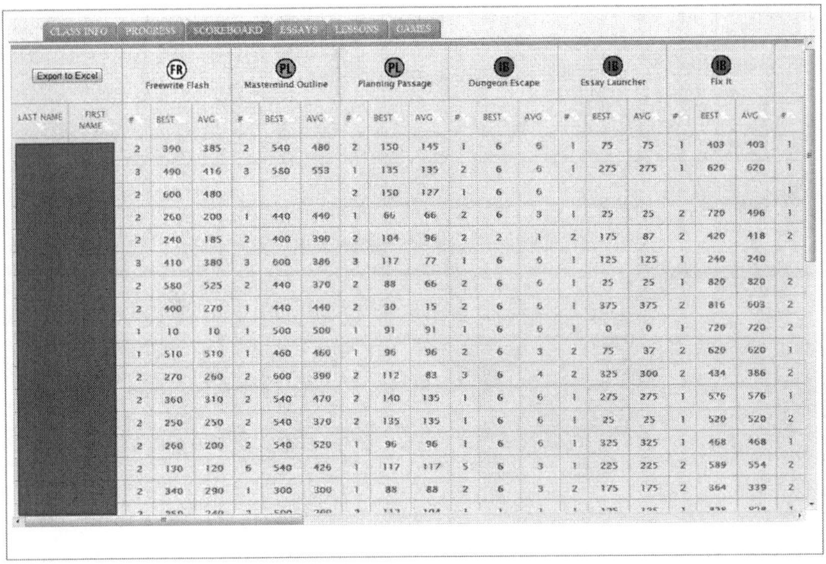

**FIGURE 12.7** Screenshot of the Scoreboard Tab.

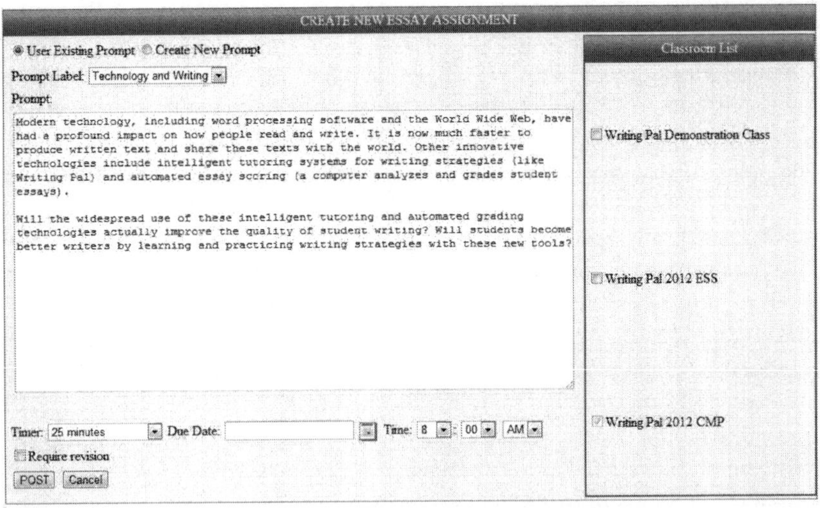

**FIGURE 12.8** Screenshot of the Assignment Creation Window.

teachers by allowing them to access what their students will see when using the system individually or in cases where they may choose to interact with W-Pal as an in-class activity (e.g., watching videos as a group or demonstrating one of the games).

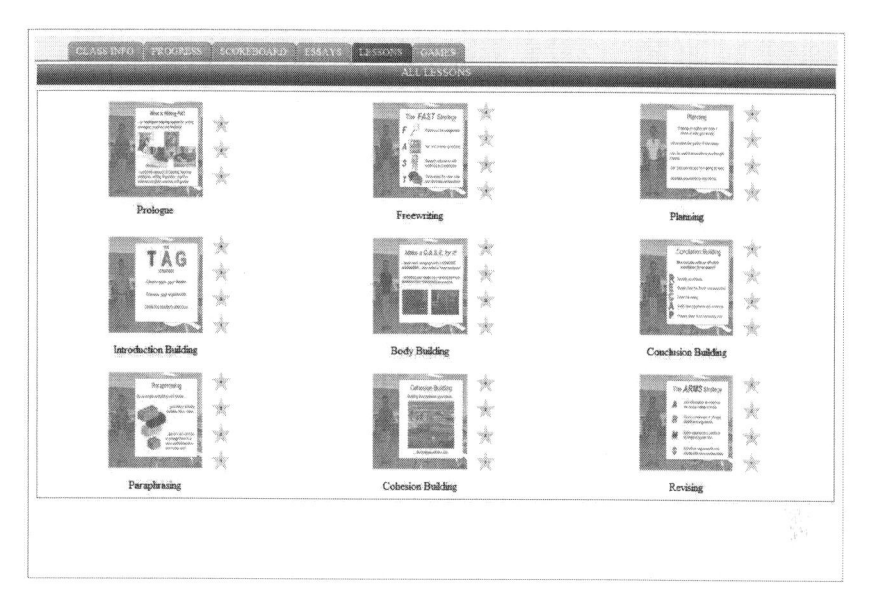

**FIGURE 12.9** Screenshot of the Lessons Tab.

## Integrating Writing Pal into the Classroom

Most, if not all, school systems are guided by standards, and many currently follow the Common Core College and Career standards. Hence, it is important to consider how a program might align with those standards. In Table 12.3, we outline some examples of how the instruction and practice with W-Pal aligns to the common core standards for writing.

It is important to note that the W-Pal system is not intended to replace the lessons offered by teachers in the classroom. Rather, the purpose of the system is to provide a supplement to classroom instruction, which can facilitate more effective writing instruction and practice. To this end, W-Pal was designed to be an open and flexible system for both teachers and students in that there is not a specific curriculum that all teachers are required to use. Such a design allows teachers to use Writing Pal in the way that they deem most appropriate for their own goals and based on the individual needs of their students.

An important question from a teacher's perspective is: how much time are students required to spend in W-Pal? Viewing all of the lessons, practicing the strategies within the games, and writing the practice essays typically requires approximately 20 hours (i.e., approximately a month, if done in class during a traditional class block). However, the amount of time spent in W-Pal can be adjusted. We have found productive uses of W-Pal in which students spent as little as 4 hours within the system, and other cases were students benefitted from interacting with W-Pal for up to 30 hours. The appropriate amount of time required

**TABLE 12.3** The Writing Pal and Common Core State Standards Alignment.

*Text Types and Purposes*

| | |
|---|---|
| **Write arguments to support claims in an analysis of substantive topics or texts using valid reasoning and relevant and sufficient evidence.** | Writing Pal uses both detailed lesson videos and practice tasks to instruct students on how they can come up with original arguments and support them with evidence in order to produce a fully rounded and supported claim. |
| **Production and Distribution of Writing** | |
| **Produce clear and coherent writing in which the development, organization, and style are appropriate to task, purpose, and audience. Develop and strengthen writing as needed by planning, revising, editing, rewriting, or trying a new approach.** | Writing Pal is composed of specific lessons that instruct strategies for organization, planning, and revising. For each set of lessons within the system, students are exposed to videos that teach useful strategies and are offered opportunities to practice these strategies. When students write an essay, they receive feedback directly related to the lessons, including planning, organization, and revision feedbacks. |
| **Conventions of Standard English** | |
| **Demonstrate command of the conventions of standard English grammar and usage when writing or speaking. Demonstrate command of the conventions of standard English capitalization, punctuation, and spelling when writing.** | Writing Pal offers a lesson video that instructs proper use of conventions of standard English grammar. The videos suggest various strategies that students can use to remember grammar and spelling rules. When students write an essay, they can select grammar check in order to verify that they did not make any unnecessary mistakes. |

depends on both the students' needs (i.e., is the student weak in many aspects of writing?) and the teacher's goals (i.e., what aspects of writing are important to the class syllabus?). In addition, since W-Pal is a web-based tool, the student need not be in the classroom to interact with the system.

There are a variety of approaches that teachers can take when integrating W-Pal into the classroom. For instance, some teachers prefer their students to progress quickly through the initial strategy lesson videos and leaving room for extended practice, such as games and essay writing, for the end when students have already had exposure to all of the strategies. On the other hand, some teachers choose to progress through W-Pal more slowly, focusing on integrating the instruction of individual strategies with extended practice opportunities.

Finally, another approach is to assign W-Pal modules to students individually based on their specific needs. In this approach, it may be the case that not all students will interact with the entire W-Pal system; rather, they will be encouraged to watch the lesson videos and practice the strategies that are most relevant to their level of writing skill.

## Limitations of Writing Pal

During the development of W-Pal, a number of limitations have become apparent. As we steadily work to improve the system, it is important to account for these current limitations to guide how teachers implement W-Pal. First, the system was developed with adolescent learners in mind. Thus, developing writers are the primary audience for W-Pal and the extendibility of the tool may not readily transfer to students in different age ranges (i.e., elementary students or advanced college students). Another limitation is that W-Pal is currently only available in English. While translating the lessons and games would be a rather simple procedure, most of the feedback algorithms used in W-Pal are based on databases and tools that are only available in English, making transition of the underlying technologies difficult. Nonetheless, W-Pal has been shown to be beneficial to English second language learners in both the U.S. (Allen et al., 2014) and abroad (Di Sano, La Caprara, Rosa, Raine, & McNamara, 2012).

In addition, W-Pal currently only focuses instruction on independent, argumentative essays (i.e., prompt-based argumentative essays that require no background knowledge of the topic). These essays are common in middle and high school curricula, but they are not the only writing tasks that students are expected to complete. However, we assume that learning the basic writing strategies that are covered in W-Pal is crucial to students' writing development and to writing in other genres (e.g., source-based writing tasks). Moreover, W-Pal affords students the opportunities to practice fundamental writing skills, which are necessary in other writing forms as well.

## Conclusion

W-Pal focuses specifically on the teaching of writing strategies and provides students woth opportunities to use these strategies in game-based practice and deliberate writing practice. These opportunities can be used to complement classroom teaching and provide students with opportunities for extended writing practice. The AWE embedded in W-Pal provides feedback to users on a number of language features that relate to the covered writing strategies (e.g., cohesion, introduction building, body building, and conclusion building) as well as a number of linguistic features related to essay quality, such as lexical sophistication, syntactic complexity, rhetorical devices, and content relevance. This feedback provides summative scores to the students as well as formative suggestions for revisions that directly link to the writing strategies that have been taught. The recursive nature of the lessons, games, writing practice, and feedback has proven effective in increasing the writing quality of essays written within the system. Continued development of the system should increase its efficacy and usability for a number of populations, tasks, and writing features.

## Acknowledgments

The research reported here was supported by the Institute of Education Sciences, U.S. Department of Education, through grant R305A080589 to Arizona State University. The opinions expressed are those of the authors and do not represent the views of the Institute or the U.S. Department of Education.

## References

Alexander, P. A., Graham, S., & Harris, K. (1998). A perspective on strategy research: Progress and prospects. *Educational Psychology Review, 10*, 129–154.

Allen, L. K., Crossley, S. A., Snow, E. L., & McNamara, D. S. (2014). Game-based writing strategy tutoring for second language learners: Game enjoyment as a key to engagement. *Language Learning and Technology, 18*, 124–150.

Barab, S. A., Gresalfi, M. S., & Arici, A. (2009). Transformational play: Why educators should care about games. *Educational Leadership, 67*, 76–80.

Boekaerts, M., Pintrich, P. R., & Zeidner, M. (Eds.). (2000). *Handbook of Self-Regulation*. San Diego, CA: Academic Press.

Burstein, J., Chodorow, M., & Leacock, C. (2004). Automated essay evaluation: the Criterion Online writing service. *AI Magazine, 35*, 27–36.

Condon, W. (2013). Large-scale assessment, locally-developed measures, and automated scoring of essays: Fishing for red herrings? *Assessing Writing, 18*, 100–108.

Council of Writing Program Administrators, National Council of Teachers of English, & the National Writing Project. (2011). *Framework for Success in Postsecondary Writing*. Retrieved from http://wpacouncil.org/files/framework-for-success-postsecondary-writing.pdf.

Craig, S. D., D'Mello, S. K., Gholson, B., Witherspoon, A., Sullins, J., & Graesser, A. C. (2004). Emotions during learning: The first steps toward an affect sensitive intelligent tutoring system. In J. Nall, & R. Robson (Eds.), *Proceedings of E-learn 2004: World Conference on E-learning in Corporate, Government, Healthcare, & Higher Education* (pp. 284–288). Chesapeake, VA: AACE.

Crossley, S. A., Roscoe, R. D., & McNamara, D. S. (2013). Using automatic scoring models to detect changes in student writing in an intelligent tutoring system. In C. Boonthum-Denecke & G. M. Youngblood (Eds.), *Proceedings of the 26th Annual Florida Artificial Intelligence Research Society (FLAIRS) Conference* (pp. 208–213). Menlo Park, CA: The AAAI Press.

De La Paz, S., & Graham, S. (2002). Explicitly teaching strategies, skills, and knowledge: Writing instruction in middle school classrooms. *Journal of Educational Psychology, 94*, 687–698.

Deane, P. (2013). On the relation between automated essay scoring and modern views of the writing construct. *Assessing Writing, 18*, 7–24.

Dikli, S. (2006). An overview of automated scoring of essays. *Journal of Technology, Learning, and Assessment, 5*(1).

Di Sano, S., La Caprara, K., Rosa, A., Raine, R. B., & McNamara, D. S. (2012). Learning to write persuasive essays: A preliminary study on the effectiveness of an intelligent tutorial system with high school students. In C. Gelati, B. Arfe, & L. Mason (Eds.), *Issues in Writing Research* (pp. 214–220). Padua, Italy: CLEUP.

Elliot, N., & Klobucar, A. (2013). Automated essay evaluation and the teaching of writing. In M. D. Shermis, J. Burstein, & S. Apel (Eds), *Handbook of Automated Essay Evaluation: Current Applications and New Directions* (pp. 16–35). London: Routledge.

Elliot, N., Gere, A. R., Gibson, G., Toth, C., Whithaus, C., & Presswood, A. (2013). Uses and limitations of automated writing evaluation software. *WPA-CompPile Research Bibliographies, 23.*

Graham, S. & Perin, D. (2007). A meta-analysis of writing instruction for adolescent students. *Journal of Educational Psychology, 99,* 445–476.

Graham, S., Harris, K., & Mason, L. (2005). Improving the writing performance, knowledge, and self-efficacy of struggling young writers: The effects of self-regulated strategy development. *Contemporary Educational Psychology, 30,* 207–241.

Grimes, D., & Warschauer, M. (2010). Utility in a fallible tool: A multi-site case study of automated writing evaluation. *The Journal of Technology, Learning and Assessment, 8,* 1–43.

Healy, A., Schneider, V., & Bourne, L. (2012). Empirically valid principles of training. In A. Healy and L. Bourne (Eds.), *Training Cognition: Optimizing Efficiency, Durability, and Generalizability* (pp. 13–39). New York: Psychology Press.

Higgins, D., Xi, X., Zechner, K., & Williamson, D. (2011). A three-stage approach to the automated scoring of spontaneous spoken responses. *Computer Speech and Language, 25,* 282–306.

Kellogg, R. (2008). Training writing skills: A cognitive development perspective. *Journal of Writing Research, 1,* 1–26.

Landauer, T., Laham, D., & Foltz, P. (2003). Automatic essay assessment. *Assessment in Education, 10,* 295–308.

McCutchen, D. (2006). Cognitive factors in the development of children's writing. In C. MacArthur, S. Graham, & J. Fitzgerald (Eds.), *Handbook of Writing Research* (pp. 115–130). New York: Guilford.

McNamara, D. S., Crossley, S. A., & Roscoe, R. D. (2013). Natural language processing in an intelligent writing strategy tutoring system. *Behavior Research Methods, 45,* 499–515.

McNamara, D. S., Jackson, G. T., & Graesser, A. C. (2010). Intelligent tutoring and games (ITaG). In Y. K. Baek (Ed.), *Gaming for Classroom-Based Learning: Digital Role-Playing as a Motivator of Study* (pp. 44–65). Hershey, PA: IGI Global.

Plant, E., Ericcson, K., Hill, L., & Asberg, K. (2005). Why study time does not predict grade point average across college students: implications of deliberate practice for academic performance. *Contemporary Educational Psychology, 30,* 96–116.

Rohrer, D. & Pashler, H. (2010). Recent research on human learning challenges conventional instructional strategies. *Educational Researcher, 39,* 406–412.

Roscoe, R. D., & McNamara, D. S. (2013). Writing Pal: Feasibility of an intelligent writing strategy tutor in the high school classroom. *Journal of Educational Psychology, 105,* 1010–1025.

Roscoe, R. D., Brandon, R. D., Snow, E. L., & McNamara, D. S. (2013a). Game-based writing strategy practice with the Writing Pal. In K. Pytash & R. Ferdig (Eds.),

*Exploring Technology for Writing and Writing Instruction* (pp. 1–20). Hershey, PA: IGI Global.

Roscoe, R. D., Varner, L. K., Crossley, S. A., & McNamara, D. S. (2013b). Developing pedagogically-guided threshold algorithms for intelligent automated essay feedback. *International Journal of Learning Technology, 8*, 362–381.

Roscoe, R. D., Allen, L. K., Weston, J. L., Crossley, S. A., & McNamara, D. S. (in press). The Writing Pal intelligent tutoring system: Usability testing and development. *Computers and Composition*.

Roscoe, R. D., Varner, L. K., Cai, Z., Weston, J. L., Crossley, S. A., & McNamara, D. S. (2011). Internal usability testing of automated essay feedback in an intelligent writing tutor. In R. C. Murray & P. M. McCarthy (Eds.), *Proceedings of the 24th International Florida Artificial Intelligence Research Society (FLAIRS) Conference* (pp. 543–548). Menlo Park, CA: AAAI Press.

Rowe, J., Shores, L., Mott, B., & Lester, J. (2011). Integrating learning, problem solving, and engagement in narrative-centered learning environments. *International Journal of Artificial Intelligence in Education, 21*, 115–133.

Rudner, L., Garcia, V., & Welch, C. (2005). An evaluation of IntellimetricTM essay scoring system using responses to GMAT® AWA prompts (GMAC Research report number RR-05–08). Retrieved from http://www.gmac.com/gmac/researchandtrends/.

Rudner, L., Garcia, V., & Welch, C. (2006). An evaluation of the IntelliMetric essay scoring system. *Journal of Technology, Learning, and Assessment, 4*, 3–21.

Shank, R., & Neaman, A. (2001). Motivation and failure in educational systems design. In K. Forbus & P. Feltovich (Eds.), *Smart Machines in Education*. Cambridge, MA: AAAI Press/ MIT Press.

Shute, V. (2008). Focus on formative feedback. *Review of Educational Research, 78*, 153–189.

Snyder, T. D., & Dillow, S. A. (2012). Digest of Education Statistics 2011 (NCES 2012–001). National Center for Education Statistics, Institute of Education Sciences, U.S. Department of Education. Washington, DC.

Warschauer, M., & Grimes, D. (2008). Automated writing assessment in the classroom. *Pedagogies, 3*(1), 52–67.

Warschauer, M., & Ware, P. (2006). Automated writing evaluation: Defining the classroom research agenda. *Language Teaching Research, 10*, 157–180.

Wilson, K. A., Bedwell, W. L., Lazzara, E. H., Salas, E., Burke, S., Estock, J. L., Orvis, K. L., & Conkey, C. (2009). Relationships between game attributes and learning outcomes: Review and research proposals. *Simulation and Gaming, 40*, 217–266.

# 13
# COMPUTER-ASSISTED RESEARCH WRITING IN THE DISCIPLINES

*Elena Cotos*

## Introduction

It is arguably very important for students to acquire writing skills from kindergarten through high school. In college, students must further develop their writing in order to continue on to graduate school successfully. To obtain their graduate degree, they have to be able to write good theses, dissertations, conference papers, journal manuscripts, and other research genres. However, opportunities to develop research writing skills are often limited to traditional student-advisor discussions (Pearson & Brew, 2002). Part of the problem is that graduate students are expected to be good at such writing, because if they "can think well, they can write well" (Turner, 2012, p. 18). Education and academic literacy specialists oppose this assumption. They argue that advanced academic writing competence is too complex to be automatically acquired while learning about or doing research (Aitchison & Lee, 2006). Aspiring student-scholars need to practice and internalize a style of writing that conforms to discipline-specific conventions, which are norms of writing in particular disciplines, such as chemistry, engineering, agronomy, and psychology.

Motivated by this need, the Research Writing Tutor (RWT) was designed to assist the research writing of graduate students. RWT leverages the conventions of scientific argumentation in one of the most impactful research genres—the research article. This chapter first provides a theoretical background for research writing competence. Second, it discusses the need for technology that would facilitate the development of this competence. The description of RWT as an exemplar of such technology is then followed by a review of evaluation studies. The chapter concludes with recommendations for RWT classroom integration and with directions for further development of this tool.

## Research Writing Competence

Writing is a skill that includes complex thinking processes and strategies. Additionally, writers need to know who their audience is, why the audience would read their texts, and in what contexts their texts are meant to appear. Writers should also be aware of the disciplinary practices of their audience, which are reflected in specific genre norms (Perelman, 2012). From the perspective of writing and genre theories, this general description is essential when considering research writing competence.

## Cognitive Writing Theory

Graduate students are novices to research writing. Theoretically, the distinction between novice and expert writers has been articulated in terms of knowledge-telling versus knowledge-transformation (Bereiter & Scardamalia, 1987). Novice writers tell their knowledge about a topic and move from one idea to the next. Expert writers, on the other hand, transform knowledge. For them, writing is a reflection-intensive activity that involves repeated planning, translating, and revising (Dunlosky & Metcalfe, 2009; Flower & Hayes, 1980; Hacker, Keener, & Kircher, 2009). Specifically, planning is considering what ideas to include and how to present them. In theoretical terms, writers create an abstract internal representation of the text by inventing ideas and setting procedural goals. Translating is putting ideas into language, or creating the written representation of the text. Revising includes evaluation and modification of the written text to ensure that it accurately renders the intended thoughts. Expert writers not only present elaborate content, but also make effective language choices to realize communicative goals.

Cognitive models of writing highlight revision as one of the most fundamental components of the writing process and expertise (Butterfield, Hacker, & Albertson, 1996; Hayes, 2000; Hayes & Flower, 1983). At this writing stage, expert writers compare their intended representation of the text with the actual written representation. When the two representations are in conflict, they detect and diagnose the problem. This stimulates a decision of what strategy to use to modify the text. Thus, competent revision principally depends on controlling the activation of these complex higher-order thinking processes. What characterizes novice writers is ineffective detection of problems in their writing. To develop expert-like problem-solving abilities, they need to practice revision guided by feedback that makes them think and detect ineffectively expressed meaning.

## Genre Theory

Research writing involves constructing, deconstructing, and reconstructing knowledge to be shared with other scientists (Badley, 2009). It is essentially a rhetorical behavior (Jolliffe & Brier, 1988) that requires novices to use the specific conventions of scientific writing. A theoretical notion that describes conventions is the notion of genres, which are classes of texts defined by a discipline's values and communicative purposes (Berkenkotter & Huckin, 1995).

The research article genre is perhaps the most wide-spread means of scientific communication. It has become a central focus in the field of English for Academic Purposes (EAP), which has embraced Swales's (1981) approach to genre theory. Swales provided a rhetorical framework grounded in the concept of *moves*, or communicative goals. For example, the Introductions of research articles are described as having three moves: establishing a territory (Move 1), establishing a niche (Move 2), and occupying the niche (Move 3). Each of these moves is realized by *steps*, or rhetorical strategies that convey specific functional meaning. For instance, to achieve the goal of Move 2, writers may use such steps as highlighting a problem or indicating a gap. The meaning of the latter can be realized using expressions such as "not previously explored," "hindered by insufficient knowledge," "scarce evidence for," etc. In such manner, this framework establishes a systematic connection between rhetorical intent and language choices, which mirror the writer's internal and written representations of the composed text.

## Need for Technology

Swales's EAP genre approach has been widely adopted in academic writing instruction, increasingly using large machine-readable collections of texts, called corpora. Many researchers recommend the use of search engines to query corpora for key words in context, co-occurrence of vocabulary items, and grammatical, syntactic, and positional patterns of search words (e.g., Friginal, 2013; Lee & Swales, 2006). However, few technologies have been created for scientific writing (e.g., DicSci, TYOS, SWoRD, MAKE, Mover, We-Write Persuasively), and they do not generate feedback to support expert-like revision. Existing automated writing evaluation (AWE) systems that do generate feedback on students' texts (e.g., Criterion, MyAccess!, Writer's Workbench, Writing Power, Writing Roadmap, Folio, etc.) are designed for essays and are thus not suitable for research writing. Plus, they have been criticized for inadequately representing the cognitive and rhetorical aspects of the writing construct (Perelman, 2012).

The need for feedback technologies to enhance higher-order aspects of writing is currently addressed by large-scale projects. For example, the U.S. Department of Education's Institute of Education Sciences has funded the development of the Writing Pal program described by Crossley, Allen, and McNamara (Chapter 12 in this volume), which enhances writing strategy instruction through automated strategy feedback. The National Science Foundation has funded two big projects: one to develop a socio-technical system for teaching written argumentation (Ashley, Litman, & Schunn, 2013), and the second to develop an intelligent ecosystem for science writing instruction (Schunn, Litman, & Godley, 2014). RWT expands these efforts to research genres and their rhetorical complexity.

## RWT

RWT was designed to complement advanced academic writing instruction. It integrates rhetorical feedback with scaffolding, or instructional techniques, derived from discipline-specific corpora of published research articles to enable students to progress toward deeper understanding and autonomous use of genre conventions. The current version of RWT contains three independent yet interactive modules for learning, demonstration, and feedback. Each of the modules aims to create conditions for practice necessary for the development of research writing competence.

### *Learning Module: "Understand Writing Goals"*

The Learning Module is designed to help teachers impart genre knowledge and to help students learn the conventions of research writing. The content of the materials included here draws from the results of a pedagogically driven study of a corpus of 900 research articles published by experts in 30 disciplines. This study yielded cross-disciplinary move/step frameworks for introduction, methods, results, and discussion/conclusion (IMRD/C) sections (Cotos, Huffman, & Link, 2015). For example, the results section contains three moves: (1) showing valid progression to findings; (2) reporting the results; and (3) establishing the meaning of results. Each move contains a series of step strategies. Move 3, for instance, may be realized by explaining specific results, suggesting reasons for what may have caused the results, reflecting on anticipated or unanticipated results, and comparing results with previous research.

The Learning Module incorporates multimodal instructional materials about the move/step conventions of each IMRD/C section. The materials define the moves, explain their purposes, provide content suggestions, specify the rhetorical functions of the steps, and supply examples from the corpus. Similar materials offer so-called *Language Focus* guidelines that highlight patterns of language use. The *Language Focus* of results, for example, describes how verbs and means of comparison are used in this section.

- Verbs: present tense is generally used to locate data in a figure or a table. Past tense is used to report specific results. Either present or past tense can be used to make strong claims about the results. Modal and tentative verbs and verb phrases are used to make less confident comments (e.g., may, might, suggest, seem, appear, tend, be possible, be likely, etc.).
- Means of comparison: adjectives are used in the comparative or superlative degrees. Verbs of variation are used to report how variables fluctuate over

time (e.g., rise, fall, increase, decrease, remain constant). Verbs of correlation are used to report the relationship between two or more variables (e.g., correlate with, associate with, related to).

Additionally, this module contains short videos where an instructor first introduces a given move and explains each step of the move using representative excerpts from the corpus. Then, the instructor prompts students to determine the steps in a series of examples and demonstrates how to interpret the functional meaning and language use in those step examples. In this way, a reflective process is modeled that students could apply when revising their own writing.

### *Demonstration Module: "Explore Published Writing"*

Numerous EAP studies show that corpus-based activities can foster enhanced awareness and writing improvement (Boulton, 2010; Henry, 2007; Tono, Satake, & Miura, 2014). Identifying similarities and differences in collections of expert writing is particularly helpful for novice second language writers (Hyland, 2004). Moreover, systematic analysis of text structure, rhetorical composition, and characteristics of language use facilitates genre learning (Tardy, 2009) and promotes critical literacy (Hammond & Macken-Horarik, 1999).

The demonstration module is designed to create conditions for such outcomes by integrating the corpora compiled and analyzed in Cotos et al. (2015). The genre conventions are illustrated through three interrelated components: *Research Articles*, *Section Structure*, and *Move/Step Examples*. The former presents complete research articles in their original published form, modeling the end documents to be prepared by students. The *Section Structure* component contains sub-corpora of separate IMRD/C section texts annotated based on the move/step frameworks introduced in the learning module. Each annotated sentence carries a color representing a move. The colors visualize the rhetorical composition of individual texts and are the same across sections to ensure consistency in the enhancement of corpus input: blue represents Move 1; red—Move 2; green—Move 3; and gold—Move 4. The structure of multiple texts can also be displayed on the same page, making it possible for students to notice patterns in the move composition of disciplinary texts. Additionally, scrolling over a sentence brings up a gloss specifying the rhetorical step it represents (Figure 13.1).

The *Move/Step Examples* component offers a search engine, known as a concordancer in EAP. Like other concordancers, it consists of a database holding the annotated sub-corpora. By hierarchically selecting a discipline, section, move, and step from respective drop-down menus, the students can retrieve all the examples of a searched step. Figure 13.2 shows examples of the step that identifies a gap. Highlighting the part that carries the step's functional meaning makes salient various language choices: "no information is available," "have not been fully understood," "there is little information available," and "are lacking

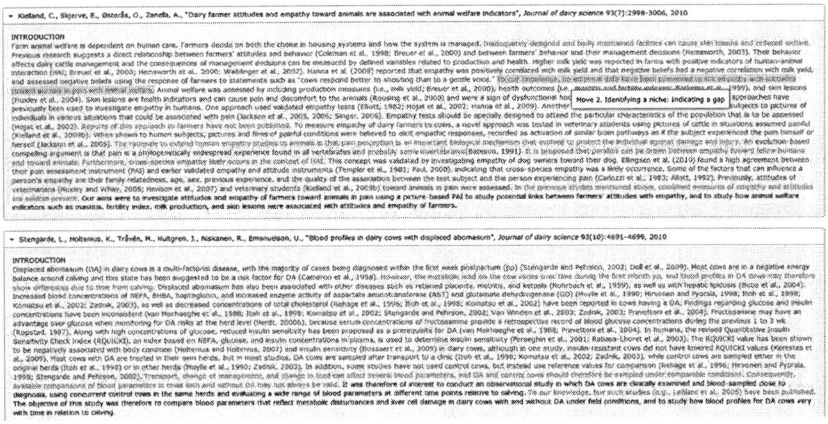

FIGURE 13.1 Screenshot Illustrating Use of Gloss.

in the literature." Furthermore, the concordance examples can be expanded by a click to show the annotated source text (similar to Figure 13.1). This allows students to observe how the given step is interwoven in the discourse and what kind of content may precede or follow it.

## *Feedback Module: "Analyze My Writing"*

Previous works demonstrate the pedagogical value of corpus-informed feedback provided as pre-cast concordance links (Todd, 2001), concordance-based teacher feedback embedded in students' texts (Gaskell & Cobb, 2004), and intelligent interactive feedback (Birch-Bécaas & Cooke, 2012; Chang & Kuo, 2011;

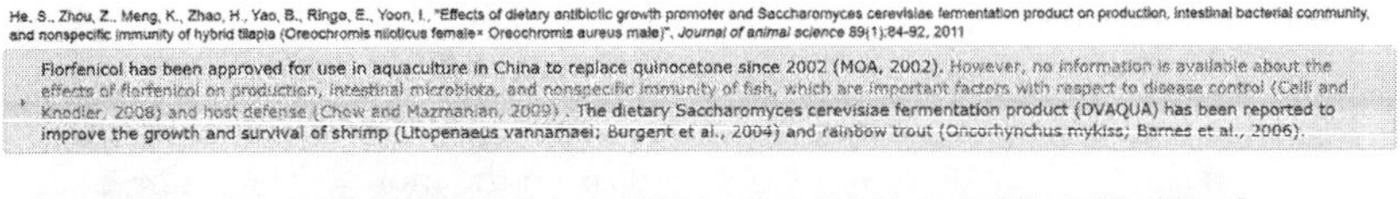
He, S., Zhou, Z., Meng, K., Zhao, H., Yao, B., Ringo, E., Yoon, I., "Effects of dietary antibiotic growth promoter and Saccharomyces cerevisiae fermentation product on production, intestinal bacterial community, and nonspecific immunity of hybrid tilapia (Oreochromis niloticus female× Oreochromis aureus male)", *Journal of animal science* 89(1):84-92, 2011

Florfenicol has been approved for use in aquaculture in China to replace quinocetone since 2002 (MOA, 2002). However, no information is available about the effects of florfenicol on production, intestinal microbiota, and nonspecific immunity of fish, which are important factors with respect to disease control (Celi and Knodler, 2008) and host defense (Chow and Mazmanian, 2009) . The dietary Saccharomyces cerevisiae fermentation product (DVAQUA) has been reported to improve the growth and survival of shrimp (Litopenaeus vannamaei; Burgent et al., 2004) and rainbow trout (Oncorhynchus mykiss; Barnes et al., 2006).

Kim, B., Gramm, B., Nimmo, R., Stein, H., "Effect of Dietary Carbadox on Apparent Ileal Digestibility of Amino Acids in Weanling Pigs", *American Journal of Animal and Veterinary Sciences* 5

Growth promoting responses have been documented for a variety of antimicrobial agents including carbadox (Thrasher et al., 1969; Yen et al., 1976; 1985). The growth promoting effects of antimicrobial agents are often associated with an improved feed efficiency, but the mechanisms responsible for these improvements have not been fully understood . Antimicrobial agents have been suggested to reduce the concentration of pathogens in the digestive tract of pigs, which will reduce the production of amines and degradation of essential nutrients and thus allow more retention time for digestion and absorption (Cromwell, 2000).

Silva, E., Meyer, P., Marino, C., Sucupira, M., Demarchi, J., Rodrigues, P., Mogentale, S., Silva, E., Meyer, P., Marino, C., "Effects of Flavomycin on Ruminal Fermentation, In Situ Degradability and In Vivo Digestibility in Bovine Fed Sugarcane Diets", *American Journal of Animal and Veterinary Sciences* 5

Nowadays, most of the products used for ruminants are ionophores and in less scale, non-ionophores antibiotics. There is little information available on the effects of non-ionophores antibiotics applied in animal nutrition. These antibiotics represent a diversified group with differences in their chemical composition, antimicrobial spectrum, mode of action, molecular weight and capacity of absorption by small intestine.

Mc Hugh, N., Evans, R., Amer, P., Fahey, A., Berry, D., "Genetic parameters for cattle price and body weight from routinely collected data at livestock auctions and commercial farms", *Journal of animal science* 89(1):29-39, 2011

Cull cows sales also contribute to the overall profitability of beef production systems. Estimates of the genetic variation in price per animal as weanlings, postweanlings, or cows are lacking in the literature. Most international dairy breeding programs have historically selected for increased milk production (Miglior et al., 2005).

FIGURE 13.2 Screenshot Showing Examples of Step Identifying a Gap.

Cho & Schunn, 2007). Writing produced by students exposed to corpora was found to improve, exhibiting patterns similar to those in published articles (Bianchi & Pazzaglia, 2007; Charles, 2014; Cortes, 2011).

The feedback module of RWT builds on these strengths. It provides students with a platform where they can receive automated feedback on their own writing. Unlike traditional AWE systems, RWT's feedback draws students' attention to the rhetorical conventions of a research genre, as opposed to grammatical correctness and elements of style in essays. The backbone of this module is an analysis engine that is trained to classify every sentence of a student text into moves and respective steps (details in Cotos & Pendar, 2016). The results of classification are translated into different types of macro and micro-level feedback generated when students submit their drafts for automated analysis.

The macro-level feedback focuses on rhetorical composition and is visually operationalized in two ways (Figure 13.3). Specifically, the submitted draft is returned color-coded for moves. This form of feedback depicts the move structure of the draft just as the demonstration module depicts the move structure of expert texts. The second form of feedback is both visual and numerical in that it summarizes the move distribution in the draft with range bars and pie charts. Here, the draft is compared with the texts from the corpus in the student's discipline. This goal-orienting feature of the feedback (Fisher & Ford, 1998) is expected to increase motivation by allowing students to monitor their writing progress in relation to published writing. If students need a reminder of what the moves entail, they can access a brief definition by hovering over the question marks next to the moves.

The concept of functional steps is operationalized through both macro-level and micro-level feedback (Figure 13.4). Expanding the range bars for each move,

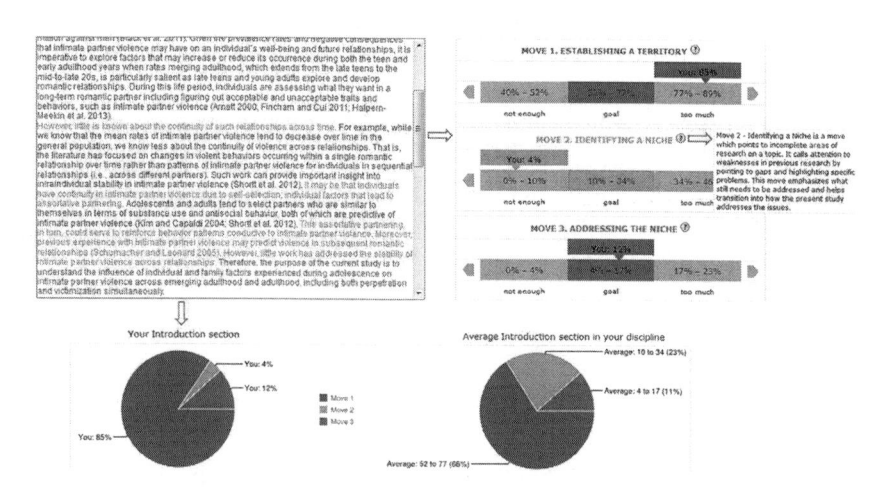

**FIGURE 13.3** Visualization of Macro-Level Feedback.

**232** Elena Cotos

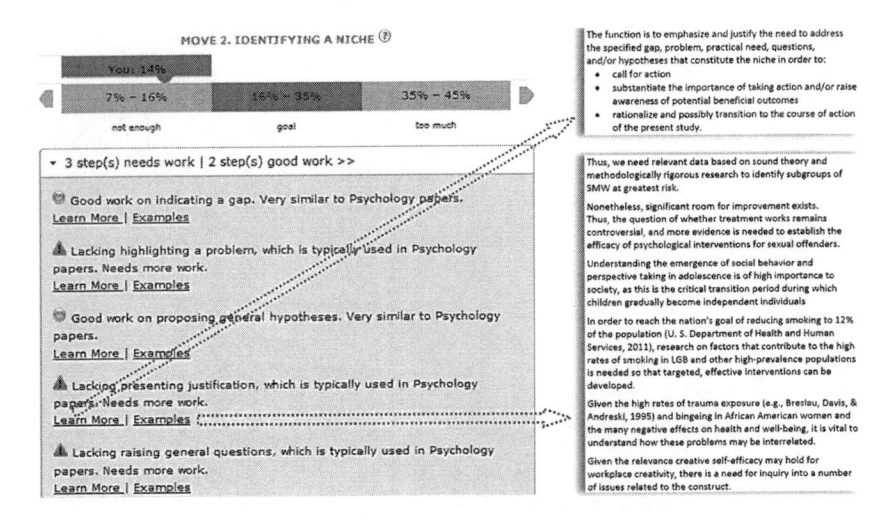

**MOVE 2. IDENTIFYING A NICHE**

| You: 14% | | | |
|---|---|---|---|
| 7% – 16% | 16% – 35% | 35% – 45% | |
| not enough | goal | too much | |

▾ 3 step(s) needs work | 2 step(s) good work >>

☺ Good work on indicating a gap. Very similar to Psychology papers.
Learn More | Examples

⚠ Lacking highlighting a problem, which is typically used in Psychology papers. Needs more work.
Learn More | Examples

☺ Good work on proposing general hypotheses. Very similar to Psychology papers.
Learn More | Examples

⚠ Lacking presenting justification, which is typically used in Psychology papers. Needs more work.
Learn More | Examples

⚠ Lacking raising general questions, which is typically used in Psychology papers. Needs more work.
Learn More | Examples

The function is to emphasize and justify the need to address the specified gap, problem, practical need, questions, and/or hypotheses that constitute the niche in order to:
- call for action
- substantiate the importance of taking action and/or raise awareness of potential beneficial outcomes
- rationalize and possibly transition to the course of action of the present study.

Thus, we need relevant data based on sound theory and methodologically rigorous research to identify subgroups of SMW at greatest risk.

Nonetheless, significant room for improvement exists. Thus, the question of whether treatment works remains controversial, and more evidence is needed to establish the efficacy of psychological interventions for sexual offenders.

Understanding the emergence of social behavior and perspective taking in adolescence is of high importance to society, as this is the critical transition period during which children gradually become independent individuals

In order to reach the nation's goal of reducing smoking to 12% of the population (U. S. Department of Health and Human Services, 2011), research on factors that contribute to the high rates of smoking in LGB and other high-prevalence populations is needed so that targeted, effective interventions can be developed.

Given the high rates of trauma exposure (e.g., Breslau, Davis, & Andreski, 1995) and bingeing in African American women and the many negative effects on health and well-being, it is vital to understand how these problems may be interrelated.

Given the relevance creative self-efficacy may hold for workplace creativity, there is a need for inquiry into a number of issues related to the construct.

**FIGURE 13.4** Functional steps Operationalized through Macro-Level and Micro-Level Feedback.

RWT details whether the steps are comparable to the target discipline. It also draws the student's attention to the steps that may be lacking or may need to be improved. In support of writer's cognitive processes, this feedback is hyperlinked with the components of the learning and demonstration modules. The *Learn More* links open a new tab with instructional materials about the step that might need to be scaffolded. The *Examples* links bring the students to the concordance with step-specific excerpts from the corpus.

The micro-level feedback is about the use of steps and appears as the student hovers over each sentence. Connected to the move color-coding of the draft, this type of feedback takes the form of interactive comments or clarifying questions about the rhetorical intent of a given sentence. The highlighted sentence in Figure 13.5 may not explicitly convey functional meaning, so the feedback prompts the student to think about it by asking whether this sentence intends to provide some general background to a claim (the step classified by the system as most probable for this sentence). Continuity to this instance of prompted reflection is maintained by the 'thumbs' and the note-taking features. In Figure 13.5, the student chose 'thumbs down,' indicating disagreement with the computer's interpretation of what she meant, and made a constructive comment that she would further use for revision. All of the sentence-level feedback prompts and student notes can be exported for self-planned revision.

## Accessing and Navigating RWT

RWT is a web-based application in continuous development, which is why, for the time being, it is only accessible at Iowa State University in the United States.

Computer-Assisted Research Writing  **233**

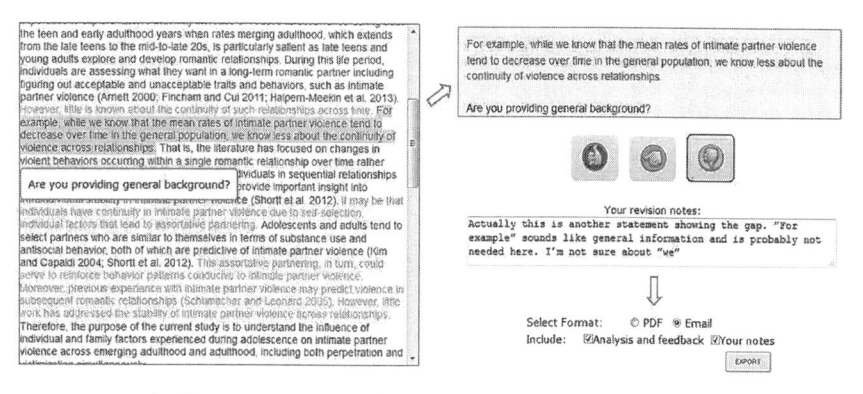

**FIGURE 13.5** Student Interaction with Micro-Level Feedback.

It is available to students and instructors at no cost. They need to create an account profile and log in with their institutional credentials (net-ID and password). The profile information includes the name, department, discipline, user status (e.g., doctoral/master/certificate/non-degree student, postdoctoral associate, or faculty), instructional setting (e.g., writing course, seminar, workshop) and English native/non-native speaker background. The homepage briefly introduces the tool, also linking to a short video demo, and encourages users to get started by creating a profile (Figure 13.6). The users can also contact the team for help if needed. Although access to RWT is restricted during ongoing development,

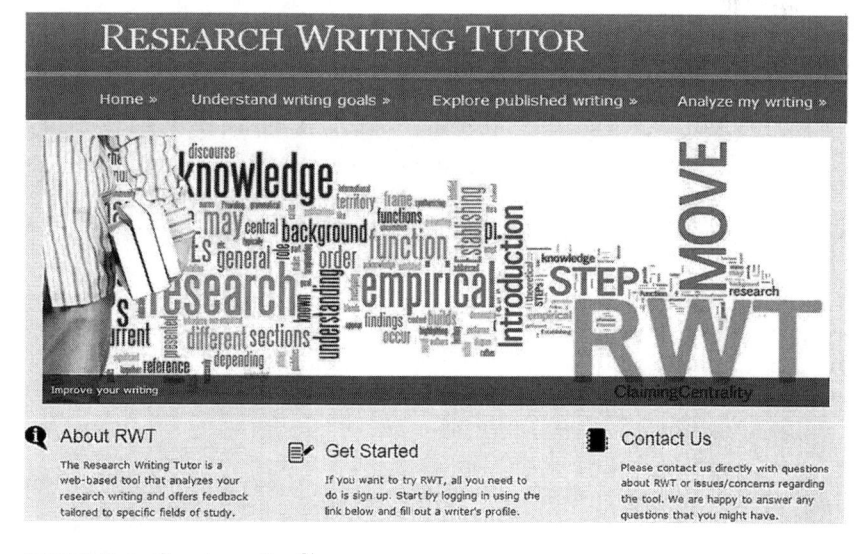

**FIGURE 13.6** Creating a Profile.

guest accounts for external users can be created upon request. Ultimately, the goal is to launch this tool as open access.

RWT's current interface is the same for all users. It is easy to navigate and is set up to engage students in greater levels of interaction. Clicking on *Understand writing goals* leads to a choice of the section the students are studying, as well as to the *Language Focus* guidelines. *Explore published writing* extends to the three components of the demonstration module, and *Analyze my writing* contains two options—to begin a new draft or continue one that is in progress. To start a new draft, students select a relevant discipline and IMRD/C section, enter the title of their paper, write or paste in the drafted content, and click on *Analyze* for feedback. When a draft for one section of their paper has been created and revised, students can add the next section. The drafts of a given section are automatically saved and can be accessed on the same editing page. The drafts of all the sections are also archived and are accessible through the *Continue draft* button according to the title of the paper.

## Evidence of Effectiveness

Empirical evidence showing how RWT can benefit novice scholarly writers is being continuously accumulated. Research results unveil its potential to trigger reflective processes and strategies, to have a positive impact on motivation and learning gains, and to suit users with the characteristics of targeted students.

### *Enhanced Cognition*

An important intended use of RWT is to activate higher-order thinking processes during revision, which is a key stage in the development of writing expertise. The various features of the tool were found to increase students' cognitive capacity in a number of ways (Cotos, 2011). Specifically, think-aloud and screen-recording data from 16 student-participants showed that the move-level feedback provided by the prototype version of RWT helped students engage in critical reading of their drafts. Most importantly, they were able to detect a mismatch between what they meant and what they actually conveyed. Students also noticed that:

- their ideas were not always explicitly stated;
- they needed more content;
- the way they organized the content was not as logical as it seemed;
- their drafts lacked some moves or steps that were commonly used by published authors in their discipline;
- their language choices were not always appropriate for their intended meaning.

Noticing these problems was triggered by both the color-coded feedback and the numerical feedback. Two other works (Chapelle, Cotos, & Lee, 2015;

Cotos, 2014) describe the cognitive reactions that were fostered by the feedback. The color-coded feedback prompted students to question what might have caused the mismatch, check whether the feedback was accurate or not, and hypothesize about what should be done to improve a problematic move. Numerical feedback facilitated setting operative goals. Because instant feedback was available for every text modification, students were able to consistently reflect and evaluate how well their ideas were translated to writing.

## Revision Strategies

Another study provides insight about the role of cognition in strategic text revision (Cotos, 2012). Open-ended questionnaires from 37 Masters and 68 PhD students specializing in a range of 34 disciplines showed that most students (90 percent) believed that the automated rhetorical feedback influenced their usual revision process and helped many of them (74 percent) develop new revision strategies. A random sample of 16 students was observed, interviewed, and their interaction with the tool was screen-recorded. Students' actions during revision showed that they first addressed the numerical feedback, trying to improve the move that was the farthest from the average in their discipline. At this point, the changes they made were sporadic, inconsistent, and often unsuccessful. Gradually, students' focus shifted to functional meaning. Their revision process turned into a very detailed self-verification, as they were checking the move colors against the intended steps sentence by sentence. When receiving feedback that was in disagreement with their rhetorical intent, students searched for move-specific phraseology in the annotated corpus. This appeared to be a constructive strategy often resulting in successful text modifications.

## Genre Learning and Writing

The macro-level feedback and corpus-based scaffolding helped students learn and apply genre concepts. Cotos (2014) reports that 80 percent of 88 students who completed questionnaires believed that they learned the moves well, 7 percent very well, and only 13 percent a little. Responses to a qualitative survey suggest that 77 percent thought they could transfer what they learned to their actual writing. Many students (59 percent) presumed that learning occurred because the corpus-based affordances helped them acquire a better understanding of the moves and steps. Another 22 percent attributed learning to the feedback and its ability to draw their attention to the rhetorical composition of their drafts. Some students (12 percent) noted that rhetorical feedback was helpful for learning how to operate with the genre concepts. An additional factor was the practice of revision exercised through multiple resubmissions of modified text. Students explained that this practice opportunity helped them consolidate their unseasoned genre knowledge. The more they revised and resubmitted, the more problems they could detect and thus the more successful modifications they were able to make.

Students' knowledge of genre conventions before and after interacting with the tool was assessed through pre and post-tests. There was a significant difference in the pre-test scores and the post-test scores, clearly indicating learning gains. Similarly, statistical analysis comparing 210 first and final drafts demonstrated that students' writing improved significantly. It is worth mentioning that students mostly improved content, language use, and structure.

## *Affect and Motivation*

Interaction with both the prototype and the current version of RWT was found to exert impact on students at affective and intrinsic levels. Most of the students (92 percent) in Cotos (2012) noted that they were excited to see improvement when new feedback was returned, and their desire to improve increased progressively. A third of these students shared a feeling of accomplishment. In some instances, repeated unsuccessful text modifications caused disappointment and frustration. As the revision continued, however, positive experience appeared to be more frequent compared to negative. This was in part because the students were coming to realize how important it is to be rhetorically and linguistically explicit. Corpus-based scaffolding features and comparison with published disciplinary texts also boosted their motivation.

## *Learner Fit*

A user study investigated the appropriateness of RWT for the revision task and for graduate students in different disciplines (Cotos & Huffman, 2013). The tool was introduced to nine students in a writing course that focused on producing a publishable quality research article. Multiple types of evidence showed that all RWT's features facilitated revision. RWT also promoted the necessary degree of learner control. Students tended to interact with its features in deliberate and exploratory ways, controlling their own pace and accessing certain types of feedback when they thought it was most appropriate. All of them evaluated the different forms of feedback as helpful, because they were directly applicable to performing the writing task. The discipline-specific nature of the feedback was perceived as suitable for individual learners.

Huffman (2015) explored 11 students' first-time interaction behaviors with RWT in a similar writing course. The results of time-on-task analysis showed that, as in Cotos and Huffman (2013), the students exercised the necessary degree of learner control by selecting what feedback and scaffolding to interact with depending on what they needed at a certain point in the revision process. Some students chose to use multiple features, and others maintained interaction with fewer features in a sequenced cyclical manner. Students' most frequently interacted with their color-coded drafts and with the 'thumbs,' taking notes on how to go about modifying specific sentences. The demonstration module was accessed particularly often. It was perceived as helpful, because the corpus-based examples illustrated how published authors compose their discourse both structurally and rhetorically. Whether opting for one or another type of interaction behavior, the students believed that RWT enabled them to self-regulate during revision.

## Utility

A study by Ramaswamy (2012) examined perceived usability and usefulness of RWT's feedback and demonstration modules, as well as the level of trust depending on the context of use. Three groups of graduate students were surveyed: one group consisted of 9 students enrolled in a graduate writing course; the second group of 24 students who participated in a month-long series of research writing seminars; and third group of 6 students who had never received any formal instruction in research writing. Interestingly, the less students knew about research writing, the more they tended to rely on the move feedback and trust the step feedback provided at sentence level. Students who had sufficient knowledge of genre conventions, but no teacher support, were more reflective. They liked having the computer provide rhetorical feedback, because it helped them think and self-analyze their writing. A participant even compared the feedback with the comments students receive from their major professors. Overall, the students' evaluated RWT as being user-friendly and easy to navigate, with consistently designed and well-integrated features, and visually appealing. In terms of usefulness, the different types of feedback were rated as comprehensible, stimulating deeper thinking, and motivating revision actions. Students expressed willingness to continue using this tool in the future, whether independently or as part of formal instruction.

## Integrating the Technology for Learning

RWT is not bound to a specific curriculum. Each of its three modules can be used to complement classroom activities in ways that are appropriate to the learning objectives, which is why RWT does not impose a pre-determined path conditioned by prerequisite steps. The materials in the learning module can be assigned by teachers as homework either before the research article conventions are introduced in class, or after that for the purpose of knowledge consolidation. In lieu of EAP corpus-based approaches, teachers can use the demonstration module to devise discovery learning tasks (see Johns, 2002), in which students explore disciplinary corpora. Their observations of how moves occur in different texts and what language is used to communicate specific shades of meaning can provide a sound foundation for class discussion and draft-planning activities.

The feedback module can be best used for the purpose of self-analysis once the students produce their first draft. In this process, note-taking in response to the sentence-level feedback can become a systematic revision strategy. It is highly recommended for teachers to model self-analysis with RWT in class in order to make sure that students engage in productive reflection and are able to detect mismatches between the mental and written representations of their texts.

Although initially designed to enhance graduate writing pedagogy, RWT can be used in other learning environments and levels of instruction. For example, it has been introduced to graduate students who seek scientific writing assistance in workshops, peer writing groups, and individual consultations with writing tutors at Iowa State. In these relatively autonomous learning environments, students can determine their own needs-based ways of interaction with RWT. Generally, they begin with the feedback module and use the other two modules when needing to understand genre concepts. RWT could also be used with advanced writers in high school, particularly where the learning of sciences includes research experiences and capstone project reports. Irrespective of the context of use, the tool's most essential advantage is integrating genre and disciplinary conventions in a platform for independent writing practice.

## Limitations and Future Directions

RWT is a pioneering genre-based system, which draws on theoretical tenets, EAP pedagogical principles, and disciplinary corpora of research writing. Its modules facilitate the learning of scientific writing conventions. The rhetorical feedback in the feedback module, in particular, warrants students' engagement in an interaction that stimulates necessary reflective processes and promotes revision for improvement.

Implementations of RWT in different contexts of use and the study of students' interactions with this tool have provided directions for future improvements. Undoubtedly, corpora from 30 disciplines are helpful to a rather broad representation of students. However, students whose discipline is not included in RWT may find it less suitable for their writing needs. Growing this tool to incorporate all possible disciplines is certainly a daunting and perhaps unrealistic endeavor. Nonetheless, empirical evidence obtained so far suggest that all three modules can be useful regardless of whether the discipline is present in RWT or not (if students are given an explanation of how existing features could be efficiently utilized). For example, the sentence-level feedback is helpful to anyone, because it can facilitate self-reflection that is needed to trigger cognitive activities important for the revision process. Similarly, because the linguistic choices expressing certain rhetorical intent are functional rather than disciplinary, the concordancer in the demonstration module can be used irrespective of the discipline. In other words, students in any discipline can choose expressions like "is well-established and rapidly expanding," "has led to significant interest," "has been at the forefront of much research," and "has received considerable attention" to claim centrality of their topic.

At this point, RWT falls short compared with other writing systems in that it does not have an interface for teachers, who might prefer to have access to all students' drafts and custom-tailored progress reports. Additionally, RWT has no technical ability to allow teachers to embed their own comments on various aspects of writing quality that fall outside genre conventions. To design new components for teachers, classroom-based investigations will be conducted, and teachers' input will take center stage. Embedded peer feedback is also a desirable addition, which could create a collaborative environment for groups of students who share similar writing goals and research interests. Furthermore, research is needed to understand better how RWT might be used more efficiently and to design new features that would help students frequently and strategically activate and monitor cognitive processes (similar to Roll, Aleven, McLaren, & Koedinger, 2007). The automated analysis performed by RWT's engine also anticipates a scale-up. While it yields acceptable move/step classification measures (Cotos & Pendar, 2016), feedback accuracy could be further improved. Also, the system classifies sentences only into one move and one step, but often sentences in published texts represent more than one rhetorical function. Another goal is to analyze step sequences and to generate feedback, comparing student writing with the sequencing preferences in their discipline. With its current features and new enhancements, RWT will help novices become experts in research writing.

## Acknowledgments

RWT was developed with support from the Computation Advisory Committee sponsored by the Office of the Senior Vice President and Provost at Iowa State University of Science and Technology, USA. Funding was also provided by the Graduate College, College of Engineering, and the English Department of the College of Liberal Arts and Sciences. The author gratefully acknowledges Dr. Stephen Gilbert's continued and invaluable contribution. Gratitude is extended to all colleagues who greatly assisted the research and development, as well as to all graduate students who worked on the RWT project at different stages.

## References

Aitchison, C., & Lee, A. (2006). Research writing: Problems and pedagogies. *Teaching in Higher Education, 11*(3), 265–278.

Ashley, K., Litman, D., & Schunn, C. (2013). Teaching writing and argumentation with AI-supported diagramming and peer review. (Project summary). Retrieved from Cyberlearning and Future Learning Technologies, National Science Foundation website: http://nsf.gov/awardsearch/showAward?AWD_ID=1122504.

Badley, G. (2009). Academic writing as shaping and re-shaping. *Teaching in Higher Education, 14*(2), 209–219.

Bereiter, C., & Scardamalia, M. (1987). *The Psychology of Written Composition*. Hillsdale, NJ: Lawrence Erlbaum Associates.

Berkenkotter, C., & Huckin, T. N. (1995). *Genre Knowledge in Disciplinary Communication: Cognition/Culture/Power*. Hillsdale, NJ: Lawrence Erlbaum Associates.

Bianchi, F., & Pazzaglia, R. (2007). Student writing of research articles in a foreign language: Metacognition and corpora. In R. Facchinetti (Ed.), *Corpus Linguistics 25 years on* (pp. 261–287). Amsterdam, Netherlands: Rodopi.

Birch-Bécaas, S., & Cooke, R. (2012). Raising collective awareness of rhetorical strategies. In A. Boulton, S. Carter-Thomas & E. Rowley-Jolivet (Eds.), *Corpus-Informed Research and Learning in ESP: Issues and Applications* (pp. 239–260). Amsterdam, Netherlands: John Benjamins.

Boulton, A. (2010). Learning outcomes from corpus consultation. In M. Moreno Jaén, F. Serrano Valverde & M. Calzada Pérez (Eds.), *Exploring New Paths in Language Pedagogy: Lexis and Corpus-Based Language Teaching* (pp. 129–144). London: Equinox.

Butterfield, E., Hacker, J., & Albertson, L. (1996). Environmental, cognitive, and metacognitive influences on text revision: Assessing the evidence. *Educational Psychology Review*, 8(3), 239–297.

Chang, C. F., & Kuo, C. H. (2011). A corpus-based approach to online materials development for writing research articles. *English for Specific Purposes*, 30, 222–234.

Chapelle, C. A., Cotos, E., & Lee, J. (2015). Diagnostic assessment with automated writing evaluation: A look at validity arguments for new classroom assessments. *Language Testing*, 32(3), 385–405.

Charles, M. (2014). Getting the corpus habit: EAP students' long-term use of personal corpora. *English for Specific Purposes*, 35, 30–40.

Cho, K., & Schunn, C. D. (2007). Scaffolded writing and rewriting in the discipline: A web-based reciprocal peer review system. *Computers & Education*, 48(3), 409–426.

Cortes, V. (2011). Genre analysis in the academic writing class: With or without corpora? *Quaderns de Filologia. Estudis Linguistics*, 26, 65–80.

Cotos, E. (2011). Potential of automated writing evaluation feedback. *CALICO Journal*, 28(2), 420–459.

Cotos, E. (2012). Towards effective integration and positive impact of automated writing evaluation in L2 Writing. In G. Kessler, A. Oskoz & I. Elola (Eds.), *Technology across Writing Contexts and Tasks, CALICO Monograph Series* (vol. 10, pp. 81–112). San Marcos, TX: CALICO.

Cotos, E. (2014). *Genre-Based Automated Writing Evaluation for L2 Research Writing: From Design to Evaluation and Enhancement*. Basingstoke, UK: Palgrave Macmillan.

Cotos, E., & Huffman, S. (2013). Learner fit in scaling up automated writing evaluation. *International Journal of Computer-Assisted Language Learning and Teaching*, 3(3), 77–98.

Cotos, E., & Pendar, N. (2016). Discourse classification into rhetorical functions for AWE feedback. *CALICO Journal*, 33(1), 92–116.

Cotos, E., Huffman, S., & Link, S. (2015). Move analysis of the research article genre: Furthering and applying analytic constructs. *Journal of English for Academic Purposes*, 17(2), 52–72.

Dunlosky, J., & Metcalfe, J. (2009). *Metacognition*. Thousand Oaks, CA: Sage.

Fisher, S. L., & Ford, J. K. (1998). Differential effects of learner effort and goal orientation on two learning outcomes. *Personnel Psychology*, 51, 397–420.

Flower, L. S., & Hayes, J. (1980). The cognition of discovery: Defining a rhetorical problem. *College Composition and Communication*, 31(1), 21–32.

Friginal, E. (2013). Developing research report writing skills using corpora. *English for Specific Purposes, 32*(4), 208–220.

Gaskell, D., & Cobb, T. (2004). Can learners use concordance feedback for writing errors? *System, 32*, 301–319.

Hacker, D. J., Keener, M. C., & Kircher, J. C. (2009). Writing is applied metacognition. In D. J. Hacker, J. Dunlosky, A.-C. Graesser (Eds.), *Handbook of Metacognition in Education* (pp. 154–172). New York: Routledge.

Hammond, J., & Macken-Horarik, M. (1999). Critical literacy: Challenges and questions for ESL classrooms. *TESOL Quarterly, 33*, 528–544.

Hayes, J. R. (2000). A new framework for understanding cognition and affect in writing. In R. Indrisano & J. Squire (Eds.), *Perspectives on Writing: Research, Theory, and Practice* (pp. 6–44). Newark, DE: International Reading Association.

Hayes, J. R. & Flower, L. (1983). *A Cognitive Model of the Writing Process in Adults* (Final Report). Pittsburg, PA: Carnegie Mellon. (ERIC Document Reproduction Service No. ED 240 608.)

Henry, A. (2007). Evaluating language learners' response to web-based, data-driven, genre teaching materials. *English for Specific Purposes, 26*, 462–484.

Huffman, S. (2015). Exploring learner perceptions of and behaviors using RWT (Unpublished dissertation). Retrieved from Iowa State University, ProQuest Dissertations Publishing, 3712448.

Hyland, K. (2004). *Genre and Second Language Writing*. Ann Arbor, MI: University of Michigan Press.

Johns, T. (2002). Data-driven learning: The perpetual challenge. In B. Kettemann & G. Marko, (Eds.), *Teaching and Learning by Doing Corpus Analysis* (pp. 107–117). Amsterdam, Netherlands: Rodopi.

Jolliffe, D. A., & Brier, E. M. (1988). Studying writers' knowledge in academic disciplines. In D. A. Jolliffe (Ed.), *Advances in Writing Research: Writing in Academic Disciplines* (vol. 2, pp. 35–77). Norwood, NJ: Ablex Publishing Company.

Lee, D., & Swales, J. (2006). A corpus-based EAP course for NNS doctoral students: Moving from available specialized corpora to self-compiled corpora. *English for Specific Purposes, 25*(1), 56–75.

Pearson, M., & Brew, A. (2002). Research training and supervision development. *Studies in Higher Education, 27*(2), 135–150.

Perelman, L. (2012). Construct validity, length, score, and time in holistically graded writing assessments: The case against automated essay scoring (AES). In C. Bazerman, C. Dean, J. Early, K. Lunsford, S. Null, P. Rogers & A. Stansell (Eds.), *International Advances in Writing Research: Cultures, Places, Measures* (pp. 121–131). Fort Collins, CO: WAC Clearinghouse/Anderson, SC: Parlor Press.

Ramaswamy, N. (2012). Online tutor for research writing. (Unpublished thesis). Retrieved from Iowa State University, ProQuest Dissertations Publishing, 1519246.

Roll, I., Aleven, V., McLaren, B. M., & Koedinger, K. R. (2007). Designing for metacognition—Applying cognitive tutor principles to the tutoring of help seeking. *Metacognition and Learning, 2*(2–3), 125–140.

Schunn, C., Litman, D., & Godley, A. (2014). An intelligent ecosystem for science writing instruction. [Project summary]. Retrieved from Division of Research on Learning in Formal and Informal Settings (DRL), National Science Foundation website: http://www.nsf.gov/awardsearch/showAward?AWD_ID=1416980.

Swales, J. M. (1981). *Aspects of Articles Introductions*. Aston ESP Reports, No. 1. The University of Aston, Birmingham.

Tardy, C. M. (2009). *Building Genre Knowledge*. West Lafayette, IN: Parlor Press.
Todd, R. W. (2001). Induction from self-selected concordances and self-correction. *System*, *29*(1), 91–102.
Tono, Y., Satake, Y., & Miura, A. (2014). The effects of using corpora on revision tasks in L2 writing with coded error feedback. *ReCALL*, *26*, 147–162.
Turner, J. (2012). Academic literacies: Providing a space for the socio-political dynamics. *Journal of English for Academic Purposes*, *11*(1), 17–25.

# 14
# WRITING TO LEARN AND LEARNING TO WRITE THROUGH SWoRD

*Christian Schunn*

## Introduction

The largest barrier to giving students opportunities to work on rich problems and tasks requiring a free text response is a feedback bottleneck: there are so many students and there is so little time to provide students with detailed and useful feedback. New automated feedback tools can address a number of those situations, but are not general enough to be applied in all contexts. By contrast, peer feedback is a highly flexible strategy that can be applied to essentially any task assigned to students. Whenever students are given a writing task, they can also be asked to evaluate their peers' work using rubrics and provide constructive criticism. Thus, students can receive detailed feedback on short or long writing tasks without always requiring instructor feedback. Further, students can also learn from evaluating their peer's writing.

To make peer feedback a viable strategy, students need to be strongly supported in the process and held accountable for their work so they provide accurate and detailed feedback rather than short and superficial feedback (i.e., "good job"). SWoRD (Scaffolded Writing and Rewriting in the Discipline) is a tool that has been iteratively improved through research (described below) to give the support students need to effectively and efficiently provide feedback on the aspects of the assignment that are important for instruction. Most saliently, it has algorithms that ensure students take the reviewing task seriously. Teachers can then assign many more rich writing-based assignments than they normally would be able to without being overwhelmed by grading/feedback workload.

## Writing as Central but Challenging

Writing is a powerful instructional tool. It can be used to support students' development of self-regulation skills, and self-regulation is a critical part of effective writing itself (Dignath, Buettner, & Langfeldt, 2008; Kliewer et al., 2011). Across diverse disciplines, in written responses, students can show that they understand how and why their answers were obtained (Miller, 1992; Rubin & Carlan, 2005), rather than potentially having guessed a correct response on a multiple-choice exam.

Recent standards in mathematics and science are full of performance indicators that require writing, and writing is likewise required in corresponding assessments. For example, in mathematics, the Common Core standards ask that students "Understand solving equations as a process of reasoning and explain the reasoning." Similarly, in science, the Next Generation Science Standards frequently refer to practices like "make and defend a claim," or "explain." Until students can turn in video answers or be interviewed one-on-one in assessments, evaluations of students' ability to explain their reasoning will likely involve writing.

English Language Arts (ELA) has always required writing, and the new Common Core standards for ELA have placed even greater emphasis on higher-level writing skills (http://www.corestandards.org/ELA-Literacy/). Many of these standards refer to writing skills that are useful across other topic areas, such as history and science. For example, these standards require that students "Cite strong and thorough textual evidence to support analysis of what the text says explicitly."

At the same time, writing is a very complex skill that students struggle to master. A main source of difficulty relates to the many layers of language that must be mastered to produce functional text. For instance, there are the complex lower levels of a language: (1) how letters form words (especially for languages like English that are filled with irregular spellings rather than languages like German); and (2) how words are sequenced to form grammatical sentences. In addition, there are the complex upper levels of language: (1) how sentences come together to form coherent arguments or narratives, building on what is already established in the text; and (2) how all of the text relates to what an intended audience member already knows about the topic. In other words, writing is an integration of many levels of skills, and developing writers need time to develop all of these skills.

Another source of difficulty comes from the integration of discipline content with these complex writing skills. Writing across disciplines takes on new forms or genres (Biber & Conrad, 2009) with each discipline potentially having their own conventions (e.g., a lab report in science). Students then have more forms to learn. But just as problematic, students are also struggling with the underlying disciplinary ideas about which they are writing (e.g., what is a phylum, how do laws shape a democracy, how do substances dissolve). This creates a fundamental working memory challenge for students (Hayes, Flower, Schriver, Stratman, & Carey, 1987; Kellogg, 1994) because of having to process complex disciplinary ideas, which are still just many isolated pieces, while also thinking about how to write text that is coherent and clear.

In sum, writing is cognitively difficult from the complexity of things to learn and from the high load on the student's working memory. These challenges are both addressed through carefully structured practice (Kellogg & Whitford, 2009), as students come to master all of the layers of text production in different genres and develop integrated conceptual understandings. Students need to be given opportunities to think through the various aspects and practice each aspect (see also Crossley, Allen, & McNamara, Chapter 12 this volume).

## The Need for Effective Peer Feedback

If such carefully structured practice with writing tasks is the answer, ironically, practice (of any kind) is what is currently most lacking. Students rarely write in general, and they especially do not very often write anything long enough to involve a real argument or an interesting narrative (Kiuhara, Graham, & Hawken, 2009). For example, a national study of writing practice in middle and high schools in the US found that students do very little extended writing in English class, and almost no extended writing at all in science, social studies, or math classes (Applebee & Langer, 2011). Further, students tend not to receive timely or effective feedback from teachers even when they do write.

As a result, student writing performance in the US is quite poor by national assessments, with most 8th and 12th graders writing at the basic or below basic levels (NAEP, 2011), and little improvement has been shown over the last 20 years (National Commission on Writing in American Schools and Colleges, 2003). Students are not entering the workplace or college ready for what is expected there (National Commission on Writing, 2004).

Why do students not get opportunities to practice? The high workload associated with grading and feedback is a primary culprit. As one teacher said quite clearly, "Well, I can't have them write two paragraphs every day because that will take me how much time to read and if I can't read it and give them thoughtful feedback, it's not very productive" (Applebee & Langer, 2011). The need for feedback for effective writing practice is obvious; what is needed is an alternative method for practice with feedback that is not dependent upon teacher feedback alone.

Automatic Essay Scoring and Automatic Writing Evaluation systems will be an important part of the solution to this lack of practice and feedback problem (see Crossley, Allen, & McNamara, Chapter 12 this volume; Ramineni & Deane, Chapter 10 this volume). However, there will likely be some forms of writing that are not easily handled using those automatic systems (e.g., ones involving integration of text and images, because those systems cannot parse images), or because of significant involvement of content understanding (e.g., distinguishing between the presence of a supporting clause and one that involves sensible content that actually is supporting).

Peer feedback can be applied to any kind of writing task assigned to students. The basic notion behind peer feedback is that if students can be reasonably expected to provide a response to the task, they can also be reasonably expected to be able to evaluate strengths/weaknesses in other students' written responses and suggest possible improvements. This follows from a general developmental pattern in which students can recognize what is needed well before they can reliably do what is needed themselves (Siegler, 1996; Vygotsky, 1978). For example, a person can talk about and recognize good/bad driving from taking a driving course well before they are good drivers. As discussed below, peer ratings of writing on clear rubrics are generally very accurate.

More importantly, giving peer feedback is another excellent learning opportunity; by evaluating responses using a rubric and by providing constructive comments to the author, students can improve their own detection and revising skills (Palincsar & Brown, 1984; Topping, 2008; Van Den Berg, Admiraal, & Pilot, 2006). Further, it emphasizes writing as a process, rather than just writing as an outcome (Katstra, Tollefson, & Gilbert, 1987), which is an important transition in mindset about writing.

However, while peer feedback can and often is implemented in classrooms without technology support (Applebee & Langer, 2011), it is frequently difficult to orchestrate, consumes an unnecessarily large amount of precious class time, and often is poorly executed. Students struggle to provide honest evaluations, worrying about threatening friendships, confronting social power dynamics, or generally not wanting to embarrass the author in public. Also, students have little incentive to put effort into the evaluations. Thus, without additional support, students typically provide short, content-free positive evaluations such as "This is awesome, dude!" (VanDeWeghe, 2004).

## The SWoRD System

There is a simple automated approach to creating effective student peer review in a wide range of classes, which has been iteratively improved over a decade of research (Cho & Schunn, 2007; Cho, Schunn, & Charney, 2006a; Cho, Schunn, & Wilson, 2006b; Kaufman & Schunn, 2011; Nelson & Schunn, 2009; Patchan, Hawk, Stevens, & Schunn, 2013). At its core, there are four elements of SWoRD:

1. A method for easily assigning anonymized documents to peers and returning reviews back to authors via the web;
2. A structured reviewing form that contains concrete suggestions for what kinds of comments are requested on specific dimensions and rating rubrics that have concrete anchors for each rating level that are also tied to specific dimensions;
3. Student authors rate the helpfulness of the reviews they receive, and these helpfulness ratings (called back-evaluations) are used to compute a reviewing helpfulness grade for the reviewers. This forces students to take the task of giving comments seriously;

4. All ratings produced by a given student are compared to the mean ratings produced by all the other student reviewers of the same documents. This is done across the multiple rating rubrics (e.g., three to eight rubrics in an assignment) multiplied by the number of peers' documents reviewed by the student for the given assignment (e.g., 4 documents x 5 rubrics = 20 ratings). If the ratings are similarly ordered (from relative weaknesses to relative strengths), then the student receives a high reviewing accuracy grade. If the ratings are very dissimilar (either by giving random ratings or all the same ratings), then the student receives a low reviewing accuracy grade. This forces students to take the rating task seriously.

These four elements work together to produce a method that is easily integrated into diverse assignments and classes to produce accurate ratings and useful comments, and ultimately good learning outcomes. In early years, SWoRD was most commonly used in college settings, as the internet was more broadly available to college-age students. In recent years, web-based methods are now much easier to use in K-12 settings, as both schools and children's homes have achieved very broad access. With growth in use at the high school level, adjustments have been made to SWoRD that support the needs of younger learners and the various obligations that high school teachers more commonly face.

## *The Student Tasks: Submission, Reviewing, Back-Evaluation*

Students complete three basic tasks for a given assignment draft, which are clearly shown to students in a timeline view (see Figure 14.1). There is also a to do list when students first log in showing what is due soon. Along the timeline, students first submit a document. Many document types are allowed, and they can be automatically converted to PDF by the system to ensure students can read the documents easily. The document submission deadline is actually a soft deadline: students can submit a document late with a per-day penalty that teachers can chose to override if there is a valid reason, such as illness or individualized education plan. Documents may be submitted up until one day before the final reviewing deadline.

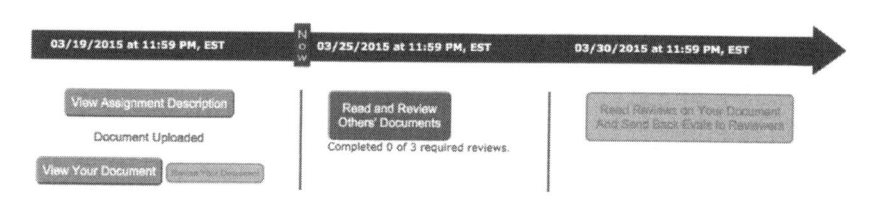

**FIGURE 14.1** The Student Assignment Time Line View. Blue buttons show optional actions/past steps, green buttons indicated what action needs to be done next, and greyed out buttons show future steps.

Second, students review between three and six peer documents. Each document is labeled only by the author's chosen pseudonym (e.g., cubsfan15 or ForestGump); real identities of authors and reviewers are always kept hidden. Teachers determine the minimum number of reviews to complete for that assignment (four or five are recommended). Students may complete extra reviews for bonus points. For a given review, students must type comments in reaction to specific comment prompts. And for each comment prompt, there are one or more rating rubrics. For example, Figure 14.2 shows a comment prompt relating to the quality of the evidence provided and a corresponding rating prompt. The rating prompts are always on a seven-point scale, but they can be customized for how many of the points on the scale have concrete anchors. The students can scroll through the submitted document while completing the review, or they can download the document for printing. Each assignment's reviewing form can have as many or as few evaluation dimensions as the teacher would like. Typically, teachers include four to eight different reviewing dimensions in a given assignment. Assignments will vary in how much time it takes to do the reviewing task, but for typical high school writing tasks, students generally self-report spending 30 minutes to an hour on all the reviewing work.

Finally, students as authors examine all the feedback they have received and rate each reviewer's comments for helpfulness on a 1–5 scale (called back-evaluations), along with a brief explanation for the rating. Students generally value comments that contain at least some critiques (i.e., are not all praise), are polite in their criticism, and include suggestions for improvement. This back-evaluation step can be done quite quickly (e.g., typically in five to ten minutes).

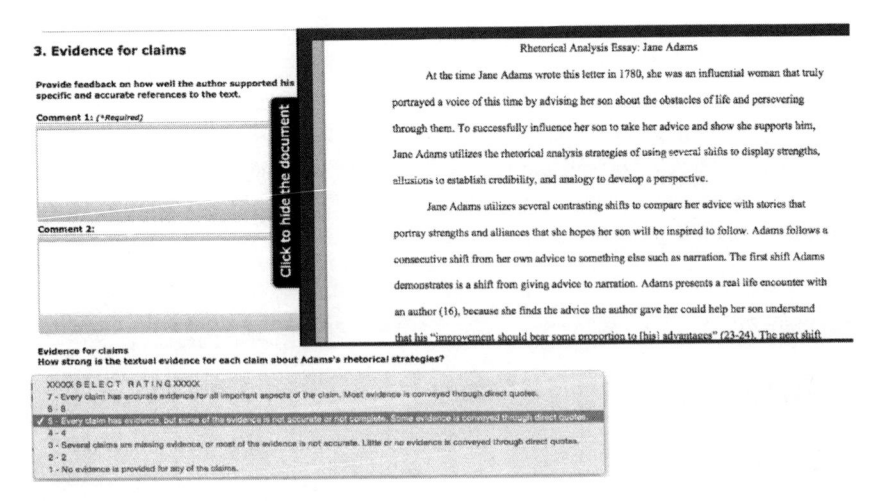

FIGURE 14.2 Reviewing form showing text boxes for constructive feedback, one corresponding rating rubric, and a scrollable viewer for reading the document to be reviewed.

Students as reviewers can then see what back-evaluations their received for each review (see Figure 14.3). They can also see what other reviewers said and the ways in which the authors did or did not appreciate these other reviews. In this way, students can see models of good reviews and receive feedback on their own reviewing skills.

Students as reviewers can also see how accurately they rated each document on each rating dimension. Figure 14.4 shows what students see. For each rating dimension, the papers the student reviewed (five in this case), are ordered from lowest to highest according to what the other reviewers thoughts; thus the dark lines always have an increasing slope. In this example, the student's own ratings and the others align well for explaining evidence and organization dimensions, but there is lower agreement for evidence for claims. Sometimes students have opposing views. In the case of high conflict, students can click to see what the other reviewers said to understand why they had a different evaluation of a given document.

## The Teacher Tasks: Assignment Setup and Performance Monitoring

The teacher interface in SWoRD has all the basic learning management system functions one would expect. Teachers can create classes, and then inside classes, create assignments, provide feedback to students (strategically as they see fit), and monitor student and assignment performance.

There are some general parameters than can be adjusted, such as number of reviewers, grading policies (e.g., late penalties), but all the parameters have default values so relatively little needs to be done to get started except for entering the assignment description and choosing/creating evaluation dimensions.

The commenting prompts and rating rubrics can be created from scratch, selected from a library of shared prompts and rubrics, or selected from the teacher's history of past prompts and rubrics. In addition, whole prior assignments can be copied, as can whole past courses; in fact, teachers can share a whole course's content with another teacher simply by letting them know the enrollment key for their course.

|   | Reviewer #1 | Reviewer #2 | GreatGatsby | Reviewer #4 |
|---|---|---|---|---|
| Explaining evidence | Goes in detail with explaining the evidence and ties it into the thesis statement. *Backevaluation(3)*: Mostly praise and no critiques. | The analysis of the evidence was sufficient enough for each section but there were varying strengths of their explainations. For example the paragraph about "personal accounts" is much weaker than the paragraph about "imagery". Develop the analysis of the personal accounts paragraph to create a more balanced essay. *Backevaluation(5)*: Very detailed and helpfull | The explanation was spot on such as in the connecting rhetorical questions to the evidence. It states how it connects to Louv's argument, and then to the authors interpretation. *Backevaluation(3)*: Thanks! How could I have furthered my textual evidence? | You interworked the quotes to where they flowed and weren't abrupt in the sentence. I dont realy have any complaints until the 4th paragraph, where I don't see any quotes. I like how you explain it, its just lacking textual evidence. Other than that you picked good evidence for everything else. *Backevaluation(4)*: How could the 4th paragraph be better? What quotes could I use. |

FIGURE 14.3   Authors rating helpfulness of received comments on a 1 (unhelpful) to 5 (helpful) scale, along with brief explanations. Here the reviewer named Great Gatsby can see the helpfulness ratings they received along with the comments and helpfulness ratings of the other reviewers for this same document.

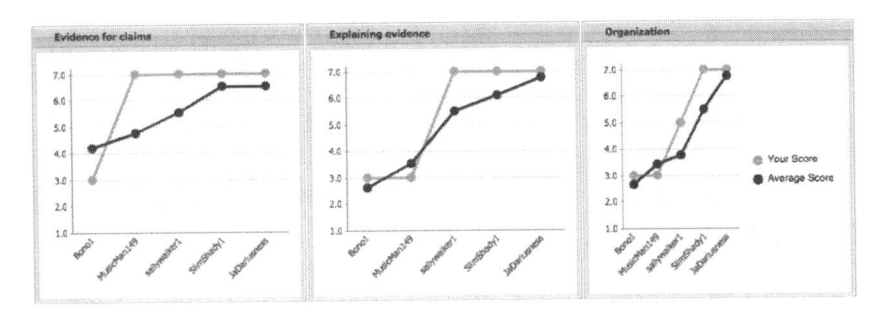

**FIGURE 14.4** Comparison of a given student's ratings to the mean ratings from the other peer reviews on those same documents.

SWoRD makes it possible for students to do all the work on their own, receiving automatic email reminders as deadlines loom or if a paper or review is now late. But it is also useful for teachers to have an overview of the class as well as simple views of which students are struggling. Figure 14.5 shows the view of a particular assignment, providing information about overall submission rates and then listing particular students who missed particular deadlines or documents that overall have not received enough ratings or have high conflict across reviewers.

Of course, teachers can also see overall student performance on each of the rubric dimensions in terms of mean ratings. More interesting, however, is the reliability performance of student ratings on each dimension: how well do students agree on a given dimension. Figure 14.6 presents an example from an English course. In this case, students had relatively low agreement on one of the evaluation rubrics, relating to describing the argument in an essay they analyzed. Two of the rating dimensions produced very high levels of inter-reviewer agreement, and the remaining dimensions were adequate, but still had areas that could be improved further. With this information, teachers can iteratively improve either their assignments or the in-class guidance they provide on the assignments. A recent analysis of all the high school writing assignments implemented in SWoRD found that a majority of the rubrics had good inter-rater agreement, suggesting that teachers quickly improve their assignments with this kind of feedback.

To understand why this dimension had lower agreement, a teacher can sort a table view of all of the submitted documents by level of agreement on that specific dimension, and from there jump to the reviews for the documents with the highest level of reviewer disagreement on that dimension (see Figure 14.7). For example, perhaps some students are not seeing certain problems at all. Or perhaps some students have a different view of how problematic certain issues are. The student comments provide teachers with insights into what the problems are, which can then lead to useful in-class discussions of the issues.

33/34 students submitted the document. Due: 02/26/2015
131/133 ratings completed. Due: 03/03/2015+1
131/133 comments completed. Due: 03/03/2015+1
121/131 backreviews completed. Due: 03/06/2015

**Missing documents**

**Late documents**

**Documents with few reviews**

**Reviewers who have much to do**

**Conflicting rating documents**

**Late Reviews**

rraci, jetmira  [Remove Penalty]

**Backevaluators who have much to do**

**All stats**

**FIGURE 14.5** Teacher display of available student activity information on a given assignment. Clicking on a bar reveals which students have that issue (e.g., submitted a document late, or completed a late review). Late penalties for valid reasons can be waived with a click.

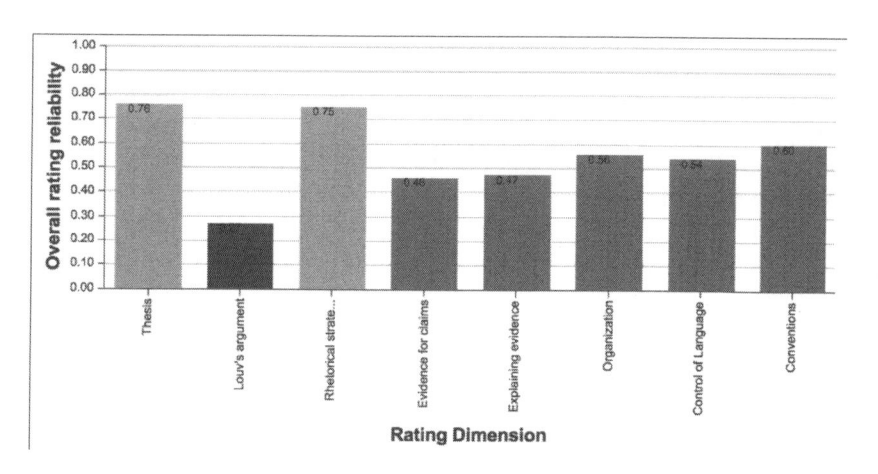

Thesis: 0.76
Louv's argument: (low)
Rhetorical strate...: 0.75
Evidence for claims: 0.46
Explaining evidence: 0.47
Organization: 0.56
Control of Language: 0.54
Conventions: 0.60

Rating Dimension

**FIGURE 14.6** Teacher display of inter-rater agreement (also called rating reliability) of each rating rubric on a given assignment.

| Louv's argument | Within the first paragraph, Louv's argument is barely stated. Only the author's argument and opinion is stated. To fix the problem, use quotes from the text that relate to Louv's opinion on the separation between people and nature.<br><br>*Backevaluation(4)*:<br>I should have more directly addressed Louv's argument. The reviewer's wording is a little strange but I understand the message. | The author doesn't ever truly state how Louv feels about the subject. They say that he believes that there is a growing separation between people and nature, yet never says how he feels. For example in the final paragraph they state that his essay is bringing "to light the thievery of real world appreciation that is being committed by the new technologies that we ourselves are creating." Here they are saying that Louv is showing this separation but yet again, not how he feels about it. The simple solution would be to include how he feels on the topic.<br><br>*Backevaluation(5)*:<br>I agree that I didn't specifically state how Louv feels about the subject nor did I elaborate on his subject very much. | Argument is accurately and properly stated and explained. The separation between people and nature that Louv proves, is portrayed well in the essay.<br><br>*Backevaluation(3)*:<br>It makes me feel good but doesn't really help me. Especially since other reviewers pointed out how I scarcely explained Louv's argument. | The opening to your Iintroductory paragraph was also very well written but I feel like it could have include done more sentence explaining Louv's negative feelings about the separation between nature and his argument.<br><br>*Backevaluation(4)*:<br>I agree I didn't outline Louv's argument very well in my introduction. |
|---|---|---|---|---|

**FIGURE 14.7** Reviewer comments in a case of high reviewer disagreement (along with author back-evaluations).

## Research on Student use of SWoRD

### Rating Accuracy

In general, peer ratings on sensible rubrics are similar to those produced by teachers, with there sometimes being a small bias in peer ratings being higher than teacher ratings (Falchikov & Goldfinch, 2000). The mean rating from four or five peers can be remarkably accurate when students are given a sensible rubric and incentives to take the reviewing task seriously. Across disciplines and student levels, the mean peer ratings from SWoRD were more similar to a teacher rating than any two teacher ratings would be to each other (correlations of .4 to .5; Cho, Schunn, & Wilson, 2006b). In a recent study (Schunn, Godley, & DiMartino, in press), we found that the mean of peer ratings in advanced placement (AP) classes using SWoRD were close to expert AP grader ratings that would meet the grading standards the College Board requires of AP expert graders. Even middle school students' peer ratings can be remarkably aligned to teacher ratings (e.g., correlations of greater than .9, or quadratic weighted Kappas of .85; Sadler & Good, 2006). These findings may seem surprising in that students clearly are generally not able to produce excellent work for the same tasks in which they are accurate raters; however, the high variability in quality across students, when combined with clear rating rubrics, makes assessing quality relatively straightforward. Further, students have received some instruction on what they should be doing (e.g., in the commenting and rubric prompts, as well in the classroom instruction leading up to the writing assignments). So, they often understand what should be done long before they have practiced enough to produce fluent and consistent outcomes in their own work.

### Peers as an Important Audience

A concern that some teachers have is that students will not take an assignment seriously if they think it will only go to peers who might have lower standards. However, students are generally quite concerned with looking bad in front of peers. There is also the problem that teachers are usually an odd audience for writing: students are asked to tell teachers things that it is clear the teacher already knows, which is a basic violation of norms of communication (Grice, 1975). Peers therefore might be a better audience than teachers for writing. A recent study with SWoRD found that first drafts of physics lab reports submitted to peers were actually stronger than first drafts submitted to teaching assistants (Cohen's d = 0.5), according to blind evaluations by experts (Patchan, Schunn, & Clark, 2011). A similar benefit from writing to peers rather than to a teacher was found in a study of writing at the middle school level (Cohen & Riel, 1989) suggesting it is a very general effect.

## *Comment Helpfulness*

Although teachers generally look upon student peer feedback as inferior to teacher feedback, in fact, students commonly see peer feedback as just as helpful. This acceptance of peer feedback was found in student's helpfulness ratings of received feedback in a study in which students did not know whether feedback came from a peer or the teacher (Cho & Schunn, 2007). Similar results are shown in student surveys and interviews (Kaufman & Schunn, 2011; Topping, 2008). It is interesting to note, however, that students have significant concerns about the fairness of grades produced by peer review processes, even if they do not dispute the grades they received (Kaufman & Schunn, 2011; Sambell, McDowell, & Brown, 1997). More importantly, when looking at what students do with feedback they receive, peer comments can be just as helpful as teacher comments. While the teacher comments are more accurate, they are often not expressed in a way that students understand. For the more complex aspects of a task, we have often seen students make documents worse in response to teacher feedback, because of such misunderstandings (Cho & Schunn, 2007). Further, receiving comments from multiple peers in SWoRD can be more persuasive then feedback from just one individual, producing much larger improvements in the document from multiple peers than from one instructor (Cohen's d = 1.2; Cho & Schunn, 2007). When only one person makes a comment, a student can dismiss the comment as erroneous or the opinion of just one potentially biased person; when many peers make the same comment, even stubborn students acknowledge there is a problem. However, students still ignore many useful peer comments, just as they ignore many useful teacher comments (Nelson & Schunn, 2009).

## *Learning from Reviewing*

Although it is important that the obtained ratings and comments are accurate and useful, a large benefit of implementing peer feedback is actually obtained from the act of providing constructive comments to peers. For example, one study found that students who provided feedback to others without themselves doing any writing actually improved their own writing more than students who wrote and received feedback (Lundstrom & Baker, 2009).

Part of the learning benefit of reviewing peer's work is that students see models of what could be done as well as examples of errors that can be made (Cho & MacArthur, 2011). Sometimes this learning from seeing errors is about noticing the importance of the error (Kaufman & Schunn, 2011). For example, it is one thing to be told that dry writing is bad for communication; it is another thing to actually see how difficult it is to read dry writing.

But the benefits of reviewing are not just about seeing useful models. There is also the act of articulating the problem clearly and describing possible revisions that address the problem. In one study using SWoRD, we examined the valued added of the commenting task in peer review. Some students were only asked to rate peer documents according to rubrics, whereas other students had to rate and comment. Subsequent submissions were significantly better in the rate and comment condition than the rate-only condition (Cohen's d = 0.9; Wooley, Was, Schunn, & Dalton, 2008).

It is for these reasons that SWoRD specifically rewards students for constructive reviewing through the helpfulness grades and that it allows bonus reviewing. Reviewing itself can be a strong learning opportunity, and having constructive comments is likely to be a critical aspect of maximizing that learning opportunity.

### *The Overall Benefits for Students*

After using SWoRD, student and teacher surveys have regularly shown that students feel better prepared for writing-based exams, in part because they have had extra opportunities to practice, but more importantly because they have had the chance to think carefully about what is being expected of them (Godley et al., in press).

The prior sections showed the benefits of each aspect of the SWoRD process. How do they add up overall, and how broadly can SWoRD be used? There have not been careful studies of cumulative long-term impact, but one case study may be of interest. There is one high school that was an early and pervasive adopter of SWoRD, and it has obtained excellent exam results with over 95 percent of the students obtaining Advanced or Proficient scores on the 12th grade state writing test. This school involves many students coming from a background that is generally not associated with high exam performance (e.g., mean performance for other schools with 60 percent of students eligible for free or reduced lunch is below 70 percent Advanced or Proficient on this state writing tests). Yet, they were able to obtain writing performance that is more typically associated with the top performing suburban schools. These results were obtained from only two teachers using SWoRD across several years of instruction; their students wrote almost every day, and used peer review throughout the year. As a result of these excellent outcomes, the whole high school is moving toward regular use of

SWoRD, even extending it to math classes. Of course, one cannot make too much of a single case study and it is likely that these teachers implemented a number of helpful writing pedagogies. Further, this case provides no insight into how much peer review is required for obtaining good outcomes; but it does show that peer review can be used to greatly increase the amount of writing with feedback that students are asked to do. Additional research will be needed to establish how much and what kinds of peer review work are needed to produce writing gains in different kinds of subjects and in various educational contexts.

## How to Access SWoRD, Now Named Peerceptiv

The first decade of SWoRD was paid for by research grant funding, and teachers throughout the world could use SWoRD for free. After a major rebuild of the system in 2009, which added many requested features and improvements to the interface, the number of SWoRD users was growing rapidly. The growth rate required the purchase of more web-servers and technical support, which were not supported by grant funding. Further grant funding is not a sustainable model for broad use of new technologies, because there can be gaps in funding for some years regardless of user demand. Since university researchers are neither skilled nor incentivized to distribute learning technologies broadly, and seeing the need to offer SWoRD on a very wide and sustainable basis of use, the University of Pittsburgh licensed SWoRD to a small company. The company renamed the tool Peerceptiv and implemented a number of additional improvements to the student and teacher interface; the user interface images shown earlier are all from the current Peerceptiv interface as of Fall 2015. There is still a version of SWoRD being used at the University of Pittsburgh for small research studies and testing new features to support student and teacher learning.

Peerceptiv is available via the web: https://go.peerceptiv.com. There is no local software installation. Any internet browser except for old versions of Internet Explorer will work. So, students and teachers can access the technology from home and school, as long as they have access to internet-enabled desktops or laptops.

Teachers and students create accounts from the main login page by click on the New Account button. Peerceptiv normally requires a valid email account, which is then used as the login ID and the destination of reminder emails for deadlines. (However, teachers can also set up a given class so that students only use teacher-provided usernames and passwords; in this case students will not get reminder emails.) At account creation, students select a pseudonym. The system checks to make sure they do not use their actual names. Because teachers can see these pseudonyms, no extra check is required that students do not select inappropriate names.

Teachers can create as many courses as they like within the system, either from scratch or copying prior courses they have created. For any schools using Blackboard, Brightside/D2L, Schoology, or Canvas, Peerceptiv will also directly integrate with those learning management systems (LMSs). Instructions on how to set up that integration are available at the Peerceptiv website (see Help:LTI Configuration on the www.peerceptiv.com website). Through this mechanism, students in the class are automatically added into Peerceptiv as well, and grades are automatically passed back to the LMS.

Otherwise, teachers have two different ways of getting students enrolled in a Peerceptiv class. When a course is created, Peerceptiv generates a simple, easy to remember course key (e.g., able7). Students select "join a course" and enter the key once to then have that course associated with their account. Alternatively, teachers can also upload a file of student names and email addresses, and Peerceptiv will add them to the course, create accounts for students who do not yet have one, and email the students to have them finish the account creation process (e.g., picking a pseudonym). It may be important to check that the school or district system administrators will allow access to Peerceptiv.com and allow student email accounts to receive email from info@peerceptiv.com.

Access to Peerceptiv can happen through four different models. First students (or parents) can pay a course fee. Second, teachers can pay a per-student fee for the course (unlimited use throughout the year). Third, a department or school can purchase a pack of student seats that can be shared with multiple teachers. Fourth, a school can purchase a site license that allows an unlimited number of students on courses for all teachers using the school email address for their account.

## Ways of Integrating Peerceptiv into a Classroom

Teachers vary greatly in the intensity of use of Peerceptiv. Some teachers use Peerceptiv two or three times a semester, whereas others have a new peer review assignment every other week. A few teachers have even done a new assignment every week, but the workload there is quite high, and students can get lost in all of the required steps when the pace is that rapid.

For students new to the technology, teachers typically have students create accounts in class, submit the first document in class, and begin doing the reviewing in class. Later students are able to do most of the work from home or other locations they use for computer access (e.g., the library). When new rubrics are introduced, it can be helpful to discuss as a whole class how a couple of example solutions match the rubric. Alternatively, teachers can use the performance diagnostics and only discuss the problem areas when they occur.

A common method is for teachers to have first drafts assessed only by students, and then second drafts be assessed by teachers, perhaps with only minimal comments. When teachers first use Peerceptiv, they are often skeptical of using the peer ratings for grading purposes. But after a few rounds of comparing their grades to the peer-provided grades, teachers quickly come to see that the mean ratings are also accurate for their classes.

Some early in-class discussions about what makes for useful comments can make the very first round of using Peerceptiv successful. Alternatively, through the back-evaluation process, students usually come to see what kinds of comments are seen as helpful and what common problems produce unhelpful comments.

## Conclusion

SWoRD/Peerceptiv is a web-based tool for implementing effective peer review assignments in a broad range of disciplines, seeking to implement writing-based assignments. A challenge for most teachers that normally prevents them from allocating sufficient assignments to produce improvements in student outcomes is that they do not have the time to provide feedback to students. Peer review, by contrast, does not burden the teacher in this way, especially when implemented using automatic distribution methods as found in SWoRD. Traditional implementation of peer review produces short superficial feedback, but using the structures and accountability mechanisms found in SWoRD, students generally produce accurate ratings and helpful comments. Further, a number of studies show that students learn from providing meaningful feedback to their peers.

There are still a number of open areas of work, however. While students feel that peer feedback is quite helpful (both providing and receiving), they are quite suspicious of grades produced by peer review, even though objective studies find these grades to be quite accurate. Additional research is required to find methods for overcoming these student concerns. Many students still ignore the peer feedback comments they receive, and thus student uptake of feedback remains a concern here just as it is a concern in their use of teacher feedback. Finally, very little is known about the cumulative impact of extensive use of such automated peer review as a pedagogical tool. Studies on this topic will need to be done in the coming years as this kind of peer review finally achieves sufficient use.

## References

Applebee, A. N., & Langer, J. A. (2011). A snapshot of writing instruction in middle schools and high schools. *The English Journal*, *100*(6), 14–27.

Biber, D., & Conrad, S. (2009). *Register, Genre, and Style*. Cambridge, MA: Cambridge University Press.

Cho, K., & MacArthur, C. (2011). Learning by reviewing. *Journal of Educational Psychology*, *103*(1), 73–84.

Cho, K., & Schunn, C. D. (2007). Scaffolded writing and rewriting in the discipline: A web-based reciprocal peer review system. *Computers & Education*, *48*(3), 409–426. doi:10.1016/J.Compedu.2005.02.004.

Cho, K., Schunn, C. D., & Charney, D. (2006a). Commenting on writing—Typology and perceived helpfulness of comments from novice peer reviewers and subject matter experts. *Written Communication*, *23*(3), 260–294.

Cho, K., Schunn, C. D., & Wilson, R. W. (2006b). Validity and reliability of scaffolded peer assessment of writing from instructor and student perspectives. *Journal of Educational Psychology*, *98*(4), 891–901.

Cohen, M., & Riel, M. (1989). The effect of distant audiences on students' writing. *American Educational Research Journal, 26*(2), 143–159.

Dignath, C., Buettner, G., & Langfeldt, H. P. (2008). How can primary school students learn self-regulated learning strategies most effectively? *Educational Research Review, 3*(2), 101–129. doi:10.1016/j.edurev.2008.02.003.

Falchikov, N., & Goldfinch, J. (2000). Student peer assessment in higher education: A meta-analysis comparing peer and teacher marks. *Review of Educational Research, 70*(3), 287–322.

Grice, H. P. (1975). Logic and conversation. In P. Cole & J. Morgan (Eds.), *Syntax and Semantics: Vol 3, Speech Acts* (pp. 43–58). New York: Academic.

Hayes, J. R., Flower, L., Schriver, K., Stratman, J., & Carey, L. (1987). Cognitive processes in revision. In S. Rosenberg (Ed.), *Advances in Applied Psycholinguistics Vol. 2. Reading, Writing and Language Processing*. Cambridge, UK: Cambridge University Press.

Katstra, J., Tollefson, N., & Gilbert, E. (1987). The effects of peer evaluation on attitude toward writing and writing fluency of ninth grade students. *Journal of Educational Research, 80*(3), 168–172.

Kaufman, J., & Schunn, C. (2011). Students' perceptions about peer assessment for writing: Their origin and impact on revision work. *Instructional Science, 39*(3), 387–406. doi:10.1007/S11251-010-9133-6.

Kellogg, R. T. (1994). *The Psychology of Writing*. Oxford, UK: Oxford University Press.

Kellogg, R. T., & Whitford, A. P. (2009). Training advanced writing skills: The case for deliberate practice. *Educational Psychologist, 44*(4), 250–266.

Kiuhara, S. A., Graham, S., & Hawken, L. S. (2009). Teaching writing to high school students: A national survey. *Journal of Educational Psychology, 101*(1), 136–160.

Kliewer, W., Lepore, S. J., Farrell, A. D., Allison, K. W., Meyer, A. L., Sullivan, T. N., & Greene, A. Y. (2011). A school-based expressive writing intervention for at-risk urban adolescents' aggressive behavior and emotional liability. *Journal of Clinical Child and Adolescent Psychology, 40*(5), 693–705. doi:10.1080/15374416.2011.597092.

Lundstrom, K., & Baker, W. (2009). To give is better than to receive: The benefits of peer review to the reviewer's own writing. *Journal of Second Language Writing, 18*, 30–43.

Miller, L. D. (1992). Teacher benefits from using impromptu writing prompts in algebra classes. *Journal for Research in Mathematics Education, 23*(4), 329–340. doi:10.2307/749309.

National Assessment of Educational Progress. (2011). *Writing Framework for the 2011 National Assessment of Educational Progress*. Retrieved from http://www.nagb.org/publications/frameworks/2011naep-writing-framework.doc.

National Commission on Writing. (2004). *Writing: A Ticket to Work . . . Or a Ticket Out: A Survey of Business Leaders*.

National Commission on Writing in American Schools and Colleges. (2003). *The Neglected R: The Need for a Writing Revolution*. New York: College Board.

Nelson, M. M., & Schunn, C. D. (2009). The nature of feedback: How different types of peer feedback affect writing performance. *Instructional Science, 37*(4), 375–401.

Palincsar, A., & Brown, A. (1984). Reciprocal teaching of comprehension-fostering and comprehension-monitoring activities. *Cognition and Instruction, 1*, 117–175.

Patchan, M. M., Schunn, C. D., & Clark, R. J. (2011). Writing in natural sciences: Understanding the effects of different types of reviewers on the writing process. *Journal of Writing Research, 2*(3), 365–393.

Patchan, M. M., Hawk, B., Stevens, C. A., & Schunn, C. D. (2013). The effects of skill diversity on commenting and revisions. *Instructional Science, 41*(2), 381–405. doi:10.1007/S11251-012-9236-3.

Rubin, R., & Carlan, V. G. (2005). Using writing to understand bilingual children's literacy development. *Reading Teacher, 58*(8), 728–739. doi:10.1598/Rt.58.8.3.

Sadler, P., & Good, E. (2006). The impact of self-and peer-grading on student learning. *Educational Assessment, 11*(1), 1–31.

Sambell, K., McDowell, L., & Brown, S. (1997). "But is it fair?": An exploratory study of student perceptions of the consequential validity of assessment. *Studies of Educational Evaluation, 23*(4), 349–371.

Schunn, C. D., Godley, A. J., & DiMartino, S. (in press). The reliability and validity of peer review of writing in high school AP English classes. *Journal of Adolescent & Adult Literacy*.

Siegler, R. S. (1996). *Emerging Minds: The Process of Change in Children's Thinking*. New York: Oxford University Press.

Topping, K. J. (2008). Peer assessment. *Theory Into Practice, 48*(1), 20–27.

Van Den Berg, I., Admiraal, W., & Pilot, A. (2006). Peer assessment in university teaching: evaluating seven course designs. *Assessment and Evaluation in Higher Education, 31*(1), 19–36.

VanDeWeghe, R. (2004). Awesome, dude! Responding helpfully to peer writing. *English Journal, 94*(1), 95–99.

Vygotsky, L. S. (1978). *Mind in Society*. Cambridge, MA: Harvard University Press.

Wooley, R., Was, C., Schunn, C., & Dalton, D. (2008). *The Effects of Feedback Elaboration on the Giver of Feedback*. Paper presented at the 30th Annual Meeting of the Cognitive Science Society.

# PART III
# Future Technologies for the Classroom

The last section of this book focuses on educational technologies for literacy that are currently under development. Like the previous parts, these chapters introduce systems that adopt innovative methods to offer supplemental instruction and practice in reading and writing. Each chapter offers a short overview that provides a basic understanding of the future technologies that will soon be available for classroom use. The first few chapters in this part describe technologies that offer training through feedback and practice in reading comprehension. The systems each differ in targeted grade level as well as audience; for example, one of these systems intends to improve the reading abilities of adult literacy learners while other systems are more directed toward young English language learners. This part ends with a chapter discussing a technology that merges both reading and writing instruction.

# 15

# PROJECT LISTEN'S READING TUTOR

*Jack Mostow*

## An Introduction and Overview of the Technology

Project LISTEN's Reading Tutor is a computer program that uses speech recognition to listen to children read (typically in grades 1 to 3). The Reading Tutor helps them learn to read by providing individual assisted practice in oral reading, somewhat like a literate, infinitely patient grandparent who listens attentively, but is somewhat hard of hearing. It detects only a quarter to a half of reading mistakes and mishears a few percent of correctly read words, but it knows how to pronounce each word correctly, gives effective forms of assistance in deciphering unfamiliar words when needed, and uses a recorded adult narration to read the sentence fluently (and expressively) when the child cannot, in order to scaffold comprehension.

Project LISTEN has iteratively developed, field-tested, and refined successive versions of the Reading Tutor since 1992, including daily use at school by thousands of children in the United States, Canada (Cunningham & Geva, 2005; Reeder, Shapiro, & Wakefield, 2007), Ghana (Korsah et al., 2010), and India (Weber & Bali, 2010). Controlled evaluations of the Reading Tutor have shown pre- to post-test gains in word identification, oral reading fluency, vocabulary, and comprehension comparable to or significantly better than independent reading practice (Mostow, Nelson-Taylor, & Beck, 2013; Poulsen, Wiemer-Hastings, & Allbritton, 2007), classroom instruction (Mostow et al., 2008), and one-on-one tutoring by certified teachers (Mostow et al., 2003).

Figure 15.1 shows a screenshot of the Reading Tutor, and the videos page at www.cs.cmu.edu/~listen shows it in action with children. For an authentic experience in assisted reading, the Reading Tutor and the child take turns picking from hundreds of stories at reading levels from kindergarten to middle school, from *Weekly*

*Reader* and other sources—including user-authored stories. In Figure 15.1, a child is reading a story written by Project LISTEN staff at a grade 3 reading level (listed as Level C to avoid stigmatizing children who read below grade level). The animated robot at the top and the mouse character Kyle at the left each provide an audience for the child's reading.

The Reading Tutor adapts Carnegie Mellon's Sphinx speech recognizer to analyze the child's oral reading by following along, detecting hesitations, crediting accepted words, and flagging miscues. It displays a sentence at a time to read aloud, graying out previous sentences and intervening if needed before the next sentence.

The Reading Tutor intervenes when it notices the reader make a mistake, get stuck, click for help, or encounter difficulty. It gives spoken and graphical responses modeled after master reading teachers, but adapted to the capabilities and limitations of the technology. In particular, the Reader Tutor was designed to elicit oral reading of a known text, rather than open-ended discussion of its meaning, so as to constrain the speech recognition problem. The Reading Tutor chooses from ten types of help on a word, such as speaking it, sounding it out, or giving a rhyming hint. It uses talking-mouth video clips as visual speech to give phoneme-level assistance such as sounding out *teach* as /T/ /EE/ /CH/, or saying "E A here makes the sound /EE/" as in Figure 15.1.

**FIGURE 15.1** Screenshot of Child Reading Story.

The Reading Tutor provides reading and writing activities at the student's estimated level in order to give assisted practice and engage the student interactively. All activities are built from the same few types of steps, namely assisted oral reading, read aloud by the Reading Tutor, talking-menu multiple choice, editing, and free-form spoken response (not recognized at runtime, but recorded for later research use). At the lowest level, activities such as *Create Your Own Scary Story* provide learner control by letting the child select, for example, a scary character from a menu, and inserting it in the ensuing text. At a higher level, activities such as *Create Your Own Sports Story* let the child type in individual words or phrases, such as the name of a player or sport to incorporate. More advanced activities such as *Create Your Own Recipe* prompt the child to type in more complex elements, such as the list of ingredients and sequence of steps. Finally, *Write Your Own Story* lets children type their own stories. To reinforce the mapping between spelling and pronunciation, the Reading Tutor's "Phonic Typewriter" feature scaffolds children's spelling by sounding out words as they type, and responding to their invented spelling by trying to guess the intended word. Children can add their voices to their stories by reading them aloud, and "publish" their narrated stories for their peers to read.

## Why the Technology is Needed

Individually guided practice in oral reading is essential in developing reading proficiency (National Reading Panel, 2000). The most effective interventions provide 30 minutes per day of guided practice (Snow, Burns, & Griffin, 1998). However, busy classroom teachers have little if any time to provide guided practice, and some parents lack the time and possibly the ability to monitor oral reading, let alone the expertise to respond appropriately.

The technology also provides a novel research tool to study children's reading at school. The Reading Tutor has served as an extensively instrumented research platform that records children's oral reading and logs its detailed interactions. The millions of read words it has logged have enabled analyses of the development of oral reading fluency and expressiveness. Its ability to administer controlled experiments automatically made it possible to test interventions to assess and teach word identification (Heiner, Beck, & Mostow, 2004; Lallé, Mostow, Luengo, & Guin, 2013; Mostow, 2008), vocabulary (Aist, 2001; Heiner, Beck, & Mostow, 2006), and explicit comprehension strategies. Its ability to automatically insert, administer, and score multiple choice comprehension cloze questions has enabled prediction of children's scores on paper tests of vocabulary and reading comprehension (Mostow et al., 2004).

## Plans for Development and Testing of Technology

Thousands of children have used the version of the Reading Tutor described above on Windows™ desktops and laptops with little or no adult assistance, but it requires technical support to install and maintain, and has therefore been available only for research use. Moreover, schools are moving away from desktop and even laptop computers. Thus the next step, already under way, is to productize the Reading Tutor on inexpensive tablets.

## Timeline for Making the Technology Publicly Available

As of autumn 2015, Carney Labs is implementing a streamlined version of the Reading Tutor on tablet computers, and another company is developing a game based on the Reading Tutor technology. One or both products should be publicly available by the end of 2015 or soon thereafter.

## References

Aist, G. S. (2001). Towards automatic glossarization: Automatically constructing and administering vocabulary assistance factoids and multiple-choice assessment. *International Journal of Artificial Intelligence in Education, 12*, 212–231.

Cunningham, T., & Geva, E. (2005, June 24). *The Effects of Reading Technologies on Literacy Development of ESL Students (Poster Presentation)*. Paper presented at Twelfth Annual Meeting of the Society for the Scientific Study of Reading, Toronto.

Heiner, C., Beck, J. E., & Mostow, J. (2004, June 17–19). Improving the Help Selection Policy in a Reading Tutor that Listens. In Proceedings of the InSTIL/ICALL Symposium on Natural Language Processing and Speech Technologies in Advanced Language Learning Systems, pp. 195–198. Venice, Italy.

Heiner, C., Beck, J. E., & Mostow, J. (2006, June 26–30). *Automated Vocabulary Instruction in a Reading Tutor*. In Proceedings of the 8th International Conference on Intelligent Tutoring Systems, pp. 741–743. Jhongli, Taiwan.

Korsah, G. A., Mostow, J., Dias, M. B., Sweet, T. M., Belousov, S. M., Dias, M. F., & Gong, H. (2010). Improving child literacy in Africa: Experiments with an automated reading tutor. *Information Technologies and International Development, 6*(2), 1–19.

Lallé, S., Mostow, J., Luengo, V., & Guin, N. (2013, July 9–13). *Comparing Student Models in Different Formalisms by Predicting their Impact on Help Success (Finalist for Best Paper Award)*. In Proceedings of the 16th International Conference on Artificial Intelligence in Education, pp. 161–170. Memphis, TN.

Mostow, J. (2008). Experience from a reading tutor that listens: Evaluation purposes, excuses, and methods. In C. K. Kinzer & L. Verhoeven (Eds.), *Interactive Literacy Education: Facilitating Literacy Environments through Technology* (pp. 117–148). New York: Lawrence Erlbaum Associates, Taylor & Francis Group.

Mostow, J., Nelson-Taylor, J., & Beck, J. E. (2013). Computer-guided oral reading versus independent practice: Comparison of sustained silent reading to an automated reading tutor that listens. *Journal of Educational Computing Research, 49*(2), 249–276. doi: 10.2190/EC.49.2.g.

Mostow, J., Aist, G. S., Burkhead, P., Corbett, A., Cuneo, A., Eitelman, S., . . . Tobin, B. (2003). Evaluation of an automated reading tutor that listens: Comparison to human tutoring and classroom instruction. *Journal of Educational Computing Research, 29*(1), 61–117.

Mostow, J., Aist, G. S., Huang, C., Junker, B., Kennedy, R., Lan, H., . . . Wierman, A. (2008). 4-month evaluation of a learner-controlled reading tutor that listens. In V. M. Holland & F. P. Fisher (Eds.), *The Path of Speech Technologies in Computer Assisted Language Learning: From Research Toward Practice* (pp. 201–219). New York: Routledge.

Mostow, J., Beck, J. E., Bey, J., Cuneo, A., Sison, J., Tobin, B., & Valeri, J. (2004). Using automated questions to assess reading comprehension, vocabulary, and effects of tutorial interventions. *Technology, Instruction, Cognition and Learning, 2*(1–2), 97–134.

National Reading Panel. (2000). *Report of the National Reading Panel. Teaching Children to Read: An Evidence-Based Assessment of the Scientific Research Literature on Reading and its Implications for Reading Instruction.* Washington, DC: National Institute of Child Health & Human Development. Retrieved from www.nichd.nih.gov/publications/nrppubskey.cfm.

Poulsen, R., Wiemer-Hastings, P., & Allbritton, D. (2007). Tutoring bilingual students with an automated reading tutor that listens. *Journal of Educational Computing Research, 36*(2), 191–221.

Reeder, K., Shapiro, J., & Wakefield, J. (2007, August 5–8). *The Effectiveness of Speech Recognition Technology in Promoting Reading Proficiency and Attitudes for Canadian Immigrant Children.* Paper presented at 15th European Conference on Reading, Humboldt University, Berlin. www.literacyeurope.org.

Snow, C. E., Burns, M. S., & Griffin, P. (Eds.). (1998). *Preventing Reading Difficulties in Young Children.* Washington, DC: National Academy Press.

Weber, F. & Bali, K. (2010, December 17–18). *Enhancing ESL Education in India with a Reading Tutor that Listens.* In Proceedings of the First ACM Symposium on Computing for Development, Paper 20. London.

# 16
# EMBRACEING DUAL LANGUAGE LEARNERS

*Arthur M. Glenberg, Erin A. Walker, and M. Adelaida Restrepo*

Dual language learners (DLLs) are becoming a significant component of the educational landscape in the United States. For example, in Arizona, Latinos constitute about a third of the population. Unfortunately, many of these children are not successfully learning to read in English, and thus find themselves unprepared for future schooling and for entering the workforce. According to the 2011 NAEP, 79 percent of Arizona's fourth-grade and 82 percent of the eighth-grade Latino students read *below* "proficient." Clearly, this is a significant local problem. At the same time, teaching DLL children is a worldwide opportunity. Consider the following: the international language of science is English. Consequently, efforts to enhance English reading comprehension may increase the number of children participating in STEM (science, technology, engineering, and mathematics) fields by a tremendous amount (e.g., approximately 300,000,000 students in China alone are attempting to learn English).

EMBRACE, an acronym for Enhanced Moved By Reading to Accelerate Comprehension in English, is designed to improve both general and STEM reading comprehension for DLL students. EMBRACE is based on the successful *Moved by Reading* intervention, which uses principles of embodied cognition to enhance reading comprehension. We will first describe the embodied cognition approach to reading comprehension, then the *Moved by Reading (MbR)* intervention, and finally the enhancements that led to EMBRACE.

## Embodied Cognition and Reading Comprehension

What does it mean to comprehend written text? Most theories (for examples, see Kintsch, 1988; McNamara, 2007) suggest that comprehension requires knowing the meanings of the words and arranging those meanings in relations that reflect the syntax (or propositional analysis) of the text. In contrast, embodied approaches (e.g., Barsalou, 2008; Glenberg & Gallese, 2012) to language comprehension in general, and reading comprehension in particular, specify that it is a *simulation* process: we use the words and the syntax to simulate the content of sentences, and that simulation process uses neural systems of action, perception, and emotion. The idea of simulation is not far from the commonsense notion that we imagine what we are reading about. Thus, when reading about a kiss on a moonlit tropical beach, comprehension is not just putting the words into the correct syntactic relations. Instead, the visual system is used to simulate the beach, waves, and palm trees; the motor system is used to simulate pursing lips; and the emotional system is used to simulate the thrill of it all. Thus, according to embodied theories, this act of imagination, although not necessarily conscious, is essential to reading comprehension.

Embodied simulation is also important in STEM fields. As one example, consider gesture in mathematics instruction. Hostetter and Alibali (2008) demonstrated that gesture reflects the underlying mental simulation. Furthermore, Alibali and Nathan (2011) documented the importance of gesture for learning both basic and advanced mathematics. For example, when teaching about linear relations using Cartesian coordinates, the teacher's gesture of a straight line facilitates student comprehension. As another example of embodiment in STEM instruction, Kontra, Lyons, Fischer, and Beilock (2015) investigated the importance of embodied simulation in learning about angular momentum. They showed that physical experience with angular momentum (obtained by holding spinning bicycle wheels) enhanced students' performance on a paper and pencil test of the concept. Furthermore, using fMRI, they found that the greater the activity in motor cortex (an index of simulation) while taking the test, the better performance.

Why should an instructor choose a technology that teaches an embodied strategy? Simulation is a key to comprehension, but most reading technologies for young children teach phonics, vocabulary, or fluency, and they leave simulation as something for children to discover on their own. However, children are rewarded mainly for correct pronunciation, not simulation. Consequently, many children do not discover simulation and their reading comprehension suffers. The goal of *EMBRACE* is to teach DLLs how to simulate while reading in English, their second language. Many DLLs have limited background knowledge and vocabulary development (Proctor, August, Carlo, & Snow, 2006), which in turn limits their ability to simulate content. Thus, supporting simulation will aid DLLs' reading comprehension in the language in which they have limited experience.

## MbR

*MbR*, the precursor to *EMBRACE*, is a two-stage, web-based intervention to teach children how to simulate text content. Children read stories that are accompanied by objects (e.g., images of toys, see Figure 16.1). In the first stage, physical manipulation (PM), the child uses a computer mouse to move the objects to simulate text content. For example, a child might read, "The farmer puts the cat in the hayloft." To simulate the content, the child moves an image of the farmer to the cat and then moves the conjoined images to the hayloft. In the second stage, imagine manipulation (IM), the children are asked to imagine moving the objects. Because the children have had experience with PM, even children in first and second grade understand this instruction to use IM.

How does *MbR* work? When children are first learning to read, the goal is to pronounce words (decoding). Unfortunately, some children have difficulty taking the next step of thinking about the meaning of the words, i.e., creating a simulation. This phenomenon is readily seen when children read without intonation and when they have little ability to describe the content of a just-read sentence. PM helps children to go beyond decoding. Manipulating the images requires the child to map the pronounced words to the images that provide some of the meaning for the words (a perceptual simulation). Perhaps more importantly, the literal manipulation of the images requires the child to map the syntax of the sentence (the who does what to whom) to their own activity, thereby creating a literal, external dynamic simulation of sentence content. Then in the second stage, IM helps to scaffold the child's skill in creating internal simulations.

**FIGURE 16.1** Images of Toys to Assist with Reading Stories.

Multiple publications (reviewed in Glenberg, 2011) support the effectiveness of *MbR* for monolingual, English-speaking children. In these studies, performance of children reading with *MbR* was compared to performance of control children reading the same texts, but without training in PM or IM. Consider Experiment 3 in Glenberg, Gutierrez, Levin, Japuntich, and Kaschak (2004), which tested children in the first and second grades. Children reading with PM recalled twice as much as control children and answered a greater proportion of inference questions. In the second stage, when reading with IM, children recalled twice as much as control children and answered inference questions more accurately. Glenberg, Willford, Gibson, Goldberg, and Zhu (2011) demonstrated the effectiveness of *MbR* for STEM texts. In that research, children in the third and fourth grades read and solved mathematical story problems. Children who read using *MbR* solved the problems more often than did control children.

## EMBRACE

The current instantiation of *MbR* is called *EMBRACE*, which is designed to improve the ability to read in English for DLL children in grades 2 to 5. *EMBRACE* works much like *MbR* in that children engage in PM and IM, but we have also designed and implemented significant additions. For one, *EMBRACE* is an iPad application, rather than web-based, so that *EMBRACE* is portable and accessible anytime and anywhere: an internet connection is not needed. In addition, the iPad affords touch-based interaction, and thus children manipulate the images using their fingers instead of a mouse, which enhances the embodied feel. Perhaps more importantly, *EMBRACE* allows logging of the children's manipulations, vocabulary requests (a child can tap on a word to hear it pronounced), and answers to comprehension questions asked at the end of each chapter. An intelligent tutoring system will use the log data to form a model of the child's skill in understanding written English. Then, the program uses the model to manipulate the syntactic complexity of the text. Thus, as the child develops skill in reading simple sentences, the child is challenged with longer, more syntactically complex sentences (and thus more complex simulations) to increase reading comprehension skills.

We are also extending the application to work across different learning activities and domains. Thus, we have developed for *EMBRACE* both story-like texts and informational (STEM) texts (see Figure 16.2). Furthermore, *EMBRACE* will function in both individual and dyadic modes. For the latter, one child reads and the other manipulates, and then they change roles. (The dyad could also be a parent and a child, a teacher and a child, or siblings.) The goal is to harness the power of social learning for teaching reading comprehension.

Finally, *EMBRACE* affords bilingual interaction, thus broadening the scope and potential impact of the application. The current version of *EMBRACE* supports

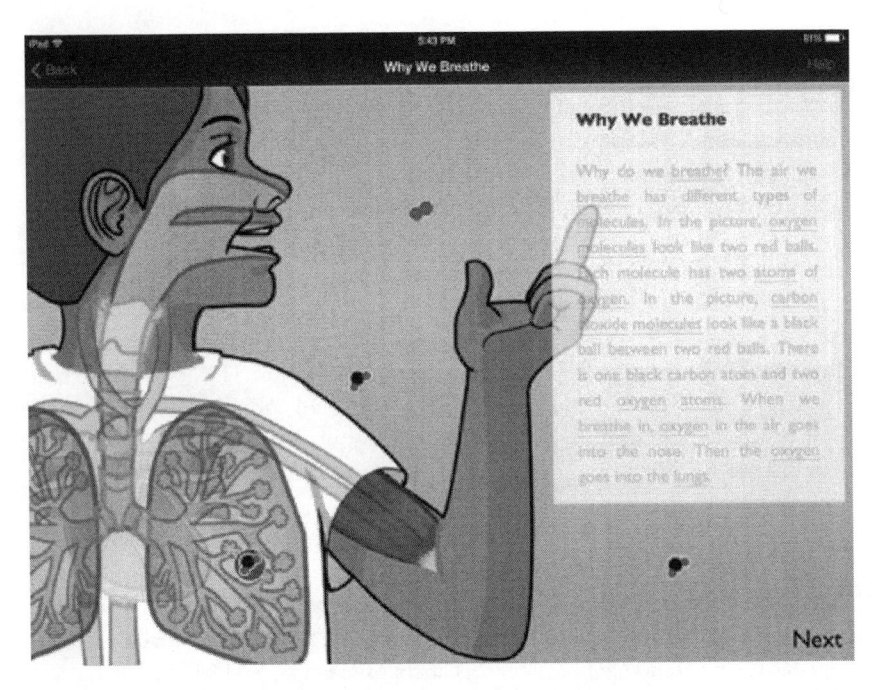

**FIGURE 16.2** Extension of *EMBRACE* for Use with Other Texts.

native Spanish speakers, although we plan to incorporate several other languages during subsequent development. In the bilingual version of *EMBRACE*, children (a) receive instruction on the system in their native language and English; (b) can tap on a word on the screen and hear it pronounced in the native language and English while the image of the referent is highlighted; and (c) hear the first chapter in multi-chapter texts in the native language (while the child manipulates the images) to encourage development of simulations. As the primary goal is to enhance comprehension of texts written in English, after the initial chapter of each multi-chapter text, all other chapters are read by the children in English (although bilingual vocabulary support is available for these chapters).

We have started testing components of *EMBRACE* with DLL children. One significant finding comes from comparing comprehension of children who use the bilingual version of *EMBRACE* to comprehension of children in a bilingual control version. In the control version, the children read the same texts with the same vocabulary help, but they do not manipulate the objects. Looking only at the texts the children read in English (i.e., disregarding the first text read to the children in Spanish), children in the EMBRACE condition answered 78 percent of the questions correctly, whereas children in the control condition answered only 47 percent correctly. Furthermore, when instructions, the introductory chapter, and the vocabulary are provided bilingually, early evidence suggests that

DLL children comprehend better than their peers in the in monolingual manipulation condition.

In summary, the goal of EMBRACE is to improve reading comprehension in English for DLL children. Evidence from previous work using MbR and the current results using EMBRACE indicate that facilitating simulation while the child reads leads to much better comprehension. But EMBRACE is not a comprehensive reading intervention program, and thus it should be combined with programs that teach phonics and decoding skills.

EMBRACE development and testing is on-going through support from the National Science Foundation. We are ensuring the readability of our texts, the benefits of bilingual and dyadic versions of EMBRACE, success of the intelligent tutor for manipulating syntactic difficulty, and that EMBRACE improves reading comprehension as measured by standardized tests. Given development plans, we anticipate having a commercially available system in 2017.

## Acknowledgments

This work was supported by NSF grant 1324807 to the authors. Any opinions, findings, and conclusions or recommendations expressed in this material are those of the authors and do not necessarily reflect the views of the funding agencies.

## References

Alibali, M. W., & Nathan, M. J. (2011). Embodiment in mathematics teaching and learning: Evidence from learners' and teachers' gestures. *Journal of the Learning Sciences*, doi: 10.1080/10508406.2011.611446.
Barsalou, L. W. (2008). Grounded cognition. *Annual Review of Psychology, 59*, 617–645.
Glenberg, A. M. (2011). How reading comprehension is embodied and why that matters. *International Electronic Journal of Elementary Education, 4*, 5–18.
Glenberg, A. M., & Gallese, V. (2012). Action-based language: A theory of language acquisition, comprehension, and production. *Cortex, 48*, 905–922. doi: 10.1016/j.cortex.2011.04.010.
Glenberg, A. M., Gutierrez, T., Levin, J. R., Japuntich, S., & Kaschak, M. P. (2004). Activity and imagined activity can enhance young children's reading comprehension. *Journal of Educational Psychology, 96*, 424–436.
Glenberg, A. M., Willford, J., Gibson, B. R., Goldberg, A. B., & Zhu, X. (2011). Improving reading to improve math. *Scientific Studies of Reading*, doi: 10.1080/10888438.2011.564245.
Hostetter, A. B., & Alibali, M. W. (2008). Visible embodiment: Gestures as simulated action. *Psychonomic Bulletin & Review, 15*(3), 495–514. http://doi.org/10.3758/PBR.15.3.495.
Kintsch, W. (1988). The role of knowledge in discourse comprehension: A construction-integration model. *Psychological Review, 95*, 163–182.
Kontra, C., Lyons, D. J., Fischer, S. M., & Beilock, S. L. (2015). Physical experience enhances science learning. *Psychological Science*. http://doi.org/10.1177/0956797615569355.

McNamara, D. S. (Ed.). (2007). *Reading Comprehension Strategies: Theory, Interventions, and Technologies*. Mahwah, NJ: Erlbaum.

Proctor, C. P., August, D., Carlo, M. S., & Snow, C. (2006). The intriguing role of Spanish language vocabulary knowledge in predicting English reading comprehension. *Journal of Educational Psychology, 98*(1), 159–169. Retrieved from http://www.sciencedirect.com/science/article/B6WYD-4JH1NN1-F/2/e8cf65685cf46a13e7d54a76f694c326.

# 17

# THE *LANGUAGE MUSE ACTIVITY* PALETTE

Technology for Promoting Improved Content Comprehension for English Language Learners

*Jill Burstein and John Sabatini*

## Introduction

### English Language Learner Issues and Teacher Capacity

Between 1997 and 2009, the number of English language learners (ELLs) enrolled in U.S. public schools increased by 51 percent (National Clearinghouse for Language Acquisition, 2011). ELLs by definition are developing English language proficiency and are typically reading *below* grade level; therefore, they may have a great deal of difficulty with academic materials in content classes. Regular classroom teachers must therefore attempt to address the learning needs of mainstreamed ELLs. This is now reinforced by the fact that the English Language Arts Common Core State Standards[1] (*Standards*) (National Governors Association Center for Best Practices and Council of Chief State School Officers, 2010) emphasizes that all learners (including ELLs) need to read progressively more complex texts across multiple genres in the content areas, preparing learners for college and careers. To maintain adequate growth toward this goal, all learners must steadily enhance their familiarity with numerous linguistic features related to vocabulary, English language structures, and a variety of English text and discourse structures. This increases content-area teachers' responsibility for language learning. Yet, most K-12 content-area teachers have little prior education in how to adapt their instructional approaches to accommodate the diverse cultural and linguistic backgrounds of students with varying levels of English proficiency (Adger, Snow, & Christian, 2002; Calderón et al., 2005; Rivera, Moughamian, Lesaux, & Francis, 2008; Walqui & Heritage, 2012). Content-area teachers already have a full plate of responsibilities in delivering instruction that covers their core curriculum content and skills, before adding responsibility for adapting that content for ELLs. Also, middle grades and secondary level teachers typically do not have comprehensive educational coursework in language and literacy development or pedagogy that would be helpful in addressing learners, such as ELLs, who are reading below grade level.

## Motivation

Content-area teachers' responsibility to support ELL language needs motivated the development of *Language MuseTM* (*LM*), a web-based application designed to offer teacher professional development (TPD) to inform and support teachers' instructional lesson planning (Burstein et al., 2014). The TPD package was intended to increase teachers' knowledge of the text-based (linguistic) challenges that ELLs face in learning from content readings, and to provide teachers with strategies and techniques that informed their lesson plans, specifically with regard to these text-based challenges. To this end, *LM* used natural language processing (NLP) to automatically identify and highlight linguistically complex or unfamiliar text elements related to *vocabulary* (e.g., academic words), *phrasal* (e.g., idiomatic expressions), *sentential* (e.g., multi-clausal, longer sentences), and *discourse* (e.g., cause-effect relations) features in texts. These features were targeted, because they are candidate linguistic obstacles that might interfere with ELLs' learning (Burstein et al., 2012, 2014). Teachers used the *LM* feedback to create language-based classroom activities. The long-term goal was to help teachers to integrate *LM* into their classroom practices to better address ELL learning needs, by providing technology-based tools that would facilitate effective and efficient instructional lesson development for busy teachers.

Burstein et al.'s (2014) findings suggested that use of the *LM* TPD package showed an increase in teachers' awareness of linguistic challenges faced by ELLs when reading content-area texts; however, the research also suggested that classroom teachers were more likely to adopt a tool that automatically generated language-based activities. To that end, the *Language Muse Activity Palette* (the *Palette*) is being developed. The *Palette* leverages *LM*'s linguistic analysis to automatically generate language-based activities for classroom texts (see Figures 17.1 and 17.2).

## The *Language Muse Activity Palette* (the *Palette*)

The *Palette* tool is being designed to automatically generate activities for middle school ELLs to support students' language skills development and content comprehension, while also considering how activities are likely to align with routine classroom practice (e.g., class discussion, independent and group work). In the final version, teachers will be able to use the *Palette* text library or classroom texts of their own choice into the system. The *Palette* text library contains social studies, science, and English language arts texts prepared by the ETS research team. The software will analyze the text and generate text-based activities, which the teacher can edit to fit their needs. The software also allows the teacher to choose the format of the activities—traditional printed activity sheets, display mode for showing on a device for classroom discussions, or digital delivery, so that students will be able to access and complete activities online.

## *Palette Activities*

Activities have been classified into four general classes based on content and language learning targets for students, as described in the following subsections. Practice with strategies to identify key information may increase students' awareness of their knowledge gaps or text misunderstanding, so they can make necessary inferences and repair comprehension breakdowns. As students read, they need to know the meaning of the words and how the words and concepts are related to each other. This information needs to be integrated with the students' prior knowledge so that it is available even when the text is removed.

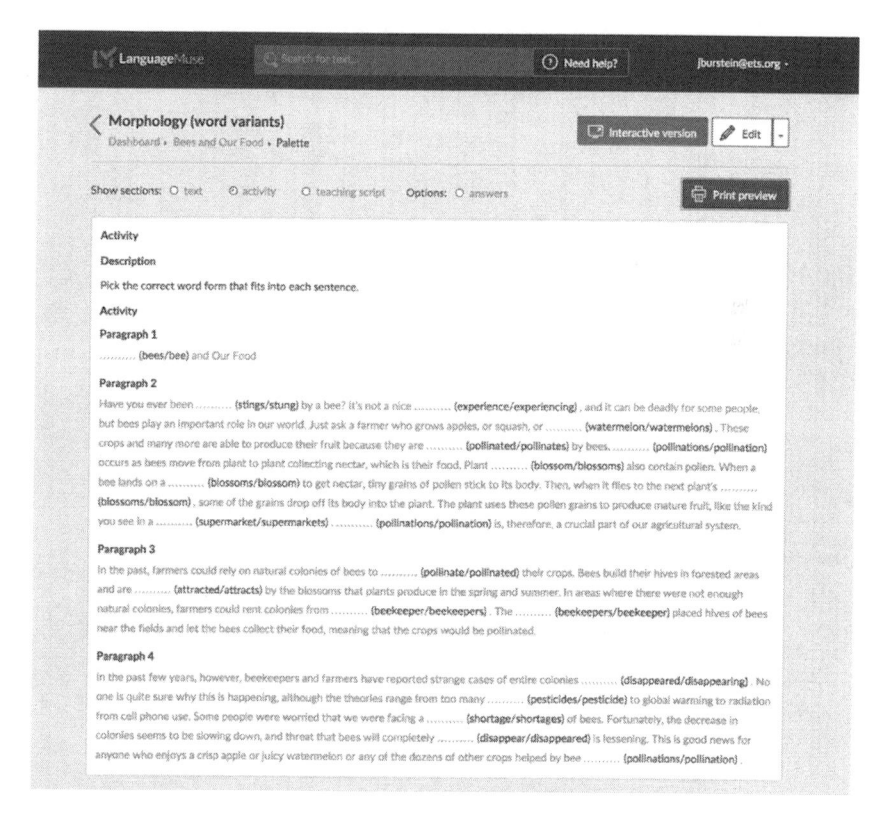

**FIGURE 17.1** Generating Language-Based Activities for Classroom Texts.

## Reading for Understanding (Passages)

Passage-based activities are designed to focus students' attention on building skills that enhance their reading for understanding, comprehension, learning, and studying. There are numerous empirically supported reading strategies that good readers apply routinely, and developing readers can learn to apply to enhance their reading and study skills (McNamara, 2007; McNamara, Ozuru, Best, & O'Reilly, 2007). The goal is to help students build coherent mental (memory) models of textual information, and to connect this model to students' existing knowledge. To construct a coherent understanding of the meaning of texts often requires that the student make meaning-level inferences (e.g., causal, referential, knowledge-based, etc.).

## Reading for Understanding (Sentences)

These types of activities are designed to focus students' attention on building meaning at the sentence level. Sentences in English can become quite complex. There may be multiple clauses, phrases, and connectors that signal relations among sentence parts. In each activity, we target a particular type of sentence feature (e.g., connectors, referents, clauses) in a content-area text.

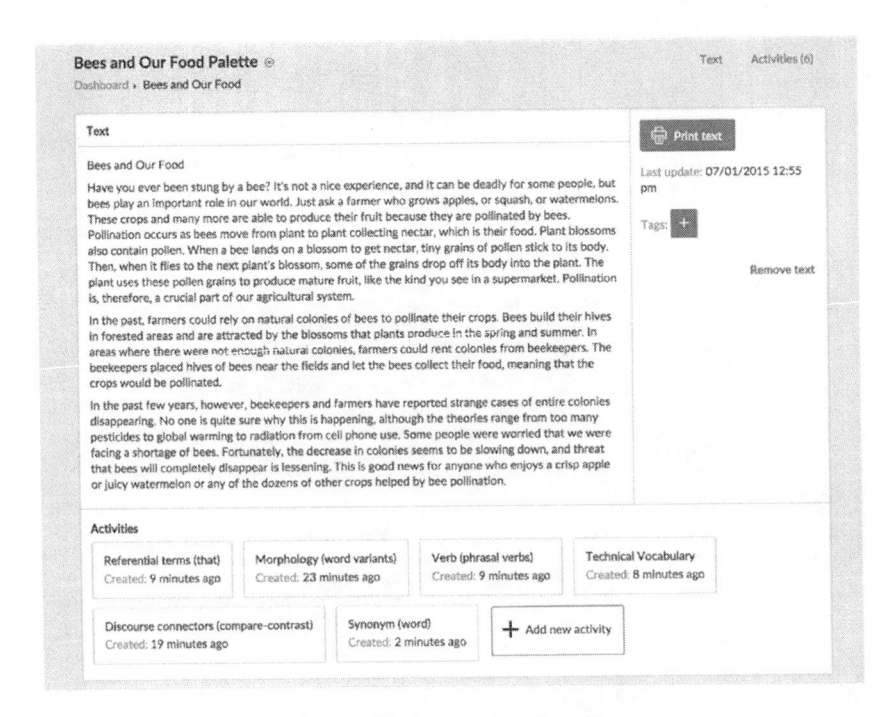

FIGURE 17.2 Illustration of Several Language Activities Types.

The goal is to build students' awareness and processing of the different parts of sentences. That is, over time students should mentally process sentence parts routinely as they construct accurate meaning of entire sentences. As this process becomes more routine, they will be able to direct attention toward inferences necessary to build coherent understanding of text information.

Students may be given sentence activities prior to being asked to read and learn from a longer passage or text, to help ensure that they are building accurate meaning of discrete sentences before tackling the more complex task of understanding the entire text. They could also practice after reading a text, drawing on their prior experience reading the full text to ease the cognitive complexity and help them confirm/evaluate that they understood meaning accurately.

## Word Meaning and Vocabulary

These types of activities are designed to focus students' attention on building word meaning. Words in English may have multiple meanings and students must determine which meaning is appropriate for any given text context. Further, words may have very specific technical meanings in a specific subject area (e.g., *prime* in mathematics). Or, there may be multiple word expressions that are different from the meaning of individual component words (e.g., hot dog). These activities typically focus on words important to the meaning of a particular content text. These may be key terms that the teacher is targeting, or more general academic vocabulary that is required for understanding of the specific text. The goal is to build students' vocabulary as well as their skills in inferring the specific meaning of words in contexts.

Students may be given word activities prior to being asked to read and learn from a longer passage or text, to help ensure that they have adequate understanding of key text terms before tackling a text. They could also practice after reading a text, drawing on their prior experience reading the full text to confirm or consolidate their vocabulary knowledge, so that it generalizes to future reading.

## English Language Syntax/Grammar/Usage/Idiom Fluency Practice

These types of activities are designed to build students' fluency in processing the meaning of routine linguistic features of the English language that affect meaning construction. In each activity, a single particular type of linguistic feature in a content-area text is targeted, so that students build an awareness that the specific targets are general linguistic features of the language. The goal is to build student fluency or automaticity. That is, students should—over time, with practice—respond to such items rapidly, accurately, and with little effort or attention. Then, they will have more memory and attention available to use in building higher level comprehension (Perfetti, 2003).

It may be beneficial for students with low accuracy or slow response rates to repeat the same activity with the express purpose of achieving high accuracy and speed at the same time. Repeated reading generally is a good habit, as it helps readers to consolidate, correct, and elaborate meaning, though this should be balanced against student motivation. Once a high level of fluency is consistently achieved across multiple passages, activities targeting the particular linguistic feature may be discontinued except as an occasional review. Students who have achieved fluency may be bored or distracted from more complex content understanding and learning.

## Evaluation

Early in 2015, as part of the *Palette* development, the application was evaluated for *activity utility* and *usability* with 14 content-area teachers and ELL specialists from middle schools in New Jersey and Texas. To evaluate *activity utility* the participating teachers reviewed a set of dynamic ("clickable") activity mock-ups for each of the 14 activity types. To evaluate the *usability* ("navigational flow") of the system, online tests were created and administered, and subsequently analyzed to identify necessary system modifications based on teacher use patterns with regard to completion of test scenarios at beginner, intermediate, and advanced levels. A post-evaluation perception survey instrument was administered. The instrument was adapted from the System Usability Scale interface and system evaluation survey (Brooke, 1996). Teacher responses to activities indicated that they were aligned with district and state standards, they would be likely to use them with their classes, and they would be engaging for ELLs. Responses with regard to system usability were also encouraging, and system development proceeded accordingly for the *Palette* Version 1 release in Fall 2015.

## Future Directions: Student Outcomes Evaluation

In the Fall 2016/Spring 2017, an large-scale evaluation study will be conducted, targeting social studies or science classrooms in middle schools with high populations of ELLs. This evaluation study will report on the promise of the *Palette* in enhancing ELLs' comprehension of content-area texts.

## Acknowledgements

Research presented in this paper was supported by the Institute of Education Science, U.S. Department of Education, Award Numbers R305A100105, R305F100005, and R305A140472. Any opinions, findings, conclusions, or recommendations are those of the authors and do not necessarily reflect the views of the IES or ETS. We also need to thank the critical team members who are contributing to the development of the *Language Muse Activity Palette*: Slava Andreyev, Kietha Biggers, James Bruno, Nitin Madnani, Diane Napolitano, Deirdre Quinn, and Hugh Wynne.

## Note

1 http://www.corestandards.org/

## References

Adger, C. T., Snow, C., & Christian D. (2002). *What Teachers Need to Know about Language*. Washington, DC: Center for Applied Linguistics.

Brooke, J. (1996). SUS: A "quick and dirty" usability scale. In P. W. Jordan, B. Thomas, B. A. Weerdmeester, and I. L. McClelland (Eds.), *Usability Evaluation in Industry* (pp. 189–194). London: Taylor and Francis.

Burstein, J., Shore, J., Sabatini, J., Moulder, B., Holtzman, S., & Pedersen, T. (2012). *The Language Muse system: Linguistically Focused Instructional Authoring* (RR-12-21). Princeton, NJ: ETS.

Burstein, J., Shore, J., Sabatini, J., Moulder, B., Lentini, J., Biggers, K., & Holtzman, S. (2014). From teacher professional development to the classroom: How NLP technology can enhance teachers' linguistic awareness to support curriculum development for English language learners. *Journal of Educational Computing Research, 51*, 119–144.

Calderón, M., August, D., Slavin, R., Cheung, A., Durán, D., & Madden, N. (2005). Bringing words to life in classrooms with English language learners. In A. Hiebert & M. Kamil (Eds.), *Research and Development on Vocabulary* (pp. 115–136). Mahwah, NJ: Erlbaum.

McNamara, D. S. (2007). *Reading Comprehension Strategies: Theories, Interventions, and Technologies*. Mahwah, NJ: Erlbaum.

McNamara, D. S., Ozuru, Y., Best, R., & O'Reilly, T. (2007). The 4-pronged comprehension strategy framework. In D. S. McNamara (Ed.), *Reading Comprehension Strategies: Theories, Interventions, and Technologies* (pp. 465–496). Mahwah, NJ: Erlbaum.

National Clearinghouse for English Language Acquisition (2011). *The Growing Numbers of English Learner Students*. Washington, DC: Author. Retrieved from https://ncela.ed.gov/files/uploads/9/growing_EL_0910.pdf.

National Governors Association Center for Best Practices and Council of Chief State School Officers (2010). *Common Core State Standards for English language Arts & Literacy in History/Social Studies, Science, and Technical Subjects. Appendix A: Research Supporting Key Elements of the Standards*. Washington, DC: Author.

Perfetti, C. A. (2003). The universal grammar of reading. *Scientific Studies of Reading, 7*, 3–24.

Rivera, M. O., Moughamian, A. C., Lesaux, N. K., & Francis, D. J. (2008). *Language and Reading Interventions for English Language Learners and English Language Learners with Disabilities*. Portsmouth, NH: Research Corporation, Center on Instruction.

Walqui, A., & Heritage, M. (2012, January). *Instruction for Diverse Groups of ELLs*. Paper presented at the Understanding Language Conference, Stanford, CA.

# 18

## THE READING STRATEGY ASSESSMENT TOOL

A Computer-Based Approach for Evaluating Comprehension Processes during Reading

*Joseph P. Magliano, Melissa Ray, and Keith K. Millis*

### Introduction and Overview of the Reading Strategy Assessment Tool (RSAT)

When teachers, administrators, and researchers think of comprehension tests, they typically picture a reading passage or set of reading passages followed by a set of multiple-choice questions. Students are expected to read each passage and then select the best answer to each question. When answering these questions, they often are able to refer back to the passages, which may have implications on what aspects of comprehension these test formats actually assess (Farr et al., 1990). They may be better suited for assessing how well students can take tests on a text, as opposed to providing a direct assessment of comprehension ability.

RSAT (Maglinao, Millis, The RSAT Development Team, Levinstein, & Boonthum, 2011) adopts a very different approach. RSAT is a computer-administered test that is designed to assess comprehension *while* students read and the *strategies* that students use to support their comprehension during reading (Gilliam et al., 2007; Magliano et al., 2011). It was originally developed in a post-secondary environment, but work is underway to develop a version that is appropriate for students in middle school. RSAT is well grounded in theory and empirical research of how students comprehend texts (Magliano et al., 2011), which indicate that readers must make connections between sentences (bridge) and use their world knowledge (elaborations) to construct a coherent text representation. These processes are assumed by most theories of comprehension in psychology to be important for building a durable memory for a text.

In RSAT, students read texts one sentence at a time. Only the sentence that they are currently reading is available onscreen, and students click a button to continue to the next sentence. While it may seem odd to have students only see one sentence at a time, this decision was made to force students to draw upon their memory for what they have read so far to answer the questions. We have shown that this approach provides a better indicator of a student's comprehension skill than allowing the student to have full access to what they have read so far (Gilliam et al., 2007), albeit it is not a naturalistic way of presenting text content (Magliano & Graesser, 1991). After pre-selected sentences are read, an open-ended question appears. When a question appears onscreen, the text title is displayed at the top of the screen, but no sentences from the text are visible. Just below the question, a textbox also appears, and students must type their responses to the questions before moving onto the next sentence.

There are two types of questions: direct and indirect. *Direct questions* are why-, what-, and how-questions that assess the extent to which students comprehend the text (e.g., "Why do we hear thunder after seeing the lightning strike?" on text about lightning). Ideal answers to direct questions can be derived from information presented in the prior text. *Indirect questions* always ask students "What are you thinking now?" Students are instructed to answer this question by typing their thoughts regarding their understanding of what they are reading and are given practice on how to do this before taking RSAT. This question answering process is akin to thinking aloud (Trabasso & Magliano, 1996). Figure 18.1 contains sample screen shots for two sentences of a text and the direct or indirect question that would appear after the second sentence (students see either a direct or an indirect

**Screen 1**

**Screen 2**

**Screen 3**

**Screen 4**

**Sentence:**
On Louis's accession, France was impoverished and burdened with debts, and heavy taxation had resulted in widespread misery among the French people.

**Sentence:**
Immediately after he was crowned, Louis repealed some of the most oppressive taxes and instituted financial and judicial reforms.

**Direct Question:**
What was Louis trying to accomplish at the beginning of his reign?

**Sample Answer:**
"He was trying to make things better for his people".

**Indirect question:**
What are you thinking now"

**Sample Answer:**
"Louis issued the reforms and tax cuts in order to restore the financial status of France.

Paraphrase = 4
Bridge = 1
Elaboration = 5

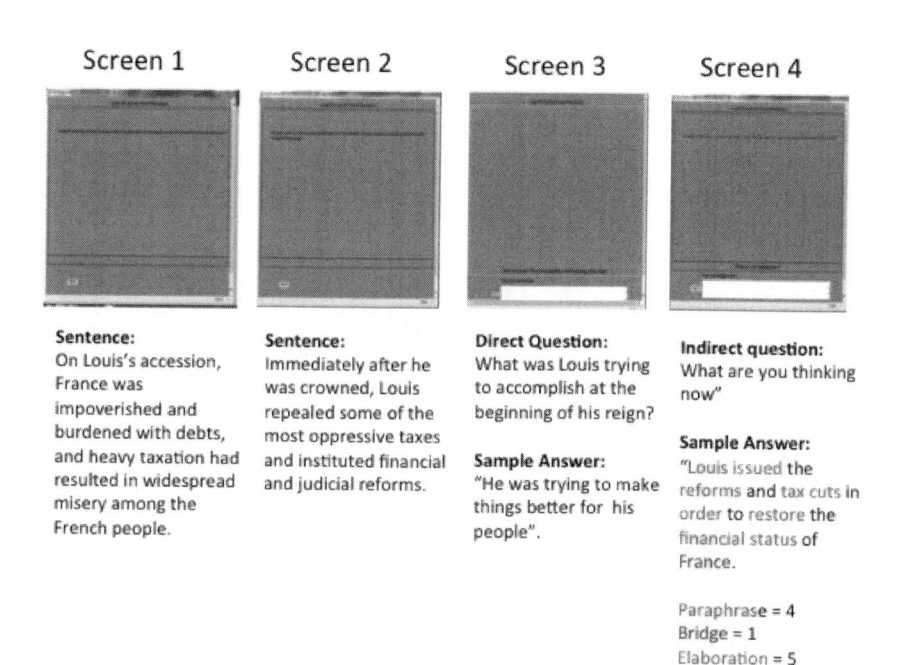

**FIGURE 18.1** Sample Screen Shots for Two Sentences of a Text and the Direct or Indirect Question that Would Appear after the Second Sentence.

question). Screen 3 contains a direct question and sample answer. Similarly, screen 4 contains an indirect question and sample response.

Answers to the direct questions feed into the global comprehension score, and answers to the indirect questions feed into the strategy scores. RSAT provides a measure of three strategies involved in comprehension: bridging inferences (connecting sentences with one another), elaborative inferences (connecting the text with what they already know), and paraphrases (producing key words from the sentence being read). The scores are derived from computer-based algorithms that automatically score answers to direct and indirect questions. Screen 4 in Figure 18.1 shows how the RSAT algorithms use the words in an answer to an indirect question to generate strategy scores: paraphrasing of the current sentences (red), bridging to prior text concepts (green), or elaborating upon the texts (blue).

The current version of RSAT contains both fiction and, informational texts (history and science). The texts have between 20 and 30 sentences, with about 6 questions per text (about half of each type of question). Some forms of RSAT only ask one type of question (e.g., only indirect questions) and other forms have both types of questions (with approximately an equal number of each). These forms were created, because researchers and practitioners may be interested in assessing comprehension or comprehension processing. Fiction texts are folktales, and informational texts are similar to brief encyclopedia articles. The texts have Flesch-Kinkaid readability scores between 9th and 10th grade. This readability level was chosen so that texts would be *within* the reading skill of college students (the population for which RSAT was developed). As a result, RSAT would be able to assess comprehension processes when students read texts within their reading abilities. With more difficult texts comprehension might be negatively affected by things such as complex sentence structure or low frequency words, which may mask or interfere with the intended strategies of bridging, elaborations, and paraphrases.

What evidence is there for the validity of RSAT? First, the RSAT approach has been shown to be correlated with curriculum-like tests of comprehension (e.g., end of chapter questions). Additionally, there is evidence that the RSAT comprehension score is correlated with performance on well-established standardized tests of comprehension, such as ACT (Magliano et al., 2011). Moreover, the strategy measures (i.e., paraphrase, bridging, and elaboration scores) are correlated with these measures of comprehension roughly to the same extent that they correlate with one another (Gilliam et al., 2007; Magliano et al., 2011). Finally, we have demonstrated that RSAT scores are highly correlated with human judgments of the use of comprehension processes (Magliano et al., 2011).

## Why is RSAT Needed?

National and international assessment data indicate that today's adolescents fail to master important skills in core areas, such as reading (Carnegie Council on

Advancing Adolescent Literacy, 2010). The development of effective screening tools that can be used by both teachers and school psychologists is needed to address this problem (see Al Otaiba & Fuchs, 2006). Practitioners are typically stuck with inauthentic multiple-choice type reading measures that provide evidence only of the outcome of reading. While such assessments are easy to administer and may have global diagnostic value, they tell little of students' strengths and weaknesses when it comes to comprehending texts. Practitioners need *formative* assessments that provide more direct evaluations of what students do as they read. Unfortunately, currently, there are few high quality formative assessments (Afflerbach, Cho, & Kim, 2015), and none that can assess the actual cognitive processes used during reading comprehension.

RSAT's assessment of comprehension "in the moment" is an important step in developing an assessment tool that fills this gap. Because it makes comprehension processes transparent, explicit, and tangible to school psychologists, teachers, students, and parents, all stakeholders can use RSAT to learn about important aspects of students' reading comprehension beyond a single score reflecting "comprehension." Additionally, McMaster and colleagues have shown that identifying different profiles of what students do when they think aloud while reading can provide a basis for tailoring interventions to the specific needs of students (McMaster et al., 2012). As stated earlier, the indirect questions in RSAT elicit think-aloud-like responses (Muñoz et al., 2006). Therefore, RSAT may provide an automated tool for generating student profiles, providing a basis for which to identify the most appropriate interventions.

In addition, the strategies measured by RSAT are similar to those emphasized in some reading interventions that focus on moment-to-moment reading, such as iSTART (see Chapter 7), which have been shown to improve both comprehension ability and class performance (e.g., McNamara & Scott, 1999). To the extent that there are multiple forms of RSAT (i.e., multiple versions of forms so that RSAT can be given multiple times to the same students), the tool has the potential to be used to monitor progress. For example, assume a student takes RSAT and essentially only paraphrases the sentences that immediately preceded an indirect prompt. This strategy has been shown to be detrimental for comprehension (Coté & Goldman, 1999; Magliano & Millis, 2003). However, if students were exposed to an intervention that promoted inference processes, then RSAT could be used to assess if students increase their inferencing skill over time.

## Plans for Developing RSAT

Current efforts are focused on making RSAT a comprehension assessment that is appropriate and available for use in middle and high schools. Because it was originally developed to assess how college freshmen comprehend text, RSAT may not be suitable for younger readers. Additionally, future versions of RSAT will be developed to contain tools that help practitioners to interpret, evaluate, and use RSAT scores. To date, RSAT's development has primarily centered on exploring the feasibility of using automated scoring of "think alouds" to assess comprehension. As a result, additional work is needed to explore the classroom applications of RSAT, which include larger tests of its reliability and validity. Finally, in order to support its use in schools, a user-friendly website will need to be developed so that practitioners and students can readily access RSAT and RSAT scores.

The current goal for RSAT development is to produce a version of RSAT that will help practitioners identify readers' initial strengths and weakness and measure how their comprehension changes over time. Because it is not a summative assessment, RSAT is likely not an appropriate replacement for traditional, high stakes tests. We believe that RSAT's greatest potential is as a tool to evaluate student progress toward developing basic comprehension proficiency.

## Timeline for Developing RSAT

We will be developing and selecting new texts and exploring different types of computer-based algorithms that can be used to generate RSAT scores for middle school aged students. Importantly, we will develop tools that will help teachers use RSAT to evaluate students in meaningful ways, and help students learn more about what they do to understand what they read. Beta version of RSAT should be available by 2017, with the intent of a scalable version available by 2019.

## References

Afflerbach, P., Cho, B. Y., & Kim, J. Y. (2015). Conceptualizing and assessing higher order thinking in reading. *Theory Into Practice, 54*, 203–212

Al Otaiba, S. & Fuchs, D. (2006). Who are the young children for whom best practices in reading are ineffective? An experimental and longitudinal study. *Journal of Learning Disabilities*, 39, 414–431.

Carnegie Council on Advancing Adolescent Literacy (2010). *A Time to Act*. New York: Carnegie Corporation of New York.

Coté, N., & Goldman, S. R. (1999). Building representations of informational text: Evidence from children's think-aloud protocols. In H. Van Oostendorp & S. R. Goldman (Eds.), *The Construction of Mental Representations during Reading* (pp. 169–193). Mahwah, NJ: Erlbaum.

Farr, R., Pritchard, R., & Smitten, B. (1990) A description of what happens when an examinee takes a multiple-choice reading comprehension test. *Journal of Educational Measurement*, 27, 209–226.

Gilliam, S., Magliano, J. P., Millis, K. K., Levinstein, I., & Boonthum, C. (2007). Assessing the format of the presentation of text in developing a Reading Strategy Assessment Tool (R-SAT). *Behavior Research Methods, Instruments, & Computers, 39*, 199–204.

Magliano, J. P., & Graesser, A. C. (1991). A three-pronged method for studying inference generation in literary text. *Poetics*, 20, 193–232.

Magliano, J. P., & Millis, K. K. (2003). Assessing reading skill with a think-aloud procedure. *Cognition and Instruction, 21*, 251–283.

Magliano, J. P., Millis, K. K., The RSAT Development Team, Levinstein, I., & Boonthum, C. (2011). Assessing comprehension during reading with the reading strategy assessment Tool (RSAT). *Metacognition and Learning, 6,* 131–154.

McMaster, K. L., Van den Broek, P., Espin, C. A., White, M. J., Kendeou, P., Rapp, D. N., . . . Carlson, S. (2012). Making the right connections: Differential effects of reading intervention for subgroups of comprehenders. *Learning and Individual Differences, 22,* 100–111.

McNamara, D. S., & Scott, J. L. (1999). Training reading strategies. In M. Hahn & S. C. Stoness (Eds.), *Proceedings of the Twenty-first Annual Meeting of the Cognitive Science Society* (pp. 387–392). Hillsdale, NJ: Erlbaum.

Muñoz, B., Magliano, J. P., Sheridan, R., & McNamara, D. S. (2006). Typing versus thinking aloud when reading: Implications for computer-based assessment and training tools. *Behavior Research Methods, Instruments, & Computers, 38,* 211–217.

Trabasso, T. & Magliano, J. P. (1996). Conscious understanding during text comprehension. *Discourse Processes, 21,* 255–288.

# 19
# READING COMPREHENSION LESSONS IN AUTOTUTOR FOR THE CENTER FOR THE STUDY OF ADULT LITERACY

*Arthur C. Graesser, Zhiqiang Cai, Whitney O. Baer, Andrew M. Olney, Xiangen Hu, Megan Reed, and Daphne Greenberg*

## Introduction and Overview of the Technology

The Center for the Study of Adult Literacy (CSAL) is a national research center that investigates reading problems in adults (those reading at the 3rd to 8th grade levels) and that develops instructional interventions tailored to their needs. A web-based instructional tutor is a practical solution for comprehension instruction, because many adults have busy schedules or transportation problems and because many literacy teachers have limited knowledge of comprehension training (National Research Council (NRC), 2011).

*CSAL AutoTutor* is an intelligent tutoring system on the web that delivers comprehension instruction. The system includes two computer agents that hold a conversation with the human and with each other (called *trialogues*, Graesser, Li, & Forsyth, 2014a; McNamara, O'Reilly, Best, & Ozuru, 2006) and thereby guide the human in learning comprehension skills and using the computer facility.

The CSAL AutoTutor curriculum has 35 lessons with trialogues that focus on specific comprehension strategies. The AutoTutor lessons each take 10 to 50 minutes to complete and are assigned by teachers on the research team (in adult literacy centers) in a hybrid intervention with both teachers and computer facilities. The strategies are aligned with a PACES intervention (see below), which teachers have successfully implemented (face-to-face) to improve reading comprehension in high school students with reading difficulties (Lovett, Lacerenza, De Palma, & Frijters, 2012). It is beyond the scope of this short chapter to cover the PACES strategies in detail, but the descriptions below sketch the main components.

1. **P**redicting the purpose and structure of the text with text signals;
2. **A**cquiring vocabulary using context clues and affix knowledge;

3. Clarifying sources of confusion of explicit text through questioning;
4. Evaluating, explaining, and elaborating texts through inferences and questioning;
5. Summarizing and using text structures.

Adults with reading difficulties typically have substantial challenges with writing, so the interface on CSAL AutoTutor tends to rely on point & click (or touch), multiple-choice questions, drag & drop, and other conventional input channels. However, the system does include some writing components that require semantic evaluation of open-ended student contributions, which is the signature feature of AutoTutor systems (Graesser et al., 2014a). CSAL AutoTutor has many pictures, diagrams, and multimedia that help grab and maintain the attention of the adult learner. The system also has the capability of reading texts aloud when the learner asks for such assistance by clicking on a screen option.

Figure 19.1 shows an example of trialogue design found in CSAL AutoTutor. There is a tutor agent at the top left and a peer agent at the top right. The passage below the agents is about receiving a General Education Degree (GED). The adult learner is asked to click on the sentence in the passage that supports the statement: "The writer did not learn about computers in high school." That would require the learner to understand the sentences in the passage and decide

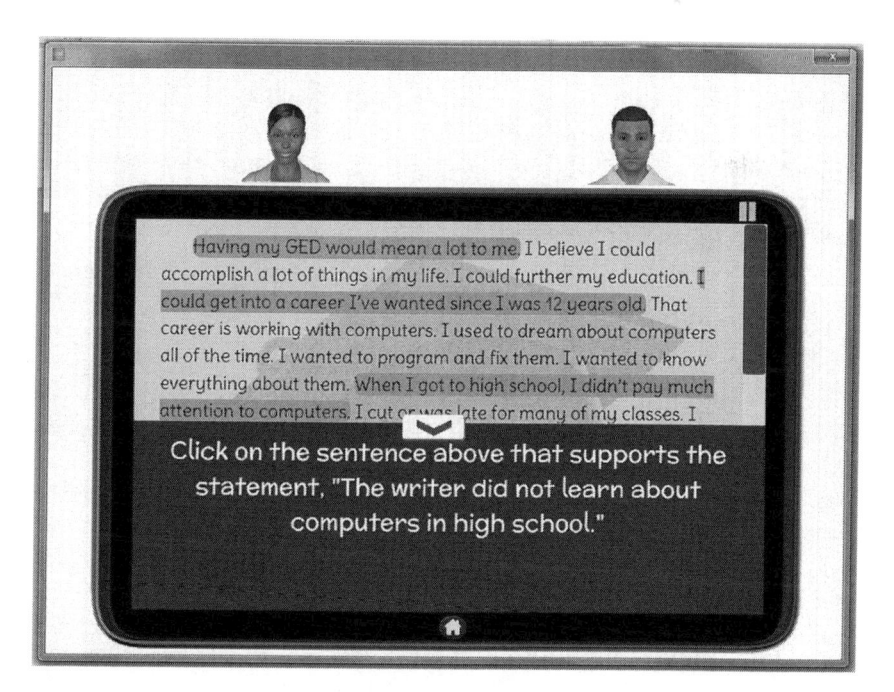

**FIGURE 19.1** Example of Trialogue Design Found in CSAL AutoTutor.

which sentence offers supportive information, which is an important comprehension skill.

There are three components of CSAL AutoTutor that provide adaptive, intelligent interaction. The first assigns texts to read (or shorter instruction episodes) that are tailored to the student's ability (not too easy or too difficult), as calibrated by prior performance of the student. A lesson starts out with a text (or set of shorter items) at an intermediate difficulty level, but then upshifts or downshifts in the difficulty of the assigned materials in a manner that is sensitive to the learner's previous performance. The difficulty level of the texts is computed by *Coh-Metrix*, a system that scales texts on difficulty by considering characteristics of words, syntax, discourse cohesion, and text category (Graesser, et al., 2014b; McNamara, Graesser, McCarthy, & Cai, 2014). After performance is scored on the questions associated with the initial text in a lesson, the next text assigned will be relatively difficult if the score of the learner is high and will be easy if the learner's score is low. The second adaptive component designs the trialogue conversations in a manner that adapts to student ability and/or motivation, as reflected in their performance scores during training. For example, the peer agent ends up losing to the human in jeopardy-like game competitions between the human and peer agent. The human and peer agent take turns answering questions and score points in the competition that is guided by the tutor agent. The human winning the competition over the peer agent is expected to boost the confidence of the adult learner. Third, the open-ended responses are assessed with computational linguistics techniques that match the student's input to expectations (Graesser & McNamara, 2012). Hint questions are generated to guide the student to fill in missing words and phrases of sentences that the learner is expected to enter.

There are auxiliary computer components of the CSAL package that augment the learning experience and motivation. Each AutoTutor lesson includes a short review video of the didactic instruction in a succinct 2–3 minute segment. The lessons are all based on practical topics that have high interest and value, such as selecting a new phone to purchase, filling out a job form, following a cooking recipe, or understanding prescription medicine. There is an electronic independent reading facility for the adult learners to use. This facility includes a text repository (i.e., a library) that has thousands of texts that are categorized on different topics (such as health, family, work, etc.) and that are scaled on reading difficulty. It also provides access to Simple English Wikipedia. They are encouraged to read documents on topics that interest them, with the guidance and encouragement of the teachers in the adult literacy centers. The hope is that the independent reading facility will increase their practice time and self-regulated learning.

A few other points need to be made about the CSAL AutoTutor series. First, assessments will be conducted on the independent reading, but it is beyond the scope of this chapter to address the independent reading facility that is designed to increase interest, motivation, and self-regulated reading. Second, there is an AutoTutor Script Authoring Tool (ASAT) for teachers and curriculum developers to develop new lessons with agents in a short amount of time. Third, the data collected during learning are organized in a data management system that is accessible in dashboards that are tailored to different stakeholders (students, teachers, and researchers).

## Why the Technology is Needed

According to the 2011–2012 international study of adult literacy (the Program for the International Assessment of Adult Competencies, PIACC), adults in the United States scored below the international average in literacy, numeracy, and problem solving in technology rich environments (Goodman, Finnegan, Mohadjer, Krenzke, & Hogan, 2013). The U.S. Department of Education reported in 2010 that over two million adults were enrolled in a federally funded adult education program to increase their skills. Unfortunately, these programs are beset with many obstacles: poor funding, little professional development for teachers and tutors, high absenteeism and attrition rates, and a wide diversity of students in terms of racial, ethnic, and gender identities, age (between 16 and 80+), as well as employment, educational, and language status. As a result of these obstacles, administering quality adult literacy instruction can be a challenge (Greenberg, 2008).

There is an increased use of computers in adult literacy classes (Kruidenier, 2002), in part because learners with varying reading skills can respond to web-based instruction (National Institute for Literacy, 2008). Technology can help overcome the obstacles in adult reading programs. Given the diversity of learners in skills and interest, as well as the inadequate professional development of instructors, well-written, adaptive, intelligent tutorial programs can be beneficial. Attendance issues can be addressed by students being able to access the learning environments in their own homes, neighborhood libraries, schools, houses of worship, and/or locations of employment. The NRC report on adult literacy instruction also states that, "technology can be leveraged to create motivating environments for acquiring reading ... that include ... animated agents" (NRC, 2011, pp. 9–13). Our web-based tutoring component includes conversational, pedagogical agents who motivate and navigate the learner through learning lessons and activities. The system also has adaptive components that are sensitive to the ability of individual learners.

## Plans for Development and Testing of Technology

The CSAL research team has already developed initial versions of 35 lessons with trialogues. These can be used on the web and are supported by most browsers. We have collected data on 52 adult learners in Toronto and Atlanta on 30 of the lessons in a feasibility study. These learners completed 71 percent of the lessons and answered 55 percent of the questions correctly. The lessons are currently being revised to accommodate feedback from teachers, adult learners, and performance data collected in log files. Between the winter of 2016 and the spring of 2017 there will be an experiment that compares an intervention with AutoTutor (plus teachers) with a comparison condition with teachers (without AutoTutor) on several hundred adult learners in Atlanta and Toronto. These assessments will guide revisions of CSAL AutoTutor so that a robust, well-tested system is developed by the end of 2017.

## Timeline for Making the Technology Publically Available

Stand-alone versions of CSAL AutoTutor will be available in early 2016, but it is an open question as to how it would be used without the support of teachers. The timeline for making a version of CSAL AutoTutor available to the public depends on the results of testing and the computer infrastructure being in place to handle different numbers of adult learners. The ideal vision is to have a web portal that can accommodate millions of adult learners.

## Acknowledgements

CSAL is funded by the Institute of Education Sciences, U.S. Department of Education (grant R305C120001). Any opinions, findings, and conclusions or recommendations expressed in this material are those of the authors and do not necessarily reflect the views of IES.

## References

Goodman, M., Finnegan, R., Mohadjer, L., Krenzke, T., & Hogan, J. (2013). *Literacy, Numeracy, and Problem Solving in Technology-Rich Environments Among U.S. Adults: Results from the Program for the International Assessment of Adult Competencies 2012: First Look* (NCES 2014–008). U.S. Department of Education. Washington, DC: National Center for Education Statistics. Retrieved from http://nces.ed.gov/pubsearch.

Graesser, A. C., & McNamara, D. S. (2012). Automated analysis of essays and open-ended verbal responses. In H. Cooper, P. M. Camic, D. L. Long, A. T. Panter, D. Rindskopf, & K. J. Sher (Eds.), *APA Handbook of Research Methods in Psychology, Vol 1: Foundations, Planning, Measures, and Psychometrics* (pp. 307–325). Washington, DC: American Psychological Association.

Graesser, A. C., Li, H., & Forsyth, C. (2014a). Learning by communicating in natural language with conversational agents. *Current Directions in Psychological Science, 23*, 374–380.

Graesser, A. C., McNamara, D. S., Cai, Z., Conley, M., Li, H., & Pennebaker, J. (2014b). Coh-Metrix measures text characteristics at multiple levels of language and discourse. *Elementary School Journal, 115*, 210–229.

Greenberg, D. (2008). The challenges facing adult literacy programs. *Community Literacy Journal, 3*, 39–54.

Kruidenier, J. (2002). *Research-Based Principles for Adult Basic Education*. Washington, DC: National Institute for Literacy.

Lovett, M. W., Lacerenza, L., De Palma, M., & Frijters, J.C. (2012). Evaluating the efficacy of remediation for struggling readers in high school. *Journal of Learning Disabilities, 45*, 151–169.

McNamara, D. S., Graesser, A. C., McCarthy, P. M., Cai, Z. (2014). *Automated Evaluation of Text and Discourse with Coh-Metrix*. Cambridge, MA: Cambridge University Press.

McNamara, D. S., O'Reilly, T., Best, R., & Ozuru, Y. (2006). Improving adolescent students' reading comprehension with iSTART. *Journal of Educational Computing Research, 34*, 147–171.

National Institute for Literacy. (2008). *Investigating the Language and Literacy Skills Required for Independent Online Learning*. Washington, DC. Retrieved from http://eric.ed.gov/PDFS/ED505199.pdf.

National Research Council (NRC). (2011). *Improving Adult Literacy Instruction: Options for Practice and Research*. Washington, DC: The National Academies Press.

# 20

# UDIO

## Rich and Authentic Literacy Experiences for Struggling Middle School Readers

*Alyssa R. Boucher, Miriam Evans, and Steve Graham*

This chapter describes a digital tool, Udio, designed specifically to support the literacy development of young adolescents who find reading and writing challenging. Educators in a middle school classroom can readily describe the challenges they experience in getting struggling readers to engage willingly and purposefully in reading text. The struggling reader prefers to stay along the sidelines when reading, whereas more skilled readers plunge directly into the reading process, extracting the core ideas, and relating them to what they already know. The struggling reader is often reluctant, even withdrawn, and the chance to engage and participate meaningfully in reading and discussing text in the classroom is limited. Overwhelmed by cognitive and emotional demands as they struggle to become literate, these students view reading as an imposing barrier resulting in fewer opportunities for active reading practice across the curriculum (Lyon, 2004).

Fortunately, we have learned much over the last several decades about how to help struggling readers become more fully engaged and successful in the process of learning to read. Essential to this process is providing students with just-in-time support so as to balance the heavy demands they perceive with resources that make the experience of learning to read more efficient, effective, palatable, and even motivating, including opportunities to: (1) discuss with others readings that are personally relevant and meaningful; (2) think about what they read by writing about it; (3) leverage embedded instruction around reading comprehension skills; and (4) read and comprehend age-relevant, grade-level texts with support like text-to-speech (Biancarosa & Snow, 2004; Carnegie Council on Advancing Adolescent Literacy, 2010; Faggella-Luby & Deshler, 2008; Graham & Hebert, 2010, 2011; Kamil et al., 2008; Scammacca et al., 2007). Digital technologies provide an especially interesting and potentially beneficial place in which to enact these principles in flexible and dynamic ways. Increasingly, literacy has shifted from page to screen (Goldman et al., 2012), providing an environment where students' reading and writing can be supported in new ways.

## Overview of the Technology

With current literacy needs at the forefront, the U.S. Department of Education's Office of Special Education Programs (OSEP) funded the Center on Emerging Technologies to Improve Literacy Achievement for Students with Disabilities in Middle School (the Center). Led by CAST (www.cast.org) in collaboration with Vanderbilt University, the Center is researching and developing a transformative approach to the problem of supporting students with low literacy skills in middle school. Specifically, the Center seeks to improve the reading comprehension skills, motivation for reading, and level of engagement in literacy activities of students who struggle with reading in middle school (see Figure 20.1). Universal Design for Learning (UDL) figures prominently in the approach. The Center has

**Theory of Change** | How Udio works to produce improved reading comprehension skill and motivation for reading.

**Strategy** → **Outcome** → **Goals Achieved**

**Motivation**
- Provide access to high-interest content.
- Allow student choice in the selection of reading material.
- Develop student understanding of their interests.
- Discuss with others readings that are personally relevant and meaningful.
- Provide UDL supports for 'just-right' reading challenges.

**Reading Comprehension**
- Provide access to text when reading skill is low.
- Leverage embedded instruction around reading comprehension skills.
- Use writing in the service of reading.

Outcomes:
- Improved engagement with reading.
- Less aversion to learning from text.
- More time spent interacting with and trying to learn from text.
- Improved understanding of grade level text with supports.

☑ Improved motivation for reading.

☑ Improved reading comprehension.

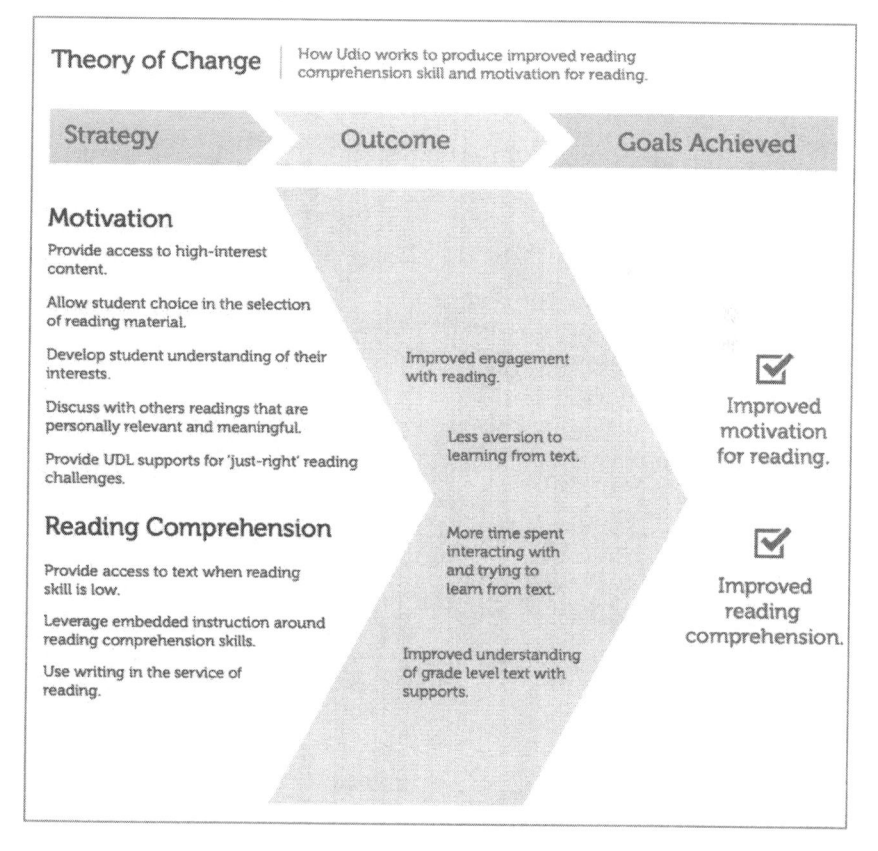

**FIGURE 20.1** Udio Theory of Change.

worked to leverage the learning sciences and emerging technologies to develop a reading environment that is highly flexible and designed to meet the needs of adolescent readers who vary substantially in their knowledge, skills, and motivation for reading. Under UDL, design decisions focus on the removal of obstacles to learning that are inherent to one-size-fits-all curricula. UDL curricula, tools, and learning environments offer flexibility through the provision of supports with multiple options for learners to access and interact with materials (Dolan, Hall, Banerjee, Chun, & Strangman, 2005; Rose & Meyer, 2002, 2006).

Udio is comprised of three main components: a wide variety of high-interest and age-relevant readings, opportunities to write projects in support of reading-related activities, and a personal dashboard to guide the student experience. Students and teachers choose from a collection of readings from publishers of print and web content who are partnering with the project (see Figure 20.2). To be included,

**FIGURE 20.2** Variety of Texts Available from Udio.

texts must be highly relevant and interesting to middle school students of varying backgrounds. These include short articles, blogs, novels, and opinion pieces covering a variety of topics, such as science, health, young adult fiction, education, sports, and technology. The flexibility of Udio allows *all* students to access the material by reading with or without audio-assisted reading supports. Dictionary and word-level translation features provide "just-in-time" support to bolster comprehension. Opportunities to engage with the text are promoted through embedded discussion areas, comprehension prompts, and interactive features enabling readers to express their reactions to the reading.

The writing project component of Udio allows students to think more deeply about what they read by developing written commentaries to share with their peers or the teacher. This can range from writing a review of a specific article to presenting a particular point of view about something presented in the article and inviting others to debate it. Udio provides students with highly supported project templates and various tools for creating different types of commentaries. Students can design a project that includes quotes and images from the reading, as well as their own responses constructed through text, voice recordings, or drawings (see Figure 20.3).

In an effort to foster personal interest and reading motivation, Udio also provides a dynamic dashboard for students to monitor their progress and view their personal topics of interest (as shown in Figure 20.4). Students can also view reading material that has been recommended to them based on their previous reading selections and recommendations from their teacher.

In addition, teachers are highly supported in Udio with a digital dashboard and teacher site that complements the student site. Here teachers can view activity in real-time during a class period and student activity over time, which includes details about the kinds of supports and features students utilize. A comprehensive teacher guide includes mini-lessons and suggestions for connecting Udio to the classroom curriculum. Included in these mini-lessons are topics that center around the theory of change: using the power of choice, building self-efficacy and metacognitive skills, supporting understanding through writing, and empowering students to discover their interests. Mini-lessons include quick teaching tips, as well as instructional procedures, references, and connections to the Common Core.

## Design and Development

Udio was designed in collaboration with middle school teachers and students using a design-based research approach. Design-based research is a formative evaluation approach to program development in which development and research take place through continuous cycles of design, implementation, analysis, and redesign (Cobb, 2001; Collins, 1992). Throughout the iterative development process, teachers and students were involved as both partners and participants, testing components as they were developed and revised, and providing feedback

FIGURE 20.3  A Student Project.

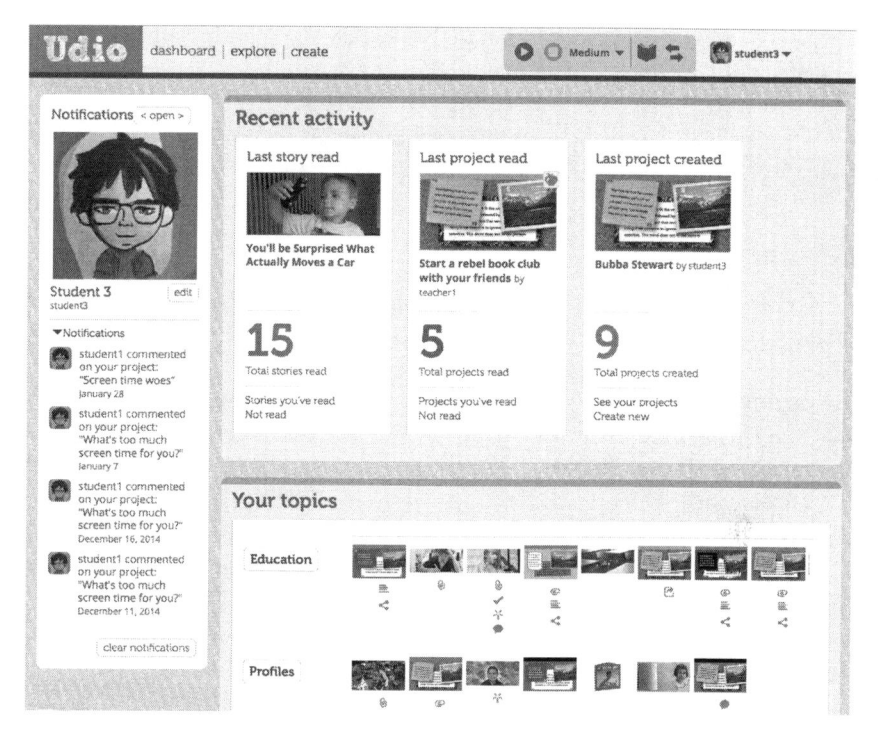

**FIGURE 20.4** Student Dashboard.

to the project team. For instance, researchers worked with middle school teachers and students to answer broad questions about how students use and interact with the internet and computers to inform the design of Udio. More targeted questions focused on the look and feel of Udio, as well as features and functions, such as making comments or projects. Once a prototype was developed, researchers observed learners as they experienced the environment and collected feedback for further development.

The process of research and development has been agile, meaning that design and development occur simultaneously, rather than in distinct phases. Instructional components of the program are rapidly prototyped and tested within two-week "sprints." Prototypes are then tested with students and teachers at the end of each two-week interval using qualitative research methodology, so that the design process stays as close to the intended users' needs as possible. Pilot testing is ongoing and initial rounds of research indicate a positive reception and enthusiasm among teachers and students with regard to quality and usefulness. A large-scale efficacy trial with approximately 1,000 students across multiple middle school settings will be conducted in preparation for public release.

With its combination of high-interest reading material, writing to encourage deeper interaction with texts, and personalization in a supported digital environment,

Udio represents a promising solution to the problem of supporting middle school students with low literacy skills. Udio offers teachers a way to help move struggling readers from the sidelines of text to active and meaningful participation with their peers. Udio is expected to be released at the conclusion of the project soon after December 2016. Visit cet.cast.org for updates and information.

## Acknowledgments

This project was supported by a cooperative agreement with the U.S. Department of Education (#H327M11000). However, the contents of this chapter do not necessarily represent the policy of the Department of Education, and you should not assume endorsement by the Federal government. Participating contributors, listed in alphabetical order, are as follows: Alyssa Boucher, CAST; Christina Bosch, CAST; Linda Butler, CAST; Peggy Coyne, CAST; Kim Ducharme, CAST; Samantha G. Daley, CAST; Miriam Evans, CAST; Graham L. Gardner, CAST; Boris Goldowsky, CAST; Steve Graham, Arizona State University; Tracey Hall, CAST; Karen Harris, Arizona State University; Ted Hasselbring, Vanderbilt University; Garron Hillaire, CAST; Christine M. Leider, Boston College; Rebecca Louick, Boston College; C. Patrick Proctor, Boston College; Gabrielle Rappolt-Schlichtmann, CAST; Kristin Robinson, CAST; and David Rose, CAST.

## References

Biancarosa, G., & Snow, C. E. (2004). *Reading Next: A Vision for Action and Research in Middle and High School Literacy: A Report to Carnegie Corporation of New York* (vol. 2). Washington, DC: Alliance for Excellent Education.

Carnegie Council on Advancing Adolescent Literacy. (2010). *Time to Act: An Agenda for Advancing Adolescent Literacy for College and Career Success*. New York: Carnegie Corporation of New York.

Cobb, P. (2001). Supporting the improvement of learning and teaching in social and institutional context. In S. Carver, & D. Klahr (Eds.), *Cognition and Instruction: Twenty-Five Years of Progress* (pp. 455–478). Cambridge, MA: Lawrence Erlbaum Associates.

Collins, A. (1992). Toward a design science of education. In E. Scanlon & T. O'Shea (Eds.), *New Directions in Educational Technology* (pp. 15–22). New York: Springer-Verlag.

Dolan, R. P., Hall, T. E., Banerjee, M., Chun, E., & Strangman, N. (2005). Applying principles of universal design to test delivery: The effect of computer-based read-aloud on test performance of high school students with learning disabilities. *Journal of Technology, Learning, and Assessment, 3*(7).

Faggella-Luby, M. N., & Deshler, D. (2008) Reading comprehension in adolescents with LD: What we know; what we need to learn. *Learning Disabilities Research & Practice, 23*(2), 70–78.

Goldman, S., Braasch, J., Wiley, J., Graesser, A., & Brodowinska, K. (2012). Comprehending and learning from internet sources: Processing patterns of better and poorer learners. *Reading Research Quarterly, 47*, 356–381.

Graham, S., & Hebert, M. (2010). *Writing to Read: Evidence for How Writing can Improve Reading: A Report from Carnegie Corporation of New York.* Carnegie Corporation of New York.

Graham, S., & Hebert, M. (2011). Writing-to-read: A meta-analysis of the impact of writing and writing instruction on reading. *Harvard Educational Review, 81,* 710–744.

Kamil, M. L., Borman, G. D., Dole, J., Kral, C. C., Salinger, T., & Torgensen, J. (2008). *Improving Adolescent Literacy: Effective Classroom and Intervention Practices: A Practice Guide* (NCEE #2008–4027). Washington, DC: National Center for Education Evaluation and Regional Assistance, Institute of Education Sciences, U.S. Department of Education.

Lyon, R. (2004). Reading disabilities: Why do some children have difficulty learning to read? What can be done about it? *Perspectives, 29*(2). Retrieved from http://www.interdys.org.

Rose, D. H., & Meyer, A. (2002). *Teaching Every Student in the Digital Age: Universal Design for Learning.* Alexandria, VA: ASCD.

Rose, D. H., & Meyer, A. (Eds.). (2006). *A Practical Reader in Universal Design for Learning.* Cambridge, MA: Harvard Education Press.

Scammacca, N., Roberts, G., Vaughn, S., Edmonds, M., Wexler, J., Reutebuch, C. K., & Torgesen, J. K. (2007). *Interventions for Adolescent Struggling Readers: A Meta-Analysis with Implications for Practice.* Portsmouth, NH: RMC Research Corporation, Center on Instruction.

# INDEX

A2i *see* Assessment-to-Instruction
Abrami, P. 19
access 14–15; A2i 47; computer-based writing systems 157–158; *Criterion* 166, 174–175; DSCoVAR 78–79; iSTART-2 114–117; ITSS 98–100; Research Writing Tutor 232–234; SWoRD 255–256; TuinLEC 136–137; We-Write 194–197; W-Pal 216–218
adjectives 228
adult literacy 3, 8, 78, 288–292
AES *see* automated essay scoring
agency 109, 180
algorithms: A2i 34, 37, 41, 43; AES systems 206; *Criterion* 169, 179; iSTART-2 109; Reading Strategy Assessment Tool 284; SWoRD 243; TuinLEC 127, 133; W-Pal 213
Alibali, M. W. 269
Allen, Laura K. 49–68, 145–162, 204–224, 227
Althoff, T. 15
Apple 17
apps 16
assessment: A2i 35, 37–38, 41–44; AES systems 146; CSAL AutoTutor 290; formative 33–34, 147, 285; ITSS 96–97; PISA 25; Reading Strategy Assessment Tool 285; self-assessment 133, 149, 184, 186–187, 188, 193, 196; web-based software 192; We-Write 185, 188, 190
Assessment-to-Instruction (A2i) 6, 33–47
Attali, Y. 172
attitudes to technology 18–20
automated essay scoring (AES) 7, 145, 146, 206–207, 245; *Criterion* 163; criticisms of 207; Project Essay Grade 154; W-Pal 204; Writing Roadmap 152
automated language processing *see* natural language processing
automated writing evaluation (AWE) 1, 7, 146–148, 206, 227, 245; *Criterion* 159, 173, 174, 179, 180; criticisms of 207; support for writing skills 164–165; W-Pal 221
AutoTutor 8, 288–292

Baer, Whitney O. 288–293
Beck, Isabel 69–70
Becker, H. J. 20
Beilock, S. L. 269
Best, R. 111
bilingual resources 166, 171, 272
Boucher, Alyssa R. 294–301
Brantley-Dias, L. 23
Bring Your Own Device (BYOD) 15
Burstein, Jill 275–281

Cai, Zhiqiang 288–293
Calico, T. 172–173
Cataldo, M. 124
CAVOCA 75
Center for the Study of Adult Literacy (CSAL) 288–292
Cerdán, R. 127
cheating 169
Chen, H. J. 173–174
Chile 24–25
CI model *see* Construction-Integration model
class sizes 9, 146, 206
cloud computing 78
cognitive writing theory 226
cohesion: CSAL AutoTutor 290; TERA 51, 53, 55–56, 62, 63, 64–65; W-Pal 209, 215
Coh-Metrix 49, 51, 59
Collins-Thompson, Kevyn 69–81
commercialized writing systems 145–162
Common Core State Standards: *Criterion* 166, 179; higher-level writing skills 244; iSTART-2 111, 112, 119; mathematics 244; persuasive writing 191–192; reading 275; TERA 51, 57, 60, 65; text structure 83; Udio 297; W-Pal 219, 220
composition 43, 164, 165, 180
comprehension 2–3, 49–50, 192, 268–269; A2i 34, 35, 37, 43; CSAL AutoTutor 289–290; *EMBRACE* 8, 268, 269, 271–273; iSTART-2 7, 104–121; ITSS 82, 85–98; Reading Strategy Assessment Tool 282–286; Reading Tutor 263, 265; structure strategy 82–85, 91–98, 99–100, 194; TERA 51, 64–65; TuinLEC 122, 124, 136; We-Write 185; WriteToLearn 149–151; *see also* reading
computer-based writing instruction 145–162
computers: access to 14–15, 158; adult literacy 291; Chile 24; Reading Tutor 265–266
confidence 19
connectives 55–56
Connor, Carol McDonald 33–48

Construction-Integration (CI) model 105
constructivism 20, 26
context, of words 70–71, 73–74, 75, 77, 78
costs 158
Cotos, Elena 225–242
Coutelet, B. 124
*Criterion* 7, 159, 163–183, 227
Crossley, Scott A. 1–12, 69–81, 204–224, 227
crowdfunding 15, 26
CSAL *see* Center for the Study of Adult Literacy
curricula development 62

Deane, Paul 163–183
decoding 34, 35, 36, 37, 39–40, 43
deep cohesion 51, 53, 55–56, 63, 64–65
deliberative practice 4, 7, 9, 145, 157; AWE systems 146–147; MyAccess! 148; reading 49–50; TPACK 23; W-Pal 207, 211; writing strategies 206; *see also* practice
diagnostics 173
digital writing 164
direct instruction 70–72
disciplinary ideas 244
discourse 186, 190, 191, 276
DLLs *see* dual language learners
Domínguez, C. 127
"double innovation" problem 20
drafts: *Criterion* 165, 170, 178; peer review 253, 256; Research Writing Tutor 231, 234; W-Pal 208, 209
dual language learners (DLLs) 268–274; *see also* English language learners
Dynamic Support of Contextual Vocabulary Acquisition for Reading (DSCoVAR) 6, 69, 71, 72–79

EAP *see* English for Academic Purposes
Educational Testing Services (ETS) 159, 166, 180
ELA *see* English Language Arts
e-learning 127
ELLs *see* English language learners
e-mails 2
embodied cognition 269

## 304  Index

*EMBRACE* (Enhanced Moved By Reading to Accelerate Comprehension in English) 8, 268, 269, 271–273
engagement 101; AWE systems 147; *Criterion* 165; iSTART-2 107, 114; TuinLEC 141; W-Pal 214, 215–216
English for Academic Purposes (EAP) 227, 229
English Language Arts (ELA) 244, 275
English language learners (ELLs) 3, 165, 268–274, 275–276; *EMBRACE* 268, 271–273; ITSS 100; *MbR* 269–271; W-Pal 221; *see also* Spanish speakers
enjoyment 114, 216
ENLACES program 24–25
enrichment lessons 97
*e-rater* 163, 165, 167–169, 174, 178, 179–180, 206
errors 145, 164; *Criterion* 166, 169–170, 174, 178, 179–180; peer review 254; TuinLEC 130
Ertmer, P. A. 15–17, 18, 19, 20, 23
essays 146, 147; *Criterion* 163; LightSide Revision Assistant 156; MyAccess! 148–149; Prentice Hall Writing Coach 151; Project Essay Grade 153–155; We-Write 191, 196–197; W-Pal 204, 207, 212–213, 215, 217, 220, 221–222; WriteToLearn 150; Writing Roadmap 152–153; *see also* automated essay scoring; writing
ETS *see* Educational Testing Services
Evans, Miriam 294–301
evidence-based instruction 4

feedback 4, 5, 7, 9, 143; AWE systems 146–147, 164–165, 227; bottlenecks 243; *Criterion* 163, 165, 166, 167–170, 173–174, 176, 178–179, 180; direct instruction 71; DSCoVAR 72, 76, 77–78; iSTART-2 111, 119; ITSS 86, 91, 96, 98; LightSide Revision Assistant 155–156; MyAccess! 148, 149; need for computer-based writing instruction 145–146; Prentice Hall Writing Coach 151; Project Essay Grade 154, 155; Project LISTEN Reading Tutor 8; Research Writing Tutor 228, 230–232,

234–235, 237–238, 239; SWoRD 8, 243, 246–257; TPACK 23; TuinLEC 122, 126, 130, 131–133, 135, 141; web-based software 192; We-Write 185, 188, 190, 192, 193, 200; W-Pal 159, 204, 207, 211, 212–214, 215, 220, 221–222; WriteToLearn 150; Writing Roadmap 152–153; writing strategies 206; *see also* peer review
Ferrer, Antonio 122–142
Fischer, S. M. 269
Flesch-Kincaid (FK) Grade Level 56, 57, 58, 284
fluency: A2i 35; *Criterion* 164, 165, 180; *Language Muse* 279, 280; Reading Tutor 263, 265
Folio 227
formative assessment 33–34, 147, 285
formative feedback 4, 9, 157, 206; AES systems 146; AWE systems 147; LightSide Revision Assistant 155–156; TuinLEC 126; We-Write 188, 192; W-Pal 159, 207, 211, 213, 221–222
Framework for Success in Postsecondary Writing (FSPW) 204–205
Frishkoff, Gwen A. 69–81
funding 15, 17, 26, 255, 291

games: iSTART-2 107–110, 111, 114, 116–117, 118; ITSS 91, 95; TuinLEC 134, 135; W-Pal 207, 208–212, 214, 216, 217, 220
genres: *Criterion* 166, 180; disciplinary practices 226; genre theory 226–227; Research Writing Tutor 235–236; TERA 56–57
GEs *see* grade equivalents
Gibson, B. R. 271
Gil, Laura 122–142
Gilabert, R. 127
Glenberg, Arthur M. 268–274
goal setting 184, 186, 187
Goldberg, A. B. 271
grade equivalents (GEs) 35, 37
Graesser, Arthur C. 288–293
Graham, Steve 147, 294–301
grammar: *Criterion* 165, 166, 169, 179; errors 145; *Language Muse*

279; MyAccess! 149; Prentice Hall Writing Coach 151, 152; W-Pal 220; WriteToLearn 150
graphic organizers 154, 186, 187, 194
Gray Silent Reading Test (GSRT) 96–97
Greenberg, Daphne 288–293
Grimes, D. 149
group work 35, 36, 39–40, 44
GSRT see Gray Silent Reading Test
Gutierrez, T. 271

hardware, access to 14–15; see also computers
Harris, C. 173
Harris, Karen R. 147, 184–203
Hebert, M. 147
help tools 131, 133, 135
Hispanics 3; see also Spanish speakers
Hodges, Leslie 69–81
Hostetter, A. B. 269
Hu, Xiangen 288–293
Huffman, S. 236

IEA see Intelligent Essay Assessor
image manipulation (IM) 270–271
independent performance 187, 191
independent reading 70–72
individualization 4, 5, 9, 145–146; A2i 36, 37, 46, 47; DSCoVAR 69; intelligent tutoring systems 15; iSTART-2 111; ITSS 97–98; reading instruction 34; writing strategies 206; see also personalization
Individualizing Student Instruction (ISI) 34, 45, 47
inferences: iSTART-2 105–106, 111, 112, 119; ITSS 7, 83, 97; *Language Muse* 278, 279; PACES 289; Reading Strategy Assessment Tool 284, 285; task-oriented reading 126; text cohesion 55, 56, 62, 63, 64–65
Ingebrand, Sarah W. 33–48
Intelligent Essay Assessor (IEA) 207
Intelligent Tutoring of the Structure Strategy (ITSS) 6–7, 82–103
intelligent tutoring systems (ITS) 1; CSAL AutoTutor 8, 288–292; DSCoVAR 69–81; individualization 15

IntelliMetric 148, 206–207
Interactive Strategy Training for Active Reading and Thinking-2 (iSTART-2) 7, 104–121, 285
International Society for Technology in Education (ISTE) 17, 24, 26
internet: access to 14; impact on reading 25; teacher training 16; TERA 60; see also online assessment; web browsers
inter-rater agreement 250
iPads 16–17, 271
Ireland, Jennifer 100
IRT see item response theory
ISI see Individualizing Student Instruction
iSTART-2 see Interactive Strategy Training for Active Reading and Thinking
ISTE see International Society for Technology in Education
item response theory (IRT) 41
ITS see intelligent tutoring systems
ITSS see Intelligent Tutoring of the Structure Strategy

Jackson, G. Tanner 49–68, 104–121
Jackson, L. 25
Jacovina, Matthew E. 13–29, 104–121
Japuntich, S. 271
Johnson, Amy M. 13–29

Kaschak, M. P. 271
KAT see Knowledge Analysis Technology
Kellogg, R. T. 173
Kim, J. E. 173
Klobucar, A. 173
knowledge 19, 22–24, 205
Knowledge Analysis Technology (KAT) 150
Kontra, C. 269

Landauer, T. K. 151
language control 164, 165, 180
*Language Muse (LM) Activity Palette* 8, 276–280
learning: constructivism 20; peer review 246, 253–254; Universal Design for Learning 295–296; see also word learning

learning management systems (LMSs) 255–256
Learning Ovations 47
Leskovec, J. 15
lesson plans 20; A2i 35, 40–41, 42; Prentice Hall Writing Coach 152; We-Write 195
*Letters 2 Meaning* 43
Levin, J. R. 271
Li, C. 172–173
LightSide Revision Assistant (RA) 155–157
literacy 2–3, 9, 33; A2i 35, 37, 47; critical 229; need for supplemental literacy instruction 3–5; screen-based 294–295; Udio 294; *see also* adult literacy; reading; writing
Llorens, A. C. 127
*LM see Language Muse*
LMSs *see* learning management systems
Lyons, D. J. 269

Magliano, Joseph P. 282–287
Maña, A. 124, 127
Martínez, T. 124
mathematics 244, 269
matrix approach 90–91, 92
Mayfield, E. 157
*MbR see Moved By Reading*
McMaster, K. L. 285
McNamara, Danielle S. 1–12, 49–68, 104–121, 204–224, 227
meaning: A2i 35, 36, 39–40, 43; iSTART-2 112; Knowledge Analysis Technology 150; *Language Muse* 278, 279; word learning 70, 75, 76, 77, 79
memorization 54, 187, 191
memory 78, 244
MESA 76, 77
Meyer, Bonnie J. F. 82–103, 184–203
Millis, Keith K. 282–287
mnemonics: We-Write 186, 187, 188, 191, 196; W-Pal 205, 208, 209, 211, 214
modeling 186–187, 190, 191, 193
Mosaic 152
Mostow, Jack 263–267

motivation: *Criterion* 165; CSAL AutoTutor 290; iSTART-2 114, 118; persuasive writing 192; Research Writing Tutor 236; self-regulated strategies development 190; TuinLEC 133, 134, 135, 141; W-Pal 214, 215–216
*Moved By Reading (MbR)* 269–271
moving window technique 126
MyAccess! 23, 148–149, 227

NAEP *see* National Assessment of Educational Progress
Nam, SungJin 69–81
narrativity 51, 53–54, 63
Nathan, M. J. 269
National Assessment of Educational Progress (NAEP) 166, 189
National Center for Education Statistics (NCES) 14
National Education Association (NEA) 15–16
National Research Council (NRC) 291
National Science Foundation 227–228, 273
natural language processing (NLP): *Criterion* 165, 168–170, 181n3; IntelliMetric 148; *Language Muse* 276; limitations of 179, 180; TERA 50, 60; We-Write 188, 193
NCES *see* National Center for Education Statistics
NEA *see* National Education Association
Next Generation Science Standards 154, 244
NLP *see* natural language processing
nonfiction texts 82–85, 284
note-taking 184, 185, 186, 193
NRC *see* National Research Council

Oakhill, J. 124
Olney, Andrew M. 288–293
online assessment: A2i 35, 37–38, 41–44; ITSS 97
oral reading 263–266
O'Reilly, T. P. 111, 113

PACES 288–289
Page, E. B. 155

partial word knowledge 76
Pearson 149, 151
pedagogical content knowledge (PCK) 22, 23, 26
pedagogy 18, 62, 63
peer review 243, 245–246; *Criterion* 163, 165, 166, 174, 178; Project Essay Grade 154, 155; Research Writing Tutor 239; SWoRD 8, 246–257; We-Write 184, 188, 193
Peerceptiv 255–257
PEG *see* Project Essay Grade
Perret, Cecile A. 145–162
personalization: iSTART-2 109, 111, 119; ITSS 86; LightSide Revision Assistant 156; Prentice Hall Writing Coach 151, 152; TERA 66; Udio 299; WriteToLearn 150; *see also* individualization
persuasive writing: *Criterion* 166, 176; ITSS 100; LightSide Revision Assistant 155, 156; MyAccess! 148, 149; We-Write 8, 184–185, 190, 191–192, 200; Writing Roadmap 152, 153
Peterson, N. S. 155
phonics 35
phonological awareness 35
physical manipulation (PM) 269–270, 271
PISA *see* Program for International Student Assessment
plagiarism 169
planning: *Criterion* 165, 166, 167, 171; persuasive writing 192; research writing 226; We-Write 193, 194; W-Pal 208, 209, 213, 220
PM *see* physical manipulation
portfolios: *Criterion* 166, 171; MyAccess! 149; Project Essay Grade 154, 155; We-Write 193
Portugal 25
POWerful strategies 184, 191
practice 4, 244–245; adaptive spacing 76–77; iSTART-2 110–111, 118–119; opportunities for 205–206; TuinLEC 125, 130–133, 135, 140; We-Write 190, 193; W-Pal 212, 215; *see also* deliberate practice
Prentice Hall Writing Coach 151–152

professional development 14, 15, 26, 189; Chile 24; ITSS 99–100; knowledge domains 23; *Language Muse* 276; TPACK 24; We-Write 195, 199
Program for International Student Assessment (PISA) 25, 122, 123
progress monitoring: A2i 33–34, 35, 36; *Criterion* 174–175; iSTART-2 116–117; LightSide Revision Assistant 156; Prentice Hall Writing Coach 152; Project Essay Grade 155; Reading Strategy Assessment Tool 285; TuinLEC 136–138, 140; We-Write 193, 196, 198; W-Pal 216–217; WriteToLearn 150
Project Essay Grade (PEG) 153–155
Project LISTEN 8, 263–267
prompts: *Criterion* 165–167, 176; LightSide Revision Assistant 156; MyAccess! 148, 149; Prentice Hall Writing Coach 151; Project Essay Grade 154; Research Writing Tutor 232; We-Write 184, 187; W-Pal 212

Quinlan, T. 173

Ramaswamy, N. 237
Ramineni, Chaitanya 163–183
Ramos, Luis 122–142
Ravitz, J. L. 20
Ray, Melissa 84, 100, 282–287
Read&Answer 126–127
readability 1, 6, 49–66, 284; *see also* text difficulty
reading 6–7, 31, 192; A2i 6, 34–47; CSAL AutoTutor 8, 288–292; deliberative practice 49–50; *EMBRACE* 8, 271–273; English language learners 268, 275–276; failure to attain literacy skills 2–3, 33, 110, 284–285; independent 70–72; internet use 25; iSTART-2 7, 104–121; ITSS 6–7; *Language Muse* 277–280; low motivation to read 101; *MbR* 269–271; need for supplemental literacy instruction 3–4; Project LISTEN Reading Tutor 8, 263–267; Reading Strategy Assessment Tool 282–287; strategies 4–5; structure

strategy 82–85, 91–98, 99–100, 190, 194; task-oriented 122–127, 135–136; TERA 6; TuinLEC 122–142; Udio 8, 294–299; We-Write 185; word learning 69–81; WriteToLearn 149–151; *see also* comprehension
*Reading 2 Comprehension* 43
Reading Strategy Assessment Tool (RSAT) 8, 282–287
Reading Tutor 263–267
Reed, Megan 288–293
referential cohesion 51, 53, 55, 63, 64
remediation: *Criterion* 173; ITSS 97; Prentice Hall Writing Coach 151
research writing 8, 225–242
Research Writing Tutor (RWT) 8, 225, 228–239
Restrepo, M. Adelaida 268–274
revision: AWE systems 164–165; cognitive writing theory 226; *Criterion* 172–173, 174–175, 176, 177; individualized feedback 4; LightSide Revision Assistant 155–157; MyAccess! 149; Research Writing Tutor 8, 235–236, 238; We-Write 184, 193, 196–197; W-Pal 204, 208, 209, 213, 220, 221–222; WriteToLearn 150
Roscoe, R. D. 215
Rose, C. P. 157
Rouet, J. F. 124
RSAT *see* Reading Strategy Assessment Tool
Russell, Devin G. 13–29
RWT *see* Research Writing Tutor

Sabatini, John 275–281
San Martín, E. 25
scaffolding: DSCoVAR 77, 78; ITSS 86, 90; Reading Tutor 265; Research Writing Tutor 228, 232, 235, 236; structure strategy 83; TERA 63, 64; web-based software 192; We-Write 185, 190, 195–196; WriteToLearn 150
Schunn, Christian 243–259
science: dual language learners 268; iSTART-2 118; ITSS 85, 100; Project Essay Grade 154; research writing 226–227, 238; Self-Explanation Reading Training 111–112, 113; writing required for 244; *see also* STEM subjects
scores: A2i 34, 35, 37–38, 40, 43–44; AWE systems 147, 206–207; *Criterion* 163, 164–165, 166, 167–170, 173, 176–177, 179; CSAL AutoTutor 290; DSCoVAR 76, 78; iSTART-2 109, 113, 116, 117, 118; ITSS 86, 96–97, 100; LightSide Revision Assistant 156–157; MyAccess! 148–149; Prentice Hall Writing Coach 151; Project Essay Grade 154, 155; Reading Strategy Assessment Tool 284, 285–286; TuinLEC 136, 137; We-Write 192; W-Pal 215, 217; WriteToLearn 150, 151; Writing Roadmap 152–153; *see also* automated essay scoring
search engines 227, 229
searching text 124, 125, 127–128, 133, 135
self-assessment: MyAccess! 149; TuinLEC 133; We-Write 184, 186–187, 188, 193, 196
self-efficacy: ITSS 96, 101; self-regulated strategies development 190; TuinLEC 134; Udio 297; We-Write 184, 193, 199
self-explanation 4, 105–110, 111–113, 116, 117–118
Self-Explanation Reading Training (SERT) 106–107, 111–113, 117
self-monitoring 71
self-regulated strategies development (SRSD) 184–188, 189–190, 191, 193, 195–196, 199–200
self-regulation 4, 188–189, 192, 243–244; Research Writing Tutor 237; TuinLEC 125, 126–127, 128, 131, 141; We-Write 184, 185, 193
self-statements 186, 187, 191
Serrano, Maria-Ángeles 122–142
SERT *see* Self-Explanation Reading Training
signaling words 83, 84–85, 86–87, 89, 91, 96, 97
simulation 269–270, 273
small group work 35, 36, 39–40, 44
Snow, Erica L. 104–121

social media 2, 23
software: access to 14; teacher training 16, 26
Soto, Christian M. 13–29
Spain 25
Spanish speakers 7, 87, 100, 122, 140, 271–272; *see also* English language learners
special education 3
speech recognition 264
spell checkers 149, 165
spelling: A2i 43; errors 145; Knowledge Analysis Technology 150; Reading Tutor 265; W-Pal 220; WriteToLearn 150
SRSD *see* self-regulated strategies development
STEM subjects 268, 269, 271
strategies 4–5, 205–206; CSAL AutoTutor 288; Reading Strategy Assessment Tool 282–287; structure strategy 82–85, 91–98, 99–100, 190, 194; We-Write 184; W-Pal 208, 211, 214, 220, 221
strategy instruction 4–5, 7–8, 9; CSAL AutoTutor 8; DSCoVAR 72–73; iSTART-2 105, 119; self-regulated strategies development 184–188, 189–190, 191, 193, 195–196, 199–200; TuinLEC 127–130, 138; W-Pal 159, 204, 205, 207–208, 214, 220
structure strategy 82–85, 91–98, 99–100, 190, 194
student-centered education 19–20, 26
summaries 150
summative feedback 206; AWE systems 207; TuinLEC 126; W-Pal 159, 207, 221
support 14, 17–18, 26, 191
Swales, J. M. 227
SWoRD (Scaffolded Writing and Rewriting in the Discipline) 8, 227, 243–259
syntactic simplicity 51, 53, 54, 63–64

TASA *see* Touchstone Applied Science Associates, Inc.
task-oriented reading skills 122–127, 135–136

teachers: A2i 33, 35–36, 41, 44, 46; attitudes and beliefs 18–20; Chile 24; *Criterion* 174–175, 176–178; direct instruction 71; English language learners 275–276; feedback on systems in development 158; iSTART-2 114–116, 117–118; ITSS 99–100; *Language Muse* 276–277; LightSide Revision Assistant 156; MyAccess! 149; need for writing technology 164; Prentice Hall Writing Coach 152; Project Essay Grade 154–155; Research Writing Tutor 239; resistance to technology 20–21; skills and knowledge 22–24; support for 17–18, 26; SWoRD/Peerceptiv 249–250, 255, 256, 257; training 15–17, 26; TuinLEC 135, 136–137, 138, 140; Udio 297; We-Write 185, 192, 194–196, 199; W-Pal 216–218, 220; WriteToLearn 150; Writing Roadmap 153
technological pedagogical content knowledge (TPACK) 22–24, 26
technology: integration of 13–29; selection of 21; teacher resistance to 20–21; teachers' beliefs about 19–20
text difficulty: CSAL AutoTutor 290; iSTART-2 112, 118; TERA 6, 49–66
Text Ease and Readability Assessor (TERA) 6, 49–68
text messages 2
text structure: genre learning 229; iSTART-2 112, 119; ITSS 6, 82–101; PACES 289; reading and writing 192; TuinLEC 125; We-Write 185, 190, 197, 200; *see also* structure strategy
texts: categorization of 123; *Criterion* 179; CSAL AutoTutor 290; *EMBRACE* 271, 272; iSTART-2 116, 118, 119; *Language Muse* 276–277; PACES 288–289; Reading Strategy Assessment Tool 282, 284; TERA 49–66; TuinLEC 123–124, 126, 130, 140–141; Udio 296–297
time constraints 20
Touchstone Applied Science Associates, Inc. (TASA) 66n3

# 310  Index

TPACK *see* technological pedagogical content knowledge
training 14, 15–17, 19, 26; DSCoVAR 72; iSTART-2 107, 113–114; knowledge domains 23; Self-Explanation Reading Training 106–107, 111–113, 117; TuinLEC 135
TuinLEC 7, 122–142
Twitter 23

Udio 8, 294–301
Universal Design for Learning (UDL) 295–296
Uruguay 25
usability: A2i 44; *Language Muse* 280; Research Writing Tutor 237; TuinLEC 134–135; W-Pal 213, 214

Vantage Learning 148
Venkatesh, V. 19
verbs 170, 228–229
Vidal-Abarca, Eduardo 122–142
virtual agents: CSAL AutoTutor 288, 290, 291; TuinLEC 128–129, 134–135, 138, 140
visualization tools 20, 26
vocabulary 69–81, 275; A2i 34, 35, 37, 43; DSCoVAR 6, 72–79; *EMBRACE* 272; iSTART-2 112; *Language Muse* 276, 279; PACES 288; Reading Tutor 263, 265; We-Write 196–197, 200; WriteToLearn 150

Walker, Erin A. 268–274
Warschauer, M. 149
web browsers 72, 74, 98, 255, 291
We-Write 7–8, 184–203
Whiteford, A. P. 173
Wijekumar, Kausalai K. 82–103, 184–203
Willford, J. 271
Wong, Y. T. 20
word concreteness 51, 53, 54–55, 63, 64
word learning 69–81; *see also* vocabulary
*Word Match Game* 43
Wozney, L. 19
W-Pal *see* Writing Pal
Writer's Workbench 227
WriteToLearn 149–151
writing 5–6, 7–8, 9, 143; commercialized writing systems 145–162; *Criterion* 7, 163–183; Framework for Success in Postsecondary Writing 204–205; ITSS 100; need for supplemental literacy instruction 4; need for writing technology 164, 206–207; research writing 8, 225–242; SWoRD 8, 243–259; TPACK 23; Udio 297, 299; We-Write 7–8, 184–203; *see also* automated writing evaluation; essays
Writing Pal (W-Pal) 8, 23, 158, 159, 204–224, 227
Writing Power 227
Writing Roadmap 152–153, 227

Zhu, X. 271